Birth Metaphors in the Book of Job

Dissertationes Theologicae Holmienses
Dissertations from Stockholm School of Theology
www.ehs.se/dth

Main editor:
Thomas Kazen

Editors:
Petra Carlsson Redell
Joel Halldorf
Jonas Ideström
Susanne Wigorts Yngvesson

No. 8

Lisa Plantin

Birth Metaphors in the Book of Job

A Blending Theory Analysis

Enskilda Högskolan Stockholm
2024

Birth Metaphors in the Book of Job: A Blending Theory Analysis

Dissertation presented at University College Stockholm, to be publicly examined in Room 219/220 at Åkeshovsvägen 29, Bromma, December 6, at 13.00, for the degree of Doctor of Philosophy in Theology (Biblical Studies: Hebrew Bible). The examination will be held in English.

Faculty examiner: Paul K.-K. Cho, Professor of Hebrew Bible, Wesley Theological Seminary.
Supervisor: Åke Viberg, Associate Professor of Biblical Studies, Hebrew Bible, University College Stockholm
Assistant supervisor: Josef Forsling, Assistant Professor of Biblical Studies, Hebrew Bible, University College Stockholm

Abstract

This dissertation offers a detailed analysis of birth metaphors in Job 1, 3, 10, 38, and 39 by using blending theory, supplemented by conceptual metaphor theory. It explores both metaphors that describe birth and those that use birth as a metaphor for other concepts, such as creation and death. It also concerns related concepts such as fetal formation, womb, and stillbirth. The metaphors are studied in their cultural and literary contexts, as well as how they are grounded in embodied experiences of birth. Blending theory explains various cognitive processes and can analyze both conventional metaphors and new, complex ones. It explains the debated expression of death as a return to the womb in Job 1:21, based on a cognitive process where something is understood through negated features of its antonym. A detailed mapping of the metaphors in Job 3 reveals, contrary to the dominant interpretation, that Job does not wish to curse all of creation but only the day he was born. Furthermore, it shows that the womb is blended with the grave and Sheol, but without projecting any positive associations of the womb to the realm of death. This study examines how conventional metaphors are replaced by new ones and demonstrates how the birth metaphors in Job 38–39 challenge the traditional combat motif, where God is seen as combating the sea and wild chaotic forces. The portrayal of God as a midwife includes an act of breaking the limit to the sea, which contradicts the combat motif. Rather than dominating creation, God is depicted as a midwife and a parent who is close to it, providing all wild creatures with food and freedom. Overall, the study underscores the central position of birth metaphors in these key chapters of Job. A close analysis of the metaphors contributes to the interpretation of the biblical text, from the understanding of specific Hebrew words to how innovative metaphors challenge both the beliefs of their time and current interpretations.

Födelsemetaforer i Jobs bok:
En analys utifrån blendingteori

Akademisk avhandling presenterad vid Enskilda Högskolan Stockholm, för disputation i sal 219/220, Åkeshovsvägen 29, Bromma, 6 december kl. 13.00, för teologie doktorsexamen i bibelvetenskap med inriktning mot Gamla testamentet. Disputationen kommer att äga rum på engelska.

Opponent: Paul K.-K. Cho, Professor, Hebrew Bible, Wesley Theological Seminary.
Handledare: Åke Viberg, Docent och högskolelektor i bibelvetenskap, Gamla testamentet Enskilda Högskolan Stockholm.
Bitr. handledare: Josef Forsling, Högskolelektor i bibelvetenskap, Gamla testamentet, Enskilda Högskolan Stockholm.

Sammanfattning

I denna avhandling analyseras födelsemetaforer i Job 1, 3, 10, 38 och 39 genom tillämpning av blendingteori, kompletterat med konceptuell metaforteori. Studien behandlar både metaforer som beskriver födelse och sådana som använder födelse som metafor i beskrivningar av andra koncept, såsom skapelse och död. Den berör också begrepp som är relaterade till födelse, såsom fostrets tillblivelse, livmoder och missfall. Metaforerna studeras utifrån kulturell och litterär kontext, samt hur de är förankrade i kroppsliga erfarenheter av födelse. Blendingteorin förklarar olika slags tankeprocesser och är väl lämpad för nyskapande och komplexa metaforer. Studien förklarar hur Jobs ord om sin död som ett återvändande till livmodern i Job 1:21, bygger på en tankeprocess där något förklaras genom att negera dess motsats. En kartläggning av metaforernas konstruktion i Job 3 visar, i motsats till dominerande tolkningar, att Job inte önskar förbanna hela skapelsen utan endast den dag då han föddes. Vidare klargörs att livmodern sammankopplas med graven och dödsriket, men utan att de positiva associationerna av livmodern överförs till begreppet död. Avhandlingen undersöker hur konventionella metaforer ersätts med nya och visar hur födelsemetaforerna i Job 38–39 utmanar det traditionella kampmotivet, där Gud anses bekämpa havet och kaosmakterna. Beskrivningen av hur Gud förlöser havet som en barnmorska skildrar hur Gud bryter upp gränsen mot havet, en provocerade bild där Gud förväntas kontrollera havet. Gud porträtteras vidare som barnmorska och förälder till de vilda djuren. Bilden som framträder är en Gud som är nära sin skapelse och förser alla dess varelser med både mat och frihet. Sammantaget understryker avhandlingen födelsemetaforernas vikt i Jobs bok. Den visar användbarheten av blendingteorin inom exegetiken. En noggrann analys av bibeltexternas metaforer påverkar tolkningen av texterna, från förståelsen av vissa hebreiska ord till hur nyskapande metaforer utmanar såväl sin tids trosföreställningar som nuvarande tolkningar.

Enskilda Högskolan Stockholm

Enskilda Högskolan Stockholm erbjuder utbildningsprogram i mänskliga rättigheter och demokrati, samt i teologi/religionsvetenskap. Högskolan grundades 1993 genom en sammanslagning av utbildningsinstitutioner med rötter från 1866, hette tidigare Teologiska högskolan, Stockholm, och har tre avdelningar: Avdelningen för mänskliga rättigheter och demokrati, Avdelningen för religionsvetenskap och teologi, samt Avdelningen för östkyrkliga studier. Forskarutbildningen i Bibelvetenskap bedrivs inom inriktningarna Gamla testamentets/Hebreiska bibelns exegetik respektive Nya testamentets exegetik. Utbildningen är både bred och djup, och innefattar bland annat filologiska, historiska, litterära, teologiska, socialvetenskapliga, ideologikritiska och hermeneutiska perspektiv

University College Stockholm

University College Stockholm offers programmes in Human Rights and Democracy and in Theology/Religious Studies. The university college was founded in 1993 through a merger of educational institutions with roots dating back to 1866, is also known as Stockholm School of Theology, and has three departments: the Department of Human Rights and Democracy, the Department of Religious Studies and Theology, and the Department of Eastern Christian Studies. The doctoral programme in Biblical Studies provides specialisations in Old Testament/Hebrew Bible exegesis and New Testament exegesis. The programme offers both breadth and depth, and includes among other things philological, historical, literary, theological, and hermeneutical perspectives, as well as perspectives from social science and ideological criticism.

Wipf and Stock Publishers
199 W 8th Ave, Suite 3
Eugene, OR 97401

Birth Metaphors in the Book of Job
A Blending Theory Analysis
By Plantin, Lisa
Copyright © 2024 by Plantin, Lisa All rights reserved.
Softcover ISBN-13: 979-8-3852-6234-2
Hardcover ISBN-13: 979-8-3852-6235-9
eBook ISBN-13: 979-8-3852-6236-6
Publication date 8/25/2025
Previously published by Enskilda Högskolan Stockholm, 2024

This edition is a scanned facsimile of the original edition published in 2024.

Preface

My interest in the Book of Job began in undergraduate school. The theme of suffering, Job's desire to bring God to court, and God's questions about the wild nature were fascinating and perplexing to me. Since then, I have spent over 20 years as a minister, often turning to the Book of Job to encourage those in pain to voice their complaints and even accuse God. Moreover, the book involves a quest for an innovative theology and new images of God when traditional ones are no longer relevant. This has challenged me in my search for images of God that resonate with our lived experience. It has also been my driving force to write this dissertation. In the early stages of my doctoral studies, I realized that the birth metaphors in Job are often overlooked or interpreted as subordinate to other metaphors, rather than on their own terms. Metaphors of God matter; we experience God through them. When I have used birth metaphors in my sermons, I have received feedback from women—daughters, mothers, and midwives—who feel recognized. Despite its profound impact, the experience of birth is often met with silence. This study explores birth metaphors in their literary and cultural contexts, alongside universal birth experiences. I believe that my own experiences of childbirth have increased my sensitivity in recognizing the experiences behind these metaphors. I am a proud mother of two children, and their births were markedly different. The birth of my daughter was complicated—she was born with her left hand first, like a little Superwoman, but she got stuck and had to be forcibly delivered. In contrast, my son's birth was easy; the labor pains were moderate, and he slipped out of my belly without complications. I have also witnessed the drama of birth from the sideline, supporting a friend as she gave birth to twin girls. In this dissertation, I will discuss ancient metaphors referring to both easy and complicated births. These metaphors communicate experiences of struggle, crisis, life, death, war, hope, mystery, protection, and care. I am convinced that we, even today, need such strong metaphors to capture our experiences of life and God.

During the years I have been working on this dissertation, I have had the opportunity to participate in projects that resulted in the acceptance of articles containing earlier versions of certain arguments in this monograph. Some years ago, I participated in the workshop "Biblical Job in the Literary Network of the Ancient Near East," and a preliminary and condensed version of my chapter 8 on Job 38, has been accepted for a volume with the same name.[1] Additionally, an article coming out of my examination of God's role with the young wild animals in Job 39, based on chapter 9, has been accepted for the forthcoming volume *Job Unveiled and Reimagined: Current Issues, New Paradigms, and Future Horizons*.[2]

This dissertation would not have been possible without the support and guidance of many individuals. I would like to express my deepest gratitude to my advisor, docent Åke Viberg. His teaching in undergraduate school laid the foundation for my interest in the Hebrew Bible, and his encouragement, expertise, and mentorship have been invaluable throughout my doctoral journey. I am also deeply grateful to my assistant advisor, teol.dr Josef Forsling, for his guidance and feedback on my texts. Many others have also contributed to this work, offering valuable feedback. I would like to extend my sincere thanks to the rest of the biblical research faculty at EHS—professor Thomas Kazen, docent Rikard Roitto, docent Hanna Stenström and docent Carl Johan Berglund—as well as my fellow doctoral students at EHS—Jessica, John-Christian, Sara, Petra, Aldar, Martin and Carl-Magnus. I have also greatly appreciated the support from the faculty and doctoral students from Uppsala and Lund. A special thanks to professor emeritus Göran Eidevall, who, as the opponent at my final seminar, carefully read the entire dissertation and provided valuable feedback for my final improvements. My proofreader Robert Rae also deserves a big thank you for his hard work in improving my English in this dissertation My thanks also go to the Sveriges Kristliga Ynglingaförening for providing financial support for conferences and for my final months of work on the dissertation.

I would also like to thank my family and friends, whose emotional and practical support was essential in completing this work. A special thanks to my husband, Jonas, for standing by my side and encouraging me to follow my dreams. My heartfelt gratitude to my daughter, Klara, for reminding me that I am not "a quitter," and to my son, Samuel, for reminding me of the importance of maintaining a social life even while writing a dissertation.

Vällingby in October 2024
Lisa Plantin

---

[1] Plantin Forthcoming-a.
[2] Plantin Forthcoming-b.

Contents

Preface 7

Contents 9

Abbreviations 15

Figures 17

1. Introduction 21
The Aim of This Study 22
Hypothesis and Method 24
The World behind the Book of Job 25
History of Research 26
    Metaphors and Biblical Research 27
    Birth Metaphors in the Hebrew Bible 31
    Birth Metaphors in the Book of Job 32
    Open Questions from Previous Research 33

2. Metaphor Theory 35
Conceptual Metaphor Theory 35
    Metaphors and Domains 36
    Metaphors Structure our Thoughts 36
    Metaphors Hide and Highlight 37
    Correlation and Resemblance Metaphors 37
    Entailments of a Metaphor 38
    Summary: Conceptual Metaphor Theory 39
Developments of Conceptual Metaphor Theory 40
    Image Schemas 41
    Conceptual Metonymy 42
Blending Theory 43
    Mental Spaces and Organizing Frames 43
    Integration of Spaces 45

    Single- and Double-Scope Networks 47
    Multiple Blends 52
    Vital Relations 54
    The Blending Process 55
    Counterfactual Blends 57
    Summary: Blending Theory 58
Two Complementary Theories 58
Context and Metaphors 61
Novel Metaphors and Creativity 64
The Interplay of Metaphors.. 67
Application of Metaphor Theory in This Study 69

3. Birth Metaphors in the Hebrew Bible 73
Descriptions of Birth... 73
BIRTH as the Target Domain 76
BIRTH as the Source Domain 77
    BIRTH and GOD 78
    BIRTH and CREATION 82
    BIRTH and PLANTS 83
    BIRTH and DEATH 85
    BIRTH and EXILE 88
Words Relating to Birth.. 89
Summary and Conclusions 91

4. Birth Metaphors in Ancient West Asia 93
Birth Metaphors in Akkadian Birth Incantations..95
Additional Birth Motifs and Metaphors 99
The Midwife 101
BIRTH as the Source Domain 104
Cross-Cultural and Culture Specific Metaphors 105
Summary and Conclusion 105

5. Birth Metaphors in Job 1 107
Text and Translation of Job 1:21 107
Literary Structure and Comments 107
Earlier Interpretations of Job 1:21...109
    Non-Metaphorical Reading 111
    Metaphorical Reading 111
    Open Questions from Earlier Interpretations 115

Birth Metaphors in Job 1:21 119
    Birth and Death Are Antonyms 119
    DEATH IS TO RETURN TO THE WOMB..120
    Returning to Dust and to the Womb 122
    Naked at Birth and Death..125
Summary and Conclusions 130

6. Birth Metaphors in Job 3 133
Text and Translation of Job 3 133
Literary Structure and Genre 135
Earlier Interpretations of Job 3 138
    Inversion of Creation 138
    Inverted Metaphors..141
    Interaction between Metaphors 142
    Job 3 as a Parody 142
    Birth Motif in Job 3 143
    Parallels to Job 3: Cursing of Days in the Past 144
    Open Questions from Earlier Interpretations 147
Metaphors in Job 3 147
    Metaphors of Light and Darkness..148
    Metaphors of Death and Exile..149
Birth Metaphors in Job 3:1–9 150
    JOB'S DAY OF BIRTH and CREATION.. 150
    The Night of Job's Conception 158
Birth Metaphors in Job 3:10–19 161
    Literary Comments 161
    Knees to Meet Me 163
    THE WOMB IS A ROOM OF DARKNESS 165
    The Womb and Death 167
Summary and Conclusions 175

7. Birth Metaphors in Job 10 179
Earlier Interpretations 179
Birth Metaphors in Job 10:8–12 181
    Text and Translation of Job 10:8–12 181
    Literary Structure and Comments 182
    GOD IS A HANDCRAFTER.. 183
    Formation in the Womb 183

  Formation of Job Is Pottery Making 184
  Formation of Job Is Curdling Milk to Cheese 191
  Formation of Job Is Dressing and Intertwining 200
  Interaction of the Metaphors in Job 10:8–12 216
 Birth Metaphors in Job 10:18–19 219
  Text and Translation of Job 10:18–19 219
  Literary Structure and Comments 219
  God Is a Midwife and a Watcher 220
  Womb and Death.. 223
 Summary and Conclusions 225

8. Birth Metaphors in Job 38 227
 Earlier Interpretations of God's Speeches 227
  A Well-Ordered Creation 228
  A Sublime World with Beauty and Danger 231
  Open Questions from Earlier Interpretations 233
 The Domains of Birth and Water 234
  The Domain of Birth.. 234
  The Domain of Water of Creation 234
 Birth Metaphors in Job 38:8–11 237
  Text and Translation of Job 38:8–11 237
  Literary Structure and Comments 237
  Earlier Interpretations of Job 38:8–11 240
  The Sea Is Amniotic Fluid and a Baby 242
  God Swaddles the Sea.. 248
  God Breaks the Water 248
  The Dual Act of Opening and Holding Back 249
  Birth Replaces the Combat Motif 253
  Summary: Birth Metaphors in Job 38:8–11 258
 Precipitation and Birth Metaphors... 259
 Birth Metaphors in Job 38:28–29 261
  Text and Translation of Job 38:28–30 261
  Literary Structure and Comments 261
  Earlier Interpretations of Job 38:28–29 262
  Formation of Precipitation and Fetuses 266
  Solidification of Water into Ice Is Formation of a Fetus 268
  Precipitation Emanating from the Womb 270
  Experiential Similarities between a Newborn and Hoarfrost 271

God's Role in Job 38:28–29 272
Summary: Birth Metaphors in Job 38:28–29 273
Birth in Job 38 and Job's Speeches 274
Summary and Conclusions 274

9. Birth Metaphors in Job 39 279
Earlier Interpretations of the Wild Animals 279
   Transformation of Conventional Metaphors 280
   Lord of the Animals 282
   Animals and Metaphors 285
   Open Questions from Earlier Interpretation 287
The Wild Animals in Job 38–39 288
   The Domain of ANIMALS in the Hebrew Bible 289
Rhetorical Questions in God's First Speech 290
Birth, Parenthood, and Young Wild Animals 291
Birth Metaphors in Job 39:1–4 292
   Text and Translation of Job 39:1–4 292
   Literary Structure and Comments 292
   Counting the Months of a Pregnancy 294
   Birth Position 294
   Breaking Out of the Womb and Untying the Bonds 294
   God and the Birth of the Wild Animals 303
   Summary: Birth Metaphors in Job 39:1–4 303
The Ostrich in Job 39:13–18 304
   Text and Translation of Job 39:13–18 304
   Literary Structure and Comments 304
   God and the Negligent Parent 305
The Young Wild Animals in Job 38–39 307
   Text and Translation of Job 38:39–41 and 39:27–30 307
   Literary Structure and Comments 308
   Earlier Interpretation of the Young Animals 309
   The Domain of YOUNG ANIMALS in the Hebrew Bible 310
   Young Wild Animals and Their Deities 311
   General Patterns in the Care for Young Wild Animals 315
   God and the Young Wild Animals in Job 38–39 316

Birth in Job 39 and Job's Speeches 324
Summary and Conclusions 325

10. Summary and Conclusions 329
The Application of Blending Theory 329
BIRTH in Ancient Texts 331
Embodied Experiences of Birth 332
New Perspectives on Job's Speeches 333
    BIRTH and DEATH 333
    BIRTH and CREATION 334
    The Formation of the Fetus Job 335
    Conceptualizations of Birth and the Womb 336
New Perspectives on God's First Speech 337
    New Understanding of Job 38:10 and 39:3 337
    Birth Replaces the Combat Motif 338
    The Cry of the Young Wild Animals 339
    The Mysteries of Creation 340
    Conceptualizations of Birth and the Womb 341
Interaction between Metaphors 341
Further Discussions 343

Appendix A: Sources for Ancient Texts 345

Bibliography 349
Dictionaries, Lexica, and Selected Text Collections 349
Literature 350

Index of Ancient Literature 367

Index of Modern Authors 379

Index of Subjects 385

Abbreviations

Abbreviations follow *The SBL Handbook of Style: For Biblical Studies and Related Disciplines,* 2nd ed. (Atlanta: SBL, 2014). In addition to this, the following abbreviations are also used.

CDA	*A Concise Dictionary of Akkadian*
CDCH	*The Concise Dictionary of Classical Hebrew*
COS-Sup	*The Context of Scripture, Supplements.*
SpbTU	*Spätbabylonische Texte aus Uruk*

Figures

Figure 2.1. Blending schema of a basic integration network....................46
Figure 2.2. Blending schema of a single-scope network of the metaphor BUSINESS COMPETITION IS A BOXING MATCH 48
Figure 2.3. Blending schema of a double-scope network of the metaphor THE SURGEON IS A BUTCHER 50
Figure 2.4. Blending schema of a multiple integration network of the metaphor DEATH IS THE GRIM REAPER 53
Figure 5.1. The counterfactual blend DEATH IS NEGATION OF BIRTH, and the metaphors DEATH IS TO RETURN TO THE WOMB and DEATH IS TO BE UN-CLOTHED...............................121
Figure 5.2. The metaphors: CHILDREN AND ANIMALS ARE CLOTHES WHICH PROTECT FROM EXPOSURE TO DEATH, THE LOSS OF CHILDREN AND ANIMALS IS TO BE STRIPPED NAKED, and GOD IS THE ONE WHO CLOTHES AND UNCLOTHES JOB...............................128
Figure 6.1. The metaphor (DESTRUCTION OF) JOB'S DAY OF BIRTH IS (DESTRUCTION OF) THE FIRST DAY OF CREATION...............................153
Figure 6.2. The metaphor JOB'S DAY OF BIRTH IS THE SEA...............................157
Figure 6.3. The metaphor THE WOMB IS A GRAVE...............................170
Figure 6.4. The counterfactual blend THE EXISTENCE OF THE DEAD IS NEGATION OF LIFE...............................174
Figure 7.1. The metaphors GOD IS A POTTER, FORMATION OF JOB IS POTTERY MAKING, and JOB IS CLAY 187
Figure 7.2. The metaphors DESTRUCTION OF JOB IS CRUSHING CERAMICS, JOB IS CLAY AND CERAMIC WARE, and FORMATION OF JOB IS POTTERY MAKING 189
Figure 7.3. The metaphors GOD IS A CHEESEMAKER, FORMATION OF JOB IS CHEESEMAKING, and JOB IS MILK AND CHEESE 197
Figure 7.4. The metaphors GOD IS A DRESSER, FORMATION OF JOB IS DRESSING, and FLESH AND SKIN ARE CLOTHES 203

Figure 7.5. The metaphors GOD IS A WEAVER, FORMATION OF JOB IS WEAVING, JOB/JOB'S INNER PARTS ARE A WOVEN FABRIC, and SINEWS AND BONES ARE TEXTILES 209

Figure 7.6. The metaphors GOD IS A ROPE PLAITER, FORMATION OF JOB IS PLAITING ROPES, JOB/JOB'S INNER PARTS ARE INTERTWINED STRONG ROPES, and SINEWS AND BONES ARE TEXTILES 211

Figure 7.7. The metaphors GOD IS A BUILDER, FORMATION OF JOB IS BUILDING A BOOTH, JOB/JOB'S INNER PARTS ARE A BOOTH, and SINEWS AND BONES ARE BRANCHES 213

Figure 7.8. The metaphor GOD IS AN UNMERCIFUL MIDWIFE WHO DELIVERS JOB 221

Figure 7.9. Blending schema of the integration of God's double roles as a midwife and a watcher 222

Figure 8.1. The Akkadian metaphor THE AMNIOTIC FLUID IS A DANGEROUS SEA 243

Figure 8.2. The Akkadian metaphor THE BABY WHO COMES FORTH FROM THE WOMB IS A RUSHING RAINFALL 244

Figure 8.3. The metaphors CREATION IS A BIRTH, THE SEA IS AMNIOTIC FLUID, and THE SEA IS A BABY 246

Figure 8.4. The metaphors GOD IS A MIDWIFE and THE SEA IS AMNIOTIC FLUID/BABY 252

Figure 8.5. The metaphors BIRTH IS A COMBAT and THE WOMAN GIVING BIRTH IS A WARRIOR, and their reversed counterparts COMBAT IS BIRTH and THE WARRIOR IS A WOMAN IN LABOR 256

Figure 8.6. The standard metaphor of God's relationship to the sea in the HB: GOD'S RELATIONSHIP TO THE SEA IS A COMBAT 257

Figure 8.7. The metaphors SOLIDIFICATION OF WATER INTO ICE IS FORMATION OF A FETUS, THE DELIVERY OF FROZEN PRECIPITATION IS A BIRTH, and THE ICE AND HOARFROST ARE NEWBORN BABIES 269

Figure 9.1. The Akkadian birth metaphors THE WOMB IS A ROOM WITH DOORS, THE WOMB IS A POT, THE BABY IS A BOAT TIED WITH MOORING ROPE, and THE MUSCLES, SINEWS AND JOINTS ARE ROPES 297

Figure 9.2. The metaphors THE WOMB IS A CONTAINER WHICH BREAKS AT BIRTH, THE MUSCLES, SINEWS AND JOINTS ARE ROPES, and THE ANIMAL IS TIED WITH ROPES DURING PREGNANCY 302

Figure 9.3. The blend of the domains of ANIMAL PARENTS and GOD, and the metaphor GOD IS A PARENT TO THE WILD YOUNG ANIMALS 317

Figure 9.4. The metaphor GOD IS THE PARENT TO THE WILD ANIMALS. An extensive blend of God's parenthood including BIRTH, HUNTING and FREEDOM 321

1. Introduction

The literary motif of birth recurs in the Book of Job, and it plays a significant role in Job's opening speeches and God's first answer to Job. This motif is central to Job 3 and 10, where Job laments his own conception, formation, and birth. He expresses his anguish by wishing that God had shut the doors of the womb so that he would have died at birth. He accuses God of being the midwife who brought him into a life of suffering. Birth imagery is also prominent in God's first speech in Job 38–39, where God describes the birth of the sea, hoarfrost, ice, mountain goats, and deer. In this speech, God is portrayed as a midwife, who breaks the water and delivers the sea, as well as a caring midwife for the wild animals. The motif of birth has often been overlooked, especially in God's first speech. God's acts as a midwife and caregiver have been downplayed in favor of God as the one who establishes order in creation and is the lord over the animals. This study explores birth metaphors in the Book of Job, which includes both those that depict birth, pregnancies, and the formation of a fetus, and those that use birth to depict death, creation, and God's relationship with Job and wild nature. It also demonstrates how analyzing these metaphors enhances the understanding of Job's speeches in Job 1, 3, and 10, as well as God's first speech in Job 38–39.

This introductory chapter outlines the purpose, hypothesis, and methodology of the study. It addresses the challenges of researching how birth was conceptualized in ancient West Asia and the questions involved in dating the Book of Job. The chapter concludes with an overview of previous research on metaphors in the Hebrew Bible (HB), with a particular focus on blending theory and studies of birth metaphors in the HB and Job, to contextualize and justify the present study. The theoretical framework, including conceptual metaphor theory and blending theory, will be detailed in chapter 2. Chapters 3 and 4 will provide an overview of birth descriptions and metaphors in the HB and other ancient West Asian texts. Chapters 5 through 9 will present the analyses of birth metaphors in Job 1, 3, 10, 38, and 39. The final chapter, chapter 10, will summarize the conclusions of the study.

The Aim of This Study

This study closely examines the construction of birth metaphors in Job 1, 3, 10, 38, and 39, focusing on what they highlight and downplay, as well as their interaction with other metaphors and motifs within their literary context.[1] The primary aim is to contribute with new insights on the interpretation of the Book of Job through the analysis of these metaphors, while also exploring the underlying conceptualizations of birth within them, and demonstrating the usefulness of blending theory in analyzing metaphors in the HB.

There are no comprehensive surveys of birth metaphors in the Book of Job. While some birth metaphors have been studied, they have not been analyzed through a theoretical framework grounded in metaphor theory. Blending theory offers a valuable interpretive tool for uncovering the construction of metaphors, potentially revealing overlooked meanings and providing new perspectives on the Book of Job. This study will build on existing research of the relevant chapters of Job, and compare the findings with previous interpretations, particularly where my conclusions offer new insights into Job's lament and God's first speech.

This study explores birth metaphors in Job 1, 3, 10, 38, and 39. These metaphors are central in the chapters in question. God's speeches are often interpreted as a response to Job's words in chapters 3 and 9–10, and the birth metaphors serve as a link between them.[2] Since birth metaphors in Job 1 and 3 are frequently discussed together, Job 1 is included in the analysis. There are other references to birth, which I consider more peripheral, that will not be covered.[3] The metaphors are analyzed within their literary context and using insights into how birth was conceptualized in ancient West Asia. The focus is on how these metaphors contribute to the discourse within their respective chapters. It considers both metaphors that directly describe birth events (use BIRTH as the target domain) and those that use birth

---

[1] In this study, I use the term "motif" to refer to both literary and mythological motifs. A literary motif is a theme that recurs within a text or texts through various expressions and images associated with the motif. This chain of imagery links different parts of the text together. A mythological motif, such as the combat motif or the "lord of the animals" motif, is a conventional motif that expresses mythological beliefs and appears in various texts. Such a motif may serve as a shorthand for an entire myth and can also function as a literary motif within a specific text. My use of "mythological motif" corresponds to how "theme" is used in literary and narrative studies (see Pyrhönen 2005, 597–98). For definitions of the term "motif," see Würzbach 2005, 322–23.

[2] Keel 1978, 44–46; Alter 2011, 129–30; Kang 2017, 57–62.

[3] Job 5:6–7; 14:1; 15:7, 14, 35; 21:10, 24; 24:20; 25:4; 31:15.

imagery to illustrate other things (use BIRTH as the source domain).[4] The birth metaphors analyzed in this study concern the domain of BIRTH and associated terms of birth, including fetal formation, the womb, infertility, miscarriage, breaking of amniotic fluid, labor pains, the birth process, delivery, women in childbirth, midwifery, the begetter, the initial care of the newborn, and God's involvement in births. A close and overlapping domain to BIRTH is the domain of PARENTHOOD, but metaphors of parenthood will not generally be analyzed unless they are intertwined with birth metaphors.

Birth metaphors will be investigated using conceptual metaphor theory and blending theory, with blending theory as the primary framework. Both theories address metaphors on a cognitive level. Understanding how birth was conceptualized during the time the Book of Job was written aids in the investigation of its birth metaphors. Thus, this study includes an examination of how other texts from ancient West Asia, particularly passages from the HB and Akkadian birth incantations, describe birth. Simultaneously, the investigation of the metaphors in Job may also offer insights into how birth was perceived in ancient West Asia.

A secondary purpose of this study is to demonstrate how blending theory serves as an effective interpretive tool for analyzing metaphors in the HB. It has been questioned, or indeed warned, that metaphor studies might become an enterprise for its own sake, failing to contribute meaningfully to the understanding of the text, or that similar insights could be gained without relying on a cognitive theoretical framework.[5] There has also been debate as to what extent conceptual theories can be applied to ancient texts when we lack direct access to the minds of the original speakers.[6] These pitfalls are avoided by being well-grounded in the theory used and by combining the cognitive approach with a close reading of the text, which considers its syntactic and semantic features, and by investigating the conceptual domains through intertextual relationships and the cultural and universal traits of the metaphors.[7]

---

[4] The terms domain, source domain, and target domain are explained in Chapter 2, see page 36.
[5] Weiss argues that the choice of metaphor theory should impact the results of the analysis, but too many biblical scholars present a specific metaphor theory and then investigate the metaphors in a general manner, without fully utilizing the potential of the theory they claim to use (Weiss 2006, 23–29).
[6] Shead 2011, 181–84.
[7] Shead 2011, 181–84; Krainer 2020, 7–8.

Hypothesis and Method

My overall hypothesis is that birth metaphors are more central to the Book of Job than has been previously acknowledged, and that they have often been misunderstood in earlier research. The experience of birth serves as a unifying literary motif between Job's complaint and God's first speech. Job challenges traditional themes such as retribution, justice, and the combat motif by accusing God of acting unjustly. I presume that the birth metaphors in Job's speeches are part of the rhetoric that accuses God and challenges traditional beliefs. God's answer to Job's complaint is to display the greatness of creation. This has been interpreted as offering Job a different perspective on the world, primarily emphasizing that God is in control over creation. In much of the existing scholarship, God's speeches are interpreted through the combat motif. However, this interpretation has been questioned, with some suggesting that God acts more as a parent or a wildlife manager in these speeches. I will suggest that the metaphors of birth and parenthood are the load-bearing metaphors in God's first speech. They are used to portray God's relationship with the untamed aspects of creation in a way that challenges the traditional combat motif, emphasizing freedom rather than control.

The birth metaphors will be studied closely by using blending theory as my main theory and method, supplemented by conceptual metaphor theory. The focus will be on understanding how birth and birth metaphors were conceptualized in ancient West Asia, rather than how they are interpreted today. By analyzing these metaphors through blending schemas, I aim to uncover how they are constructed, the associations they invoke, and the aspects they highlight and downplay. The theoretical framework, including both conceptual metaphor theory and blending theory, will be thoroughly presented in the next chapter, which will also discuss their application in this study.[8]

The meaning of a metaphor is dependent on its cultural and literary context.[9] An analysis of metaphors must therefore be combined with a literary analysis of the text, considering its semantic, syntactic, and structural features. Metaphors interact with these features and the overall meaning of the text, and the meaning of the metaphors is dependent on these interactions. My analysis of the metaphors begins with a close reading and translation of the text, and an analysis of the immediate context of the metaphors. This involves a semantic analysis of the key terms, identifying ambiguities in the text, and a structural analysis based on both

---

[8] See Chapter 2, especially "Application of Metaphor Theory in this Study," pages 69–72.
[9] See Chapter 2, pages 61–63.

syntactical and semantic content. The translations of the biblical texts in this thesis are my own unless otherwise specified.

The text as we have it in the Masoretic form in BHS, serves as the starting point for my analysis. I propose that the Masoretic text of Job can generally be read as a coherent whole, even if the poetic sections may have been added to the prose, and certain chapters might have been added at a later date. I will rarely discuss redaction criticism or textual criticism, except insofar as these issues relate to the metaphors. While I am aware of discussions regarding the book's compositional history—such as the relationship between the prose and poetic sections, the structure of the third cycle of dialogue, and the potential later interpolations of Job 28 and Elihu's speech—these major discussions do not impact the interpretation of the birth metaphors in this study.

The World behind the Book of Job

This study uses conceptual metaphor theory and blending theory and discusses the conceptual background to the metaphors. Understanding these metaphors requires insight into how birth was conceptualized in ancient West Asia. While the HB offers some understanding, this must be supplemented with additional sources from the region. Sumerian and Akkadian birth incantations are particularly valuable. They reveal that the conceptualization of birth seems to have been consistent over time, as Sumerian and Neo-Assyrian texts present similar imagery. These images are also coherent with the depictions of birth in Genesis, Psalms, and Isaiah. Additionally, several of these images appear in other cultures and historical periods.

The dating of the Book of Job, including its various layers, is debated, and there is no consensus. Clines notes that most scholars date the Book of Job to between the seventh and second centuries BCE, with the possibility that the prose may stem from an older folktale about a pious sufferer.[10] Habel examines linguistic expressions, literary links, and various themes used in efforts to date the book, and concludes that the arguments are ambiguous. He suggests that the most likely period is the exilic period or the aftermath of the exile.[11] I agree with this assessment, which places the writing of the Book of Job during a time of theological creativity when old beliefs were reconsidered, aligning with the creativity evident in Job. Another argument for dating the Book of Job to this period is its use of legal language,

---

[10] Clines 1989, lvii.
[11] Habel 1985, 40–42.

which is similar to that found in the prophets. The *rîb* pattern (רִיב, "lawsuit") is used in Micah, Jeremiah, and Deutero-Isaiah (Mic 6; Jer 12; Isa 41, 43). In this study, I will propose that there are allusions to Jeremiah, but that the Book of Job precedes Ecclesiastes. However, textual dependency is difficult to establish, as allusions to other texts may trace back to other common sources or shared traditions. The book of Job addresses themes and ideas that are relevant across different eras. The motif of a sufferer claiming innocence and lamenting before the gods is present in several ancient West Asian texts, such as Let Me Praise the Lord of Wisdom (Ludlul-Bel-Nemeqi), the Babylonian Theodicy, and older poems like the Sumerian Man and His God.[12] The author of Job might have been familiar with these older traditions.

The difficulties in dating the composition of the Book of Job make it challenging to determine with any certainty which texts might provide background knowledge on how the author(s) of Job perceived different concepts or ideas. However, conceptualizations of birth seem to remain consistent across various ancient time periods. Giving birth is also a shared experience among mothers throughout history and across cultures. Despite differing conditions, there are common physical experiences associated with birth, such as the breaking of water, labor pains, the process of pushing the baby out, and the assistance provided by others during labor. In this study, I primarily seek background information on birth from written sources in ancient West Asia, but occasionally refer to experiences that appear to be universal or nearly universal, even if they are not described in ancient texts.

History of Research

This study relates both previous research of birth in the HB, and the broader field of metaphor studies within the HB. Prior studies of metaphors as conceptual have demonstrated the benefits of these theories, and methods by which to approach the challenges of studying ancient texts by using cognitive theories. I will provide an overview of this research field, with a particular focus on studies using blending theory. I will then discuss how birth metaphors and descriptions have been explored in the HB and in the Book of Job.

---

[12] The second tablet of Ludlul-Bel-Nemeqi is often called the Babylonian Job. For an overview of the content and composition of these texts, see Oshima 2014, 1–28. Oshima also refers to Akkadian prayers to Marduk and an Ugaritic text, Ugaritica 5, no. 162, with the same theme.

Metaphors and Biblical Research

Metaphor studies of the HB is today an extensive area of research. Metaphors are studied from different perspectives, and both cognitive and literary approaches are employed. Cognitive approaches have had a tremendous impact on metaphor studies of the HB, and the insight that metaphors are not only literary tropes but also operate on a cognitive level and structure our thoughts has taken root.[13] At the same time, questions have been raised about how cognitive methods can be applied to a text in an ancient language when we do not have access to the minds of the native speakers. Shead refutes this critique by emphasizing that if meaning is conceptual, cognitive methods are necessary for interpreting a text. He argues that interpreting a dead language is more challenging than interpreting a living one; therefore, we need to combine different methods in our exegesis. Research into human cognition is one resource; others include the text itself, its history of interpretation, comparative linguistic, and semantic and syntactic analysis. By integrating these methods, we will gain a better understanding of how terms and expressions were conceptualized, and thus achieve a clearer understanding of the text's meaning.[14]

I will provide an overview of cognitive metaphor research, focusing on the application of blending theory in the exegesis of the HB.[15] Conceptual metaphor theory has been applied to a variety of metaphors. Embodiment has been studied in metaphors of the body, emotions, and in spatial metaphors.[16] Metaphors involving God as the target domain, relational metaphors, and plant metaphors have all received extensive attention.[17] Additionally, many other areas have been explored

---

[13] For a literary approach to metaphors in the HB, see Caird 1980; Macky 1990; Soskice 1985; McFague 1987; Eidevall 1996. For examples of various approaches to metaphor studies over the last 20 years, see the three anthologies on metaphors in the HB: Van Hecke 2005; Van Hecke and Labahn 2010; Verde and Labahn 2020.

[14] Shead 2011, 181–84.

[15] For a comprehensible overview of metaphor research and the HB, see Lancaster 2021. I will refer to several studies that employ cognitive methods in their investigation of various metaphors; however, these should be regarded as examples rather than an exhaustive inventory list.

[16] Metaphors related to the sensory system: Tilford 2017; Boris 2020. Other body metaphors: Gault 2019; Van Hecke 2010. Metaphors of emotions: Kotzé 2009; Basson 2009; Schlimm 2011, 75–88; Kruger 2015. Spatial metaphors: de Joode 2018; Lamprecht 2021.

[17] Images of God: Basson 2006a. God as a parent and family metaphors: Dille 2004. God as a king: Brettler 2009 (originally 1989); Osborne 2018. Sexual and marriage metaphors: Moughtin-Mumby 2008; Green 2012. Plant metaphors: Basson 2006b; Eidevall 2019; Jindo 2010; Osborne 2018. God as a planter: Pantoja 2017.

using conceptual metaphor theory, such as birth, animals, exile, sin, light, and darkness.[18]

Interest in how different metaphors interact and work together has increased over the last twenty years. Dille's study on metaphors depicting God as a father and a mother in Isaiah, and Jindo's study of metaphors in Jeremiah, demonstrate how metaphors interact and must be interpreted collectively.[19] Hawley's book, *Metaphor Competition in the Book of Job,* explores how metaphors in the Book of Job interact, cohere, and compete, with a particular focus on animal and speech metaphors.[20] In 2020, Verde and Labahn edited an anthology on networks of metaphors in the HB, which includes many insightful studies on how metaphors interact, share entailments, and trigger each other.[21]

In Lancaster's overview of metaphor research in studies of the HB, he argues that biblical scholars still mainly refer to Lakoff and Johnson's book, *Metaphors We Live By,* when they apply conceptual metaphor theory. He accentuates the need to develop cognitive methods according to more recent research.[22] The application of blending theory in research of the HB is not extensive. However, Van Hecke explored the advantages of using blending theory as early as 2005.[23] He argues that blending theory is a simple descriptive tool for displaying complex metaphorical structures. His application of blending theory in interpreting Hos 4:16 shows that, although blending theory was not originally developed for biblical exegesis or the study of ancient texts, it proves to be an effective hermeneutical tool. However, interpreters must reconstruct the conceptual domains and incorporate the common knowledge of the ancient context.[24] Also, DesCamp and Sweetser applied blending theory in their 2005 research on metaphors of God.[25] Both Hawley and Kim refer to blending theory as a complementary method to conceptual metaphor theory, necessary for interpreting several complex metaphors in their respective works.[26]

---

[18] Sin: Lam 2016; DiFransico 2016. Life is a way: Jäkel 2002. Birth: Bergmann 2008; Dille 2010. Exile: Halvorson-Taylor 2010. Animals: Hawley 2018. Light and darkness: Janowski 2010; Schmidt and Nel 2016; Van Hecke 2011, 95–98.
[19] Dille 2004; Jindo 2010.
[20] Hawley 2018.
[21] Verde and Labahn 2020.
[22] Lancaster 2021, 241.
[23] Van Hecke 2005.
[24] Van Hecke 2005, 230–31.
[25] DesCamp and Sweetser 2005.
[26] Hawley 2018, 125–27; Kim 2018.

An important resource for blending theory and exegesis is the anthology *Cognitive Linguistic Exploration in Biblical Studies*, edited by Howe and Green.[27] This volume explores how cognitive methods can be integrated with syntactic, semantic, and cultural contextual analysis. Sweetser and DesCamp challenge the notion in conceptual metaphor theory that mappings are unidirectional from the source domain to the target domain. By employing blending theory, they demonstrate that conventional metaphors may also lead to their reversed counterparts; for example, the metaphor GOD IS A FATHER might induce the metaphor THE FATHER IS GOD. They also emphasize that the selection of source domains is driven by experience rather than being less abstract than the target domains.[28] Robinette illustrates how understanding conceptual structures within an integration network can clarify ambiguous textual passages, applying this approach to Jer 17:5–8.[29] Andrews examines how God's silence can be interpreted as a negated (counterfactual) blend of God's activity and speech.[30]

Besides this anthology, there are several articles that apply blending theory to the analysis of texts from the HB. Grohmann uses blending theory to analyze metaphors of miscarriages in the Psalms. She demonstrates how blending theory can integrate both the literal and metaphorical meanings of miscarriages, and remains effective even when it is unclear which space is the target and which is the source.[31] De Hulster and Strawn use blending theory to understand mixed metaphors in Deuteronomy 32 and interpret images from "Mischwesen" iconography.[32] Ross argues for the conceptual unity of Ps 51 by showing how different conceptual networks overlap within the psalm.[33] Krainer analyzes Ps 102, discussing how a successful application of blending theory requires a close reading, thorough analysis of syntactic and semantic features, and consideration of parallelism in the text.[34] Viberg examines metaphors depicting enemies as dangerous animals; using blending theory, he explains how these metaphors derive from experiences of predator behavior and how the abstract concept of evil is concretized in the dangers posed by predators.[35] Kazen employs blending theory in his discussion of purity laws,

---

[27] Howe and Green 2014.
[28] Sweetser and DesCamp 2014.
[29] Robinette 2014.
[30] Andrews 2014.
[31] Grohmann 2010.
[32] de Hulster and Strawn 2015.
[33] Ross 2019.
[34] Krainer 2020.
[35] Viberg 2021.

arguing that the emotion of disgust helps to explain what is considered pure or impure and clarifies several purity regulations in the priestly codes.[36] He also analyzes the marital metaphors in Malachi; by unpacking these metaphors, he argues that the marriage is not considered to be a covenant, but that the metaphor of God as a wife is used within the framework of the covenant.[37]

There are only a few monographs that use blending theory as their primary method for investigating biblical metaphors, and none of these focus on the HB. DesCamp's monograph explores images of women in Philo's works and examines how blending theory can be applied to exegetical studies. By comparing blending theory with narrative and rhetorical analysis, she argues that blending theory offers insights into how and why rhetorical devices, such as repetition and metaphors, function. She also explains how mapping between input spaces has required her to engage more closely with the text, avoiding the imposition of her own views and recognizing when the text presupposes shared background knowledge.[38] Lundhaug employs blending theory to analyze the metaphors THE SOUL IS A WOMAN and CHRISTIANS ARE CHRIST in two Nag Hammadi texts. Among other contentions, he argues that these texts are soaked with scriptural allusions and citations from Scripture, which weave a conceptual web essential for understanding the metaphors.[39] Gomola uses blending theory to analyze pastoral metaphors in patristic writings. He explores how the church fathers creatively employed the metaphor THE CHURCH IS GOD'S FLOCK and how it influenced early Christian doctrines, demonstrating how the metaphor GOD IS THE SHEPHERD was extended by the church fathers to support theological arguments against their opponents.[40]

To summarize: Analyzing metaphors from a cognitive perspective is a well-established area of research in biblical studies. Conceptual metaphor theory is employed to investigate both unconscious conventional metaphors and more conscious, less established ones. Since 2005, blending theory has been used as a tool in biblical research, primarily as a complement to conceptual metaphor theory to explain complex metaphors. Exegetical works demonstrate that blending theory is an effective descriptive tool for unpacking metaphors, and that it should be combined with syntactic and semantic studies of the text, as well as background information on the concepts used in the metaphors. Additionally, blending theory has

---

[36] Kazen 2014.
[37] Kazen 2023.
[38] DesCamp 2007.
[39] Lundhaug 2010.
[40] Gomola 2018.

Birth Metaphors in the Hebrew Bible

Birth metaphors in the HB have primarily been studied within the prophetic literature and the Psalms. A more detailed discussion of specific metaphors will be presented in Chapter 3, "Birth Metaphors in the HB."

Dille explores metaphors depicting God as a father and a mother in Deutero-Isaiah in *Mixing Metaphors: God as Mother and Father in Deutero-Isaiah*.[41] Her exploration includes portrayals of God as the one who begets, gives birth, and knows the babies in the womb. She also discusses the simile "like a woman in labor." Additionally, in her article on Deut 32, Dille examines images of God nursing and giving birth.[42] Grohmann's book *Fruchtbarkeit und Geburt in den Psalmen* investigates the motif of birth and fertility in the Psalms. She explores various images related to birth and fertility, including the formation of a human in Ps 139, God as a midwife in Ps 22, and God giving birth in Pss 2:7, 90:2, and 110:3. She also addresses the depiction of miscarriage in several psalms. While Grohmann approaches the metaphors from a linguistic standpoint, she also considers the experience of birth and womanhood as contextual background for the imagery of birth.[43] She has also published two articles on birth metaphors, one on God and birth in Pss 90:2 and 110:3, and the other on miscarriages in the Psalms.[44] Another significant monograph on birth metaphors is Bergmann's *Childbirth as a Metaphor for Crisis*.[45] In this book, she explores how birth is employed in the HB, primarily in Isaiah and Jeremiah, to represent various crises, both personal and national. She gives considerable attention to the simile "like a woman in labor." Claassens emphasizes the portrayal of God with female attributes in her book *Mourner, Mother, Midwife: Reimagining God's Delivering Presence in the Old Testament*.[46] She explores how images of God as a mourner in Jeremiah, a mother in Isaiah, and a midwife in Pss 22 and 71, offer a contrasting perspective to the depiction of God as a violent war-god.

---

[41] Dille 2004.
[42] Dille 2010.
[43] Grohmann 2007.
[44] Grohmann 2010; Grohmann 2019.
[45] Bergmann 2008. See also her articles Bergmann 2007; Bergmann 2010.
[46] Claassens 2012.

Birth Metaphors in the Book of Job

I will here present the major research on birth metaphors in the Book of Job. Additionally, my analytical chapters include a thorough investigation on existing research of the metaphors studied.

Alter recognizes the dominance of birth metaphors in Job 3 and their recurrence in God's first speech in Job 38. He presents a short examination of how these metaphors interact with metaphors of light and darkness in Job 3, and how Job's inversion of creation in Job 3 is reordered in Job 38.[47] Vall's dissertation *From Womb to Tomb: Poetic Imagery and the Book of Job* discusses links between the womb and the tomb in the Book of Job. It includes a theoretical discussion of poetic imagery and an overview of all references to the womb, Sheol, and the grave in Job. Vall closely investigates Job 1:21, arguing that Sheol is depicted through the image of the womb and that the womb of Mother Earth encompasses both the unborn and the dead.[48] In a later article, Vall provides a more extensive analysis of the birth metaphors in Job 38:28–29.[49] Zwan examines the image of the womb from a psychoanalytic perspective, highlighting Job's ambivalence towards it. Job expresses negative feelings about the womb, yet simultaneously desires a return to it. According to Zwan, the image of Sheol as a womb brings positive associations to death.[50]

Greenstein demonstrates that the metaphor of the womb as a room with doors, used in Job 3:10 and 38:8–10, is also present in Akkadian texts.[51] Building on Greenstein's work, Langton argues that Job 3 represents an inversion of Akkadian birth incantations. She also points out that both Job and Akkadian texts portray birth as the baby being brought into light.[52] Eckstein claims that Job 3:12a depicts a birth, suggesting that the expression "knees to receive me" represents the baby seeing their mother's knees when they are being born.[53] Schifferdecker discusses the motif of procreation in her book on creation theology, *Out of the Whirlwind: Creation Theology in the Book of Job*. She examines how procreation serves as a unifying

---

[47] Alter 2011, 123–29.

[48] Vall 1993. His discussion on Job 1:21 is also presented in condensed form in an article (Vall 1995a). Job 1:21 has been cited by other scholars, including Keel and Schroer, Stordalen, and Meyer, as evidence supporting the idea of Sheol as a womb and the concept of Mother Earth (Keel and Schroer 2015, 84–85; Stordalen 2010, 113–14; Meyer 2021, 139–40).

[49] Vall 1995b.

[50] van der Zwan 2019a.

[51] Greenstein 2017, 147–49.

[52] Langton 2012. Langton refers to Greenstein's paper presented at the SBL meeting in 2008.

[53] Eckstein 2019.

theme throughout the prologue, dialogue, God's speeches, and the epilogue. In the prose and dialogue, procreation is used to signify both God's blessing and punishment, while in God's speeches it symbolizes God's nurturing of all creation, including wild animals and the sea.[54] Newsom explores various voices and metaphors in her book *The Book of Job: A Contest of Moral Imaginations*. She interprets the reference to the mother's womb in Job 1:21 as bringing associations of protection to Job's experience of exposure and death.[55] Additionally, she argues that the birth metaphors in God's speeches add a caring perspective on God's relationship with the wild parts of creation.[56] Both Newsom and Schifferdecker discuss the portrayal of God as a midwife who delivers the sea but also restricts it and sets boundaries for it.[57]

To summarize: Previous studies have noted similarities between the metaphors in the HB and Akkadian texts, particularly in how both depict the womb as a room with doors, and birth as going out into the light. There are some recurring interpretations and discussions in previous studies of birth metaphors in the Book of Job. One interpretation is that Job 1:21 uses the image of the womb to portray death as a protective and secure place. Another interpretation highlights how Job 3 combines the language of procreation and creation, which is interpreted as if Job inverts the order of creation. Additionally, the metaphor of God as a midwife in God's first speech is recognized as adding a caring dimension to God's relationship with the sea and the wild parts of creation.

Open Questions from Previous Research

Previous metaphor studies demonstrate the importance of using cognitive methods to analyze metaphors. If metaphors are cognitive, they should be studied accordingly. However, cognitive methods need to be complemented by a close reading of the text and an understanding of its cultural context. Existing research underscores the necessity of examining how metaphors interact, and blending theory as a valuable tool for interpreting complex metaphors, creativity, and ambiguous texts. Despite its potential, blending theory remains underutilized in biblical research. This study will consider these insights from previous research and contribute by providing a systematic application of blending theory to a large number of metaphors.

---

[54] Schifferdecker 2008, 121–27.
[55] Newsom 2003, 57.
[56] Newsom 2003, 244.
[57] Newsom 2003, 244; Schifferdecker 2008, 76–77.

Earlier studies have pointed out that the motifs of birth and procreation are central in Job's lament in Job 3 and in God's speeches. However, there has not yet been a thorough examination of how these birth metaphors are constructed, which is a necessary prerequisite to studying their interaction or understanding them from other perspectives, such as using a psychoanalytical framework. The birth metaphors in Job have often been interpreted intuitively, without a solid grounding in metaphor theory, leading to assumptions such as viewing the womb as a protective space, or birth in positive terms, even when this is neither stated nor implied in the text. Other debatable assumptions include references to Mother Earth, the idea that the birth metaphors in Job 3 imply an inversion of creation, and that God as a midwife limits the sea. Recognizing the similarities between Akkadian birth incantations and the Book of Job is crucial for this study. I will demonstrate how the Book of Job shares several metaphors with these incantations and uses presumed standard metaphors in a new creative way. Finally, previous research on birth metaphors has largely overlooked how new metaphors challenge conventional beliefs, and how the metaphors under investigation here function in this regard. The image of God as a midwife has been acknowledged in earlier studies, but it is worth exploring whether, or to what extent, this metaphor challenges traditional beliefs.

2. Metaphor Theory

In my research, I want to explore how birth metaphors are constructed, their purpose, the associations and thoughts they presuppose, what they highlight, and their impact on the discourse in the Book of Job. I will primarily use blending theory, complemented by insights from conceptual metaphor theory. Both theories assert that metaphors are conceptual, integral to our thinking, and construct our reality. Conceptual metaphor theory emphasizes that metaphors are grounded in embodied experience and structure our cognition. Blending theory provides a flexible and comprehensive framework for understanding the complexities involved in constructing metaphors. In this chapter, I will present these two theories, along with contextual factors influencing the construction of metaphors, and how to analyze novel metaphors and the interaction between metaphors.

Conceptual Metaphor Theory

Conceptual metaphor theory, also called cognitive metaphor theory, holds that metaphors are cognitive and structure the way we think. Metaphors are not only seen as ornamental or as rhetorical expressions, but as crucial in order to understand the world that surrounds us. In 1980, Lakoff and Johnson published their book *Metaphors We Live By*, in which they presented a systematic analysis of how linguistic expressions are derived from conceptual metaphors that structure our thinking.[1] Their book has had a tremendous influence on metaphor research, and also on how metaphors are analyzed in biblical research.[2] It will serve as my point of departure, complemented by later research, particularly the developments by Kövecses, who integrates conceptual metaphor theory with blending theory.[3]

---

[1] Lakoff and Johnson 2003.
[2] See Chapter 1, pages 27–31.
[3] Kövecses has published several books and articles on metaphor theory. In my work, I use his metaphor handbook (Kövecses 2010) and his studies on creativity in metaphor production and the influence of context (Kövecses 2005; Kövecses 2015; Kövecses 2020).

Metaphors and Domains

Lakoff and Johnson primarily focus on metaphors in our everyday language and explore underlying, mainly unconscious, metaphors that structure the way we think. They define a metaphor as "understanding and experiencing one kind of thing in terms of another."[4] Not only are two different concepts brought together in the metaphor, but also two domains. A *concept* is a basic unit of mental representation, and its meaning depends on how it relates to other concepts. A *domain* is the network of the associated concepts of a unifying concept. It could be understood as the background knowledge structure of a concept stored in the long-term memory. Domains are rich in information and include both associated concepts and the relationships between them.[5] A domain can be broad, like the domain of LOVE, or more specific like, the domain of HUSBAND. The domain of HUSBAND is part of the broader domain of MARRIAGE which in turn can be part of the domain of LOVE. (Small capital letters are used in conceptual metaphor theory to mark that the domains, or the metaphors, operate on a conceptual level.)

The two domains in a metaphor are called *source domain* and *target domain*, with the target domain being understood and experienced in terms of the source domain. A metaphor is typically expressed in the formula THE TARGET DOMAIN IS THE SOURCE DOMAIN. The process in which different aspects, characteristics, and structures, from the source domain are transferred to the target is called *mapping*. Lakoff and Johnson describe the mapping as selective; for instance, not all associations of the domain of WAR are mapped onto the domain of ARGUMENT in the metaphor ARGUMENT IS WAR.[6] They also claim that the mapping is unidirectional, it goes from the source domain to the target, and from a more concrete domain to a more abstract one.[7]

Metaphors Structure our Thoughts

The conceptual metaphor ARGUMENT IS WAR makes us conceptualize ARGUMENT in terms of WAR, leading to linguistic expressions such as "he attacked every weak point in my argument," "okay, shoot," and "I've have never won an

---

[4] Lakoff and Johnson 2003, 5.
[5] My definition is based on how domains are discussed in Langacker 2008, 44–47; Evans 2019, 402; Kövecses 2020, 53–54. Lakoff and Johnson discuss domains as the overall experience of something, including both embodied experience and the way it is shaped by interactions with people within a specific culture and context (Lakoff and Johnson 2003, 117).
[6] Lakoff and Johnson 2003, 12–13; Kövecses 2010, 93–96.
[7] Lakoff and Johnson 2003, 112.

argument with him."[8] The domain of WAR thus functions not only as an image of what an ARGUMENT might be, but also shapes the way we think about arguments and how we act when we argue with each other.

Metaphors Hide and Highlight

Metaphors always both highlight and hide aspects of their target domains. The metaphor ARGUMENT IS WAR hides the cooperative aspects of arguing and highlights the opposition between the debaters. To highlight other aspects of argument, we need to combine it with other metaphors such as ARGUMENT IS A BUILDING and ARGUMENT IS A CONTAINER, which highlight the construction and the content of argument. That the source domain only structures parts of the target domain is a natural consequence of the nature of the metaphor. If the structuring were total, the source domain would essentially become the target domain, and then there would be no metaphor.[9]

Correlation and Resemblance Metaphors

Lakoff and Johnson show how our metaphors are based on experience. They distinguish between metaphors that arise from correlations within our experiences, and those that are based on experiential similarities.[10] The metaphor GOD IS A KING is based on experiential similarities, on resemblance, as both God and a king are seen as figures of authority and power. The metaphor DANGER IS DARKNESS is not based on resemblance but on our experience of being more exposed to danger during the dark night than in bright daylight. The distinction between correlation metaphors and resemblance metaphors has become a standard categorization for defining metaphors within conceptual metaphor theory.[11] Resemblance metaphors have been the focus of traditional metaphor research, but conceptual metaphor theory reveals that many of our fundamental metaphors are grounded in co-occurrence in our embodied experience. The term embodied experience refers to inner physical reactions and to how we interact with the world around us, with other objects, humans, animals, and nature. The human body and body parts are common source domains, and so also are physical experiences such as illness,

---

[8] Lakoff and Johnson 2003, 4–6.
[9] Lakoff and Johnson 2003, 10–13. For further discussion of selective mapping and how a metaphor highlights and hides aspects of a target domain, see Kövecses 2010, 91–96.
[10] Lakoff and Johnson 2003, 147–55.
[11] For a more detailed presentation of correlation and resemblance metaphors, see Kövecses 2010, 78–86.

sleeping, giving birth, and eating.[12] Two concepts or domains are correlated if they are combined repeatedly in human experience. The metaphor MORE IS UP is based on the experience that when we pile something up, or pour water into a glass, there is a correlation between quantity and height.[13] The metaphor ANGER IS HEAT is based on our embodied experience of becoming warm when anger is aroused.[14]

It is important to Lakoff and Johnson to discuss resemblance metaphors as grounded in experiential similarity. The similarity is not inherent but experiential, and we tend to create similarities between the two domains involved in the metaphor. Lakoff and Johnson refer to the metaphor LIFE IS A GAMBLE as one grounded in experiential similarity. Users of this metaphor create similarities between life and gambling: actions in life are likened to playing cards or bluffing, the outcomes of one's actions are framed as winning or losing, and the likelihood of events is referred to in terms of odds.[15]

The similarities between target and source domains in conventional metaphors have become part of our conceptual system. Lakoff and Johnson show that metaphors based on our embodied experience of space and objects can also be used to create similarities in more complex metaphors. The metaphors BODY IS A CONTAINER and MIND IS A CONTAINER OF IDEAS lead to an experienced structural similarity between FOOD and IDEAS—they are objects that enter our bodies as a bounded space. We recognize parallels between food and ideas: just as we chew, swallow, and digest food, we use similar expressions for ideas, saying that we chew over, swallow, and digest them, reflecting how we process an idea intellectually.[16]

Entailments of a Metaphor

A metaphor establishes a basic mapping between two domains, with its structure shaped by the source domain. In the metaphor LIFE IS A JOURNEY, the basic mapping involves viewing life as a journey that begins with birth, significant life events as destinations, life choices as different paths, and dreams for the future as goals. However, we know much more about journeys than is used in the basic selective mapping between the domains. We know that when we travel by car, the driver needs to follow certain traffic rules and that there are roundabouts and speed bumps on the road. This knowledge of certain kinds of journey might be used in

---

[12] Lakoff and Johnson 2003, 56–60, 117–18; Kövecses 2010, 18–23.
[13] Lakoff and Johnson 2003, 14–21, 151–52.
[14] Kövecses 2010, 79–81.
[15] Lakoff and Johnson 2003, 153–55; Kövecses 2010, 81–82.
[16] Lakoff and Johnson 2003, 147–55; Kövecses 2010, 83–84.

an elaboration of the metaphor LIFE IS A JOURNEY. We can describe an experience in life as a road bump that made us go slower, or that our life is like driving round a roundabout without knowing which exit to choose. This rich knowledge of source domains that can be used in metaphorization is called the *entailment* of the metaphor.[17] Entailment can include the structure of the source domain, logical implications of the metaphor, and more specific or more general metaphors which can be derived from the metaphor. The metaphor TIME IS MONEY entails the more general metaphor TIME IS A LIMITED RESOURCE. Metaphors that share entailments are easily combined and Lakoff and Johnson call them *coherent metaphors*.[18]

Summary: Conceptual Metaphor Theory

Conceptual metaphor theory holds that metaphors are cognitive. We think in metaphors, and they are grounded in our embodied experience. Lakoff and Johnson's definition of a metaphor is "understanding and experiencing one kind of thing in terms of another."[19] Not only are two different concepts brought together in the metaphor, but also two domains. A domain is the network of associations of a concept and how they relate to each other. The target domain is understood in terms of the source domain and expressed in the formula THE TARGET DOMAIN IS THE SOURCE DOMAIN. In conceptual metaphor theory the mapping is said to be unidirectional, and the target domain is more abstract than the source domain. Not all characteristics of the source domain are used in the metaphor. The mapping from the source to the target is selective, and the metaphor always highlights certain aspects and downplays other aspects of the target domain. There are two different kinds of metaphors. One is based on correlation of experience and the other is based on experienced similarities between the two domains. In correlation metaphors, the link between domains is strong, but the mappings between domains in conventionalized resemblance metaphors also become entrenched in our conceptual system.

---

[17] Kövecses 2010, 121–26. In conceptual metaphor theory, the entailment only concerns the rich knowledge of the source domain; however, in blending theory it also includes the knowledge of the target domain.

[18] Lakoff and Johnson 2003, 91–96.

[19] Lakoff and Johnson 2003, 5.

Developments of Conceptual Metaphor Theory

Many of the insights presented by Lakoff and Johnson in *Metaphors We Live By* are still important to metaphor research, including their basic insights on how metaphors are conceptual, structure our thoughts, involve domains, highlight aspects of the targets, and how general metaphors can be elaborated and specified. However, conceptual metaphor theory has been developed, modified, and tested since they published their book.[20] Blending theory is one of these developments. Image schema and primary metaphor theory have further explored how metaphors are grounded in experience. Primary metaphor theory holds that only a few basic primary universal metaphors are grounded in embodied experience; however, from these, more complex metaphors are constructed.[21] Metonymic research discusses how correlation metaphors are mainly created from metonymic relationships. These explorations of the relationships between general and specific metaphors also relate to questions about which of the conceptual metaphors may be considered universal across cultures, and which ones appear to be more context-dependent.[22] Neuroscience has demonstrated the connection between embodied experience and metaphors. By exploring which brain areas and neurological paths are activated during metaphor comprehension, we can examine how certain conceptual metaphors activate sensorimotor areas together with areas of abstract thinking.[23] The focus on conceptual conventional metaphors influenced by *Metaphors We Live By* has been complemented by discussion on how conceptual metaphors are used in literary texts, how new metaphors are created, and the influence of

---

[20] I will refer only to some of the developments in conceptual metaphor theory. Others that could be mentioned are class inclusion theory by Glucksberg and Keysar 1990; deliberate metaphor theory by Steen 2017; career metaphor theory by Bowdle and Gentner 2005.

[21] For an introduction to primary metaphor theory, see Grady 1997a. Grady also discusses primary metaphors in an article analyzing the conceptual metaphor THEORIES ARE BUILDINGS (Grady 1997b). For another clarifying overview, see Evans 2019, 320–34.

[22] We can never definitively claim that a metaphor is used in every culture around the world. Referring to metaphors as universal is based on the assumption that these metaphors are so fundamental to human experience that they are likely used and understood universally, or almost universally. However, even embodied experiences are shaped by specific cultural frameworks, and so-called universal metaphors can be interpreted differently depending on the cultural context. This will be discussed below, see pages 61–63.

[23] For an overview on neural theory of metaphors, see Lakoff 2008.

context in metaphor production.[24] In the following section of this chapter, I will first briefly present theories of image schemas and conceptual metonymy, and then turn to my main theory: blending theory.

Image Schemas

Lakoff and Johnson develop conceptual metaphor theory by discussing *image schemas*, the basic recurring patterns in our embodied experiences.[25] Image schemas are often acquired in early childhood and formed from our sensorimotor skills, our interactions with other humans and objects, and the way in which we experience spatial relations. Because image schemas are recurring patterns which are crucial in the development of every child, they can be assumed to be universal. Examples of image schemas are SOURCE-PATH-GOAL, CONTAINMENT, PART-WHOLE, and BALANCE. For example, the image schema BALANCE is used in metaphorical expressions such as "the balance of justice" or "he is mentally imbalanced."[26] An image schema that we receive early is CONTAINMENT. From experience we know that a container needs an opening to be filled or emptied, and when the container moves, its contents stay in the container. The metaphor THE BODY IS A CONTAINER is a universal metaphor. For example, the head is seen as a container of ideas and the mouth as a container of words.

The recognition of image schemas, or recurring embodied patterns, helps us recognize conceptual metaphors that are used cross-culturally. It also helps us in discussions about how metaphors cohere and interact.[27]

---

[24] Two scholars who have significantly developed conceptual metaphor theory are Kövecses and Gibbs. Kövecses has contributed through his research on the context of metaphors and the integration of conceptual metaphor theory with blending theory, most notably presented in his book *Extended Conceptual Metaphor Theory* (Kövecses 2020). Gibbs discusses how different metaphor theories often represent various stages of metaphorical production, each offering a useful perspective on the process. He argues that these theories should be viewed as complementary rather than competing (Gibbs 2017, 15–17, 213–21, 262–68).

[25] The development of the theory of image schemas was developed by Lakoff and Johnson, and is closely related to their metaphor theory. Each of them published a book on image schemas (Lakoff 1987; Johnson 1987). For an overview of this theory, see Evans 2019, 221–40.

[26] Gibbs 2017, 23–25.

[27] Lakoff refers to image schemas in his discussion of how target and source domains are paired in the construction of metaphors. He suggests that the structure of the image schema from the source domain must be preserved in the mapping and remain consistent with the inherent structure of the target domain. He calls this the *invariance principle* (Lakoff 1993, 215). This principle is useful for understanding how domains can easily be integrated within general conceptual metaphors. However, it is important to recognize that we are also capable of understanding and creating metaphors from domains with conflicting structures.

Conceptual Metonymy

Metonymy is when we use something closely related to a concept to refer to it. For example, saying "I read Astrid Lindgren to my children" refers to her books rather than the author herself. Similarly, "he seeks comfort in the bottle" uses "the bottle" to stand for alcohol, and "the White House has decided" uses the building to represent its residents. A synecdoche is a type of metonymy that expresses a part-whole relationship, where a part, such as "the wheel," is used to refer to the whole, in this case, the entire car. Metonymies are not only linguistic devices, but also conceptual constructs.[28] One suggestion is that metonymy is more fundamental to our cognitive system than metaphors.[29] It is not always easy to separate metonymy and metaphors. The following distinction of Kövecses is clarifying:

> A common definition of metaphor in conceptual metaphor theory is that in metaphor we conceptualize one domain in terms of another (Lakoff & Johnson, 1980). In metonymy, an element in a domain, or frame, provides mental access to another element within the same domain, or frame.[30]

Metonymy only concerns one domain, and a metaphor involves at least two domains. However, it seems that metaphors and metonyms interact, and it has been argued that correlation metaphors involve a metonymic state.[31] The metaphor HAPPY IS UP could be seen as a correlation metaphor based on the co-occurrence in experience of being happy and being up, as when someone who is happy jumps up and down. However, it could also originate from the metonymy, where UP represents the whole experience of HAPPINESS. This is a metonymy, as long as being up is part of the experience and the domain of HAPPINESS. However, when it is generalized to describe the happiness of someone who is sitting down, it becomes a metaphor that combines the two separate domains: SPACE (being up) and EMOTION (happiness). Kövecses describes this process as a process of generalization and argues that at least some of the correlation metaphors pass a metonymic stage when they are produced.[32] Not all metaphor theorists approve of this theory of metonymic stage in correlation metaphors. Even so, recognizing the metonymic stage in correlation metaphors is illuminating, and explains why it can be difficult to

---

[28] For an overview of conceptual metonymy, see Evans 2019, 334–48.
[29] Evans 2019, 341.
[30] Kövecses 2013, 78.
[31] Evans 2019, 339–42. Goossens discusses the interaction between metaphor and metonymy in Goossens 2002.
[32] Kövecses 2013, 87. Kövecses also discusses the metaphors ANGER IS HEAT, SADNESS IS DOWN, and KNOWING IS SEEING.

discern whether an expression is based in a correlation metaphor or a metonymy. For instance, referring to darkness as something dangerous can be explained either by the correlation metaphor DANGER IS DARKNESS, grounded in the experience of having encountered dangers in a dark night, or as a metonymy where darkness represents all the dangers lurking in the darkness of the night.

Blending Theory

Blending theory, also called conceptual integration theory, was developed by Fauconnier and Turner.[33] Like conceptual metaphor theory, it presupposes that metaphors are part of our cognitive structure, and are processed by combining different areas of meaning and experience. However, blending theory does not define a metaphor as understanding one thing "in terms of another," but as understanding one thing by blending it with one or several other things. Blending theory holds that a metaphor is a more complex network than a unidirectional mapping from the concrete source domain to a more abstract target domain. The simplified pattern of a metaphor presented by conceptual metaphor theory is a pattern of many metaphors, but not of all. There are more complex metaphors that cannot be explained by this pattern. Consider the metaphor THE SURGEON IS A BUTCHER, which expresses that the surgeon is incompetent and a danger to the patient.[34] The notion of incompetence is not part of the source domain and cannot be explained by the mapping from the source to the target. It is created from the disanalogy between the two domains. A surgeon's goal is to heal, and the butcher's is to kill and dismember. These kinds of metaphors can be explained by blending theory, which is a suitable tool for complex metaphors, and to describe creativity present in metaphor production.

Mental Spaces and Organizing Frames

Blending theory, rooted in mental space theory, explores how the mind processes sensory impressions and information by integrating various areas of meaning, so called mental spaces. According to this theory, a metaphor involves at least two input spaces that are integrated into a space of shared generalized features, the

---

[33] The Fauconnier and Turner book *The Way We Think* is a comprehensive presentation of blending theory (Fauconnier and Turner 2002). They had previously presented their theoretical framework in two articles (Fauconnier and Turner 1996; Fauconnier and Turner 1998).

[34] This has become a classic example in descriptions of blending theory, as mentioned in Grady, et al. 1999, 103. See pages 49–51.

generic space, and a new area of meaning, a new space, the blended space, which encompasses the metaphorical meaning. The metaphor is a new construction which is formed from the interaction between these different spaces.

Mental spaces are defined by Fauconnier and Turner as "conceptual packets constructed as we think and talk, for purposes of local understanding and action."[35] Mental spaces are partial and temporary when compared with domains that are stable and contain all forms of frames and entities related to a concept. Mental spaces are concerned with the thoughts we have in the present moment, and correspond to neuronal assemblies. The integration of these mental spaces corresponds to the neurological co-activation of different brain areas.[36] The spaces contain different elements, and often a frame which structures the element and relates them to each other. The concept of a frame is used somewhat differently by various scholars within cognitive linguistics.[37] In their description of blending theory, Fauconnier and Turner refer to the organizing frame of mental spaces. The *organizing frames* go back to the schematic organizations of the domains from which the mental spaces are derived, and they are entrenched in the long-term memory and recruited to structure the relations and roles of the elements in the spaces. The organizing frame specifies and relates the agents, activity, and events of the space to each other. For example, the organizing frame of BOXING frames the scenario of two boxers who fight in a ring, where the one who knocks the other down wins, and the one who is knocked down loses. The BOXING frame is a subframe to the more general frame FIGHTING, which in turn is a subframe to COMPETITION. The organizing frame often includes different scales of time, space, quality, and quantity. The organizing frame of BOXING contains thoughts such as: how good are the boxers? how long does a match last? how many people are in the audience? how hard do the contestants hit?[38]

A mental space is operating in the working memory but can be entrenched in the long-term memory. If someone refers to a teacher we may automatically think

---

[35] Fauconnier and Turner 2002, 40.

[36] Fauconnier and Turner 2002, 102.

[37] There are no clear shared definitions in cognitive linguistics for terms such as frames and domains. The term *frame* is sometimes used interchangeably with *domain* to refer to a network of concepts tied to a particular idea. Kövecses, however, distinguishes frame as a level between domain and space which is more specific than a domain but less specific than a mental space (Kövecses 2020, 51–56). Frame semantics use frame as a collective term for concepts that belong together because they are associated in experience. For an introduction to "frame semantics" and a discussion of the overlap between frame and domain, see Croft and Cruse 2004, 7–21.

[38] Fauconnier and Turner 2002, 104–5.

of students, education, or of our favorite teacher in school. These spaces are then co-activated, and relations between them are entrenched. A mental space can activate entrenched structures such as organizing frames, blended spaces, and the whole network of the blend. Conventional metaphors are entrenched blends which we easily activate while novel metaphors involve new blending processes.

Integration of Spaces

Blending theory describes how our thoughts are built on networks of mental spaces.[39] When two or more *input spaces* interact, it leads to a generic space and to a blended space. The *generic space* contains shared characteristics of the input spaces. These characteristics need to be generalized and abstracted enough to correlate to both input spaces. The fourth space in the integration network is the *blended space,* also just called the blend. This space is related to the generic space. Some of the elements and frames of the input spaces are projected from the input spaces to the blend. The generic space guides which elements and structures are projected from the input spaces; however, additional elements and structures from any of the input spaces may also be projected to the blend. The context also guides the selective projection from the input spaces to the blend. New elements and structures which do not exist in the input spaces, or their frames, can also emerge in the blend. The new structure of the blend, which is not found in the input spaces, is called an *emergent structure*. This will explain how the element of incompetence emerges in the metaphor THE SURGEON IS A BUTCHER, even if neither the input space SURGEON nor BUTCHER contains the notion of incompetence.[40]

The projections and the interactions between the spaces are often mapped out in a so-called *blending schema* displaying the *integration network*. A blending schema of the integration network helps us to unpack the metaphors we analyze and see what characteristics and structures are combined between the spaces. A basic integration network is typically displayed as in Figure 2.1.

---

[39] For the elements of blending, see Fauconnier and Turner 2002, 40–50.
[40] See pages 49–51.

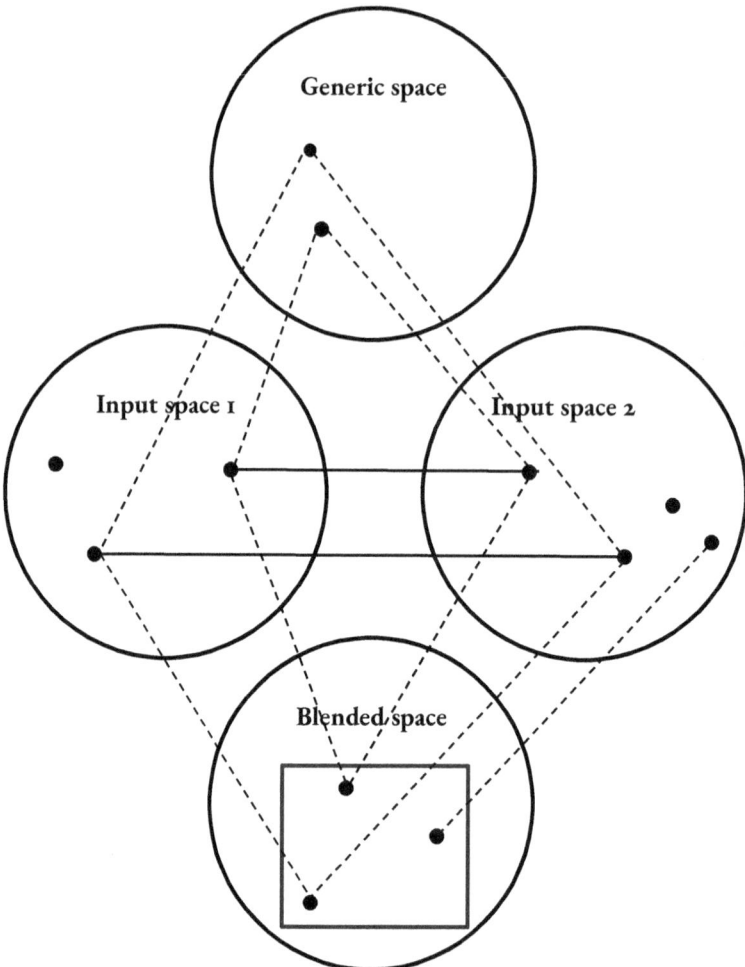

Figure 2.1 *Blending schema of a basic integration network.*[41]

The dots represent the elements of the spaces. The correspondences between the input spaces are linked with solid lines. The dotted line shows how elements in the input spaces are generalized in the generic space or projected to the blended space. The square indicates the emergent structure. Since lines between the different elements of the input spaces often make the map of the network cluttered, scholars

---

[41] Adapted from Figure 3.6 in Fauconnier and Turner 2002, 46.

often simplify the schemas in various ways. Some scholars skip the blending schema altogether and instead use columns to represent the different spaces. Others may omit the connecting lines or only include them when absolutely necessary. Additionally, the round circles may be replaced with squares for a clearer presentation.[42] In my presentations of the integration networks, I have simplified the blending schema, using squares with rounded corners, and only drawing lines between the elements when I consider it necessary to point out how the elements correlate. I use squares not only to point out the emergent structure of the blend, but also to mark the organizing frames of the input spaces when this allows for a better understanding of the network (see below in Figure 2.2).[43]

Single- and Double-Scope Networks

Blending theory is not only concerned with metaphors but with cognition in general. Fauconnier and Turner describe different kinds of integration networks depending on the organizing frames of the input spaces and the blended space. The networks, called single-scope networks and double-scope networks, are essential for exploring metaphors formed from two input spaces.[44] A *single-scope network* has two input spaces with different organizing frames, but only one of them structures the blend. This type of network corresponds to how conceptual metaphor theory describes the pattern of metaphors in terms of a target domain which is understood through a source domain. The input space which projects its frame to the blend corresponds to the source domain. Fauconnier and Turner refer to the input space containing the organizing frame as the "framing input" and the other as the "focus input" but also identify them as the "source" and "target."[45] The single-scope network is always asymmetrical. The framing input space organizes the

---

[42] The dotted and solid lines are often simplified or reduced, as seen in Robinette 2014, 44. Dancygier and Sweetser use squares with rounded corners instead of circles (Dancygier and Sweetser 2014, 75, 83, 92). Sweetser and Descamp use columns as a complement to a simplified network model in DesCamp and Sweetser 2005, 227–28, and only columns in Sweetser and DesCamp 2014, 16–18. Some scholars, however, use the standard map of the blend, as demonstrated by Goering 2014, 137, 140, Gomola 2018, 163, 166, 175.

[43] Evans and Lundhaug use squares to point out organizing frames of the input spaces (Evans 2019, 532–33, 537; Lundhaug 2014, 81).

[44] Other types of networks are simplex and mirror networks, which are presented together with single- and double-scope blends in Fauconnier and Turner 2002, 119–35. In my presentation, I will use standard examples which are used in the presentation of these networks in Fauconnier and Turner, but also by Kövecses and Evans (Kövecses 2005, 267–82; Evans 2019, 550–56).

[45] Fauconnier and Turner 2002, 127.

terms in the blend and plays a major role in what elements of the input spaces are projected into the blend, while the target does not structure the blend.

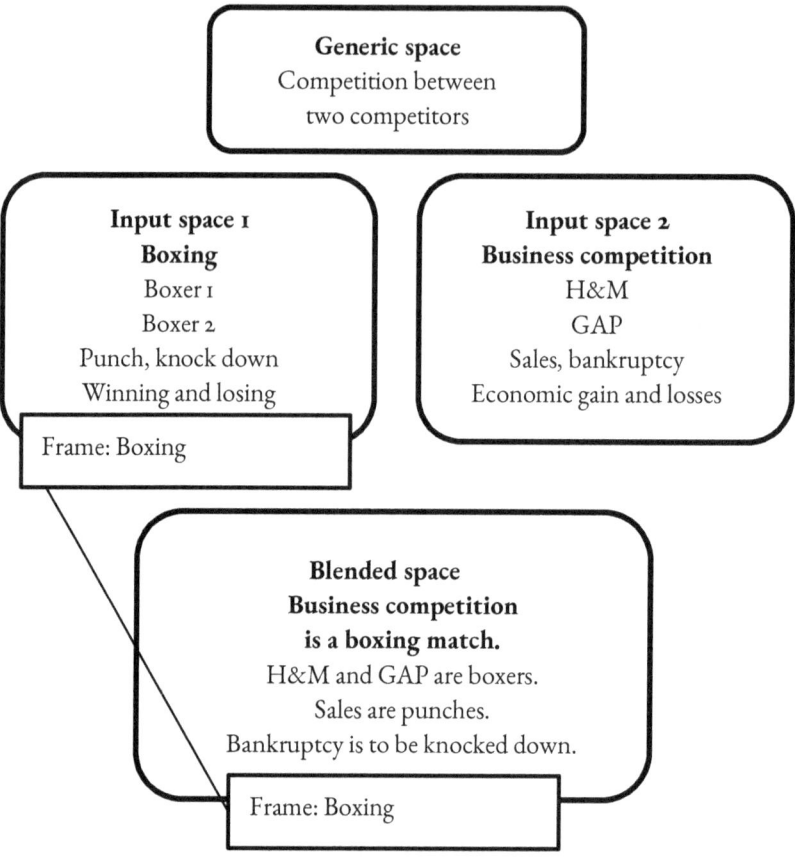

Figure 2.2 Blending schema of a single-scope network of the metaphor BUSINESS COMPETITION IS A BOXING MATCH.[46]

The metaphor BUSINESS COMPETITION IS A BOXING MATCH is a single-scope network. The frame BOXING organizes the blend, in which the business competitors, here the clothing companies H&M and GAP, are two boxers that punch each other. The goal for the boxers is to win and to knock the other down. The more

---

[46] Adapted from Figure 7.2 in Fauconnier and Turner 2002, 128.

general frame COMPETITION is a shared frame between both boxing matches and business competition, and is part of the generic space. This shared frame makes the analogy between BOXING and BUSINESS COMPETITION possible, but it does not organize the blend. The business competition is understood in the structure of a boxing match. The difference between the two organizing frames of the input space is solved by only letting one of the input spaces organize the blend. It is also common that frames of the targets are diffuse, as in abstract targets, which then need to be structured by the sources. For instance, DEATH, which has a diffuse organizing frame due to our uncertainty about what happens when we die, is structured through the metaphor DEATH IS SLEEPING by the more concrete source domain of SLEEPING. This approach aligns with how metaphors are presented in conceptual metaphor theory.

The *double-scope network* is a network where the blend has an organizing frame of its own that is constructed from the organizing frames of both input spaces or from an interaction between them. The interaction between the frames of the input spaces may result in new frame structures that are not part of the original frames of the input spaces. The organizing frames of the input spaces often clash, which leads to creative new constructions of the blends. When the frames of the input spaces are more compatible, they are more smoothly combined in the blend. An example of a double-scope network with high asymmetry and different organizing frames is the metaphor THE SURGEON IS A BUTCHER, which I have mentioned above. The input space of the surgeon has the organizing frame SURGERY which states that the surgeon cuts the patient with precision in order to heal the patient. The input space of the butcher has the organizing frame BUTCHERY which states that the butcher kills and cuts the dead animal to dismember it. These two frames collide with respect to the purpose of the action. There is a disanalogy in why the surgeon and the butcher cut the body, between cutting with precision to heal on the one hand, and dismembering the body on the other. This collision between the frames leads to new structures in the blended space, resulting in the surgeon being perceived as incompetent. The blend visualizes a surgeon performing surgery as if they were a butcher. A surgeon who uses the scalpel as a cleaver, who cleaves the body instead of healing the body, is not a competent surgeon. The image and frame INCOMPETENCE is the emergent structure in the blend.

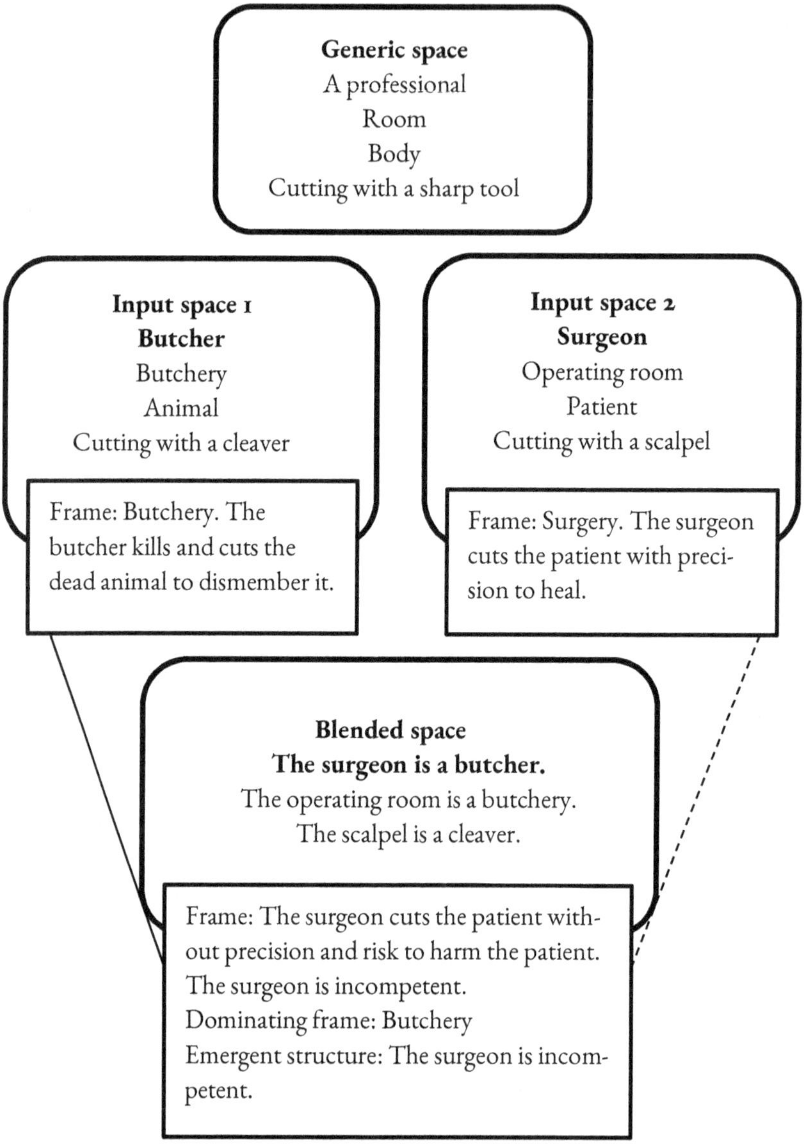

Generic space
A professional
Room
Body
Cutting with a sharp tool

Input space 1
Butcher
Butchery
Animal
Cutting with a cleaver

Frame: Butchery. The butcher kills and cuts the dead animal to dismember it.

Input space 2
Surgeon
Operating room
Patient
Cutting with a scalpel

Frame: Surgery. The surgeon cuts the patient with precision to heal.

Blended space
The surgeon is a butcher.
The operating room is a butchery.
The scalpel is a cleaver.

Frame: The surgeon cuts the patient without precision and risk to harm the patient.
The surgeon is incompetent.
Dominating frame: Butchery
Emergent structure: The surgeon is incompetent.

Figure 2.3 Blending schema of a double-scope network of the metaphor THE SURGEON IS A BUTCHER.[47]

---

[47] Adapted from Figure 1 in Grady, et al. 1999, 105.

In this blend we have a clear asymmetry: the input space SURGEON is the target, and the input space BUTCHER is the source of the metaphor. The frame BUTCHERY dominates the blend even if it also includes an emergent structure. Here, I use solid lines to mark the dominant frame, which mainly structure the blend, and dotted lines to indicate the non-dominant frame, which also contributes to the organizing frame of the blend and its emergent structure. Solid lines will also be used in double-scope blends, when I want to mark that both input spaces project significant parts of their organizing frames into the blend.

The double-scope networks can also be more symmetrical, at which point it is not meaningful to discuss the network in terms of target and source. The expression "smoke is coming out of his ears," reflect a more symmetrical network where one of frames of the input spaces does not dominate the blend. In the metaphor ANGER IS HEAT, various elements from the input space HEAT are projected to the blend to structure ANGER. For example, the container of the heated fluid becomes the image of the angry person, and the intensity of the heat structures the intensity of the anger. The image of an angry person with smoke coming from their ears combines aspects of both the angry person and the container of heated fluid. This blend incorporates structural elements from both input spaces, from both the angry person's body (the ears) and the steam from the heated fluid.[48]

Recognizing that both input spaces may contribute to the organizing frame of the blend is crucial. For example, the metaphor THE GRAVE IS A WOMB would be interpreted differently depending on whether it is considered a single-scope or double-scope network. If it were considered a single-scope metaphor, only the organizing frame of the womb would structure the blend. The structure of the womb depicts the baby lying in the protective womb until birth, and when this structure is applied to the grave, it presents the grave as a protected place of transition to a new life. In this view, the grave is seen as a place where the dead are sheltered and nurtured until they are (re)born. However, if the metaphor is treated as a double-scope network, where both the frame of the womb and the frame of death contribute to the blend, the metaphor could incorporate additional ideas. This could include the notion of death as an eternal sleep, combined with projections from the womb, resulting in the metaphor depicting the grave as a sheltered place of eternal rest. Guidance from the context of the metaphor is essential for determining how the metaphor is constructed, and which frames and elements are projected into the blend.

---

[48] Kövecses 2005, 278–79.

Single-scope networks are easily modified and turned into double-scope networks in which the targets also influence the frame of the blends. Consider the metaphor THE LORD IS A SHEPHERD, which is modified in the parable of Jesus as the good shepherd who leaves 99 sheep to search for the lost one. Here, Jesus' concern for the lost sinner structures the blend, together with the frame of the input space SHEPHERD. One needs to be aware that many metaphors with high asymmetry and clear target and source input spaces are, in fact, double-scope networks. Turner expresses this as follows: "single-scope networks sit atop a very slippery slope and slide easily into double-scope structure."[49] The slippery slope is important to acknowledge. There is no strict line between single-scope and double-scope blend. The analysis of metaphors needs to be pragmatic, focusing on the most important details for interpretation, which depend on both the purpose of the analysis and the specific context in which the metaphor is used. This must also determine whether the blend is interpreted and displayed as a single-scope network, even if it could be argued that the organizing frame of the target has some minor influence on the organizing frame of the blend.

Multiple Blends

Integration networks do not need to consist of only two input spaces; they can involve multiple input spaces. An example of a multiple blend is provided by Fauconnier and Turner with the concept of the Grim Reaper.[50] It is a conventionalized blend in which DEATH is personified as the GRIM REAPER. The Grim Reaper is typically envisioned as a skeletal figure clothed in a dark hooded cloak, holding a scythe. At first glance, one might expect the Grim Reaper to be a double-scope network combining the elements A REAPER and DEATH, where characteristics from both input spaces merge in the blend. However, a closer examination reveals that it is a complex blend involving interactions between multiple input spaces and processes of metonymy. It involves input spaces of a dying person, of a murderer killing victims, a reaper cutting down crops, and a religious figure wearing a cowl. Additionally, it involves a metonymic relationship between death and a skeleton, and it incorporates a blend where the abstract concept DEATH is personified and blended with the cause behind the death of a person. The central integration network displaying the Grim Reaper is a network of the three input spaces REAPER, KILLER, and DEATH, which all share the general frame of AN AGENT CAUSING SOMETHING TO DIE.

---

[49] Turner 2008, 15.
[50] Fauconnier and Turner 2002, 291–95.

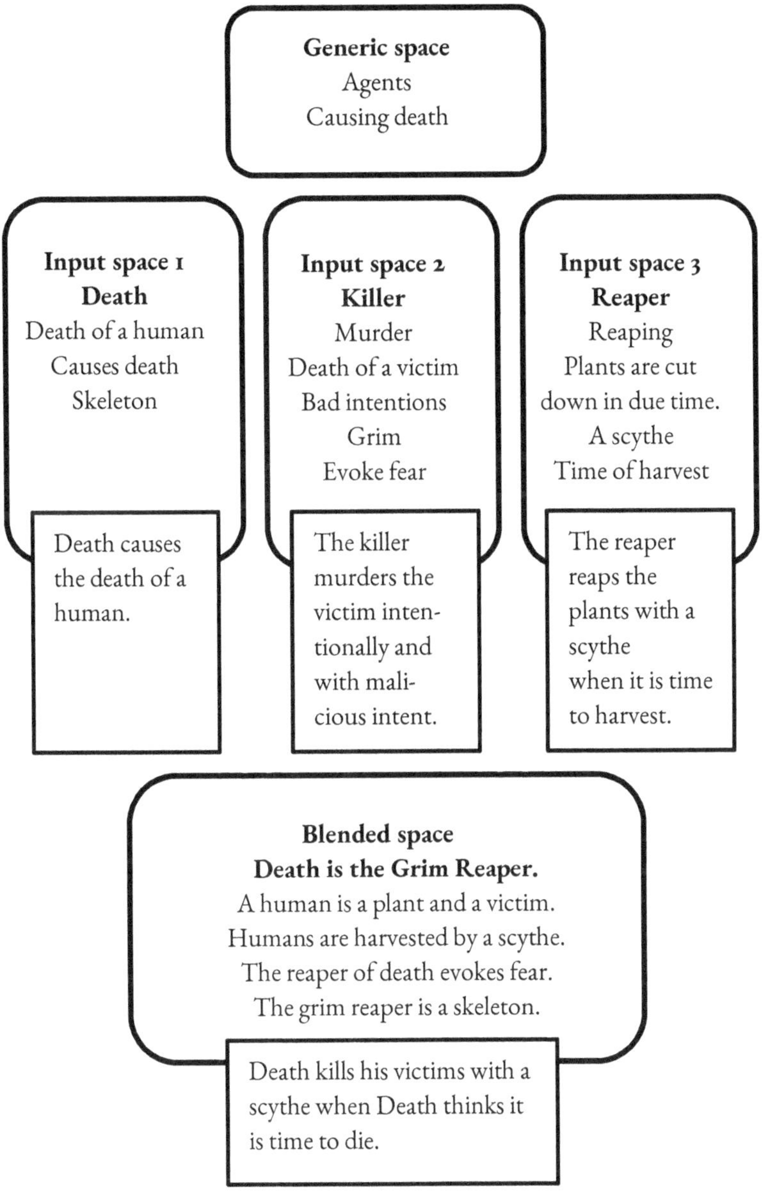

Generic space
Agents
Causing death

Input space 1
Death
Death of a human
Causes death
Skeleton

Death causes the death of a human.

Input space 2
Killer
Murder
Death of a victim
Bad intentions
Grim
Evoke fear

The killer murders the victim intentionally and with malicious intent.

Input space 3
Reaper
Reaping
Plants are cut down in due time.
A scythe
Time of harvest

The reaper reaps the plants with a scythe when it is time to harvest.

Blended space
Death is the Grim Reaper.
A human is a plant and a victim.
Humans are harvested by a scythe.
The reaper of death evokes fear.
The grim reaper is a skeleton.

Death kills his victims with a scythe when Death thinks it is time to die.

Figure 2.4 Blending schema of a multiple integration network of the metaphor DEATH IS THE GRIM REAPER.

Input space 1, in which DEATH is seen as an agent who causes the death of a human, is a blended space of a former network in which DEATH is blended with CAUSE OF DEATH. This is not an uncommon process and explains why we say that "sleep causes sleeping," and "love causes people to fall in love," or "smell causes smell." DEATH is personified to be able to be blended with the input space KILLER and REAPER. The organizing frames between REAPER and CAUSE OF DEATH are coherent. The reaper cuts down his plants when they have grown, and it is time to harvest. The personified Death causes death as a natural part of the lifecycle of a human. The conceptual metaphor HUMANS ARE PLANTS makes it easy for us to blend the reaper harvesting crops with the personified Death causing the death of humans. While it is natural to associate plants being cut down when they have fully grown with people dying of old age, the image of the Grim Reaper extends beyond natural death, as it also reaps when someone's life is taken too early. Death is described as grim, a feature that is not present in either the DEATH or the REAPER input spaces. This is a feature from a third space, a space of a murderer who kills with malicious intent. From this space, we also derive the idea that humans are victims who attempt to negotiate or escape their fate when confronted by the Grim Reaper. The authority of the Grim Reaper and the notion that he is sent by God are symbolized by the cloak, which is traditionally worn by priests and monks. This would be an additional blend between THE GRIM REAPER and A RELIGIOUS MAN where the Grim Reaper is portrayed as sent by God. The cloak might also be associated with funerals, as it is the garment of priests, who officiate at funerals.

The Grim Reaper is a multiple blend and shows that an expression might allude to more than two input spaces, and to input spaces which are not explicitly mentioned in the metaphorical expression.

Vital Relations

Mental spaces are structured by organizing frames. These relate the different elements in the input spaces to each other. The links between elements within a space and between the spaces are called *vital relations*. Fauconnier and Turner refer to several vital relations, such as ANALOGY, DISANALOGY, TIME, SPACE, ROLE, IDENTITY, CAUSE-EFFECT, CHANGE, REPRESENTATION, PART-WHOLE, PROPERTY, CATEGORY, INTENTIONALITY, and UNIQUENESS.[51] When a face on an old photo is identified with the person in front of us, then we run a blend which links the input space of the photo to the input space of the person: it is a link of IDENTITY

---

[51] Fauconnier and Turner 2002, 92–102, 312–19.

and PART-WHOLE. In the metaphor BUSINESS IS BOXING, the two input spaces are primarily linked by ANALOGY, and in THE SURGEON IS A BUTCHER by both ANALOGY AND DISANALOGY. (Both metaphors are also linked by other vital relations such as ROLE and INTENTIONALITY.) Vital relations from the input spaces are projected to the blend. The input spaces usually do not need to share the value or the scale of the vital relations. They could refer to different times or to different places around the earth but still be blended. The input spaces LIFE and JOURNEY are linked by the vital relation TIME, which is projected to the blend of the metaphor LIFE IS A JOURNEY. A lifetime and a journey operate on different scales, and the metaphor LIFE IS A JOURNEY compresses a lifetime into the more manageable scale of a journey.

The governing principle for integration networks is to make things easier to understand, to use familiar experiences to understand complicated matters. We tend to scale down to a timeline we can grasp, simplify complicated cause and effect relations to one or two major causes, or combine a diffuse order of events into the plot of a story with a few key elements. Fauconnier and Turner call this process a scaling down to *the Human Scale* which they see as a guiding principle of all blending processes.[52]

The Blending Process

In the blending process, we work with all the spaces (input, generic, and blended spaces) simultaneously. Elements of the spaces are projected between the different spaces and in different directions. They move primarily from the generic space and input spaces to the blend, but elements can also be projected backward, from the blend to the input spaces and generic space.[53] The blending process is done unconsciously, and the description of the process in an integration network is a way of unpacking the metaphor, and of displaying how the cognitive process behind linguistic expressions might have taken place. With this in mind, I will describe the process in sequences in order to get a better overview of the process of blending.[54]

---

[52] Fauconnier and Turner 2002, 322–25.

[53] Projection from a blend to the generic space occurs when a metaphor creates similarities between the two input spaces that would not be apparent without bringing them together. Backward projection from the blend to the input spaces mainly concerns the elaboration process (see below) when the blend modifies and strengthens cross-mapping between the input spaces and projection to the blend. Additionally, the emergent structure of the blend can be projected to the input spaces and influence which vital relations the input spaces employ within the integration network. For backward projection from the blend, see Evans 2019, 533–35.

[54] The blending process is described in sequences in Fauconnier and Turner 2002, 44–50.

If the blending process is seen in sequences, it can be said to start with a cross-matching between the input spaces. Corresponding elements and frames are identified and connected to each other based on different vital relations. The shared roles and structure of a paired match are generalized and projected into the generic space, which in turn projects them back to the input spaces and strengthens the connection between the two matched elements. The projections from the input spaces into the blend are selective, only a few elements and vital relations are projected into the blend.[55] Some matched counterparts are projected together into the blend. At times, only one counterpart is projected, and it is also possible for an element without any counterpart in the other input space to be projected to the blend. The whole network influences the selection. The blend and the generic space are correcting and modifying the selection of the input elements and frames. The context of the discourse, as well as the cultural and social context, impacts the blending process and the selective projection. When the focus in the network shifts, other characteristics may be highlighted. Even entrenched metaphors are modified by their context.

Frames, or parts of frames, are projected to the blend. A new frame, an emergent structure, can also be created in the blend. The emergent structure contains structures that are not copied from the input spaces. Instead, a new structure can be created by composition, completion, and elaboration.[56] *Composition* is when a new structure is created to arrange the elements in the blend. Parts of the frames of the input spaces may be composed into a new frame. *Completion* is done when a frame of the input spaces is too partial to be able to embrace the elements in the blend. In this case, the frame in the blend will fill out the missing part needed to structure the elements of the blend. The *elaboration* of the network continues until it makes sense to us, and the network reaches some sort of equilibrium. During this modification process we tend to *run the blend*. For instance, we might imagine a scenario where the surgeon operates on the patient using the tools and techniques of a butcher. The elaboration leads to modifications of the frame but also of the whole network.

An important insight is that a shift in one of the mental spaces modifies the whole system. Let us consider the two metaphors THE SURGEON IS A BUTCHER and THE BUTCHER IS A SURGEON. These two have the same input spaces but their blends differ, and the emergent structure of their blends would be opposite. That the butcher cuts the meat with the precision of a surgeon makes him more

---

[55] Fauconnier and Turner 2002, 47.
[56] Fauconnier and Turner 2002, 48.

competent. However, if the expression is said in a context in which the butcher is portrayed as slow and too meticulous, the metaphor will have another meaning.[57] If a butcher takes as much time to dismember a slaughtered animal as a surgeon takes to perform a complicated surgery, then he is not a good butcher. The context helps us select the elements we project into a blend.

Counterfactual Blends

A *Counterfactual blend* is not a new type of network from the ones mentioned above, but a blend that displays the cognitive process of counterfactual utterances.[58] Evans explains a counterfactual utterance: "it sets up a scenario that runs counter to a presupposed reality."[59] It can be a conditional or a modal statement like "if only," "if I were you," "if you ask me," "maybe," "I will," and "you should." The conditionals present an alternative future to the present state, as in "I would buy a larger house, if I won millions on lottery." It refers to a state that is counterfactual to the present state. We are involved in counterfactual blending when we plan our week or when we think of what might have happened if we had acted differently in the past. Compound nouns such as a child-safe beach, caffeine headache, money problem, and oven-proof dish can also be explained by counterfactual blends. Counterfactual compound nouns describe something in reversed terms of something else. When we comprehend the sentence "that beach is child-safe," we first visualize what kind of dangers there might be on a beach for a child, and then we imagine the beach without these dangers. The same process is detected in descriptions of death in the HB. Death is often described as non-life and in negated characteristics of the terms of life, such as death being an existence where you have no possessions, no memory, no knowledge, no joy, no light, and no relationships.[60] Fauconnier and Turner claim that counterfactual blends are very hard to notice because we do them effortlessly and they are part of our "backstage cognition."[61]

---

[57] For further discussion on metaphors created by reversing the source and target of other metaphors, see pages 64–67.

[58] For further discussion on counterfactual blends, see Fauconnier and Turner 2002, 25–27, 224–30; Evans 2019, 498–99.

[59] Evans 2019, 498.

[60] This will be further explored in Chapters 5 and 6, discussing birth metaphors in Job 1 and 3. For expressions of death as a negation of life in the HB, see Tromp 1969, 187–96.

[61] Fauconnier and Turner 2002, 229.

Summary: Blending Theory

Blending theory is based on mental space theory, which explains the way we think as an integration of different areas of meaning, called mental spaces. A mental space correlates to the momentary thoughts we have of a certain concept at a specific time. It only concerns some specific parts or features of a larger domain. These features are often organized by the structure of the domain, and this structure is called the organizing frame of the mental space. The integration network of a metaphor consists of at least two input spaces, a generic space, and a blended space. The shared features of the input spaces are generalized and projected to the generic space. The generic space guides which features are projected from the input spaces to the blended space, but some non-shared features may also be projected from the input spaces to the blend. According to blending theory, a metaphor is not about experiencing one thing through another; rather, it involves bringing together both things, or more accurately all input spaces, and blending them to create a new image. The metaphor is something new. The organizing frame of the blend may originate from one of the input spaces, in which case the network is referred to as a single-scope blend. Alternatively, if the organizing frame is a blend of the frames from both input spaces, it is known as a double-scope blend. The frame in a double-scope blend may also be a new frame, not found in any of the input spaces but created from how the input spaces interact or collide. This is called an emergent structure. The integration network is mapped out in so called blending schemas. They visualize what features and frames are selected and projected to the blended space, the metaphor. In blending theory, the target domain can be less abstract than the source domain. This is often the case in reversed metaphors which have switched the source and the target of a conventional metaphor. Blending theory also explains mental processes other than metaphors. Counterfactual blends depict how we think when we make up plans, think in conditional clauses, or think of something in negated terms of something else.

Two Complementary Theories

Conceptual metaphor theory and blending theory share many features. In both theories, metaphors are considered to be cognitive, and to have a selective mapping that highlights and hides certain characteristics of the topic, including both elements and structure. I will use conceptual metaphor theory and blending theory as complementary theories, but blending theory as my main theory.[62] Each bring a different perspective on metaphor. The recurring cognitive patterns and entrenched structures of general metaphors are best understood through the lens of conceptual metaphor theory. This theory also applies to correlation metaphors, as it explains how embodied recurring patterns influence metaphor production.[63]

Conceptual metaphor theory relies on domains and is more schematic in its mapping of metaphors compared to blending theory. While domains in conceptual metaphor theory are static and encompass broad networks of knowledge, mental spaces in blending theory are more specific, partial, and temporary. Blending theory explains metaphorical creativity and complex metaphors better than conceptual metaphor theory. It explores the way we think at the moment when we construct or interpret the metaphor. It is flexible, recognizes the context of the metaphor, and is also usable when the metaphor is derived from many spaces or when a metaphor is structured by the frames of both target and source. Single-scope blends are compatible with how resemblance metaphors are described in conceptual metaphor theory. Such metaphors are structured by their source domains; however, the network model offers a more comprehensive understanding of how all the spaces in the network interact and influence the construction of the metaphor. In blending theory, one thing is not spoken of in terms of another, but the source and the target blend into the metaphor. The metaphor is always considered a new creation, something other than its input spaces. This is most evident in double-scope blends, which can have structures and elements not found in either input space, which emerge when they are blended. This explains the entailments of the metaphor which one would not expect based on the input spaces. Blending schemas of the integration network are good descriptive tools to unpack metaphors and display their construction. The schemas are especially important in explorations of new metaphors which do not fit our previous metaphorical experience well.

Conceptual metaphor theory holds that the mapping is unidirectional. The unidirectional mapping from source to target is not compatible with the network integration of double-scope blend. Blending theory also modifies the idea that the source should be more concrete than the target. It is a common pattern of metaphors but does not always apply. The need to structure an abstract concept using the framework of a more concrete target aligns with blending theory's view that

---

[62] For a clarifying comparison of blending theory and conceptual metaphor theory, see Grady, et al. 1999. The complementary approach is also discussed in Fauconnier and Lakoff 2009.

[63] Kövecses 2020, 133–36.

we aim to scale down complex and obscure matters to a more manageable human scale in our blending processes.[64]

Kövecses refers to different levels of metaphors in which the image schema is the most schematic level, the mental space the most specific, and the domain is something in between.[65] All levels contribute to the construction of metaphors. While structures are inherited from more schematic levels, they can be elaborated within mental spaces and blends. This elaboration is influenced by contextual factors and may involve a combination of several domains. Kövecses' acknowledgment of different levels of metaphors, that they both concern more stable domains and temporary mental spaces, helps us to combine conceptual metaphor theory and blending theory. The level of domain is overlooked in blending theory. If the specific metaphor ARGUMENTS ARE WEAPONS is explained according to blending theory, then the focus will be on the specific concepts ARGUMENTS and WEAPONS. Conceptual metaphor theory, on the other hand, will instead focus on the domains behind the specific concepts and the general metaphors DEBATE IS WAR. General metaphors are important, both to understand how new metaphors are created from conventional metaphors and how different metaphors in a text call back to the same general metaphor. Likewise, the knowledge of the domain helps us in the interpretation of specific mental spaces. The input spaces show what parts of the domain are used in a specific metaphor, but to understand collisions of frames and implied elements of the spaces, one needs to have knowledge of the domains.

To summarize: Blending theory is more specific and holistic than conceptual metaphor theory with respect to how metaphors are constructed, and its integration network displays how new metaphorical meaning is created. A blending schema is a clarifying descriptive tool to visualize the construction of a metaphor. The insights of blending theory are important to understand the complexity of metaphors, that a metaphor is something more than its input spaces and how metaphors can combine targets and sources which organizing frames collide. At the same time, conceptual metaphor theory is important for discussing metaphors on the level of domains and how metaphors are created from more general metaphors.

---

[64] Instead of arguing that the source domain should be more concrete, Sweetser and DesCamp claim that the source domain of a metaphor is rather more closely related to our direct experiences compared to the target domain (Sweetser and DesCamp 2014, 10–12).

[65] Kövecses argues that a metaphor involves four different cognitive structures or levels, namely image schemas, domains, frames, and mental space. The frames are not only structural but, like domains, are also propositional in nature and rich in information. Kövecses acknowledges that his use of the term frame and domain often overlap (Kövecses 2020, 51–80).

Another important insight from conceptual metaphor theory is how metaphors can be derived from embodied experience and how to explain correlation metaphors.

Context and Metaphors

Even though the primary focus of Lakoff and Johnson's *Metaphors We Live By* is to demonstrate how metaphors are conceptual, it also briefly addresses the idea that metaphors depend on the cultural context in which they are used. They claim that metaphors express cultural values, and that new metaphors can change our perceptions, thoughts, and actions.[66] However, the emphasis on cross-cultural embodied experience has led to a neglect of contextual factors within conceptual metaphor theory, and it has often been criticized for treating metaphors as independent of their literary and cultural context.[67] Gibbs and Kövecses respond to this critique, and they both claim that metaphors are created from an interaction between many factors, including those that are biological, historical, cultural, and cognitive.[68] Kövecses argues that when we use metaphors, we do not simply recruit pre-stored mapping between domains. Instead, metaphors are created through an interaction between the context and our conceptual system. This system is not static, but is shaped and modified by the context in which it is used.[69]

Kövecses discusses four different contexts that influence how we create and understand metaphors: situational, conceptual-cognitive, discourse, and bodily contexts.[70] These different contexts have an impact on how our conventional metaphors and our cognitive system are structured, but also on how individuals use metaphors. Exposure to certain source domains makes us use them more than others. A person's use of metaphors is dependent both on contextual factors that form and modify the conceptual metaphors, and on the immediate situation in which metaphors are used. It should be noted that these contexts are dependent on each other and overlap.

Situational context: This includes physical environment, as well as social and cultural context. The physical environment encompasses the landscape and

---

[66] Lakoff and Johnson 2003, 9, 22–24, 57, 67.
[67] Gibbs summarizes some of the critique in Gibbs 2017, 9–16.
[68] Kövecses 2005; Kövecses 2015; Kövecses 2020; Gibbs 2017.
[69] Kövecses 2015, 49.
[70] The presentation in this chapter follows Kövecses' presentation of different contexts in Kövecses 2020, 95–100, but it is complemented by Kövecses' earlier works, in which he also discusses contextual factors (Kövecses 2005; Kövecses 2015).

climate we live in, our access to water and food, and our overall living conditions. The social context relates to social hierarchies and classes shaped by factors such as gender, education, occupation, ethnicity, sexual orientation, and more. For instance, the social context can explain why women might use different metaphors than men or why different cultures and time periods experience the same metaphor differently.[71] The cultural context concerns both the shared knowledge embedded in our conceptual system and the more immediate influence of cultural expressions found in media, art, and science. Specific metaphors tend to be more culturally sensitive than more general ones.

Conceptual-Cognitive context: Kövecses refers to our entrenched conceptual metaphors as a context, along with memory, history, ideology, interests, and concerns, which shape our metaphorical thinking. A shared history of a nation or a culture influences the use and preference for certain conceptual metaphors.[72] Personal memories can also shape our preferences for specific metaphors. Studies have shown how life-transforming events in the lives of poets have influenced the metaphors they use.[73] Different groups and individuals have varying interests and concerns that affect their choice of metaphors.

Discourse context: The discourse context involves previous discourse on the same topic, knowledge about the topic, surrounding discourse, and the main elements in the discourse. Earlier expressions and metaphors in the discourse could be repeated, trigger new metaphors, or be used for a creative metaphorical elaboration. When we discuss the discourse context of a text, we need to consider the immediate literary context of the metaphor and its intertextual relationships. Different genres and traditions have different dominant metaphors and preferences for how to combine metaphors.[74] The linguistic context also includes how words relate to each other as homonyms, hyponyms, synonyms, and antonyms, or by syntactic and semantic structures.[75]

---

[71] For instance, many cultures share the general metaphor ANGRY PERSON IS A PRESSURIZED CONTAINER, although they specify it differently. In Japanese, the container is the belly; in Zulu, it is the heart; in Chinese, the anger is depicted as gas; and in English and Swedish, it is seen as a fluid (Kövecses 2005, 68–69).

[72] Kövecses discusses how the experience of war explains why Hungarians tend to use metaphors that describe life as a war, struggle, and compromise, while Americans prefer metaphors that depict life as a precious possession or a game (Kövecses 2005, 241).

[73] Kövecses 2015, 120–22.

[74] For discussions on genre and metaphor, see Caballero 2017.

[75] Kövecses presents how the poet Plath uses different meanings of "medusa" as an example of how a homonym induces the use of specific metaphors (Kövecses 2015, 127).

Bodily context: That embodied experience is the ground for many of our conceptual metaphors is an essential part of conceptual metaphor theory. Often overlooked is the fact that our individual physical experience also becomes a factor in the use of metaphors. Illness, our bodily strength, weakness, dysfunctional body parts, and whether we are left or right-handed could influence which metaphors we prefer. When discussing embodied experience, it is crucial to recognize that our perception of our bodies and our embodied experience are also shaped by our cultural context. Our body perception, values, and prior experiences influence even the most basic sensorimotor skills. Therefore, we cannot assume that a basic embodied experience will necessarily lead to the exact same conceptual metaphor.[76]

Conceptual metaphor theory demonstrates that our metaphor production is grounded in our conceptual system. Kövecses identifies three additional contexts—situational, discourse, and bodily—that also influence metaphor creation and use. These contexts act both as sources of inspiration and as constraints with respect to how we use and create metaphors. Kövecses argues that conceptualizers try to seek coherence between the different contexts; however, one or several contexts will emerge as stronger than the others. The strongest context(s) will induce the metaphors that are most fitting to use, even if they conflict with other contexts.[77] The understanding of how different contexts influence our metaphorization reveals that metaphorical expressions in speech and text are not merely the recruitment of conventional metaphors or references to established lexical meanings. Instead, they involve a process where various contextual factors are integrated and processed together.

Semino and Steen give several examples of literary studies that use metaphorical patterns to detect the worldview and values of the writer. They also refer to a study demonstrating how Shakespeare uses distinct metaphorical patterns for different characters, reflecting their individual worldviews and values.[78] These studies offer insight into how context influences metaphorical patterns in texts, and that authors deliberately select specific metaphors to characterize their characters.

To summarize: Contextual factors influence the comprehension and production of metaphors. These can be summarized as situational, conceptual-cognitive, discourse, and bodily contexts. These various contexts inspire us to use certain source domains and metaphors, but they also have a limiting function. They make us use and create new metaphors that are meaningful and possible to understand.

---

[76] Kövecses 2005, 42–43.
[77] Kövecses 2015, 51; Kövecses 2020, 100–104.
[78] Semino and Steen 2008, 238–41.

Novel Metaphors and Creativity

The main purpose of conceptual metaphor theory has been to seek general patterns in metaphorization, and it has been argued that the boom of conceptual metaphor theory has led to a neglect of study regarding specific metaphors, novel metaphors, and creativity in metaphor elaboration. Kövecses has expanded conceptual metaphor theory by exploring not only different contextual factors but also creation of new metaphors. He argues that new metaphors, whether in texts or everyday life, are inspired by the immediate context of the metaphor producer. New metaphors are created when we need to say something that cannot be said using conventional metaphors. The need occurs when the influence of the situational, discourse, or bodily contexts becomes stronger than the constraints of the cognitive system. Novel metaphors are constructed both in everyday language and in literature. The same processes can be detected in both.[79]

The different contexts impact our choice of metaphors and work both as inspiration and constraint in the production of new metaphors. Metaphors and cognitive structures based on correlation in experience execute a strong constraint on our metaphorical creativity, stronger than conventional metaphors based on resemblance.[80] The constraints ensure that our metaphors are comprehensible and remain consistent with our cognitive structures and conventional language. When we hear or read a text with a new metaphor, we tend to spend a millisecond longer processing novel metaphors compared to conventional ones.[81] When interpreting new metaphors, we need to create a new blend and establish a new selective projection, whereas with conventional metaphors, we only need to modify the entrenched blend to fit the new context. Novel expressions and metaphors stand out from the context, and the more novel a metaphor is, the more likely we are to remember it. We also tend to perceive novel metaphors as more metaphorical compared to conventional ones.[82] For example, we tend to see GOD IS A MOTHER as more metaphorical than GOD IS A FATHER.

---

[79] It has been discussed whether literature contains more complex new metaphors than everyday language. Lakoff and Turner state that there are more novel and elaborated metaphors in literature than in everyday language (Lakoff and Turner 1989, 67–72). Fauconnier and Turner demonstrate that complex and novel metaphors are also present in everyday language (Fauconnier and Turner 2002, v). Semino and Steen discuss how readers' expectations influence metaphor recognition, noting that readers tend to identify more metaphors in poetic texts than in newspapers (Semino and Steen 2008, 241–44).

[80] Kövecses 2005, 264.

[81] Philip 2016, 225.

[82] Philip 2016, 224–25.

New metaphors are created either out of a need to express something new or as a reaction to conventional metaphors. They involve new combinations of input spaces or of domains. Metaphors that are created from entirely new combinations of domains are perceived as more novel compared to specific new metaphors that are derived from general conventional metaphors.

Lakoff and Turner discuss how conventional metaphors are used in new creative ways in their book *More than Cool Reason* (1989). They demonstrate how poets use conceptual conventional metaphors of everyday life in new ways in their poetic works. Even though their book aims to analyze metaphors in poetry, their conclusions can also be applied to everyday language. They refer to four ways poets use conventional metaphors in new creative ways: questioning, composing, extension, and elaboration.[83] *Questioning* is to use the absurdity of a metaphor to prove its inappropriateness, or to highlight the absurdity of a situation.[84] It could also be done, according to Kövecses, by negating a conventional metaphor or by replacing it with another.[85] Questioning is a device used by poets and creative writers to reflect on our values and worldviews. *Composing* is when conceptual metaphors are combined in new ways into complex metaphors, as in the network of "Grim Reaper."[86] Extension and elaboration are two practices for constructing new metaphors from conventional ones by modifying which parts of the domains are used in the metaphor. I will discuss these methods below, and introduce reversed metaphors as another way to create new metaphors from conventional ones.

Extension: Extending a metaphor involves using parts of the source domain that are not normally used in the conventional metaphor. Lakoff and Turner give the example of how the conceptual metaphor DEATH IS SLEEP is extended in Hamlet, when Shakespeare refers to death as dreaming and creates the metaphor DEATH IS DREAMING. Dreaming is part of the source domain of SLEEP but normally not used in the metaphor DEATH IS SLEEPING.[87]

---

[83] Lakoff and Turner 1989, 67–72.

[84] Lakoff and Turner give the example of how Catullus questions the metaphor LIFETIME IS A DAY by expressing that "Suns can set and return again, but when our brief light goes out, there's one perpetual night to be slept through." The metaphor A LIFETIME IS A DAY is not appropriate because, unlike a day which is followed by a new day, the end of a lifetime does not lead to a new life (Lakoff and Turner 1989, 69).

[85] Kövecses 2005, 262.

[86] Lakoff and Turner 1989, 70–72. For a more extensive description of the metaphors involved in the metaphor DEATH IS THE GRIM REAPER, see pages 52–54.

[87] Lakoff and Turner 1989, 67.

Elaboration: Elaboration is when the metaphor is specified in a new way. For example, the Roman poet Horace refers to death as "an eternal exile on a raft." This is an elaboration of DEATH IS DEPARTURE which usually does not say how the departure is achieved. In the metaphor DEATH IS AN ETERNAL EXILE ON A RAFT, the raft is presented as a vehicle for the departure. A raft often drifts and cannot be easily controlled. The concept EXILE adds the meaning of a forced unwanted departure. This leads to new meanings beyond the content of the general metaphor DEATH IS DEPARTURE.[88]

Another way to create a new metaphor is to reverse the conventional metaphor. For example, the reversed metaphor of SURGEONS ARE BUTCHERS is BUTCHERS ARE SURGEONS. Metaphors that are based on two nouns are possible to reverse.[89] According to conceptual metaphor theory, a more concrete domain is used to structure the more abstract domain, but research has shown that even if the mapping goes from a more abstract domain to a concrete domain, the metaphor is still easily understood.[90] What happens is that the interpreter perceives it as more metaphorical. The difference in abstractness varies among metaphors; for example, SURGEONS ARE BUTCHERS has a smaller difference in abstractness than LIFE IS A JOURNEY. Research has shown that when the difference in abstractness between the two domains is smaller, it is easier to reverse the metaphor.[91] It is easier to understand BUTCHERS ARE SURGEONS than THE JOURNEY IS A LIFE, but it is possible to understand both. Campbell and Katz investigate how interpretation of metaphors is facilitated by the context of the discourse. In one study, they let a group interpret twelve different metaphors and their reversed counterparts, both in isolation and in the context of a short discourse. The results showed that 2 % of standard mappings and 8 % of reverse mappings are uninterpretable in a context, compared to 10 % and 24 % when read in isolation.[92] Blending theory is suitable to cope with reversed metaphors. It modifies the selective projection depending on the context and what the topic of the blend is.[93]

---

[88] Lakoff and Turner 1989, 67–69.
[89] Kövecses 2010, 28.
[90] Kövecses holds that conceptual metaphors are primarily unidirectional in their mapping, typically moving from a concrete source domain to a more abstract target domain. If this direction is reversed, it results in metaphors that are generally absent from our everyday language (Kövecses 2010, 27–28).
[91] Dunn 2015, 18–19.
[92] Campbell and Katz 2006, 5–11.
[93] The reversal of the metaphor THE SURGEON IS A BUTCHER is discussed on pages 56–57.

To summarize: New metaphors are created both in everyday language and literature. They are created when we need to say something which conventional metaphors cannot express. Our different contexts work as both inspiration and constraint in metaphor production. New metaphors can be created from conventional metaphors, or from new combinations of domains or input spaces. I have referred to five ways which conventional metaphors are used in creative ways: extension, elaboration, questioning, composing, and reversing.

The Interplay of Metaphors

Metaphors in a text always interact with the literary context, as discussed above in the section on the context of the discourse. This also implies an interaction between the various metaphors in the text. The different metaphors may allude to each other, illuminate different aspects of the topic, or relate to the same concepts and domains.[94] The associations between metaphors in a text contribute to its flow and plot. New metaphors may be created from other metaphors within the text or from intertexts. The interpretation of one metaphor can be modified by the understanding of other metaphors in the same text. A metaphor may be reused in new ways later in the text, and its new context would bring new meaning to it. The closer together the metaphors are placed in a text, the more we can anticipate that they should be interpreted together. However, we must also be aware that an author may reuse and allude to other metaphors throughout the entire text.

Questions to consider when investigating interaction of metaphors in a text include: Do they share an input space or general structure? Do they collide, cohere, or complement each other? There are different ways that metaphors relate to each other. The most prominent relation is shared input spaces. The metaphors RAIN IS STORED IN STOREHOUSES and RAIN IS STORED IN POTS share the target, the input space RAIN, while the metaphors A CLOUD IS A POT and the A WOMB IS A POT share the source, the input space POT. There are also networks where a blended space becomes an input space in another network, creating a chain of interconnected networks. For instance, the blend of the Grim Reaper integrates the input spaces DEATH, REAPER, and KILLER, where the input space DEATH is a blend in which Death is personified as an agent causing the death of a person.[95]

---

[94] Ricoeur argues in his 1975 study that "a metaphor never comes alone" and discusses how more general metaphors, so-called root metaphors, give rise to more specific, partial metaphors (Ricoeur 1975, 94).

[95] See pages 52–54.

Several specific metaphors may also relate to the same more general domain. The metaphors GOD IS A PARENT, GOD GIVES BIRTH, and GOD IS FEEDING AND RAISING ISRAEL refer to the same conceptual domain, the domain of PARENTHOOD. Metaphors are on a scale from general to specific. A specific metaphor is derived from a more general metaphor, and it inherits its structure from the general one.[96] In an analysis of metaphors, it is not necessary to go back to the most general level, but rather to focus on the general metaphor that reveals the meaningful structure of the specific metaphor or serves as the lowest common denominator among several metaphors. Another way to relate metaphors to each other is by their organizing frames. Metaphors that have organizing frames that are derived from the same general frame are called *family metaphors*. Domains that share the same general frame could easily be combined in metaphors. For instance, the frame of competition is the general frame of domains of WAR, SPORTS, BUSINESS, and ARGUMENT, and these can be combined into the metaphors ARGUMENT IS WAR, SPORT IS WAR, ARGUMENT IS A SPORT, and BLACK FRIDAY IS A BATTLE BETWEEN THE STORES.[97]

Metaphors that share domains, derive from the same general metaphor, or entail similar structures are considered coherent. Such metaphors can be integrated and mixed easily due to their shared entailments.[98] When combined, these metaphors provide background information that can fill gaps in the interpretation of these metaphors and their specific integration networks. Authors often use coherent metaphors to emphasize a point, or as a pedagogical tool.[99] In an analysis of metaphors, we can assume that coherent metaphors also are used together to modify each other and to give different perspectives on a topic.

Older metaphor research claims that only coherent metaphors can be used together effectively. However, more recent studies have demonstrated that we can easily understand, and often mix, non-coherent metaphors within the same text or speech.[100] A text, or a discourse, seldom contains only coherent metaphors.[101] Noncoherent metaphors can be mixed even when their frames and conceptual

---

[96] Dancygier and Sweetser 2014, 71.
[97] Dancygier and Sweetser 2014, 67–69.
[98] See Lakoff and Johnson 2003, 9, 94–105.
[99] One example of a text with only coherent metaphors is Jesus' parable of the Sower. It contains metaphors derived from the same source domain. An investigation of sermons and classroom teachings reveals that they often contain a high number of coherent metaphors (Kimmel 2010, 97–99).
[100] Gibbs 2016, 68–70.
[101] Kimmel 2010, 97–99.

contents clash with each other. Although they may not modify each other with the same strength as coherent metaphors, they are still easily understood and offer complementary perspectives on the topic. When metaphors are combined in the same clause, we feel a need to interpret them together; however, if they are further apart, we tend to interpret noncoherent metaphors separately. Our selective mapping of the source domain usually helps us to avoid the clashes between them. The syntactic rules guide us in how to understand these metaphors. It becomes easier when they are combined in a scenario, or in a temporal or causal chain of events.[102] A biblical example of how noncoherent metaphors can be used together is found in Deut 32:18, which refers to God as a rock giving birth.[103]

Application of Metaphor Theory in This Study

In my investigation of metaphors, I use a combination of conceptual metaphor theory and blending theory, with blending theory as my main theory. I will present metaphors in the formula THE TARGET DOMAIN IS THE SOURCE DOMAIN. Correlation metaphors and general metaphors will only be expressed using this formula, and I will treat correlation metaphors as metaphors, but with an awareness that they are close to metonymy. The more specific resemblance metaphors that are the focus of my analysis will be illustrated through blending schemas, showing the input spaces, generic space, and the blended space with its elements, and, when necessary, the organizing frames. When I refer to a frame, I mean the organizing frame of a mental space, as the term is used in blending theory by Fauconnier and Turner. When the network has high asymmetry, a clear topic, and a framing input space, I refer to the input spaces as target and source and the domains they belong to as source domain and target domain. This is always the case in single-scope networks, but also in asymmetrical double-scope networks. Metaphors typically have high asymmetry. The blend is modified depending on which input space is the target and which is the source, and therefore it is necessary to identify them. The terms target and source are standard expressions in cognitive theories of metaphors, and also among biblical scholars using blending theory.[104] Even if I use the terms target and source domain, I interpret the metaphor as a blend where the two domains or

---

[102] Kimmel 2010, 97–99.
[103] Deut 32:18 is discussed in de Hulster and Strawn 2015, 131–32; Dille 2004.
[104] Van Hecke 2005, 221–28; DesCamp 2007, 24–38; Hawley 2018, 58–59; Gomola 2018, 157–59; Lundhaug 2010, 75, 98.

the input spaces interact and are blended. The mapping is not unidirectional, and it does not demand that the source is more concrete than the target.

I will discuss metaphors both on the level of mental spaces and of domains. This diverges from blending theory, which only refers to mental spaces. I am using a wide definition of domain as the background knowledge of a concept, consisting of associated concepts and structures of how these concepts relate to each other. I will survey the domains that are used in the metaphors by exploring how they are expressed in the Book of Job, the HB more broadly, and in other texts from ancient West Asia, as well as discussing the embodied experience associated with them. Elements and structures of the input space are derived from the domains, which are essential for understanding the metaphor. In the interpretation of a metaphor, I start with the linguistic expression containing the metaphor, which guides me when I unpack the metaphor, the blend, into the input spaces and the generic space. What is explicitly stated in the text helps identify the contents of the input spaces and the specific parts of the general domain that are utilized. However, knowledge of the domains from which these input spaces are derived is essential for understanding the implied associations and the structures of the spaces. I will visualize my conclusions about the specific features of the input spaces used in the metaphors through blending schemas. I will map out the metaphors in networks based on what I discern to be the most probable way of mapping the network, though I acknowledge that a metaphor can be interpreted and mapped in various ways.

I will discuss the creativity of metaphors by drawing on Lakoff and Turner's insights into how conventional metaphors are used to create new ones. In this context, the relationship between the input spaces and their domains is crucial. I will also explore reversed metaphors. They are explained effectively by blending theory, because it accommodates the possibility that the target can be more abstract than the source, and describes the elaboration of the whole integration network when the target and the source are switched.

I refer to metaphors as conventional or standard metaphors when they are common in the HB or in other texts from ancient West Asia, and call them new or creative metaphors when they occur rarely or when they clearly are created from more conventional metaphors. I am aware that the metaphors I categorize as new may have been conventional in ancient West Asia, even if they do not, or only seldom, appear in the texts I have access to. As Philip points out, novelty is a subjective matter, and we can only say that a metaphor is novel in relation to our own experience.[105] Metaphors may be conventional in one context but regarded as new in another, where they are used to challenge existing metaphors. Metaphors grounded in the experience of women, for example, may function as new metaphors in a patriarchal context. I will discuss the creativity in shaping new metaphors by referring both to how the new can be seen as built on conventional metaphors, and how new metaphors challenge conventional metaphors and beliefs.

I will consider various contextual factors, with a primary focus on the literary context. This includes examining both the immediate context of the text and its intertextual relationships. My analysis will involve a close reading of the text, paying attention to its syntactic and semantic features, and exploring how birth metaphors interact with other metaphors and expressions within the text. I will discuss how these interactions can highlight certain values and elucidate the meanings of particular metaphors or linguistic expressions. The terms image schema, entailment, and coherence are useful in the discussion of how metaphors relate to each other in a discourse.

I will work as closely as possible with what we can know of how the domains were conceptualized in ancient West Asia, rather than what they generate for us today. My best source of the situational and conceptual cognitive context is through texts, either the HB or myths and incantations from other parts of ancient West Asia. This can be complemented by the knowledge we have of the climate and landscape of the area. Embodied experience is important in conceptual metaphor theory, especially experiences that could be presumed to be universal. Giving birth is a shared experience among birth mothers across history and cultures. While this experience is influenced by contextual factors such as social norms and access to medical care, it includes universal components like contractions, labor pains, pushing, and birth complications. I will refer to universal embodied experiences of birth in my interpretation of the birth metaphors, but when I do, I will also be clear whether they are also documented in texts from the HB or in other texts from ancient West Asia.

The analysis of metaphors needs to consider their specific context and content. Therefore, my analysis will be adapted to the metaphors I analyze. For instance, in Job 1 and 3, there are metaphorical expressions that are best understood through the structure of a counterfactual blend. In Job 10, a close investigation of ancient embryological knowledge is necessary. In Job 38 and 39, the focus will be on the

---

[105] Philip 2016, 226.

creativity of new metaphors and how birth metaphors interact with other metaphors and motifs.

3. Birth Metaphors in the Hebrew Bible

This chapter provides an overview of how the domain of BIRTH is expressed in the HB. It concerns both how births are illustrated in narratives and how the domain of BIRTH is used in images referring to God, creation, death, exile, and plants. In the next chapter, I will discuss how birth is described in Akkadian birth descriptions, which will provide a broader understanding of how birth was conceptualized in ancient West Asia. Descriptions of actual births in the HB are not detailed and do not reflect the perspective of women. However, metaphors that use birth as one of their input spaces seem to draw on the experiences of birth, including struggle, screaming, agony, and death, as well as the experiences of trusting the midwife and receiving the baby as a gift of life.

Descriptions of Birth

Births are commonly referred to with a short formula וַתַּהַר וַתֵּלֶד בֵּן, "she conceived and bore a son." Descriptions of births are often used in narratives to mark the significance of the one born. Miraculous pregnancies and complicated births imply that the one born will become a prominent man. They are seen as expressions of God's power, election, and care. The stories of Isaac, Moses, and Samuel pay attention to the special circumstances around their births. The special election of the prophets Jeremiah and Isaiah are accentuated by saying that they were elected already in the womb.

Fathers are not depicted as present at the birth of their children. Jeremiah 20:15 refers to a messenger who brought the news of Jeremiah's birth to his father. The women in labor are instead said to be assisted by other women or by a midwife. Two Egyptian midwives, Shiphrah and Puah, are mentioned by name in Exod 1:15. They resist the decree to kill the Hebrew male infants in Egypt, and deliver Moses. The decree refers to birth as when the women are "on the stones," (עַל־הָאָבְנָיִם) (Exod 1:16). These stones serve as a birth stool, helping the women to kneel in a good birth position.[1] The biblical text does not describe the actual birth of Moses.

---

[1] Stol 2000, 120.

There are a few shorthand descriptions of labor and births in the HB (Gen 35:16–18; 38:27–30; 1 Sam 4:19–22). Genesis 35:16–18 describes how Rachel dies giving birth to Benjamin. The birth is described as hard, and the midwife comforts Rachel by telling her that she is giving birth to a son. The complications at birth are not described, and neither are the actions of the midwife, nor Rachel's pain. Rachel names her baby Ben-Oni, but later the father changes it to Benjamin. The delivery of Tamar's twins in Gen 38:27–30 is the most detailed description of a birth in the HB. One of the twins, Zerah, puts out his hand before the actual birth and the midwife then ties a red string to the hand. The hand is drawn back into the womb and instead Zerah's twin brother, Perez, is born first. His birth is commented upon by the midwife saying "'What a breach you have split by yourself,' and he was given the name Perez" (מַה־פָּרַצְתָּ עָלֶיךָ פָּרֶץ וַיִּקְרָא שְׁמוֹ פָּרֶץ). The root פרץ is used as a verb, a noun, and a name in this description. The verb means "split in two" or "break," the noun means "breach," and his name, Perez, means "the breacher."[2] The act of breaking is accentuated and must imply that he caused severe tears in the vaginal tissue or in the perineum. The narrative of the birth of Perez then describes two kinds of birth complications: limb presentation and perineal tears. There are no references to how the midwife acts to help the mother with these complications. It is said that the midwife ties a red string around Zerah's hand, which could be interpreted as a magical charm, but is more likely a narrative device to indicate that Zerah is the rightful firstborn.[3] Limb presentation is a dangerous condition, and the baby risks being stuck in the womb, which would endanger the life of both the mother and the baby. Bergmann discusses the possibility that the act of breaking during Perez's birth may be a reference to a surgical removal of the twins.[4] The discussion of ante-mortem C-section in ancient times is, however, speculative. There are no known texts describing ante-mortem C-sections from ancient Rome, Egypt, Greek, or Mesopotamia. Furthermore, the story in Gen 38:27–30 narrates that it is Perez who breaks out, not that the midwife splits open the belly.

---

[2] *HALOT*, s.v. "פרץ I."

[3] Scurlock discusses how strings and knots of different colors were used as magical charms to stop vaginal bleedings in Mesopotamia (Scurlock 1991, 139). The red string may allude to a similar tradition.

[4] Bergmann 2008, 64, n. 21. Boss claims that Mishnah and Tosefta (second century CE) refer to women who have recovered from "opening of the body wall" which he interprets as a reference to C-section, arguing that the Hebrews learned this procedure between the exile and the Bar Kochba revolt (Boss 1961, 128). However, the meaning of the expression "opening of the body wall" has been debated, with some suggesting that it refers to a laparotomy (Stol 2000, 131).

A birthing position is described in 1 Sam 4:19–22 when the wife of Pinehas is in labor. She is said to be in great pain, and she kneels when she gives birth. The verb כרע, "kneel down," refers to a birth position in which the woman kneels or sit on a birth stool. The reference to the pain of a woman in labor is unusual in birth narratives in the HB. The labor of Pinehas's wife starts when she receives the message of the death of her husband and her father-in-law, and that the ark was captured. Her body reacts to the shocking news, and she gives birth. She dies at childbirth, but she names her son before she dies, and the son survives. The women who assist her comfort her by saying that she has given birth to a son. Besides this, the text does not mention what the assisting women did to help the birthing mother.

The appropriate care of a newborn is presented in a description of an abandoned baby in Ezek 16.

> As for your birth, on the day you were born your navel cord was not cut, nor were you washed with water to cleanse you, nor rubbed with salt, nor wrapped in cloths. No eye pitied you, to do any of these things for you out of compassion for you; but you were thrown out in the open field, for you were abhorred on the day you were born.[5]
>
> Ezek 16:4–5

Cutting the cord, washing and rubbing the baby, and swaddling it are universal acts in the care of a newborn, and also common practices in ancient West Asia.[6] The rubbing of salt is culture specific, but it is also described in other texts from ancient West Asia.[7] The naming of the baby is often mentioned in the HB. Both mothers and fathers could name their child (Gen 4:25–26; 1 Sam 1:20; 1 Chr 7:23).

Miscarriages are mentioned in the HB (Exod 23:26; 2 King 2:21; Ps 58:9). If someone causes a miscarriage, then the father of the baby must be compensated economically (Exod 21:22). Ecclesiastes 6:3 states that a stillborn baby is better off than an old man who is not buried, which may imply that stillborn babies are buried.

To summarize: Descriptions of births in the HB primarily signal the importance of the one being born. Women gave birth in a kneeling position, with

---

[5] NRSV.

[6] Bergmann and Malul suggest that the washing is a legal act of confirmation of the child (Malul 1990, 109–10; Bergmann 2008, 48). Stol argues that this can only be inferred indirectly. While there are legal texts that refer to the adoption of a child "in its birth fluid and blood," no extant texts confirm that washing the baby served as a legal confirmation of the adoption (Stol 2000, 178).

[7] Stol 2000, 177.

assistance from other women. The use of birthstones as birth stools is confirmed in the HB. While the specifics of how midwives handled difficult complications are not detailed, there are references to issues such as limb presentation, the baby causing tears, and maternal death during childbirth. Miscarriages are also mentioned, and those who caused a woman to miscarry were required to pay a fine.

BIRTH as the Target Domain

There are recurring patterns of how conception, miscarriage, and birth are described, and which metaphors are used in these descriptions. Conception and the formation of the fetus are described using different metaphors. Both offspring and semen are called זֶרַע, "seed" (Gen 38:9; Lev 15:16). The man's semen was seen as the source of life, while the womb contributed a space in which the new life could grow.[1] The woman is depicted as the space where the man sows his seeds (Num 5:28), and the baby is called the fruit of the belly (Gen 30:2; Deut 28:4; Isa 13:18). These different metaphors of the growth of the child inside the womb are derived from the more general metaphor GESTATION IS GROWTH OF A PLANT and the conceptual metaphor HUMANS ARE PLANTS. These lead to the metaphors CONCEPTION IS SOWING, SEMEN IS SEED, THE WOMB IS A FIELD, and THE BABY IS A FRUIT. The characteristics of the womb as giving nourishment and growth are highlighted in these metaphors. Psalm 139 and Job 10 describe the formation of a fetus as an action of God. God pinches the fetus out of clay (Job 10:9) and intertwines the fetus in the womb (Job 10:11; Ps 139:13, 15). They use the general metaphors CREATION OF HUMANS IS A HANDCRAFT and GOD IS A HANDCRAFTER, which is specified in the metaphors GOD IS A POTTER and GOD IS A WEAVER.[2] These highlight God's freedom to form a human according to God's will.

The fertility of a woman is discussed in the HB using the metaphors of a closed and an open womb. A barren woman is said to have a locked or restrained womb which only God could open. God opens (פתח) the wombs of Leah (Gen 29:31) and of Rachel (Gen 30:22). The verb עצר, "restrain" or "lock up," is used in the description of God preventing Sara from bearing children, and God locking all the womb of the house of Abimelech (Gen 16:2; 20:18). God has closed (סגר) Hanna's

---

[1] Lev 12:2 may refer to the woman as active at conception by causing the seed to grow (Hiphil 3 fem sing impf of זרע).

[2] Job 10:10 and Ps 139:13 may not refer to the formation of humans as an act of weaving; other forms of craftsmanship are also possible. See Chapter 7, "God Intertwines Job with Sinews and Bones," pages 200–216.

womb in 1 Sam 1:5. The verb סגר, "close," "shut," mainly refers to the shutting of doors, but may also be used to describe the closure of a wound or a breach (Judg 3:22; 1 King 11:27).³ It may imply that the womb is thought of as a room with doors. These different descriptions of God's involvement at conception are grounded in the metaphor GOD IS THE OPENER AND THE CLOSER OF THE WOMB. It highlights God's control over procreation, and also over the bodies of women. The story of the birth of Perez shows how birth could be seen as an act of breaking out of the womb and as an act of tearing. This is also implied in the common word פֶּטֶר, "firstborn," derived from the root פטר, "split," "open."⁴ These expressions show how births are imagined as the act of a fetus breaking itself out. It is based on the experience that the babies tear vaginal tissue and perinea on their way out. It is used metaphorically in instances where it is used to describe any birth as an act of tearing, even when the baby does not cause damage.⁵

The word for miscarriage is נֵפֶל, which refers to the fetus as something that has fallen out of the womb (Job 3:16; Ps 58:9; Eccl 6:3). The miscarried fetus is described a couple of times, once as a melting snail (Ps 58:9) and once as a baby whose skin is half consumed (Num 12:12).

To summarize: Several metaphors which use BIRTH as their target domain have been identified: GESTATION IS GROWTH OF A PLANT, FORMATION OF A FETUS IS A HANDCRAFT MADE BY GOD, GOD IS THE CLOSER AND THE OPENER OF WOMBS, and BIRTH IS AN ACT OF BREAKING. The metaphor of God opening and closing wombs may also imply the metaphor THE WOMB IS A ROOM WITH DOORS.

BIRTH as the Source Domain

Birth metaphors are used in the HB for different purposes. These purposes determine what kind of characteristics of the womb and birth are accentuated in the metaphors. The domain of BIRTH is used in metaphors describing creation, plants, God, coronations of kings, death, care, war, fear, precipitation, hardship, and liberation. I will discuss five domains used in blends with the domain of BIRTH: GOD, CREATION, PLANTS. DEATH, and EXILE. I will present how BIRTH is blended with these domains in the HB as a background to my discussion of how it is achieved in the Book of Job. In the Book of Job, there are metaphors depicting God as an agent at Job's birth and describing the origin of the creation of specific parts of nature,

---

³ *HALOT*, s.v. "סגר I."
⁴ *HALOT*, s.v. "פטר," "פֶּטֶר."
⁵ See discussion on Conceptual Metonymy in Chapter 2, pages 42–43.

such as the sea and ice. The blend between DEATH and BIRTH is used several times, reflecting Job's wish to be released from the hardships of his life. The birth metaphors in Job also relate to metaphors based on the domains of PLANTS and EXILE, even though these domains are not explicitly blended with BIRTH in the metaphors examined in this study.

BIRTH and GOD

Metaphors that associate God with birth and procreation have often been rejected in exegeses of the HB. Grohmann argues that many translators and interpreters avoid the birth imagery in Ps 90:2.[6] Schreiner argues that birth imagery involving God must be understood figuratively:

> Begettings and births of deities like those recorded (sometimes in coarse detail) in Ugaritic mythology are foreign to Yahwism; according to the OT, Yahweh has neither mate nor children. The few passages (Dt. 32:[15], 18; Ps 2:7; LXX 110:3 [LXX 109:3]) in which God appears as subject of yld must be interpreted figuratively against a mythological background.[7]

He is, of course, correct that these descriptions need to be interpreted as metaphors; however, even as metaphors there has been reluctance to attribute them to the domain of GOD. Clines discusses 22 passages which have been used as examples of how God is portrayed in female roles, such as a mother giving birth (Deut 32:18; Isa 45:9–10), a midwife (Job 38:8; Isa 66:9), or a nursing mother (Num 11:12). He concludes that only 2 of the 22 instances compare God with a woman, and that God in the HB is always a male god with the pronoun he.[8] When investigating metaphors, it is important to remember that all metaphors contain a lie or an absurdity. The purpose of a metaphor is not to say that A is everything B is, but to highlight some characteristic of both A and B in a new image which permits a new experience of both A and B. Not all characteristics of the different input spaces are projected to the metaphor. Using the imagery of conception and birth does not imply that God is thought to have sexual intercourse or to possess a womb. God can be depicted as both a male deity and a midwife simultaneously. This insight regarding how metaphors are constructed is often overlooked in discussions of metaphors that refer to God as a man or a woman.

---

[6] Grohmann 2010, 25.
[7] Schreiner, "ילד," *TDOT* 6:80.
[8] Clines 2021.

GOD IS A PARENT, BEGETTER, AND A WOMAN IN LABOR

Metaphors describing God as a parent, a father or a mother, are not dominant metaphors in the HB. God is called father approximately ten times in the HB. The Israelites are, accordingly, said to be God's sons and daughters.[9] The special relationship between the king and God is also described as a parent-son relationship.[10] There are also a few examples of the metaphor GOD IS A MOTHER. God is an ideal mother who never forgets her children (Isa 49:15) and comforts them (Isa 66:13).[11] God is also portrayed as an ideal parent in Ps 27:10, in which the psalmist says that God will never abandon them even if their father and mother may forsake them. Moses implies with rhetorical questions that God should start to behave as a mother to the people when he complains of his task of leading them (Num 11:12–14). He asks if he conceived (הרה) or gave birth (ילד) to the people, that God could expect him to carry them in his bosom (חֵיק) as a suckling child (יוֹנֵק). It is implied that God is the one who conceived and gave birth to the people and therefore needs to carry them. The birth metaphor is here used as an appeal to make God remember God's responsibility for the people. As their mother, God should carry them and feed them.

The references to God as the begetter and the one who gives birth are often combined with descriptions of God as a parent. The birth metaphors with God as the subject are generally relational metaphors which depict God's relationship with the people, the king, or Wisdom. The metaphors of parenthood and birth are used for different purposes. The main purpose is to make the people recognize God as their God. The people are reminded of how God once created them and cared for them in the past. As a mother, God shows the people the love of a mother and comforts them. As the children of God, they are carried, protected, healed, and fed by God. God's parenthood also highlights God's authority: the children should obey God's commandments. The people are also described as rebellious children whom God disciplines as a father disciplines his children.[12]

---

[9] The Bible portrays God as a Father (Deut 32:6; Pss 27:10; 68:6; 103:13; Prov 3:12; Isa 45:10; 63:16; 64:7; Jer 3:4, 31:9; Mal 1:6; 2:10) and the Israelites as God's sons (Deut 32:5; Isa 1:2; 30:1, 9; 45:11; 63:8; Jer 3:19; Hos 2:1; 11:1). The Israelites are also referred to as God's sons and daughters (Isa 43:6) and as God's firstborn (Exod 4:22; Jer 31:9).

[10] For the king as God's firstborn and son, see 2 Sam 7:14; Pss 2:7; 89:27.

[11] For a comprehensive study of parent metaphors in Isaiah, see Dille 2004.

[12] Examples of biblical references to God's actions as a parent include showing compassion/love (Ps 103:13; Hos 11:1), providing comfort (Isa 66:13), carrying (Num 11:12; Deut 1:31; Hos 11:3), offering protection (Deut 32:10; Ps 68:6), healing (Hos 11:3), and feeding (Num 11:13; Deut

The song of Moses (Deut 32) combines many of these elements of parenthood. The people are asked to remember their childhood, when God acted as their parent. Then God elected the people of Israel, and the people were dependent on God's guidance and providence. The description of God as a caring parent starts with a reference to God as a father and creator of the people (v.6) and ends with an image of God in labor: "You forgot the rock that gave birth to you, you forgot the God who was in labor with you" (צוּר יְלָדְךָ תֶּשִׁי וַתִּשְׁכַּח אֵל מְחֹלְלֶךָ) (v. 18).[13] The birth metaphor of God giving birth is mixed with the metaphor of God as a rock. The birth metaphor accentuates the origin of the people, the closeness between them and God, and God's willingness to struggle for the children. It is used as an appeal to the people to remember and return to God. The song of Moses also depicts God as an eagle or a vulture who uncovers the nest when it is time for the chicks to leave it, but still protects them with its wings and carries them on its back. This image is close to the images of the young animals and their parents in Job 39.

The metaphors GOD IS A WOMAN IN LABOR and GOD IS A BEGETTER are combined with the metaphor GOD IS A POTTER in Isa 45:9–10. Verse 9 suggests the woe of the one who contends with God, and asks if the clay could question the work of its potter. Verse 10 continues, "Woe to the one who says to a father, 'What are you begetting?' or to a woman, 'With what are you in labor?'" (הוֹי אֹמֵר לְאָב מַה־תּוֹלִיד וּלְאִשָּׁה מַה־תְּחִילִין).[14] It is followed by a description of how God has created heaven and earth, and that God has chosen Cyrus to liberate the Israelites. The purpose of the birth metaphor is to make the people acknowledge God's superiority and not question God's choice of Cyrus. The father image, and that of God as the potter, is also combined in Isa 64:7 in an appeal to God to remember God's people.

God is depicted like a woman in labor in Isa 42:14. This is combined with a warrior simile, in which God is said to be like a warrior who cries before his enemies to show them his might. The woman in labor cannot stop her cries or the birth, just as God cannot refrain from intervening on behalf of the people. The simile of a woman in labor (כַּיּוֹלֵדָה) is often used to depict how warriors cry and are in agony "like a woman in labor" (Ps 48:7; Isa 13:8; Jer 30:6). This imagery commonly

---

32:13–14). Additionally, God disciplines (Deut 8:5; Isa 28:26). The children respond with both obedience (Deut 8:6) and rebellion (Deut 32:5; Isa 1:2, 4; 30:1, 9).

[13] The word תֶּשִׁי in the MT is probably a textual corruption. My translation follows the Samaritan Pentateuch that has תַּשָּׁא, possibly from the root נשׁה, "forget." *HALOT*, s.v. "שׁיה."

[14] NRSV.

signals a crisis, but in Isa 42:13–14, it also conveys the hope of God's deliverance.¹⁵ The purpose of the simile is not to portray God as a mother but to emphasize the urgency of the situation and the need for God's response to the crisis.

To summarize: Metaphors of God as a parent are used in the HB, but they are not dominant metaphors. God is depicted as an ideal parent. The metaphors of God as a parent highlight God's close and compassionate relationship with the people or the king. The purpose of portraying God as a parent is typically to remind both God and the people of their close relationship, and to encourage them to act in accordance with that relationship.

GOD IS A MIDWIFE

The metaphor GOD IS A MIDWIFE is used a few times in the HB. God is never called a midwife with the feminine form of the Piel participle of ילד, but in Isa 66:9b God is referred to as a הַמּוֹלִיד, the masculine form of the Hiphil participle of ילד, as the one who makes the women give birth.¹⁶ This has been recognized as a male midwife by some interpreters.¹⁷ The reference to God as the one opening the womb is here used in a context which accentuates God's will to save the people.

Isa 66:9	הַאֲנִי אַשְׁבִּיר וְלֹא אוֹלִיד	Shall I make it break but not deliver,
	יֹאמַר יְהוָה	says the Lord;
	אִם־אֲנִי הַמּוֹלִיד עָצַרְתִּי	shall I, the one who delivers, shut it?
	אָמַר אֱלֹהָיִךְ	says your God.

The act of opening of the womb is here referred to with the word שבר, "break." God delivers a baby and takes it out of the womb also in Pss 22:10; 71:6.¹⁸ The verb used in Ps 22:10 is גחה, "take out," and Ps 71:6 uses the verb גזה, "cut."¹⁹ The references to breaking and cutting out the baby correspond to how Perez is described

---

¹⁵ Bergmann investigates the simile "like a woman in labor" in Bergmann 2008; Bergmann 2010. For discussion on metaphors relating to birth and exile, see pages 88–89.

¹⁶ The Hiphil participle of ילד is used to refer to the fathers who beget children in Jer 16:3, but it would not fit the context in Isa 66:9.

¹⁷ Franke 2009, 44–45; Green 2019, 278–79.

¹⁸ For further discussion of the image of God as a midwife in the Pss 22 and 71, see Grohmann 2007, 50–69; Claassens 2012, 71–79.

¹⁹ These verbs are *hapax legomena*. The root of גֹחִי in Ps 22:10 is uncertain. It may be derived from נחה, possibly meaning "pull out" from the Arabic *jaḫḫa* or "uproot" from the Arabic *jhw*, or it could be related to גזה, which is used in Ps 71:6, likely meaning "cut up" in accordance with the Arabic *jz'*. (*HALOT*, s.v. "גחה"). These verbs are also similar to גיח and גוח, meaning "burst out," which is used in reference to birth in Job 38:8 and Mic 4:10 (*HALOT*, s.v. "גיח").

as breaking himself out of the womb (Gen 38:29). Isaiah 66:9 is used in the context of the exile to describe God's intervention and redemption. Psalms 22:10 and 71:6 use the birth metaphor in pleas asking for God's mercy and care. These references to God's involvement at birth are used to accentuate characteristics of God's mercy and ability to save those who suffer.

To summarize: God is portrayed as a midwife in the HB. As a midwife, God needs to open the womb to deliver the baby. The examples of God as a midwife are used to accentuate God's mercy and ability to save, both in promises from God and in appeals from the ones in need.

BIRTH and CREATION

The domain of BIRTH is used in metaphors to describe God's formation and election of humans. Furthermore, Wisdom is said to be born in the beginning of the creation (Prov 8:23–24). However, metaphors depicting God as giving birth to creation are unusual in the HB. An exception is Ps 90:2, which states that God gives birth to the earth and the mountains.

Ps 90:2	בְּטֶרֶם הָרִים יֻלָּדוּ	Before the mountains were born
	וַתְּחוֹלֵל אֶרֶץ וְתֵבֵל	and you were in labor with the earth and the world,
	וּמֵעוֹלָם עַד־עוֹלָם אַתָּה אֵל	from eternity to eternity, you are God.

The purpose of the birth metaphor in this verse is to emphasize that God is the creator of the world and existed before everything was created. Grohmann argues that the passive form of ילד always means "be born."[20] The verb חיל in Polel usually means "bring forth (through labor pain)" (Deut 32:18; Isa 51:2). The subject of וַתְּחוֹלֵל in Ps 90:2 is either אֶרֶץ, "earth" (3rd fem sing) or God (2nd masc sing). Grohmann points out that the object תֵבֵל, "the world," is usually paired with God as the subject. Her argument leads her to the conclusion that God is the one who gives birth to the earth and world and therefore it is most likely that God is also the agent who gave birth to the mountains.[21]

Psalm 110:3 reads that the dew emanates from the womb of the dawn. It may also contain a metaphor of God giving birth to the king. It is a royal psalm which addresses the king. Psalm 110 has several text variants, and it has been interpreted

---

[20] Grohmann 2010, 25.
[21] Grohmann 2010, 25–28. The earth is also described as being born in Isaiah 66:8, but here "earth" refers to the Israelites as a people, and the birth metaphor concerns the birth of them.

as either a military description of the king or as a description of the birth of the king and the dew. Hossfeldt and Zenger argue that Ps 110 originally depicted the enthronement of a king as a birth, but that redactors of the text have preferred the military language.[22]

Ps 110:3	עַמְּךָ נְדָבֹת בְּיוֹם חֵילֶךָ בְּהַדְרֵי־קֹדֶשׁ מֵרֶחֶם מִשְׁחָר לְךָ טַל יַלְדֻתֶיךָ׃	Your people are willingly on the day of your birth on the holy mountains. From the womb of the dawn comes the dew and your youth to you.

There have been different interpretations of חיל in verse 3a, regarding whether should be understood as "birth" or "strength."[23] The word for dawn, מִשְׁחָר, is a *hapax legomenon*, and can be interpreted as a special form of שַׁחַר or as שַׁחַר with the preposition מִן, which could be a duplication of the preposition in מֵרֶחֶם, "from the womb."[24] It has also been discussed whether ילדתיך should be vocalized with the Masoretic vocalization יַלְדֻתֶיךָ, "our youth," or יְלִדְתִּיךָ, "I gave birth/begat you" (cf. Ps 2:7).[25] Regardless of these different interpretations, this verse refers to the dew emerging in the morning and uses a metaphor depicting the dew as coming from the womb of the dawn. Ancient Israel had long, dry summers, and the dew was essential to moisten vegetation. The dew is often used metaphorically in the HB as a revitalizing gift from God (Hos 14:6–8). In this context, it describes God's blessing and care of the king.

To summarize: Metaphors depicting creation of specific parts of nature in terms of a birth are almost non-existent in the HB. Apart from the Book of Job, such metaphors appear only in Ps 90:2, where God gives birth to the mountains and the earth, and in Ps 110:3, where the dew is born from the womb of the dawn.

BIRTH and PLANTS

Plant metaphors are used to describe conception, pregnancy, and birth. The metaphor behind these plant metaphors is the cross-cultural metaphor HUMANS ARE

---

[22] Hossfeld, et al. 2011, 142–43, 149. For further discussion see Grohmann 2010, 28–32. The NRSV adopts a military translation of Ps 110:3: "Your people will offer themselves willingly on the day you lead your forces on the holy mountains. From the womb of the morning, like dew, your youth will come to you."

[23] Grohmann 2010, 30; Hossfeld, et al. 2011, 142.

[24] Ruppert, "שַׁחַר," *TDOT* 14:577.

[25] Grohmann 2010, 31; Hossfeld, et al. 2011, 142.

PLANTS.[26] It is a dominant metaphor in the HB.[27] Its reversed counterpart, PLANTS ARE HUMANS, is not common; however, it may be implied in a few descriptions of planting, irrigating, and drought (Isa 55:10; Gen 49:25–26).

The correlation between HUMANS and PLANTS is expressed in the Hebrew language. Vall points out that there are many words that can refer both to procreation and to the growth of plants, such as זֶרַע, יָצָא, יָלַד, and פְּרִי.[28] When the verb יָלַד is applied to humans it means "give birth," but when it is used for plants it means "sprout." The verb יָצָא is used both to describe a baby going out from the womb and a plant sprouting and emerging from the ground. The noun זֶרַע, "seed," is also used for semen and offspring, and the noun פְּרִי, "fruit," is applied to the offspring of humans; the verb פרה can also be applied both to humans and plants.[29] Frymer-Kensky also refers to the nouns יוֹנֵק and יוֹנֶקֶת, which can refer to an infant, a suckling child, and to a tender plant, a shoot.[30] These expressions show that the domains of HUMANS and PLANTS are often cross-mapped onto each other. Plants are not explicitly described as growing from a womb in the HB.[31] It could be implied in the description in Isa 55:10, in which the rain begets the earth (Hiphil of ילד) to make plants sprout. Psalm 139:13–15 refers to the formation of the fetus both in the mother's womb and in the depth of the earth, which may imply that the depth of the earth is imagined as a womb.

The fertility blessings in Gen 49:25–26 and in Deut 28:3–6 are good examples of how HUMANS and PLANTS are used in parallel expressions without necessarily being blended. The fertility of humans is described together with the fertility of the fields; the birth of children together with the sprouting of plants; the gift of children together with generous harvests. They are part of the same blessing, and are both affected if God withdraws God's blessings. This shows how plants and humans correlate in experience—when the plants flourish, then the humans thrive.

---

[26] Lakoff and Turner 1989, 84.

[27] Weiss refers to an approximation of 250 plants images in the HB (Weiss 1984, 135).

[28] Vall 1993, 41–43.

[29] Examples of ילד: Giving birth: Gen 3:16; Judg 13:5. Plants sprouting: Isa 55:10. Examples of יצא: Giving birth: Gen 25:6; Job 1:21. Plants sprouting: Gen 1:12; Isa 11:1. Examples of זֶרַע: Semen/offspring: Gen 38:9; Lev 15:16. Seeds of plants: Gen 1:11; Exod 16:31. Examples of פְּרִי: Children of humans: Gen 30:2. Fruits of plants: Gen 1:11; Lev 26:4. Examples of פרה: Be fruitful (humans): Gen 1:28. Bear fruit (plants): Isa 32:12.

[30] Frymer-Kensky 1987, 22.

[31] In Atraḫasis (Late Assyrian version) the earth is described as a womb, and drought as a constricted womb that does not give birth to plants (Foster 2005, 272).

It has been suggested that the concept "Mother Earth" is an underlying metaphor behind expressions of a birth from the earth in Isa 26:19 and the formation in the depths of the earth in Ps 139:15.[32] I will discuss this further in chapter 5, "Birth Metaphors in Job 1." Here, I want to point out that the plant metaphor HUMANS ARE PLANTS is a dominant metaphor in the HB, and the relationship between PLANTS and HUMANS must be seen as an entrenched relationship, easy to retrieve when metaphors depict humans as growing out of the earth, thriving, bearing fruit, withering, and returning to dust. The plant metaphor can be developed to the image of Mother Earth; however, in the HB the earth is not called mother and there are no explicit references to the womb of the earth. The depths of the earth, being a source of fertility and growth, share these features with the womb, which can be used to construct metaphors of the womb of the earth.

To summarize: The correlations between the domains of PLANTS and HUMANS are strong. The same words are often used to describe the growth of both humans and plants. The fertility and barrenness of the ground are frequently paralleled with expressions describing the fertility and barrenness of humans. The metaphor HUMANS ARE PLANTS is dominant in the HB, while the metaphor PLANTS ARE HUMANS is only implied when plants are described with terms typically applied to humans. Plants are never said to come from the womb of the earth, but the depths of the earth are viewed as a source of fertility.

BIRTH and DEATH

Birth and death are antonyms, but both are transitional phases between life and non-life. Births are dangerous and might be life-threatening to the baby and their mother. The experience of women dying in childbirth is used in the simile "like a woman in labor," which is generally used to depict warriors at war. The domain of WOMB is blended with the domains of GRAVE and SHEOL into metaphors which describe death and hardship. Some of these metaphors depict an unborn child trapped in the womb, illustrating the hardship of exile or expressing a desire to have died at birth. These metaphors blend BIRTH and DEATH, and WOMB and GRAVE. Metaphors of the grave as a womb have often been interpreted as if the positive associations of the womb are projected to the grave, and as depicting the grave as a place of protection and compassion.[33] This is rarely the case in the HB.[34]

---

[32] Vall 1993, 41–70; Stordalen 2010; Keel and Schroer 2015, 86.

[33] Keel 1987, 53; Lévêque 1970, 200–201. Newsom 2003, 59. van der Zwan 2019a, 10. Their arguments are summarized in Chapter 5, pages 113–15.

[34] This is discussed in Dille 2010, 58–59.

The metaphor THE WOMB IS A GRAVE is explicitly stated in Jeremiah's lament, where he wishes he had never been born or had died in the womb (Jer 20:14–18). Jeremiah cries out "because he did not kill me in the womb; so my mother would have been my grave" (Jer 20:17).[35] Job 3:10–11, 16 and 10:18–19 also allude to the close connection between death and the womb.

Sheol is compared to a barren, life-consuming womb. Proverbs 30:15–16 refers to Sheol, the closed womb (עֹצֶר רָחַם), the dry land, and the fire, as things that never are satisfied (see also Prov 1:12; 27:20; Isa 5:14). This proverb links the domain of SHEOL with both the WOMB and the EARTH. In Hos 13:13–14, Ephraim's apostasy is depicted as a rejection of life through the metaphor of refraining from birth. God, therefore, would not deliver them from death or Sheol. The choice of death is described as being trapped in the womb, where a baby stuck in the womb is doomed to die. Both Sheol and the womb are portrayed negatively here. The womb is depicted not as a nurturing space but as a place of death, akin to the womb of a stillborn or a miscarriage. This imagery contrasts with the nurturing womb of a healthy pregnancy. The image of a baby stuck in the womb is also used in Isa 26:17–20, but from the mother's perspective.

> [17]Like a woman with child,
> who writhes and cries out in her pangs
> when she is near her time,
> so were we because of you, O LORD;
> [18]we were with child, we writhed,
> but we gave birth only to wind.
> We have won no victories on earth,
> and no one is born to inhabit the world.
> [19]Your dead shall live, their corpses shall rise.
> O dwellers in the dust, awake and sing for joy!
> For your dew is a radiant dew,
> and the earth will give birth to those long dead.
> [20]Come, my people, enter your chambers,
> and shut your doors behind you;
> hide yourselves for a little while
> until the wrath is past.[36]

The righteous here complain that God brings hardship upon them even though they have pleaded for salvation. They are likened to a woman in labor who suffers and cries but never gives birth. This simile illustrates both the pain and the fruitlessness of their labor. Despite their suffering and righteousness, they have not

---

[35] NRSV.
[36] NRSV.

found peace. Moreover, the simile underscores the critical situation: if the mother cannot push the baby out of the womb, both her life and the baby's life are at risk. The righteous are given a promise in Isa 26:19 that their dead shall live, and the earth will give birth to the dead spirits. They are identified both as the one who gives birth in vain (vv. 17–18) and as the dead ones who are born (v. 19). They cannot give birth, but the earth can. Here, as in Hos 13:13–14, the inability to give birth is equated with death. In contrast to Hos 13:13–14, God promises that the dead will be delivered from Sheol. The earth is described as a woman capable of giving birth to the dead. This is the only instance in the HB where the earth is depicted as giving birth to humans, even if they are dead spirits (רְפָאִים). In the next verse, Isa 26:20, we have a third image: the people are asked to enter the chambers and close the door behind them and wait for the wrath of God to pass. The chambers are presumably grave chambers (cf. Job 14:13). However, if viewed as a continuation of verse 19, they may also refer to graves as wombs that hide and protect the dead.[37] In this case, the positive attributes of the womb are projected to death. In short, there are three different birth metaphors in Isa 26: 17–20. The first depicts suffering and death as a fruitless labor; the second refers to the delivery from death as a birth; the third explicitly refers to the grave but may also implicitly refer to the womb as a space to hide and be protected.

There is a reference to בֶּטֶן שְׁאוֹל, "the belly of Sheol," in Jonah 2:3. The word בֶּטֶן can refer to the "belly," to the "womb," and also to interior parts of the body or the interior of a space.[38] The belly of Sheol may here refer to the belly of the fish, but more probably to the interior of the sea. Verse 3 continues the description by referring to the depth of the sea and describes how the water of the depth captures Jonah and how he is enclosed behind the bars of the land of the dead. The word בֶּטֶן does not bring any good associations to the description of Sheol.

Sirach 40:1 depicts the hardship of life, which starts when humans leave their mothers' wombs and ends when they return to "the mother of all living" or "the mother of all."[39] The expression used in the Greek text of Sirach is "mother of all," which is a common reference in Greek texts to Gaia, Mother Earth.[40] Sirach 40:1

---

[37] Keel and Schroer 2015, 86.

[38] *HALOT*, s.v. "בֶּטֶן I."

[39] Note that the Greek text in LXX differs from the Hebrew fragments LXX: εἰς μητέρα πάντων, "to the mother of all." Hebrew fragment (SirB 9v:10): כל חי <[א]ל אם >שובו אל אם, "the mother of all living."

[40] The expression "mother of all" is used in *Homeric Hymns* as well as in Hesiod's *Works and Days* (trans. Hine 2005, 42, 193).

describes the hardships of life, and neither the womb nor death is described as good nor bad.

The texts that blend the domains BIRTH and DEATH, or WOMB and GRAVE/SHEOL, generally do not use the positive connotations of the womb to present Sheol as a safe place. Instead, characteristics of death are transferred to the womb. The womb of Sheol is depicted as a place of infertility and as a life-consuming womb. This agrees with the common belief in HB that Sheol is a place of destruction, despair, and negation of life.[41]

To summarize: The domains BIRTH and DEATH are blended in the HB on several occasions. The womb is used as both a source and a target domain for the grave and Sheol. Jeremiah's wish to die in the womb is visualized by the metaphor of the womb as a grave. When the grave and Sheol are depicted in the image of the womb, it commonly refers to a womb which cannot give life. It might be a barren womb or a womb that entraps the baby inside it.

BIRTH and EXILE

Birth metaphors are used to depict the hardships of the exile and the rescue from it. Death, exile, and hardship are depicted through similar metaphors in the HB, such as imprisonment, darkness, and destruction.[1] As shown, birth complications are used in Isaiah and Hosea to describe the disaster of exile, particularly through the metaphor of a child being stuck in the womb, which would lead to death. Additionally, birth metaphors in Isaiah are also used to describe hope and God's deliverance from the exile.

The exilic state is depicted as Zion being a barren woman without any children, while God's salvation from exile is portrayed as Zion becoming a fertile woman who gives birth without pain and becomes the mother of many (Isa 49:20–21; 66:7–14). The image of God as a midwife in Isa 66:9 is part of a description of God's liberation of Israel from exile. Green claims that this depiction of God as a midwife signifies a new exodus, with the restored mother Zion illustrating a renewed covenantal relationship.[2] Maier points out that Isa 66:7–14 is a counterimage to the simile "woman in labor," which usually describes a situation of war.[3]

---

[41] For a presentation of how death was conceptualized, see Tromp 1969.

[1] Halvorson-Taylor 2010, 127–35.

[2] Green 2019, 293. The metaphors of birth and motherhood in this passage have been interpreted from various perspectives, see also Franke 2009; Maier 2012.

[3] Maier 2012, 231.

Claassens writes about the images of God as a mother and a woman in labor in Isaiah and Jeremiah.[4] She discusses the simile "God is like a woman in labor" in Isa 42:14, God as the comforting mother in Isa 49:13–15, and God as the nurturing mother in Isa 66:9–13, and argues that these images depict "God's delivering presence."[5] She claims that the simile "like a woman in labor" depicts both the trauma of the exile and God's redemption. It carries connotations of struggle, but at the same time it "reminds the reader of the ultimate goal of labor, i.e., to bring new life into the world."[6] Bergmann does not interpret the simile "like a woman in labor" as a hopeful image except once, when God is described as the one who gives birth in Isa 42:14.[7] It is instead used to depict a crisis which is unavoidable and life-threatening. Warriors are compared to women in childbirth, and Bergmann points out that they share similarities in their physical experiences, such as changes in appearance, breathing patterns, and encounters with life-threatening situations characterized by pain, tears, cries, sweat, and blood.[8] Isa 42:14 depicts God in the simile "like a woman giving birth," and this is the only time, according to Bergmann, that a birth metaphor depicts the outcome of the crisis of birth as something productive and positive. She argues that the simile in Isa 42:14 transforms the conventional meaning of the simile—as depicting a crisis—into a simile of hope.[9]

To summarize: Birth metaphors are used to depict the crisis of the exile. Metaphor of being entrapped in a womb equates exile with death. The simile "like a woman in labor" refers to a crisis which cannot be avoided. The act of giving birth is compared to being at war. It is often used to depict warriors as scared, trembling, and screaming. It uses the association of birth as a life-threatening bloody struggle. The good connotations of birth are used when God is said to deliver the baby who is stuck in the womb, when Zion gives birth with no pain, and when God cries out like a woman in labor in the struggle to save the people.

Words Relating to Birth

There are central words relating to birth in the HB whose meanings are crucial for interpreting the birth metaphors in the Book of Job. Here, I present the central

---

[4] Claassens 2012; Claassens 2014.
[5] Claassens 2012. See especially pp. 41–63.
[6] Claassens 2014, 69.
[7] Bergmann 2010, 39. The simile "like a woman in labor" is used in Ps 48:7; Isa 13:8; Jer 6:24; 30:6; 49:24; 50:43; Mic 4:9–10. Similar images are also found in Isa 21:3; 26:17; Jer 4:31; 13:21; 48:41.
[8] Bergmann 2010, 47–48.
[9] Bergmann 2010, 39, 52.

words that will occur several times in my metaphorical analysis. Other words referring to birth will be explained continuously as the metaphors are analyzed.

יָלַד, *"bring forth," "give birth," "beget."* The Qal stem of יָלַד is mainly used with a female subject and means "bear" or "give birth." It is also used with a male subject in genealogies with the meaning "beget." The Hiphil mainly refers to a male subject, also with the meaning "beget." The passive stems Niphal and Pual mean "be born." The Hiphil may also mean "bring forth," as in "bring forth a child" in Isa 66:9 and "bring forth rain" in Isa 55:9. The Niphal is used in genealogies together with the preposition לְ, meaning "someone being born to someone." The Piel means "assist at birth," and its participle refers to the one who assists at birth, the midwife.[1]

הָרָה, *"conceive," "be pregnant."* This has both female and male subjects and means "conceive" and "be pregnant." The passive Qal and Pual mean "be conceived." The verbs הָרָה and יָלַד are often used together in the phrase "she conceived and bore a son." The adjective הָרָה means "pregnant."[2]

יָצָא, *"go out."* This is a general verb used in Qal to describe something going out from or to a place. It can be applied to humans and things that come forth, such as rivers, years, words, and plants. It is used to describe a baby who goes out from the womb (מִבֶּטֶן or מֵרֶחֶם). It is also used in references to miscarriages, the birth of the afterbirth, and the emission of semen. Additionally, descendants can be said to go out from the father of the clan. The Hiphil means "cause to go out" or "bring out." It can convey the sense of "saving" or "sending out." This form applies to both objects and people being brought out. God is said to bring out water, wind, and stars. *TDOT* does not mention birth in its overview of יָצָא in Hiphil, but, as I will show, it is used in the context of birth in Job 10:18.[3]

בֶּטֶן, *"interior," "belly," "womb."* The noun בֶּטֶן is a general term which refers to the interior part of a human and may also be a synecdoche for the whole body. It may refer to the belly, the digestive organ, or to male and female reproductive organs. Children can be said to come from the בֶּטֶן of a man, but more commonly from the בֶּטֶן of a woman. It is used in parallel with the more specific term רֶחֶם, "womb." The noun בֶּטֶן is used 16 times in Job, with 9 of these instances referring to the womb. Also, the innermost cosmos or the inner parts of a building can be referred to with the word בֶּטֶן.[4]

---

[1] Schreiner, "יָלַד," *TDOT* 6:67–77.
[2] Ottosson, "הָרָה," *TDOT* 3:458.
[3] Preuss, "יָצָא," *TDOT* 6:225–30.
[4] Freedman and Lundbom, "בֶּטֶן," *TDOT* 2:94–97.

רֶחֶם, *"womb."* This is often found in parallel with the more general term בֶּטֶן, but רֶחֶם only refers to the female body. It might refer to the female genitalia as a whole, but it mainly refers to the uterus where babies are formed and from where they go out at birth. It occurs 25 times in the HB, five times in the Book of Job. The synonyms רַחַם, רַחֲמָה are not used in Job.[5]

Summary and Conclusions

This chapter started with an overview of how births are described in the HB. They are commonly referred to with the formula she "conceived and bore a son." More extensive descriptions of birth usually signal the prominence of the one born, or are needed in the narratives to explain something else. The descriptions of birth do not focus on the experience of the mother and her labor, and the birth itself is seldom described. However, some information about birth can be derived from them, such as the fact that the mother is assisted by other women and sometimes a midwife, that she kneels when giving birth, the practice of using birthstones, that both the mother and the father can name the baby, that the news of a newborn son is better than that of a daughter, the practice of rubbing the newborn with salt, and that many women died while giving birth. I have pointed out four major metaphors with BIRTH as their target domain: GESTATION IS GROWTH OF A PLANT, GOD IS THE CLOSER AND OPENER OF WOMBS, BIRTH IS AN ACT OF BREAKING, and CREATION OF HUMANS IS A HANDCRAFT MADE BY GOD.

The second and major part of this chapter discusses how the domain of BIRTH is used as a source domain that is blended with the domains of GOD, CREATION, PLANTS, DEATH, and EXILE. God is described as a parent, begetter, a woman giving birth, and as a midwife. These metaphors mainly highlight God's care for the people, and are used in appeals to the people to remember God, and to God to remember the people. They accentuate the close relationship between God and the people, while also highlighting God's authority over them and God as their creator. The domain of BIRTH is rarely used in descriptions of the creation of earth, but God is said to give birth to the earth and the mountains, and the dew is said to be born from the womb of the dawn. The closeness between the domain of PLANTS and HUMANS is expressed in the metaphor HUMANS ARE PLANTS. The reversed metaphor is rare in the HB, but the fertility of the ground and the fertility of humans are often described together and in similar terms. The domains of DEATH and BIRTH are blended in the HB. When the womb and the grave or Sheol are

---

[5] Kronholm, "רֶחֶם," *TDOT* 13:454–58

blended, the metaphor usually highlights the characteristics of death and destruction. These blends are used in wishes of having died in the womb and in descriptions of exile as being stuck in the womb. Isaiah also uses birth metaphors to portray liberation from exile. The images of the restored mother Zion giving birth without pain, God as a midwife, and God giving birth are all used to depict God's act of liberation. The simile "like a woman in labor" otherwise highlights the characteristics of war, death, blood, trembling, fear, and struggle.

Metaphors that blend BIRTH with the domain of PLANTS highlight characteristics of growth and nourishment. In these metaphors, the womb is implied to be soil where seeds grow, and to bear fruit. Semen is referred to as seed, and children are seen as the fruit of the womb. In contrast, metaphors blending BIRTH with DEATH emphasize the characteristics of a barren womb that causes death. The simile "like a woman in labor" illustrates birth as a life-threatening situation. When applied to humans, it depicts an extreme crisis such as war. However, when applied to God, it can also carry positive associations of birth as a struggle that leads to new life. The domain of BIRTH and its metaphors in the HB encompass various associations, and it is crucial to consider these different associations when analyzing birth metaphors. One must be cautious of the context to understand the specific characteristics each metaphor highlights.

4. Birth Metaphors in Ancient West Asia

The HB provides some insights into how birth was conceptualized in ancient Israel. In this chapter, I will offer a more comprehensive background by examining depictions of birth in other ancient West Asian texts, particularly Akkadian birth incantations. While I do not suggest a direct intertextual connection between the Book of Job and these other texts, I argue that they share a cultural context regarding the conceptualization of birth and the depiction of gods as midwives assisting in childbirth. The various texts I will refer to originate over a long period of time. I will discuss Sumerian texts as well as Akkadian texts from the Old Babylonian to Neo-Assyrian periods; however, all share metaphors, which shows that these metaphors were consistent over time. One might even argue that many of the metaphors used in the HB, as well as in other ancient texts, are also used throughout history in different parts of the world.

Existing research on birth descriptions and imagery in ancient West Asia primarily concerns Sumerian and Akkadian texts. Births are described in Mesopotamian myths, as well as medical and magical texts. They share motifs and metaphors with birth descriptions in the HB. For instance, the births of great kings are often depicted as complicated events, yet the babies miraculously survive. Other shared elements include gods controlling procreation by opening and closing wombs, gods forming humans from clay, references to the kneeling position of the woman giving birth, the use of birthstones, and the presence of a midwife assisting the woman in labor. Stol explores the conceptualization of birth in ancient West Asia, examining how conception, gestation, birth, and midwifery are represented across various texts.[1] Van Dijk transliterated and translated several Sumerian and Akkadian birth incantations in the 1970s and examined various motifs within them.[2] Scurlock has compiled and investigated several Assyrian-Babylonian medical texts of obstetrics and gynecology which prescribe treatments for problems during pregnancy and childbirth.[3] Veldhuis has analyzed the literary features of the Neo-

---

[1] Stol 2000.
[2] van Dijk 1972; van Dijk 1973; van Dijk 1975.
[3] Scurlock 1991; Scurlock 2014.

Assyrian compendium for a woman in childbirth, a well-preserved collection of myths, incantations, rituals, and prescriptions related to childbirth.[4] The compendium is a crucial source for understanding how birth was conceptualized in ancient times. Two major copies of the compendium have been found: one from Assur and the other from Nineveh. Parts of it are present in Middle Assyrian texts, and a small fragment has even been discovered in the Hittite archives at Boğazköy. There is also a commentary text from Nippur. The manuscript from Assur is the most well-preserved and consists of a tablet with four columns of text.[5] These different manuscripts show the significance of the compendium and that it had spread over a significant area. The compendium also shares imagery and phraseology with Sumerian texts. Common motifs and metaphors in Sumerian and Akkadian texts have been identified and discussed in several articles and books. Couto-Ferreira summarizes them and lists the following recurring motifs: knots, knotting, bars, bolts, doors, paths, ships, sailing, cow giving birth, butting, crouching, crying, darkness, light, falling, breaking like a vase, death, streaming water, and divine assistance.[6]

Greenstein identifies similarities between the descriptions of the womb in the Book of Job and Akkadian birth incantations, noting that these are generic similarities.[7] A common metaphor in the incantations is the image of the womb as a room with doors that can be closed and opened. These doors are opened at birth by gods who act as midwives. Both Job 3:10 and Job 38:8–11 use this image. Inspired by Greenstein's findings, Langton identifies additional shared features, such as the

---

[4] The compendium from Assur was transliterated and translated by Ebeling in 1923 (Ebeling 1923). Veldhuis has reconstructed the Akkadian text in Veldhuis 1989. He has translated the myth A Cow of Sîn from both the Neo-Assyrian compendium and other texts that share the same tradition in Veldhuis 1991. Farber translated the myth Cow of the Sîn from the compendium from Assur in *TUAT* II/2, 274–77. Stol has translated parts of the compendium from Assur in Stol 2000, 64–66. A translation of major parts of it is provided by Foster in Foster 2005, 1007–9.

[5] Veldhuis 1991, 1–3.

[6] Couto-Ferreira 2014, 310–11. Van Dijk identifies several motifs such as the cow and a god, the boat, and helping spirits in van Dijk 1972. Veldhuis also discusses shared motifs. In addition to those listed by Couto-Ferreira, Veldhuis identifies motifs such as the baby slipping out like a snake or a gazelle, the baby emerging into the light, female and masculine symbols, and the quay of death (Veldhuis 1989, 250–51; Veldhuis 1991, 41–42). Bergmann also provides an overview of texts and motifs of birth in the ANE in Bergmann 2008, 9–59.

[7] Greenstein 2017, 147–50. Greenstein suspects that the author of Job uses Aramaic sources rather than Babylonian texts.

reference to darkness inside the womb and the imagery of the baby being born into the light.[8]

In this chapter I will first note several metaphors used in Akkadian incantations and rituals that are relevant to my investigation of the birth metaphors in Job. I will also discuss two motifs present in various myths: "the cow of Sîn" and "counting the months." Next, I will survey the role of the midwife and how gods are portrayed in this role. Finally, I will briefly explore how the domain of BIRTH is used to depict creation and death in texts from ancient West Asia.

Birth Metaphors in Akkadian Birth Incantations

Birth incantations are magico-medical texts which invoke the gods to help at births. They are often combined with rituals performed at childbirth. I will present three examples of incantation texts that use metaphors similar to those found in Job, particularly in Job 38–39. The most striking example is an Old Babylonian birth incantation:

> In the water of intercourse, the bone was created;
> in the flesh of muscles, the baby was created.
> In the ocean waters, fearsome, raging,
> in the far-off waters of the sea:
> where the little one is – his arms are bound!
> inside which the eye of the sun does not bring light.
> Asalluḫi, the son of Enki, saw him.
> He loosed his tight-bound bonds,
> he made him a path, he opened him a way:
> 'Opened are the paths for you, the ways are ... for you.
> The ... is sitting for you,
> she who creates ... she who creates us all.
> She has spoken to the doorbolt: You are released.'
> Removed are the locks, the doors are thrown aside.
> Let him strike [...] like a *dadum*, bring yourself out!'[9]

In this incantation, the water that surrounds the fetus, the amniotic fluid, is portrayed as a sea. This sea is described as fearsome and raging, highlighting the danger

---

[8] Langton 2012. Langton refers to Greenstein's oral presentation at the SBL meeting in 2008, where he demonstrated these generic similarities. Paul also points out that both Akkadian birth incantations and Job 3 depict the womb as a room with doors (Paul 2013, 171–74).

[9] YBC 4603 (YOS 11, 86), line 1–28, (trans. Stol 2000, 11). The Akkadian word *dadum* could both mean "beloved one" or "a fish" (Stol 2000, 11). This incantation is found on a tablet containing two birth incantations. There is only one copy discovered so far, and it is partly damaged. Its provenance is uncertain. For the Akkadian text, see van Dijk 1973, 503.

of being pregnant and giving birth. The womb is a dark room with doors. They need to be opened at the time of birth, and they are here opened by the god Asalluḫi and the mother goddess.[10] The baby is described as tied with bonds that need to be untied. The gods act as midwives who release the baby, and they also speak to the child in the womb, telling it to bring itself out. The Akkadian verbs used to describe the release of the baby are *paṭarum* and *ramum*.[11] They can mean "let someone free," referring to untying ropes and removing locks. These verbs can also relate to the slackening of joints and sinews in the body. In this incantation, they are used within the metaphor of opening bonds and removing door bolts, but the underlying reference is to the physical process in which body parts need to be slackened to allow the baby to be born. The words *paṭarum* and *ramum* are thus applicable to both the source and target domain in this metaphorical description.

I identify five metaphors in this Old Babylonian incantation: THE WOMB IS A ROOM WITH DOORS, GODS ARE MIDWIVES WHO OPEN THE DOORS OF THE WOMB AT BIRTH, THE AMNIOTIC FLUID IS A SEA, THE UNBORN IS TIED WITH BONDS, and GODS ARE MIDWIVES WHO UNTIE THE BONDS OF THE UNBORN AT BIRTH.

The amniotic fluid as a sea is also implied in the compendium from Assur. One of the incantations depicts the baby as a ship and their movements through the birth canal as a boat journey. The ship departs from the quay of death and hardship, heading for the quay of health and wellbeing.

> May the ship (arrive) well in the ...
> may the barge (arrive) felicitously in the ...
> May her taut mooring rope be slackened,
> and her closed door be opened,
> the mooring rope of the boat for the quay of well-being,
> the mooring rope of the barge for the quay of health.
> May the limbs be relaxed, the muscles loosen,
> may the sealed one ease, may the creature come forth.
> The separate bone, the human form,
> may it come forth soon and see the sunlight!
> Like rainfall from heaven, may it not turn back,
> like what has fallen from the wall, may it not return,*
> like a streaming gutter, may its waters not stay behind.

---

[10] Van Dijk claims that the woman in this incantation is the mother goddess (van Dijk 1973, 504). This is confirmed by two similar Old Babylonian birth incantations, presented by George, which explicitly refer to the mother goddess, one to Belit-ili and the other to Ninḫursaga (George 2016, 140–42).

[11] *paṭarum*: "He *loosened* his tight-bound bonds," "*removed* are the locks." rāmûm: "the doors *are thrown aside.*" *CDA* translates *paṭarum*, "release," "loosen," and "cut off," and *ramum* "throw" "cast down," "slacken" and "release locks" *(CDA* s.v. "paṭāru(m)"; "rāmûm I, II, III").

> When Asalluḫi heard this,
> he became anxious, he worried for her life,
> on the word of Ea he exalted his name;
> he threw the incantation of life, the formula of well-being.
> He loosened the mooring rope, he untied her k[not].
> The closed doors were o[pened].
> The sealed were eased, [the creature came forth]
> The separate bone, the human form,
> may it come forth soon and see the sunlight![12]

The god Asalluḫi is here the midwife who unties the mooring rope, opens the doors, and brings the baby out into the sunlight. This incantation refers to limbs and muscles being loosened, as well as the mooring ropes and doors being opened.[13] It is hoped that the delivery of the baby will be like a rainfall. If the baby comes out with the speed and power of a rainfall or a streaming gutter, then it will be a safe and successful birth. It is most likely that the delivery of the baby, rather than the amniotic fluid, is depicted as a streaming rainfall, as the preceding sentence expresses the wish for the baby to come forth and see the sunlight. However, it is not far-fetched to think that the experience of the amniotic fluid breaking could be behind this metaphor. When the water breaks during birth, it flows out without any effort by the mother, and one might wish that the baby would come forth with the same ease. The compendium also describes a ritual in which the midwife uses a mixture of hailstones, dust from a collapsed wall, and dust from a broken vessel to rub on the abdomen.[14]

The metaphors of birth as a boat journey, the baby born as a rainfall, and the womb as a broken pot, are found in two Sumerian texts. In these texts, however, the woman in labor is the one depicted as the boat carrying precious cargo, the baby.[15] One of these texts describes how Enki instructs Asalluḫi to smear the vulva with fat, which would open the door and untie the knots, while reciting an incantation: "may it be released like the showers of heaven, may it run like the waters of

---

[12] VAT 8869 (BAM 248) ii 47–60 (trans. Stol 2000, 65). For the Akkadian text, see Ebeling 1923.

[13] The Akkdian verbs are here *paṭārum* ("may her taut mooring rope be *slackened*," "may the limbs *be relaxed*"); *petûm*, "open" ("and her closed door *be opened*," "the closed doors *were o[pened]*); *ramûm* ("the muscles *loosen*," "he *loosened* the mooring rope"); *pašārum* ("may the sealed one *ease*," "the sealed *were eased*"). The verb *petûm*, "open," may refer to the act of opening of doors, ties, locks as well as parts of the body such as the mouth and ears (*CDA* s.v. "petū(m) I, II"). The verb *pašārum*, "free," "release," may refer to the release of captives but it can also denote the release of illnesses, evil forces, and loosened knots (*CDA* s.v. "pašāru(m)").

[14] Veldhuis 1989, 251.

[15] UM 29-15-367, VAT 8381 (VS 17, 33), van Dijk 1975, 53–65.

gutter of the roof, may it [stream] like a canal pouring into the lake, may it be broken like a broken pot."[16]

The compendium from Assur and the Sumerian texts add five metaphors to the list of Akkadian birth incantation: THE BIRTH IS A BOAT JOURNEY, THE BABY IS TIED WITH MOORING ROPES, BEING BORN IS TO SEE SUNLIGHT, THE BABY WHO COMES FORTH FROM THE WOMB IS A RUSHING RAINFALL, and THE WOMB IS A POT.

The examples cited above refer both to the doors of the womb and the importance that they are opened at birth. The complication of a baby being stuck in the womb is a life-threatening condition for both the baby and the mother, and such a terrifying scene is described in a middle Assyrian medical text from the Ligabue Library tablets.[17]

> The woman in labor is having a difficult labor,
> Her labor is difficult, the baby is stuck,
> The baby is stuck!
> The door bolt is locked, about to end life,
> The door is fastened against the suckling kid...[18]

Here we have the metaphor BIRTH COMPLICATIONS ARE LOCKED DOORS, and it is Marduk who is asked to open them. This text also compares the woman in labor to a warrior in battle. The domains of COMBAT and BIRTH share associations of danger, screaming, blood, struggle, and death.

> The woman giving birth is covered with death's dust,
> She is covered with the dust of battle, like a chariot...
> She sprawls in her own blood, like a struggling warrior.[19]

The description above can be expressed in the metaphor A WOMAN IN LABOR IS A WARRIOR. The reversed counterpart A WARRIOR IS A WOMAN IN LABOR is found in the HB. They both highlight the danger, the blood, and struggle experienced both in war and childbirth.

The incantation texts quoted above highlight the danger of birth and the wish that the baby should be delivered safely. The danger is expressed by references to

---

[16] UM 29-15-367 (trans. Stol 2000, 61).

[17] This incantation is from a well-preserved single-column tablet containing prescriptions for a pregnant woman who suffers from colic and two birth incantations. Its provenance is unknown. It is transliterated and translated in Lambert 1969. For a similar Middle Assyrian text, see Veldhuis 1991, 10–11.

[18] Trans. Foster 2005, 1006. For the Akkadian text, see Lambert 1969, 31.

[19] Trans. Foster 2005, 1006. For the Akkadian text, see Lambert 1969, 31.

darkness, death, warriors, locked doors, being tied, and the fearsome sea. The gods are described as midwives who loosen the bonds, open the doors, relax the muscles, and urge the baby to bring itself out.

To summarize: The birth incantations above use several metaphors in the descriptions of births. I have identified eleven birth metaphors in them: THE WOMB IS A ROOM WITH DOORS, GODS ARE MIDWIVES WHO OPEN THE DOORS AT BIRTH, THE AMNIOTIC FLUID IS A SEA, THE UNBORN IS TIED WITH ROPES, GODS ARE MIDWIVES WHO UNTIE THE ROPES, THE BIRTH IS A BOAT JOURNEY, BEING BORN IS TO SEE SUNLIGHT, THE BABY WHO COMES FORTH FROM THE WOMB IS A RUSHING RAINFALL, THE WOMB IS A POT, BIRTH COMPLICATIONS ARE LOCKED DOORS, and THE WOMAN IN LABOR IS A WARRIOR. These metaphors provide a more extensive background to how birth was conceptualized than we find in the HB alone.

Additional Birth Motifs and Metaphors

There are two birth motifs from ancient West Asia which are prominent in the myths: the motifs "Cow of Sîn" and "counting of the months." These are particularly important for the investigation of birth metaphors in Job 39, which describes births among animals and uses the motif of the "counting of the months."

The myth of the Cow of Sîn is retold in the compendium from Assur and in other Akkadian and Sumerian texts concerning birth.[20] The myth narrates how the moon god Sîn, in the form of a bull, impregnates a cow. When the cow goes into labor it trembles, crouches, and cries for help. Sîn sends two helpers from heaven, two helping spirits or the two daughters of Anu, to help the cow.[21] The Akkadian word for cow (*littu*) is similar to the word of a woman in childbirth (*alittu*) and the wordplay signals that the cow is seen as a prototype for the woman in childbirth.[22] The description of the cow trembling, crouching, and crying out reflects

---

[20] The oldest Sumerian text referring to the Cow of Sîn dates to the Fara period in the middle third millennium BCE. Another more comprehensive text, UM 29-15-367, dates to the UR III period in the late third millennium (van Dijk 1975; Stol 2000, 60). The motif also appears in an Old Babylonian text, KUB IV. 13, Middle Assyrian texts (Ligabue tablets) and the Neo-Assyrian compendium for a woman in childbirth (Veldhuis 1991, 4). For the Ligabue tablets, see Lambert 1969. The motif of a god impregnating a cow also appears in a Hittite myth and in the Baal Cycle, but these myths do not include references to a woman in childbirth. The Hittite myth is called The Sun God and the Cow (Stol 2000, 68), and the episode from the Baal Cycle is found in *KTU* 1.5 v 17–25.

[21] In the Neo-Assyrian compendium, the helpers are two helping spirits, the Lamassus, and in the earlier Ligabue tablets they are identified as daughters of Anu (Veldhuis 1991, 22).

[22] Veldhuis 1991, 22.

traits one might typically expect from a woman in labor rather than a cow. The narrative of the Cow of Sîn is combined with medical prescriptions and incantations in the compendium for a woman in childbirth. The texts imply a wish that the woman in labor would give birth as easily as the cow. Other expressions in birth incantations also refer to animals, such as wishing for the baby to be born like a gazelle, fish, or snake.[23] These animals are used to illustrate a rapid, smooth, and effortless birth because the gazelle symbolizes speed, and the snake and fish would easily slide out from the womb.

The theme of counting the months, or the days, of a pregnancy is a well-known motif in Akkadian, Ugaritic, and Hittite birth texts. Bergmann has pointed out that this motif often dominates over the actual description of the birth.[24] In Atraḫasis the mother goddess Nintu supervises the pregnancy of the first human couple. She is then said to sit down to count the months and later performs midwifery by opening the womb.[25] The myth Enki and Ninḫursaga emphasizes the counting of the days of Ninḫursaga's nine-day pregnancy, explaining that each day of her pregnancy corresponds to a month of human pregnancy. The birth itself is briefly described, stating that on the ninth day, she gave birth to Ninmu, like oil.[26] In the Ugaritic text describing the birth of Dawn and Dusk, El sits down to count the months of his wife's pregnancy. Similarly, in the Aqhatu legend, the father Dani'ilu is depicted as counting the months.[27] In the Hittite Songs of Kumarbi, the impregnated Kumarbi is described as sitting down to count the months.[28] This motif also appears in the myth Appu and His Two Sons.[29] Although the motif is consistent across these texts, the role of who counts the months varies; it is performed either by the mother goddess or the father.

---

[23] For instance, "Run hither to me like a gazelle. Slip out to me like a little snake! I, Asalluḫi, am the midwife, I will receive you" from VAT 8869 (BAM 248) iv, (trans. Foster 2005, 1008). Discussion on the symbolism of the gazelle, see Veldhuis 1991, 41. For discussion of the fish and snake, see Stol 2000, 10–11.

[24] Bergmann 2008, 14.

[25] "Atraḫasis" I 278 (trans. Lambert, et al. 1999, 62–63).

[26] Kramer and Albright 1945, 12–15; Rodin 2014, 332.

[27] "Dawn and Dusk" (COS 1.87:282). "Aqhatu legend" (COS 1.103:345).

[28] "Song of Emergence" §8 (COS-Sup 4.6A:42).

[29] "Appu and His Two Sons" (COS, 1.58:154).

The Midwife

In Akkadian texts, midwives were referred to as "wise" women. The Akkadian term for midwife is *šabsut remin*, which translates to "knowing the inside of the womb."[30] Midwives were recognized as experts in managing normal pregnancies and births, but detailed texts about their work and methods are scarce. The primary sources of information about midwives come from myths depicting gods in the role of midwives. Medical texts describe treatments for complicated births, bleeding, and severe postpartum complications, but these procedures might have been carried out by exorcists rather than midwives. It is difficult to distinguish the roles of midwives and exorcists. From the depictions of divine midwives, it appears that midwives recited incantations and performed rituals as part of their work. These rituals and incantations played a crucial role in ensuring a safe and successful birth.

The divine midwives were from the beginning birth or mother goddesses. The Sumerian Akkadian mother goddess has many names, the most common being Mama, Nintu, Ninḫursaga, and Belit-ili. The god Asalluḫi, also known as Marduk, was regarded as a midwife in the Old Babylonian period, and this role continued into the period of the Ligabue tablets and the Neo-Assyrian compendium for a woman in childbirth. Asalluḫi was the god of incantations, which may explain why birth incantations were directed towards him.[31]

A description of the work of the mother goddess Nintu when she performs midwifery is found in Atraḫasis.

> The birth-goddesses were assembled
> And Nintu [sat] counting the months.
> [At the] destined [moment] the tenth month was summoned.
> The tenth month arrived
> And the elapse of the period opened the womb.
> With a beaming joyful face
> And covered head she performed the midwifery.
> She girded her loins as she pronounced the blessing,
> She drew a pattern in meal and placed the brick,
> 'I have created, my hands have made it. ...'[32]

---

[30] The Akkadian word for midwife is *šabsutu* which originates from the Sumerian *šá.zu*, "knowing the inside (of the body)." Its extended form *šabsutu remim* means "midwife of the womb." implying that she knows the inside of the womb (Stol 2000, 171).
[31] Sommerfeld 1928, 368.
[32] "Atraḫasis" I 277–89 (trans. Lambert, et al. 1999, 62–63).

The mother goddess Nintu oversees the pregnancy, counting the months, and, in the tenth month, preparing to open the womb.[33] During childbirth, she covers her head, girds her loins, and exhibits a joyful expression. The joyful face would, according to Scurlock, bring good luck to the birth and the baby.[34] The drawing of a circle in the meal may also have a magical explanation, while the brick probably refers to the birthstones used as a birth stool.[35] We learn about the work of the midwives from this description, but the specific method by which the midwife opens the womb is not explicitly described. The phrase "and the elapse of the period opened the womb" is acknowledged as difficult to interpret. Stol and Jacobsen suggest that it refers to the breaking of the water and the opening of the membrane of the amniotic sac.[36] Another practice described in Akkadian birth incantations is the midwife opening the womb by massaging the belly and putting pressure on it. Special oil was made for these purposes and the midwife should roll a stick over the woman's belly. The Neo-Assyrian compendium prescribes that the midwife should rub the abdomen with a mixture of hailstones, dust from a fallen wall, and water from a drainpipe. These correspond to the wish that the baby should be delivered like streaming water and something that has fallen from a wall.[37] Although these ingredients have symbolic value, they indicate that the midwife performed a form of abdominal massage on the woman in labor. Additionally, the compendium advises the midwife to smear the vulva with oil, as a way to open the womb. This act of smearing is a well-known practice in many cultures to prevent perineal tears when the baby breaks through.

The midwife also helped the woman with the afterbirth and cut the umbilical cord. The cutting of the umbilical cord was regarded as an important moment that could influence the baby's future.[38] She also wiped and rubbed the baby and

---

[33] Some myths say pregnancy lasts 10 months, others 9, due to different calendars—some using lunar months, others solar (Stol 2000, 24).

[34] Scurlock 1991, 167, n. 56.

[35] Stol 2000, 118–22.

[36] Jacobsen 1973, 290 (see n. 63); Stol 2000, 115. The Akkadian word *silitu*.translated as "womb" may also mean afterbirth. Stol interprets it here as "womb" or "membrane," translating the line: "and she slipped into (?) the *palu*, opened the membranes." Stol is uncertain of the meaning of *palu* suggesting "stick" or "garment." The stick could be used to break the membrane of the amniotic sac (Stol 2000, 115).

[37] Stol 2000, 65–66. See also Veldhuis 1989, 251. Scurlock discusses how the words for these ingredients sound similar to terms associated with birth. For instance, the word for hailstone correspond to words for create and giving birth (Scurlock 1991, 145).

[38] Stol 2000, 143.

cleared their airways.³⁹ In a description of Nintu in Enki and the World Order, she is said to bring birth bricks, an umbilical cord lancet, leeks, and vessels.⁴⁰ The vessels Nintu brings may have two functions, one for bringing water for the cleaning of the baby and the mother, and the other as the vessel in which the afterbirth was placed.⁴¹ The purpose of the leek is not entirely clear, but it may have been used in postpartum care, possibly for disinfection or to stop bleeding.⁴² The midwife was responsible for assisting the mother in expelling the placenta and managing postpartum complications, such as infections and fever. Several cures have been documented, including drinking infusions, rubbing the genitals with different mixes, or having the mother sit over jars of smoking herbs.⁴³

In Mesopotamian literature there are descriptions of Lamaštu, an evil demon who was believed to attack children.⁴⁴ She was considered to complicate births and bring disease and death to infants and their mothers.

> She is fierce, she is wicked, she is [...]
> She slinks about, she is un[canny].
> Though no physician, she bandages,
> Though no midwife, she wipes off the babe.
> She reckons off the month(s) of pregnant women,
> She likes to block the dilation of women in labor.
> She dogs the livestock's footsteps.
> She spies out the country with demonic fierceness.
> She seizes the young man in the roadway,
> The young woman in play,
> The little one from the wet nurse's shoulder.⁴⁵

This incantation describes the wiping of the baby as one of the midwife's tasks. In this text, the evil demon Lamaštu is depicted as acting like a midwife; she counts the months and wipes the baby. However, unlike a benevolent midwife, Lamaštu obstructs the birth canal and closes the womb. This portrayal underscores the belief in evil demons and spells that could hinder childbirth, explaining the necessity of birth incantations and divine assistance to ensure a safe delivery.

---

³⁹ Scurlock 1991, 149–51; Stol 2000, 111–12, 143–45, 177.
⁴⁰ Stol 2000, 111, 141–42.
⁴¹ Scurlock 1991, 149–51.
⁴² Scurlock 1991, 149.
⁴³ Scurlock 1991, 150.
⁴⁴ She is a daughter of Anu, just as the helping spirits in the Cow of Sîn (Veldhuis 1991, 22).
⁴⁵ YOS 11, 19 (YBC 4601), "Against Lamashtu" (trans. Foster 2005, 174). For Akkadian text, see Dijk, et al. 1985, 25–26.

To summarize: Midwives were seen as wise women. They assisted women with practical support, recited incantations, and performed rituals. Their practical assistance included breaking the amniotic sac, massaging the belly and vulva, cutting the umbilical cord, clearing the baby's airways, and providing postpartum care for the mother.

BIRTH as the Source Domain

I have given a more extensive background above to how birth was conceptualized in ancient West Asia than could be deduced from the HB alone. I will here briefly discuss how BIRTH is used as a source domain in metaphors in texts from ancient West Asia. It is not the aim of this study to investigate them, but I want to show that the domain of BIRTH is used with the domains of CREATION, PLANTS, and WAR in metaphors in other texts besides the HB. I have already shown how a woman in labor is compared with a warrior at war. To portray creation of specific parts of nature in terms of birth is more common in Mesopotamian texts than in the HB. Birth metaphors are used in descriptions of planting, irrigating, growing crops, and drought. In Enki and the World Order, Enki's semen fills the Euphrates and Tigris, irrigates the fields, and makes the landscape flourish.[46] The Babylonian myth the Creation of Pickax depicts the creation of humans as if they were plants growing in a field.[47] Atraḫasis refers to the womb of the earth in a description of drought. When it is constricted, no plants will come forth.[48] Couto-Ferreira discusses the similarities of how the room of death and wombs are depicted. They are seen as dark enclosed rooms, as prisons with bolted doors.[49] She states that this relationship has been mainly studied in the Hymn to Nungal, in which the concepts of womb, the netherworld, and prison are combined in metaphorical expressions such as "my house gives birth to the right man, it kills the criminal man."[50] The relationship between the womb and tomb is more distinguished in Egyptian sources, which accentuate that the dead are reborn by the mother goddess into a new life.[51] These examples provide insights that the domain of BIRTH was a

---

[46] Dickson 2007.
[47] Simkins 2014, 42–44.
[48] "Atraḫasis" I iv 46–49 (Late Assyrian Version), (trans. Foster 2005, 272).
[49] Couto-Ferreira 2018, 48–50.
[50] Couto-Ferreira 2018, 49–50. The quote is from Hymn from Nungal 103. For the Sumerian text, see Sjöberg 1973, 28–37.
[51] Spieser 2018; Hays 2012.

significant domain for constructing metaphors, particularly in relation to creation and death. Similar metaphors are present in the Book of Job.

Cross-Cultural and Culture Specific Metaphors

I have in this chapter identified several birth metaphors used in Akkadian birth incantations. Some of them are also found in other cultures while others seem to be more culture specific. The metaphor of imagining the baby coming forth as a rainfall can be assumed to be more culturally dependent than depicting a baby sitting in a dark room. Couto-Ferreira gives several examples of different cultural contexts in which the metaphor THE WOMB IS A ROOM WITH DOORS is used. She refers to Greek comedies, the Latin word "vulva," Japanese childbirth rituals, and notes that the etymology of the Japanese term for womb translates to "child's palace."[52] The list of examples can be extended. A study of birth metaphors in South Sudan shows that the womb is called "the house of childbirth" which is said to have an entrance with doors; additionally, the study finds that the womb is imagined as a pot.[53] Medieval English birth charms used the biblical story of the resurrection of Lazarus, especially the words "Lazarus, come forth!" which reflect a concept of the womb as a grave in which the baby is enclosed.[54] Legends of Bodhisattva (the future Buddha) describe his fetal life in the womb as living in a jeweled palace illuminated by his radiance.[55] A study of how viewing an ultrasound affects parents' thoughts and emotions towards their unborn baby describes the experience of the ultrasound as looking through a window into the womb or as a journey to the womb. It also mentions other metaphors parents use for the womb, such as calling it a home, a bedroom, or a nursery.[56] In my investigation of the metaphors in the Book of Job, I will refer to the metaphors I have identified in Akkadian birth incantations as Akkadian birth metaphors, but I am aware of that some of these are also cross-cultural metaphors.

Summary and Conclusion

This chapter provides a background to how birth and midwifery were conceptualized in a wider context than the HB. It focuses mainly on identifying birth

---

[52] Couto-Ferreira 2018, 50.
[53] Boddy 1982, 693.
[54] Jones and Olsan 2015, 415–16.
[55] Sasson and Law 2008, 55–59.
[56] Krolokke 2010, 149–51.

metaphors in Akkadian texts, and how midwifery is expressed in these incantations, myths, and medical texts. The womb is depicted as a dark room with doors that the gods need to open at birth. It is said to be a pot that needs to be cracked to let the baby out. A dreaded birth complication is when the baby gets stuck in the womb, enclosed behind bolted doors, and tied to the womb. A successful birth is expressed as the baby being born into the light, with the power of rainfall, the speed of a gazelle, and as smoothly as a fish sliding out of the womb. A woman in difficult labor is described as a warrior who struggles in blood. The midwives were seen as wise women who assisted at birth, both by reciting incantations and with practical help such as massaging the belly, cutting the umbilical cord, wiping the newborn, delivering the placenta, and giving postpartum care to the mother.

There are clear parallels between how birth is described in the HB and in Akkadian texts. The motif of a womb as a container that could be opened and closed are present both in the HB and in the Akkadian texts. God is commonly said to open or close the womb at conception in the HB, while the incantations refer to the opening of the wombs at birth. The use of the verb סגר, "close," "shut," may imply that the womb is shut by doors in the HB also, because this verb usually refers to doors. The act of breaking the doors in Akkadian descriptions corresponds to the way in which Perez breaks himself out at birth, and how God is said to break open the womb in Isa 66:9. In my investigation of the birth metaphors in Job, I will also show other links between them and Akkadian birth metaphors.

5. Birth Metaphors in Job 1

At the beginning of the Book of Job, in the first chapter, in the first words Job utters, there is a reference to Job's birth and his mother's womb. Job has been deprived of all his belongings and his children, and the question is whether Job will curse God or if he will hold on to his integrity. Job 1:21 answers this question. Job does not curse God. Instead, he describes his loss and blesses God's name. His answer is "Naked I went out from my mother's womb, and naked I will return there. The Lord gives, and the Lord takes. May the name of the Lord be blessed!" What the expression "return there" refers to has been debated. The expression has been called an "enigma" and has been interpreted as a return to Job's mother's womb, Sheol, dust, or Mother Earth. This single verse has received a great deal of attention in discussions of whether death is imagined as a womb in the HB. Therefore, it is also a good point of departure for the analysis of birth metaphors in the Book of Job.

This chapter starts with a translation of the text and some literary remarks. Then follows a presentation and a discussion of existing research. Then the expression "Naked, I went out from my mother's womb, and naked I will return there" will be analyzed closely with blending theory.

Text and Translation of Job 1:21

21aa	וַיֹּאמֶר עָרֹם יָצָתִי מִבֶּטֶן אִמִּי	And he said: "Naked I went out from my mother's womb,
21ab	וְעָרֹם אָשׁוּב שָׁמָּה	and naked I will return there.
21ba	יְהוָה נָתַן וַיהוָה לָקָח	The Lord gives, and the Lord takes.
21bb	יְהִי שֵׁם יְהוָה מְבֹרָךְ	May the name of the Lord be blessed."

Literary Structure and Comments

Job 1:1–22 concerns the first test of Job, in which the Accuser is allowed to stretch out his arm to touch all Job's possessions. It begins with the introduction of Job as a wealthy and pious man. In this introduction there is a non-metaphorical reference to birth, the birth of Job's children. They are said to be born to Job and are enumerated among Job's possessions of animals and servants (vv. 2–3). The children are also used to portray him as pious, and it is said that he makes offerings on their behalf in case they have sinned and cursed God in their thoughts (vv. 4–5). The references to Job's children depict Job as wealthy and pious and set the scene for the question of whether Job will curse God when he loses his wealth and children. The answer in Job 1:21 contains the second reference to birth in the Book of Job. It refers to Job's own birth and emphasizes that Job was *naked* when he went out from his mother's womb and that he will return there *naked*. Job does not curse God for his loss; instead, he acknowledges the fact that God gives and takes.

Job's first response to his sufferings is non-verbal. He reacts to his loss by tearing his clothes and cutting his hair (Job 1:20). His actions follow traditional rituals to express grief. Job 1:21 is Job's first verbal response, and his words might reflect conventional sayings to express loss. They have been interpreted as a combination of a general proverbial saying (v. 21a), a religious saying (v. 21ba), and a blessing (v. 21bb).[1] Verse 21a and verse 21ba are parallel statements which both use antonymic expressions. The verbs יצא, "go out," and the verb שוב, "return," correspond to the verbs נתן, "give," and לקח, "take." The antonyms are united in verse 21a by both relating to the mother's womb, and in verse 21ba by both referring to the Lord as the one who both gives and takes.

The verb יצא is used in images of going out of the womb in the Book of Job (Job 10:18; 38:8, 29). It is a general verb meaning "go out," and it is often contrasted with the verb שוב, "return" (Gen 8:7; Job 39:4; Isa 55:11). The verb שוב is either used to describe a return back to an original place or a radical change in direction. The preposition and descriptions of where someone turns to designate whether it is a turn or a return.[2] Here, the verb שוב is followed by the adverb שָׁמָּה, "there" (a locative, with the particle ה indicating direction), which refers back to the mother's womb, making "return" the most appropriate understanding of שוב. The verb שוב is used in several reference to death in sayings of returning to dust (Gen 3:19; Job 10:9).[3]

The adjective "naked," עָרֹם, is highlighted in Job 1:21a. It is repeated twice and placed first both in the clause of Job's birth (v. 21aa) and in the clause of Job's return (v. 21ab). Ecclesiastes 5:14 uses the word עָרֹם to depict the newborn and the

---

[1] Vogels 1994, 370–71.
[2] Lambert 2015, 73–74.
[3] For discussion on the expression "Returning to Dust," see pages 122–24.

dead in a similar proverbial saying. Job 1:21 and Eccl 5:14 are the only instances in the HB where the word עָרֹם is explicitly used to describe the state of a newborn or of a dead person. The word עָרֹם is also used in an implicit reference to a newborn in Hos 2:5, when God declares how he will treat the adulterous wife Israel: "I will strip her naked and expose her as in the day she was born."[4] The closest parallel in the HB to Job 1:21 is Eccl 5:14.

Eccl 5:14	כַּאֲשֶׁר יָצָא מִבֶּטֶן אִמּוֹ	Like he went out from his mother's womb
	עָרוֹם יָשׁוּב	naked, so he shall return naked.
	לָלֶכֶת כְּשֶׁבָּא	He shall go like he came;
	וּמְאוּמָה לֹא־יִשָּׂא בַעֲמָלוֹ	he will carry nothing from his toil,
	שֶׁיֹּלֵךְ בְּיָדוֹ׃	which he may bring in his hand.

Ecclesiastes 5:14 and Job 1:21 are the only texts in the HB that share the expression יָצָא מִבֶּטֶן אִמּוֹ, "went out from my mother's womb," and they both use the word naked as a reference to the newborn, and the word שׁוּב as the reversal of יצא. Schulz argues that the rarity of these expressions shows a dependence between the texts, and that it is probable that Ecclesiastes has borrowed the expression from the Book of Job. The author of Ecclesiastes then erases the word שָׁמָּה, "there," and simply writes "return" (יָשׁוּב). The word שָׁמָּה has been seen as problematic, and Schulz proposes that Eccl 5:14 solves this problem by erasing it.[5] The context of Eccl 5:14 describes the loss of wealth (v. 13) and emphasizes that everything a man has earned by their toil is in vain (v. 15). This would imply that the loss of wealth corresponds to the word nakedness in Eccl 5:14.

Earlier Interpretations of Job 1:21

Vall has undertaken a thorough investigation of the research of Job 1:21 conducted in the twentieth century.[6] He identifies two different main strategies in interpretations of Job 1:21: one which argues that the concept of Mother Earth is implicit in Job 1:21a, and one which does not.[7] The major discussion concerns אָשׁוּב שָׁמָּה, "I

---

[4] NRSV.
[5] Schultz 2013, 193–95.
[6] An extensive exploration from Nöldeke (1905) to Clines (1989) is undertaken in Vall's dissertation (Vall 1993, 9–29). He summarizes his discussion in an article (Vall 1995a).
[7] Vall 1993, 9–29; Vall 1995a, 325–29. Vall speaks of the different interpretations as two camps. In the Mother Earth camp, he refers to scholars including Augé, Dhorme, Tromp, Pope, Horst,

will return there," and whether it implies a metaphor in which death is understood in terms of the womb, or if it is a non-metaphorical description where the adverb שָׁמָּה is a euphemism for Sheol or an abbreviated expression of "return to dust."[8] Based on the two main strategies presented by Vall, I identify three different readings of Job 1:21 in earlier interpretations, one non-metaphorical and two metaphorical interpretations.

1. There are no metaphors. The expression "my mother's womb" (בֶּטֶן אִמִּי) only refers to the physical womb of Job's mother. The word שָׁמָּה, "there," is a euphemism for Sheol or the expression אָשׁוּב שָׁמָּה "I return there," is an abbreviation for "I return to dust."[9]
2. Verse 21aa should be read in its literal sense; however, שָׁמָּה refers to "my mother's womb," which leads to a metaphorical interpretation of verse 21ab, either as the metaphor THE DESTINATION OF DEATH IS MY MOTHER'S WOMB or THE DESTINATION OF DEATH IS MOTHER EARTH.[10]
3. Verse 1:21aa is first read in its literal sense; however, after recognizing the metaphor THE DESTINATION OF DEATH IS MOTHER EARTH in verse 21ab, the reader also needs to metaphorize the mother's womb in 1:21aa. MY MOTHER'S WOMB is then blended with MOTHER EARTH into the metaphor MY MOTHER'S WOMB IS MOTHER EARTH. Mother Earth is then seen as both the womb of origin and death, embracing both the unborn and the dead.[11]

A common conclusion drawn from a metaphorical reading is that the positive associations of the womb are transferred to death in the metaphor THE DESTINATION OF DEATH IS MY MOTHER'S WOMB/MOTHER EARTH. Below follows a more detailed presentation of the three different readings of Job 1:21 and the discussion of the safe womb of death.

Lévêque, Terrien, Habel, and Stier. In the opposing camp, he identifies scholars including Tur-Sinai, Fohrer, Andersen, Driver-Gray, Buttenwieser, Rowley, and Gordis. He refers to Clines in his dissertation as opposing the Mother Earth interpretation, but he does not mention him in his article. Clines rejects the contention that Job 1:21 describes a belief of Mother Earth (Clines 1989, 36). Seow refers to the Mother Earth in his interpretation of Job 1:21 (Seow 2013, 281–82). Stordalen, Purdue, and Keel and Schroer refer to 1:21 as an example of the concept Mother Earth in the HB (Perdue 1991, 56, 187 n. 2; Stordalen 2010, 113, 117–18; Keel and Schroer 2015, 38–39).

[8] Vall 1995a, 326. Vall traces the euphemistic use back to Buttenwieser (1922) (Vall 1993, 12).
[9] Tur-Sinai 1957, 20; Andersen 1976, 88.
[10] Hartley 1988, 78; Balentine 2006, 57.
[11] Vall 1995a, 326–31, 335–37; Newsom 2003, 57.

Non-Metaphorical Reading

Those who advocate for the euphemistic interpretation of שָׁמָּה, "there," reference Egyptian and Greek sources to demonstrate how שָׁם and שָׁמָּה, "there," refer to the underworld, and they also identify examples of this usage in the HB (Job 3:17, 19; 34:22; Ezek 32:22–30). They argue that neither שָׁמָּה, "there," nor בֶּטֶן אִמִּי, "mother's womb," can have a dual function in the sentence. The word שָׁמָּה, "there," cannot simultaneously serve as a euphemism for the netherworld and refer to "the mother's womb." Likewise, "the mother's womb" cannot be understood both metaphorically and literally as the physical womb of Job's mother. Therefore, they argue that verse 21a refers exclusively to the womb, while verse 21b concerns only the underworld. An alternative interpretation is to view שָׁמָּה, "there," as a euphemism for the netherworld, and then equate the netherworld with Mother Earth.[12] Vall criticizes those who reject the concept of Mother Earth and favor a euphemistic reading, arguing that they never adequately explain how the adverb שָׁמָּה, "there" (with the directional ה), and the verb שׁוּב, "return," can be interpreted without implying that Job's origin and death refer to the same place.[13]

Tur-Siani opposes the interpretation that "my mother's womb" refers to the womb of Mother Earth, or that שָׁמָּה is a euphemism for the underworld. Instead, he argues that the expression "I will return there" is a shortened form of the idea of returning to dust, as stated in Gen 3:19.[14] Clines argues that שׁוּב, "return," should not "be pressed too literally," citing Pss 9:18 and 146:4 to demonstrate that references to returning to Sheol or the earth need not be accompanied by explanations of how it constitutes a return, or imply that humans also originate from Sheol.[15] Instead it is the word שׁוּב, "return," in itself that carries the connotations of death.

Metaphorical Reading

The metaphorical reading of Job 1:21a either only concerns death and the expression "return there," or it interprets both "return there" and "my mother's womb" metaphorically. The presumed metaphors are then DEATH IS TO RETURN TO THE WOMB OF ONE'S MOTHER/MOTHER EARTH and BEING BORN IS TO GO OUT FROM MOTHER EARTH.

---

[12] Pope 1973, 16.
[13] Vall 1995a, 327.
[14] Tur-Sinai 1957, 19–20.
[15] Clines 1989, 37. See also discussion in Vall 1993, 19–20, 24; Vall 1995a, 327.

Mother Earth Is Implied in Job 1:21

Vall argues that the primary strategy of those who support the Mother Earth interpretation of Job 1:21 is to demonstrate the presence of the concept Mother Earth in the HB, with Ps 139:13–15 playing a key role in their argument.[16] This passage refers both to the mother's womb and the depths of the earth as the place where a fetus is formed. If Job's birth and death are understood as relating to the womb of Mother Earth, it would resolve the enigma of 1:21a. In this interpretation, "my mother's womb" refers both to Job's physical mother and to Mother Earth, implying that Job will return to Mother Earth. Vall follows Augé, Sicre Diaz, and Habel in their description of the shift from a literal to a figurative reading of Job 1:21aα. They explain that שָׁמָּה, "there," is a double entendre, referring both to Job's mother's womb and to Mother Earth. According to Vall, this leads to a reinterpretation of "mother's womb" as also having a double entendre, signifying both the physical womb and Mother Earth.[17]

Job 1:21 is often compared to Sirach 40:1, which states that humans come from their mother's womb and return to the "mother of all" or to "the mother of all living."[18] The explicit reference to death as a return to the "mother of all" has been used to support the interpretation of "return there" in Job 1:21 as a reference to Mother Earth, and thus to interpret "my mother's womb" as also referring to Mother Earth. Others argue that Sir 40:1 rather points out that the womb of a mother and the womb of the "mother of all living" are separate places and therefore "my mother's womb" in Job 1:21 should not be fused with the womb of Mother Earth.[19] Clines contends that Sir 40:1 cannot be used to interpret Job 1:21 because, while Job 1:21 fuses the concepts of womb and death, Sirach explicitly separates them into two distinct places.[20] The expressions "taken from" and "return to dust" in Gen 3:19 have been cited as evidence that the earth was conceptualized as both the origin and final destination of humans, and hence as a mother's womb from which humans are born and to which they return at death.[21]

There has also been debate over whether Job 1:21 uses language originally intended for the first humans. Opponents of the argument that the concept of Mother Earth is present in the HB contend that the idea of an origin from the

---

[16] Vall 1995a, 325.
[17] Vall 1995a, 328–32. See also Habel 1985, 93; Newsom 2003, 57.
[18] For a discussion on Sir 40:1 see chapter 3, pages 87–88.
[19] Vall 1993, 13–14, 17.
[20] Clines 1989, 37.
[21] Dhorme 1984, 13; Vall 1995a, 327; Seow 2013, 282.

earth cannot be applied to individual humans. They argue that only the first humans are described as being taken from the earth and created from dust, whereas their descendants are described as being formed in their mothers' wombs. Therefore, must expressions that might suggest the formation of individuals in the earth, as in Job 1:21 and Ps 139:13–15, be evaluated as merely poetic expressions, rhetorical in nature, and not reflecting actual beliefs.[22]

Keel and Schroer argue that the belief in Mother Earth existed in ancient Israel, primarily by referring to burial customs and womb motifs in iconography; however, they also cite Job 1:21 to support their claim. They point to the omega-shaped symbol, representing the womb and the mother goddesses Nintur and Ninḫursaga, which is found on seals in Judean graves dating to Iron Age IIC (ca. 700–586 BCE). They also interpret the burial custom of placing graves under sacred trees as reflecting the belief in the earth's regenerative powers.[23] Keel interprets the omega-shaped headrests in the bench tombs at Ketef Hinnom as symbols of the Mesopotamian mother goddess, leading him to conclude that the ancient Israelites viewed the graves as representations of the womb.[24] His interpretation of the omega-shaped headrests has been challenged. These headrests are found in only a few graves at Ketef Hinnom, where most graves contain horseshoe-shaped headrests. According to Barkay, the headrests served only the practical function of supporting the head. He interprets the omega-shaped headrests as elaborations of the horseshoe-shaped iterations, possibly inspired by similar designs in Egypt. In Egypt, omega-shaped headrests had a symbolic function, representing the wig of the goddess Hathor, but Barkay argues that in the Hebrew context, they were purely decorative.[25]

The Womb of Death Is a Safe Place

The metaphor DEATH IS TO RETURN TO MY MOTHER'S WOMB has been interpreted to contend that Job views the grave and death as places of protection and compassion. Lévêque argues that Job 1:21 portrays Job's life as a journey from one mother to another—from his birth mother to Mother Earth—both of whom represent protection and peace.[26] Keel interprets the headrests at Ketef Hinnom as symbolizing wombs, reflecting a belief or wish that the grave is a place of care,

---

[22] Clines 1989, 37; Vall 1993, 15, 17–18; Vall 1995a, 330–31.
[23] Keel and Schroer 2015, 38–39, 84–87.
[24] Keel 1987, 50–53; Keel and Uehlinger 1998, 367.
[25] Barkay 1988, 50.
[26] Lévêque 1970, 200–201.

compassion, and motherly warmth. He refers to Job 1:21 and say that the Israelites "wanted to return to the womb from whence they came at the time when they had been as helpless as they now were in death."[27] Hays incorporates Barkay's interpretation in his discussion of Job 1:21, claiming that the concept of the grave as a womb alludes not to Mother Earth but to Egyptian beliefs. In this context, the grave was considered the womb of a goddess, such as Nut, Neith, or Hathor, with death understood as a form of rebirth. He suggests that Job's mother is assimilated with the mother goddess, similar to how earthly mothers are identified with mother goddesses in Egyptian texts. Hays further argues that Job's reference to being naked at death reflects the Egyptian tradition of burying the dead naked, contrary to the ancient Judean custom of burying the dead in cloaks. Job's words in Job 1:21a express hope for the comforting return to the womb and the possibility of rebirth, alluding to Egyptian beliefs. However, according to Hays, Job conveys that such hopes are not meant for him, as he submits himself to the Lord, Yahweh.[28]

Newsom argues that Job 1:21 challenges the image of death as "nothingness," instead portraying Sheol as something more than an abyss. The image of a mother's womb suggests that "something experienced as protective and loving frames existence even in loss, even in death."[29] Schifferdecker follows Newsom, asserting that the womb signifies protection, and she interprets Job 1:21 as referring to the Mother Earth.[30] Vall argues that the word "naked" is highlighted in Job 1:21, conveying vulnerability, while the womb suggests concealment and protection. He stresses that it is the word "mother" that brings the allusions of protection to the image of the grave.[31]

There are also psychoanalytic interpretations of Job 1:21 that describe the womb as protective. Van der Zwan analyses the references to the womb from a psychoanalytic perspective. He claims that Job wishes to return to the womb in Job 1:21 and Job 3 and argues that the image of death as a womb would "sugar-coat" death.[32] Rancour-Laferriere claims that this verse refers to Mother Earth, but interpret it from a psychoanalytic perspective, suggesting that Job whishes death to be a comforting womb.[33]

---

[27] Keel 1987, 53.
[28] Hays 2012.
[29] Newsom 2003, 59.
[30] Schifferdecker 2008, 26–27.
[31] Vall 1993, 162–63.
[32] van der Zwan 2019a, 10. For a longer discussion of van der Zwan's arguments, see Chapter 6, pages 143–44.
[33] Rancour-Laferriere 2021, 2–6.

Mathewson does not interpret the reference to the womb in Job 1:21 as a depiction of death as a sheltered place.[34] Instead, he discusses how this verse remythologizes the concept of the womb and transforms the traditional notions of birth and death. He notes that, in the HB, references to the womb typically represent an intimate relationship between God and humans, symbolizing blessings—but not in Job 1:21. Here, God is acknowledged as the giver of life, but not as the protector of creation. Mathewson argues that Job's portrayal of the womb minimizes God's involvement in human life: "The womb now is no longer a metonymy for abundant life, but for bare, minimal biological existence."[35] God's role in human lives is thus reduced to bringing them into existence and ultimately bringing them to death. Mies notes that Job 1:21 does not attribute any specific characteristics to Job's mother's womb, neither portraying it as a sheltered place nor as a stifling prison.[36]

Open Questions from Earlier Interpretations

I have outlined the central arguments in the three common interpretations of Job 1:21. Interpreters are generally more inclined to view the grave as a womb of the earth than to suggest that humans originate from the womb of the earth.[37] This is not surprising, given that the idea of Sheol being located in the netherworld is well established in the HB, while references to creation within the earth are rare. The so-called enigma of returning to the womb in Job 1:21a has been addressed by interpreting "my mother's womb" as a metaphor depicting Job's origin from the womb of the earth. The concept of a womb that embraces both the dead and the unborn has generally been explained through references to Mother Earth and mother goddesses. I agree that if the concept of Mother Earth had been an established belief in the HB, it could potentially explain Job 1:21. However, I have my doubts about this, and I will discuss my reasoning below.

Vall concludes that the willingness to recognize the metaphors in 1:21 depends on the acceptance of Mother Earth as a belief present in the HB. I am critical of how those who refer to Mother Earth as an established concept in the HB often do so without clearly defining its meaning. There are sweeping references to Mesopotamian, Greek, and Latin sources, and to "pagan beliefs."[38] Vall highlights the

---

[34] Mathewson 2006, 53–55.
[35] Mathewson 2006, 55.
[36] Mies 2022, 35.
[37] Hartley 1988, 78; Balentine 2006, 57; Clines 1989, 37.
[38] Pope 1973, 16; Dhorme 1984, 13; Vall 1993, 31–32.

connection between the womb and the earth in the HB by citing shared expressions from procreation and agriculture. However, he acknowledges that references to Mother Earth are subtle, and he discusses how the HB contains "vestiges" of the concept of Mother Earth and argues that Mother Earth "is almost unconsciously, part of the Hebrew way of thinking."[39] In his discussion of Job 1:21 and Mother Earth he says that the author of the Book of Job "reaches down below the surface of his own tradition to a connection that is very deeply embedded in the thought and literature of many peoples, a connection that is so deeply rooted in human condition and human common experience that one may call it archetypical."[40] He argues that the image of the earth as a mother is cross-cultural and that this image is transposed in biblical thought so that it is not valued as a mythological deity and rarely personified.[41] Vall and others who discuss the presence of the Mother Earth motif refer to the dust-to-dust theme (Gen 3:19), parallels between the womb and the grave and between women and gardens, metaphors of humans as plants, and passages such as Ps 139:13–15, Job 1:21, Eccl 5:14, and Sir 40:1.[42] They assume that these examples are rooted in a conventionalized image of the earth as a mother and use this perspective in their interpretation of Job 1:21. I question whether these examples, and other images of the womb in the HB, form a coherent image of the earth as a mother whose womb is the source of all life and a room for the dead. I suspect that the image of Mother Earth used to explain Job 1:21 is more influenced by the Greek belief in Gaia than in anything found in the HB. The HB uses different associations for the womb when describing the womb of life versus the womb of death, and it never presents a unified womb that encompasses both the dead and the unborn.

The Greek concept of Gaia as Mother Earth would resonate well with the imagery that Vall and others refer to in their interpretations. She is the mother of all, who both creates all living beings and embraces them at death. Hesiod's *Theogony* describes her as the primordial mother to many gods.[43] She was also believed to give life to humans, animals, and plants, and when they die, they return to her. She was revered as the sustainer and was assigned characteristics of compassion and care. Aeschylus (ca. 525–456 BCE) refers to her "Earth herself, who gives birth to all things, nurtures them, and then receives that fruit of her womb back into

---

[39] Vall 1993, 63–64, 69–70; Vall 1995a, 329, 332–33.
[40] Vall 1993, 63.
[41] Vall 1993, 31–34.
[42] Vall 1993, 41–70; Stordalen 2010.
[43] Hesiod, *Theog.* 126–45 (trans. Most 2018, 12–15).

herself."⁴⁴ The Greek concept of the "mother of all" appears in Sirach (Sir 40:1), but this does not substantiate an assumption that it is present in the earlier books of the HB.⁴⁵ The Greek assimilation of a mother goddess with the earth into the image of Mother Earth, who both gives life and embraces the dead, cannot be considered universal. This was not the predominant image in Assyrian and Babylonian texts. The concept of a mother goddess in Mesopotamian contexts is complex and encompasses a wide range of goddesses, who were seen as creators of humankind, patrons of midwifery and childbirth, or mothers to gods, humans, and animals.⁴⁶ The mother goddesses have connotations of death, and there are myths depicting mother goddesses lamenting their dead children and how they destroy or kill the ones they have created.⁴⁷ A few mother goddesses are counted among the gods of the netherworld, although not the majority.⁴⁸ Krebernik argues that birth and netherworld goddesses were originally separate, but that the use of the epithet mother for both groups led to a confusion between them.⁴⁹ Rodin, on the other hand, suggests that the mother and netherworld initially were the same. She claims that mother goddesses were originally viewed as both bringers of life and death as part of their role in decreeing destinies for the newborn.⁵⁰ Rodin points out the contradiction between being a goddess of the netherworld and a goddess of birth. In the netherworld, there is no fertility, and its inhabitants cannot procreate.⁵¹ The diversity of beliefs and the multiplicity of Mesopotamian mother goddesses show that we cannot take for granted that there is one shared image of Mother Earth in ancient West Asia that depicts earth as the mother caring for both the unborn and the dead.

---

⁴⁴ Aeschylus, *Cho.*, 127–29 (trans. Sommerstein 2008, 226–27).

⁴⁵ For a discussion on Sir 40:1 see chapter 3, pages 87–88.

⁴⁶ In the well-known god-list An-Anum from Middle Assyrian period, the mother goddess is mentioned by 45 different names. These names represent different deities, yet they were also used interchangeably (Rodin 2014, 90–95). For an overview of different names of mother goddesses, see Krebernik 1993, 502–16.

⁴⁷ Rodin 2014, 107–9.

⁴⁸ Rodin describes how both Ninḫursaga's daughter Ninnisi and her granddaughter Ninkura are portrayed as both birth goddesses and goddesses of the netherworld. Ninnisi is capable of giving life but is also identified as the wife of Nergal. Additionally, she is paralleled with Ereškigal in a god list (Rodin 2014, 137–41). Ninḫursaga is mentioned once on a god list of netherworld gods, but this is considered an exception and is viewed as a reuse of another list that identifies the ancestors of Enki (Katz 2003, 367).

⁴⁹ Krebernik 1993, 516.

⁵⁰ Rodin 2014, 140, 169–76.

⁵¹ Katz and Rodin point out that the reference to Ereškigal as a birth mother contradicts her identity as a netherworld deity (Rodin 2014, 138–41; Katz 2003, 387–89).

Vall gives several examples of how death and the womb are associated with each other in the HB. However, he never discusses the fact that the metaphor HUMANS AND PLANTS ARE BORN FROM THE WOMB OF THE EARTH uses different characteristics of the womb than SHEOL IS A WOMB. The womb of birth is used metaphorically to display fertility and growth of life. The barren womb and the womb of a stillborn are used to depict Sheol. Even if the metaphorical womb of life and Sheol are both said to be located in the earth, they are still each other's counter-images. Psalm 139:13–15, which refers to the formation of a fetus in the depths, and Gen 49:25, which may imply a womb in the depths, do not refer to a common womb of the dead and the unborn. The two opposing images of the womb of the earth in the HB are noted by Stordalen, who argues that Mother Earth is both the good mother who gives life and the bad mother who consumes life.[52] These opposing views of the mother and the womb clarify why the image of a mother, or a womb, does not inherently evoke associations of life and protection. The womb of the dead and the womb which gives life may be fused once in the HB, in Isa 26: 17–19, but the womb of the earth is then used to depict the exile, and the birth is then a liberation from the exile. It is not used to depict newborn babies. It is, therefore, hard to argue that the idea of a womb encompassing both dead and unborn humans is supported by biblical texts. Expressions such as those found in Job 1:21, Ps 139:15, and Eccl 5:14 may have contributed to a development of a belief in Mother Earth, but they do not convey this belief themselves. I suggest that within the HB, the metaphor HUMANS ARE PLANTS is the most effective metaphor for encompassing both birth and death. It effectively accommodates the belief in humans being born from the ground and returning to it. However, neither the concept of Mother Earth nor the plant metaphor is necessary to solve the so-called enigma of Job 1:21, which my analysis below will show.

To summarize: The interpretation of Job 1:21 as referring to a unified Mother Earth embracing both the unborn and dead is problematic, likely influenced more by the Greek concept of Gaia than by HB traditions. Interpreters often use "Mother Earth" without clear definition, overlooking how the HB uses the womb differently when depicting death versus its use in the context of birth and fertility. Mesopotamian mother goddess imagery differs from Gaia, and without textual evidence from the HB, it is unclear whether the concept of Mother Earth was an established belief among the ancient Israelites.

---

[52] Stordalen 2010, 126–27.

Birth Metaphors in Job 1:21

Several biblical scholars have said that Job 1:21a is difficult to explain, and the expression "return there" has been described as an enigma. It has been potentially solved by references to Mother Earth, or as reading "return there" as a euphemism for Sheol or as an abbreviated statement for "return to the ground." Imagine reading Job 1:21a for the first time, or asking someone with little knowledge of the Bible and no awareness of the concept of Mother Earth to explain this verse. Do you think they would understand it as a description of how we are born and die with no possessions? I believe they would, and if so, then it would not be an enigma.

Fauconnier and Turner discuss how we can understand complex expressions almost effortlessly.[53] This seems to be such an example. I will analyze Job 1:21 by first exploring how we understand birth and death as an antonymic word pair, and then displaying the comprehension of "return there" in a so-called counterfactual blend. Following this, I will analyze the metaphorical meaning of the word "naked" in Job 1:21.

Birth and Death Are Antonyms

The word pair "birth and death" is a general word pair in our minds. They form an *inclusio* of a life: birth is the beginning and death is the end. Birth and death are antonyms used to describe opposite states. If birth and death are described through metaphors, then their metaphors must also be each other's antonyms: if birth is light, then death is darkness; if birth is joy, then death is sorrow; and if life is day, then death is night. There are many descriptions of death as negation of life in the HB. Death is depicted as non-movement, sleeping, laying down, night, and darkness while life is seen as movement, being active, day, and light. Death is being cut off from relationships with other humans and from God, while life is being part of a community. Birth is associated with a fertile womb, and death with a barren one.[54] In our thought, death and birth are antonyms, and could also be understood as negated forms of each other. Therefore, we understand that the author refers to the beginning of life and the end of it, death, in the words of 1:21a. We are used to think of death in negated features of birth. If birth is described as "go out from the womb" then death could be described as "return there."

---

[53] Fauconnier and Turner 2002, 17–18.

[54] For death as lie down or sleep, see Job 20:11; Ps 13:4; for death as darkness and night, see Job 10:22 and Lam 3:6. Psalm 88 contains images of death as being laid down (v. 6), in the darkness (v. 7), and cut off from the community (vv. 6, 15). For the barren womb and death, see Prov 30:15–16. For further discussion, see Chapter 3, pages 85–88.

DEATH IS TO RETURN TO THE WOMB

The expression "Naked I went out from my mother's womb, and naked I will return there" depicts birth and its antonymic state. The word עָרוֹם, "naked," is highlighted as the shared characteristic between the two opposing states, represented by the antonyms יצא, "go out," and שׁוב, "return." Job's birth is explicitly stated in the phrase "I went out from my mother's womb" and when the antonymic verb is expressed in "I will return there," the reader naturally searches for the antonymic state of birth, which logically leads to thoughts of death. Another antonymic state of birth is remaining in the womb, but the verb יצא, "go out," makes it clear that Job did not stay in the womb. The word "naked" also implies that death is viewed as the negation of birth. Nakedness is indeed presented as a shared characteristic of the newborn and the dead, but the act of dressing is reversed. Humans are born naked, but a newborn baby is clothed by their caretakers. To describe the ones who die as naked would imply that someone has unclothed them. The reversal of actions is also described in 1:21ba, in which Job declares that the Lord is the one who gives and takes. The antonyms נתן, "give" and לקח, "take," strengthen our search for antonymic states in verse 21a. The expression of the Lord as the one who both gives and takes implies that God is the one who clothes and unclothes Job.

This interpretation of Job 1:21a can be described as a counterfactual blend, a cognitive process used to understand something by reversing the characteristics of another concept.[55] Applied to Job 1:21, this approach reveals how we first think of birth, then negates its characteristics and thereafter blends them with death. In Job 1:21, the description of birth is that Job goes out of the womb and that he is born naked. The negation of going out of the womb is returning to the womb, and the negation of being clothed is being unclothed. These negated terms are then blended with the domain of DEATH as displayed in Figure 5.1.

---

[55] For a presentation of counterfactual blends see Chapter 2, page 57.

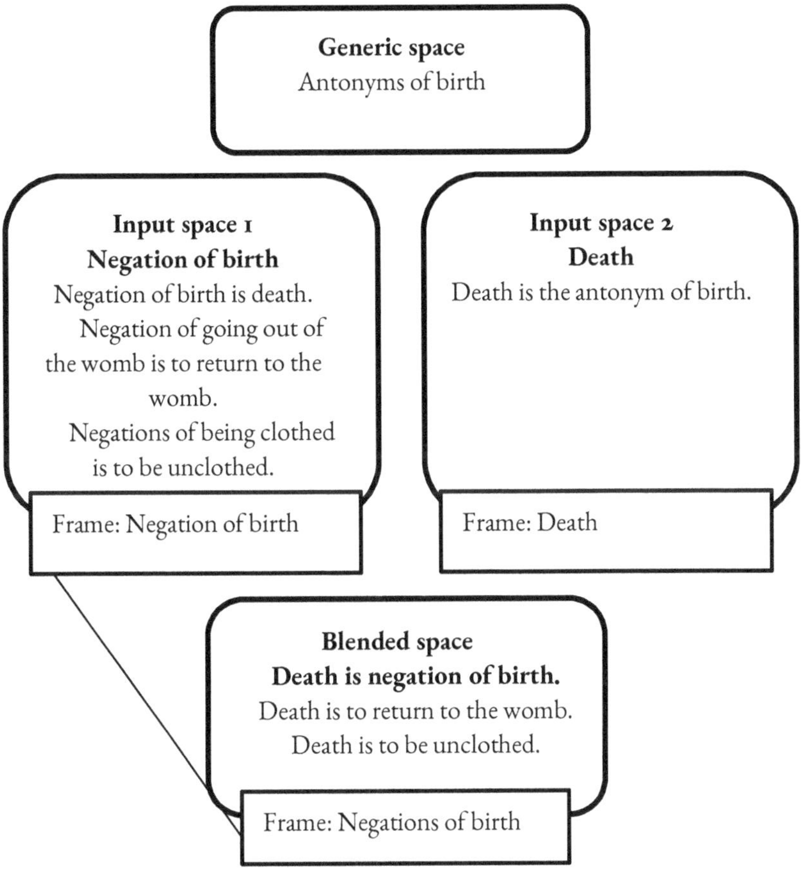

```
                    ┌─────────────────────────┐
                    │      Generic space      │
                    │    Antonyms of birth    │
                    └─────────────────────────┘

┌─────────────────────────────┐   ┌─────────────────────────────┐
│       Input space 1         │   │       Input space 2         │
│     Negation of birth       │   │           Death             │
│  Negation of birth is death.│   │ Death is the antonym of birth.│
│   Negation of going out of  │   │                             │
│    the womb is to return    │   │                             │
│         to the womb.        │   │                             │
│   Negations of being clothed│   │                             │
│      is to be unclothed.    │   │                             │
├─────────────────────────────┤   ├─────────────────────────────┤
│  Frame: Negation of birth   │   │       Frame: Death          │
└─────────────────────────────┘   └─────────────────────────────┘

              ┌─────────────────────────────┐
              │        Blended space        │
              │  Death is negation of birth.│
              │ Death is to return to the womb.│
              │   Death is to be unclothed. │
              ├─────────────────────────────┤
              │ Frame: Negations of birth   │
              └─────────────────────────────┘
```

Figure 5.1 *The counterfactual blend DEATH IS NEGATION OF BIRTH, and the metaphors DEATH IS TO RETURN TO THE WOMB and DEATH IS TO BE UNCLOTHED.*

The input space DEATH is viewed as an antonym to BIRTH, and is therefore structured by the frame NEGATIONS OF BIRTH and by different antonyms to different concepts of the domain of BIRTH. To perceive death as structured by antonyms to birth, or negations of birth, is a metaphorical step. Death is not literally a negation of birth. Death is not the same as not being born and there are several features of death that cannot be explained by negated terms of birth. The metaphor DEATH IS NEGATION OF BIRTH uses the frame of negated birth to structure how death is conceptualized. The input space DEATH has a diffuse and abstract frame which is filled with content by the inverted frame BIRTH.

Counterfactual blends could also be described in conditional clauses. The blend above could be expressed in clause: "If birth is to go out of the womb and death is negation of birth, then death is to return to the womb." The description of death as a return to the womb is a logical consequence of viewing death as a negation or as an antonym of birth. The metaphor DEATH IS TO RETURN TO THE WOMB is a more specific metaphor which is derived from the more general metaphor DEATH IS NEGATION OF BIRTH. The metaphor DEATH IS TO BE UNCLOTHED is also derived from DEATH IS NEGATION OF BIRTH and could be expressed by the clause "If newborns are clothed and death is a negation of birth, then the dead are unclothed." Those who see 1:21a as an enigma do not acknowledge the metaphor DEATH AS NEGATION OF BIRTH and, therefore, they do not understand the more specific metaphor DEATH IS TO RETURN TO THE WOMB. The counterfactual statements and the blend above show that the metaphors DEATH IS A NEGATION OF BIRTH or DEATH IS TO RETURN TO THE WOMB do not highlight any characteristics of the womb. No characteristics of the womb are stated in Job 1:21, nor are there any references to features of Sheol. Job 1:21a does not describe death in the image of a comforting womb nor does it express an image of earth as a mother carrying the unborn and the dead in her womb. The counterfactual statement in Job 1:21 instead highlights death as a reversal of birth, just as God's action of taking is the reversed action of giving in 1:21b. Job 1:21 is part of Job's pious response to his loss. In Job 1:20, Job tears his robe, cuts his hair, bows down in worship, and then utters the words in 1:21. The sayings in 1:21 are words of acceptance of the duality of life—that life contains birth and death, acts of going out and of returning, and that the Lord both gives and takes away.

To summarize: Job 1:21 should be understood as a counterfactual blend which depicts death in negated terms of birth. The antonymic verbs "go out" and "return" guide the reader to think of an antonymic state of "going out of the womb" and to interpret "return there" as a reference to death. The term naked also fits into the thinking of death as a reversal of being newborn.

Returning to Dust and to the Womb

The common expression of death as a return to dust has been used to explain Job 1:21. Genesis 3:19 expresses death in these terms, while also referring to dust as the origin of humans. It has been argued that "return there" in Job 1:21a is an abbreviated form of "return to the ground," and Gen 3:19 is often cited as an example of how the earth is conceptualized as a mother from whom humans originate and to whom they return in death.

Gen 3:19	בְּזֵעַת אַפֶּיךָ תֹּאכַל לֶחֶם	With the sweat of your face, you shall eat bread,
	עַד שׁוּבְךָ אֶל־הָאֲדָמָה	until you return to the ground,
	כִּי מִמֶּנָּה לֻקָּחְתָּ	for from it you are taken
	כִּי־עָפָר אַתָּה	because you are dust
	וְאֶל־עָפָר תָּשׁוּב׃	And to dust you will return

Gen 3:19 uses the fact that birth and death are antonyms—one can be described in the negated terms of the other. The reference to death as a return to dust (עָפָר) or to the ground (הָאֲדָמָה) is common in the HB. It is far less common to describe humans as originating from the dust or the ground. Genesis 3:19 refers both to dust as the material from which the human body is made and to the idea that humans come from and return to dust. This aligns with the descriptions that when humans give up their breath, they return to dust (Pss 104:29; 146:4; Eccl 12:7; c.f. Gen 2:7). To say that mortals are both coming from and returning to dust is also stated in Eccl 3:20 (הַכֹּל הָיָה מִן־הֶעָפָר וְהַכֹּל שָׁב אֶל־הֶעָפָר, "all are from the dust, and all return to dust"). Job 10:9 describes the lifecycle in similar terms. God is there said to form Job out of clay (חֹמֶר) and then return him to dust (עָפָר). Death, without references to birth, is described as a return to אֲדָמָה, "the ground," in Ps 146:4, to עָפָר, "dust," in Job 34:15 and to דַּכָּא, "crushed things," in Ps 90:3. The dead are also referred to as dwellers of dust and as going down into the dust (Job 17:16; 21:26; Isa 26:19). These expressions connecting death and dust are mainly used without being integrated into extensive metaphorical descriptions, except Ps 90:3, Job 10:9, and Gen 3:19. Psalm 90:3 connects the expression with the metaphor HUMANS ARE PLANTS, and Job 10:9 uses it together with the metaphor GOD IS A POTTER. The context of Gen 3:19 implies the metaphor GOD IS A POTTER as well as the metaphor GOD IS A GARDENER. The expressions of coming from and returning to dust in Gen 3:19 can be explained by both the potter and the gardener metaphor. Potters shape their products from clay, and they can return the formed objects to unformed clay or crush the ceramic ware into dust. The metaphor GOD IS A GARDENER entails the metaphor HUMANS ARE PLANTS. In the metaphor HUMANS ARE PLANTS, humans are likened to plants that grow in moistened ground and eventually wither, die, and decompose back into dust.

Together, the examples above demonstrate that it is easier to envision death as a return to dust than to imagine birth as originating from dust. The experience of witnessing dead bodies decomposing forms the basis for the expression "returning to dust" and the metaphor HUMANS ARE DUST. The depiction of humans being created from dust also stems from this experience. If death is understood as returning to dust, then birth is seen as being formed from it, as expressed in Gen 3:19 and Eccl 3:20. However, it seems less problematic seeing birth as coming from dust than seeing death as returning to the womb. One might wonder why biblical scholars view the lifecycle of a human as coming from dust and returning to dust as unproblematic, but the image of a lifecycle as coming from and returning to the womb as an enigma? Both expressions are understood by the same blending process which recognizes death and birth as antonyms and then views one of them in the inverted terms of the other. The concept of Mother Earth can be explained through counterfactual thinking, which combines the blend of death as returning to the womb with birth as coming from the ground. It can also be understood through the conceptual metaphor HUMANS ARE PLANTS. which encompasses the idea of humans originating from the earth and returning to dust.

The relationship between death and birth as antonyms describes how we can think of humans as both coming from and returning to the ground or the womb. The recurring description of death as returning to dust also contributes to the understanding of Job 1:21. In the HB, when the human lifecycle is mentioned, the word "return" is associated with death. This association with death becomes an entrenched association of the word שוב, "return," and it facilitates our understanding of "return there" in Job 1:21. However, this understanding could arise even without knowledge of how the HB commonly refers to death as a return to dust, because we process counterfactual blends easily and often do so unconsciously.[56]

To summarize: It is more common to express death as a return to dust than to refer to birth as coming from dust. The experience of witnessing dead bodies decompose has led to the metaphor DEATH IS RETURNING TO DUST. The expression that humans also come from dust is based on a counterfactual blend. The relationship between death and birth as antonyms describes how we can think of humans coming and returning both from the ground and the womb. The widespread use of the expression "return to dust" in descriptions of death has entrenched the association between the word "return" and death, which may facilitate the interpretation of Job 1:21ab as a reference to death.

---

[56] Fauconnier and Turner 2002, 229.

Naked at Birth and Death

In Job 1:21 the images of birth and death share the characteristic of nakedness. I have explained how this also reflects that death reverses the actions taken to clothe a newborn. These actions correspond to the second saying in Job 1:21b, that the Lord gives and takes away. God is the one who clothes Job at birth and strips him naked at death. The word עָרֹם, "naked," is emphasized and serves as the only descriptive term for both the newborn and the one approaching death. While a baby's nakedness at birth is natural, the nakedness at death should be understood metaphorically, as we will explore further.

The Domain NAKED

Oorschot presents five perspectives on nakedness which are used in the HB.[57]

1. Nakedness is a natural characteristic of a newborn baby and is used metaphorically to describe the first humans at the time of creation, symbolizing their initial state before being socialized into culture.
2. Nakedness symbolizes a "borderline situation" and the margins of human life. Oorschot suggests that nakedness represents a potential threat to human existence, signifying vulnerability, powerlessness, and exposure to danger, without necessarily being associated with sin, death, or a loss of status. He categorizes Job 1:21 and Eccl 5:14 within this framework.
3. Nakedness symbolizes the deterioration of human life, encompassing grief, shame, and death, as well as the loss of political and social status. When someone loses power and status, they become exposed and vulnerable. Outcasts and the poor are often depicted metaphorically as being naked.
4. Nakedness is used positively in the Song of Songs to depict the erotic relationship between lovers, where love, instead of clothes, provides protection.
5. Nakedness needs to be covered in a cultic setting, as nudity entails a social threat that must be avoided. Oorschot suggests that these threats are mitigated by specific clothing restrictions in the cult.

All these perspectives on nakedness include references to vulnerability and exposure. Even though point 1 discusses the natural nakedness of a newborn, it also

---

[57] Oorschot 2019, 238–48.

highlights the infant's vulnerability. A newborn left unclothed signals abandonment and neglect (Ezek 16:4). These various perspectives on nakedness also correspond to different implications of undressing someone. The act of undressing someone as a means of depriving them of protection aligns with the ideas in point 2, while the act of shaming through undressing relates to point 3. The act of shaming by undressing is well attested-to in biblical imagery, such as God stripping his adulterous wife, Jerusalem (Hos 2:5, 12; Ezek 16:37–39; 23:29), and captives being stripped (Isa 20:3–4). The act of undressing someone approaching death is illustrated in the narrative of Aaron being stripped of his priestly garments as he nears death (Num 20:26–28).[58] Niehr discusses how clothing represented power in Mesopotamia, referring to the myth Descent of Ishtar, in which Ishtar needs to remove a piece of jewelry or clothing each time she passes a gate on her way down to the netherworld. By the time she arrives, she is naked, and her sister inflicts diseases upon her, and she dies. This undressing is interpreted as a loss of power.[59] This would match Oorschot's discussion of nakedness as a borderline state, and as representing the vulnerability of the dying person.

In the Book of Job, there are descriptions of Job being stripped of his clothes as a symbol of losing power. Job 19:9 depicts his fate by stating that God has stripped him of his glory and his crown. Additionally, Job describes counselors, priests, and other mighty men as being stripped by God (Job 12:17–21). This theme is further reflected in the portrayal of outcasts as naked in Job 24:5–12. Quick argues that there is often a connection between "damaged clothing and damaged bodies" (Ps 102:27; Isa 50:9).[60] She argues that Job's sickness is described in terms of his clothing and being unclothed and clothed.[61]

The various applications of metaphors where nakedness signals exposure go back to the experience that clothes protect the body from physical threats such as the sun, wind, cold, and wounds. The characteristics of protection and exposure are then transferred to various domains. In the domain of MORALITY, clothes protect from shame; in the domain of SEXUALITY, they protect from sexual abuse; in the domain of SOCIAL STATUS, clothes protect from humiliation; and in the domain of WARFARE, clothes protect from defeat, weakness, vulnerability, and the loss of power, ethnicity, and identity. They can all be summarized in and are

---

[58] For a further discussion of the symbolic value of dressing someone, see Chapter 7, pages 201–2.
[59] Niehr, "עָרוֹם," *TDOT*, 11:350. For the myth, see *COS* 1.108: 381–84.
[60] Quick 2022, 55.
[61] Quick 2022, 57–62.

derived from the general metaphor CLOTHES ARE PROTECTION FROM SOCIAL THREATS.

The Metaphor of Nakedness in Job 1:21

Job's reference to his nakedness signifies his vulnerability and lack of protection. A comparison between the naked Ishtar in the myth Descent of Ishtar and Job 1:21 is illuminating. Job's losses leave him exposed and vulnerable, much like Ishtar was made vulnerable when she was stripped. Nakedness serves as a metaphor for Job's loss of wealth and relationships, while also signaling that he is approaching death.

In Job 1:10–19, we learn that Job has lost his animals, servants, and children. These losses are triggered by a challenge from the Accuser, who asks God to remove God's protection from Job (Job 1:10). God is depicted as protecting Job and his possessions by fencing him in. Just as clothes serve as protective barriers, so do fences, and when God removes them, Job loses his possessions. The next time the Accuser challenges God, he goes a step further by attacking Job's skin. Job's loss of his children, servants, and animals has made Job vulnerable to the attacks on his body. Combined with the expression of nakedness in Job 1:21, this implies that Job is metaphorically naked as a result of these losses. The things Job has lost correspond to clothing, leading to the metaphor: JOB'S CHILDREN, SERVANTS, AND HIS ANIMALS ARE CLOTHES. Job's loss of wealth and children will eventually lead to a loss of status and identity within his community. This becomes evident later in the book, during Job's final speech (Job 29–31), where he reflects on his life before his losses, when he was highly respected in society. However, this loss of social status is not explicitly expressed in Job 1. In the immediate crisis, he does not yet experience a loss of status. His friends have not turned against him, and he has not yet been humiliated; it is the actual loss of his animals and children that is acute in Job 1:21. This loss is portrayed as bringing him closer to death. The children and wealth are thus seen as a protection from death in Job 1:21—when he loses them, he begins to speak about his own death.

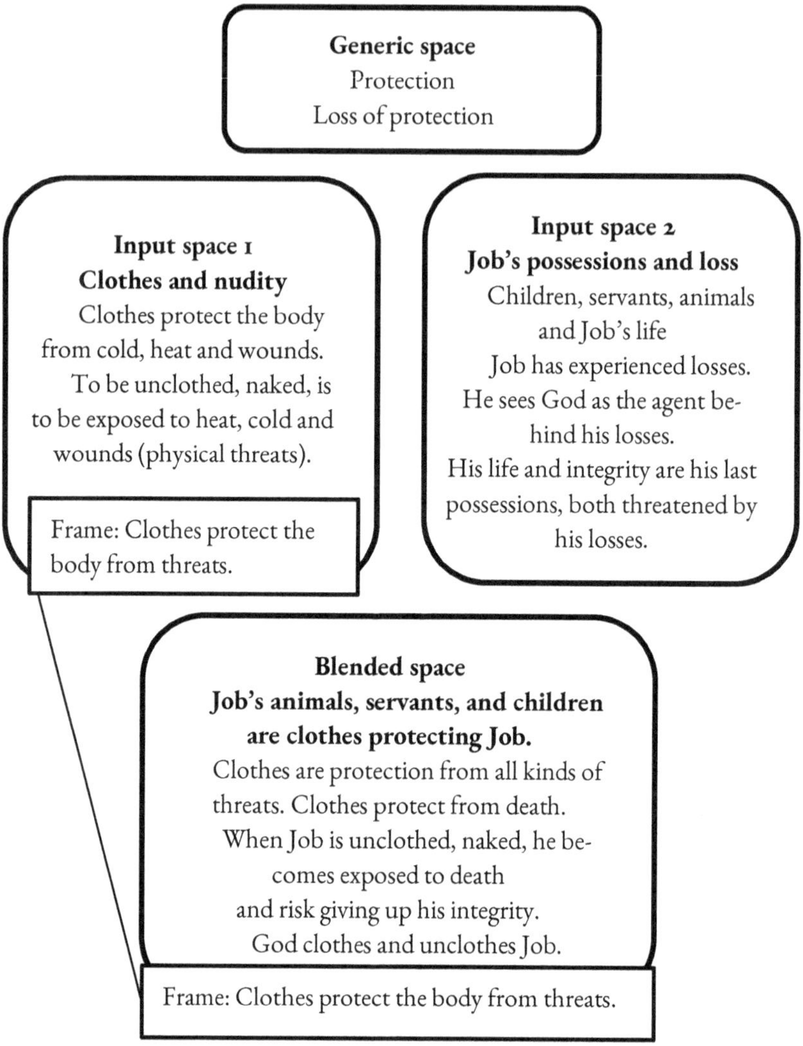

```
                    ┌─────────────────────────┐
                    │     Generic space       │
                    │      Protection         │
                    │   Loss of protection    │
                    └─────────────────────────┘
```

Input space 1
Clothes and nudity
Clothes protect the body from cold, heat and wounds.
To be unclothed, naked, is to be exposed to heat, cold and wounds (physical threats).

Frame: Clothes protect the body from threats.

Input space 2
Job's possessions and loss
Children, servants, animals and Job's life
Job has experienced losses. He sees God as the agent behind his losses.
His life and integrity are his last possessions, both threatened by his losses.

Blended space
Job's animals, servants, and children are clothes protecting Job.
Clothes are protection from all kinds of threats. Clothes protect from death.
When Job is unclothed, naked, he becomes exposed to death
and risk giving up his integrity.
God clothes and unclothes Job.

Frame: Clothes protect the body from threats.

Figure 5.2 *The metaphors:* CHILDREN AND ANIMALS ARE CLOTHES WHICH PROTECT FROM EXPOSURE TO DEATH, THE LOSS OF CHILDREN AND ANIMALS IS TO BE STRIPPED NAKED, *and* GOD IS THE ONE WHO CLOTHES AND UNCLOTHES JOB.

The blending schema in Figure 5.2 interprets the expression and "naked I will return there." The death of Job's children not only causes him grief but also leaves him exposed, prompting him to talk about his own death. In the dialogue between the Accuser and God, Job's children, servants, and possessions are depicted as parts of God's protection. The Accuser holds that they are a prerequisite for Job's integrity and claims that once they are taken away, Job will curse God to God's face. But Job does not curse God, he expresses his exposure to death and blesses God's name. Job's wife questions why he still holds on to his integrity and urges him to curse God and die (Job 2:9). Her words link Job's death with the act of abandoning his integrity by cursing God. Thus, Job's loss not only makes him vulnerable to death but also exposes him to the risk of cursing God.

Ecclesiastes 5:14 uses the saying regarding humans leaving this world naked to illustrate the futility of human labor and wealth. However, neither Job 1:21 nor Eccl 5:14 state that their possessions are lost at the time of death. Ecclesiastes 5:13 describes the loss of a man's fortune, so that there is nothing left to pass on to the son. Similar to Job, this man loses his possessions during his lifetime. This is the background to these sayings of dying naked. While one might expect these sayings to suggest that death strips a person of their possessions, Job declares that it is God who gives and takes away. Job's possessions are taken away at the height of his life, instead of at death. Psalm 49:18 depicts death as separating humans from their possessions: "For when they die, they will carry nothing away; their wealth will not go down after them."[62] Job is not dead yet, but losing his children and wealth brings him closer to death. This underscores his lament; his loss is as great as if he had gone down into the land of the dead.

Job's sense of being exposed to death has been interpreted as if Job identifies himself with his children, experiencing their death as his own.[63] It is then argued that Job's children are portrayed as an extension of Job in Job 1:2–5, and by describing their death as his own, Job again views them as integral parts of his identity. This interpretation suggests that Job's children are not merely metaphorical "clothes," but rather, they represent a part of Job himself, reflecting the metaphor THE DEATH OF MY CHILDREN IS MY DEATH. This interpretation is empathetic and resonates with the experience of many parents who have suffered the loss of a child. However, it does not align with the rest of the prologue. In Job 1:2–3, the children are portrayed as extensions of Job's possessions. They are described as born to him and are listed alongside his servants and animals. This view is reinforced in the dialogue between God and the Accuser, where the death of Job's children occurs when the Accuser stretches out his hand to destroy Job's possessions, not when he strikes Job directly.

---

[62] NRSV.
[63] Clines 1989, 36; Rancour-Laferriere 2021, 12.

To summarize: Job 1:21 describes Job as both being born naked and eventually dying naked. While the nakedness of a newborn is natural, Job's nakedness as he approaches death must be understood metaphorically. Nakedness is associated with vulnerability. Clothes provide protection from physical threats such as heat and cold, and are often used in metaphors to represent protection from other dangers in life. Job's lack of clothes symbolizes the loss of his children and wealth; without them, he is vulnerable to death. The nakedness of Job can be understood in the metaphors CHILDREN, ANIMALS, AND SERVANTS ARE CLOTHES WHICH PROTECT FROM DEATH and THE LOSS OF CHILDREN, ANIMALS AND SERVANTS IS TO BE NAKED AND VULNERABLE TO DEATH.

Summary and Conclusions

This chapter has engaged previous interpretations of Job 1:21, particularly the idea of death as a return to the womb. I have proposed that it can be understood as a counterfactual blend, where death is described in negated terms of the characteristics of birth. The analysis also demonstrates how the word naked is highlighted and how it is used to depict Job's vulnerability and exposure to death.

Earlier interpretations have called the expression "Naked I went out from my mother's womb and naked I will return there" an enigma. It has been resolved by seeing "return there" as a reference to dust or Sheol or by arguing that Mother Earth is implied, with the belief that all humans are born from her and return to her in death. I question whether the concept of Mother Earth is truly established within the texts of the HB. While it may have been developed from passages such as Job 1:21 and Ps 139:15, these and other images of the womb associated with death and fertility in the HB do not form a coherent image of a unified womb of the earth that embraces both the unborn and the dead. I have shown that Job 1:21 is not an enigma and that the concept of Mother Earth is unnecessary for its interpretation. The discussion of Mother Earth has obscured the fact that this verse highlights the word naked, and hence Job's loss. Job 1:21ab does not describe death as a sheltered womb. It is only the characteristic of nakedness that is projected from the experience of the newborn to the state of death, while the characteristics of the womb as a sheltered place or a place of fertility are not transferred at all.

The so-called enigma of Job 1:21 is explained by mapping it as a counterfactual blend, where the characteristics of DEATH are the negated terms of BIRTH. Birth is used as an antonym to death, and if birth is described as going out of the womb, then death is returning to the womb. This explains the metaphor DEATH IS TO RETURN TO THE WOMB, which is derived from the more general metaphor DEATH

IS NEGATION OF BIRTH. Furthermore, the shared characteristics of being naked can be understood by understanding death in negated terms of birth: if the naked newborn is clothed, then those approaching death are unclothed and stripped naked. The cross-cultural metaphor of clothes as protection from different threats in life implies that when you are unclothed and naked you are vulnerable to these threats. Job 1:21b makes it clear that God is the one who has removed Job's protection, effectively undressing him. The implied clothes taken away in Job 1:21 are Job's possessions, including his children. Their loss leaves Job exposed to death and the risk of losing his integrity. The Accuser believes that Job would curse God to God's face, but instead, Job expresses his grief by using a proverbial saying regarding being born and dying naked, acknowledging that God gives and takes, and ending with a blessing. However, the pious expression of dying naked is slightly off target. The loss occurs while Job is still alive, yet he frames it in terms of his own death. The incongruence between Job 1:21 and the more typical experience of losing possessions at death highlights Job's deep sense of loss and gives his words of acceptance a tone of lament.

In Job 1, the character of Job does not express a longing for death, nor does he wish he had died in the womb. He does not envision the womb—whether his mother's or that of death—as a protective place. Instead, the expressions of birth and death are used to articulate his loss and to depict his vulnerability. In the prologue, Job's words are concise, and his statements in Job 1:21 resemble conventional expressions. However, in Job 3, the narrative shifts to poetic language, with Job's first speech turning into an intense lament where he curses the day of his birth. Here, Job speaks freely, with many references to birth, the womb, and death. The blending of WOMB and DEATH will be richer, and Job will not only refer to his birth but also wish that it never had taken place.

6. Birth Metaphors in Job 3

Job 1:21 expresses Job's grief, vulnerability, and his exposure to death, but no wish to be dead. This changes in Job 3: Job curses the day he was born and the night he was conceived, and describes his suffering and his longing for death. Job articulates a strong wish that he had died in the womb, desiring to be among the dead. It is within this lament that the birth metaphors are expressed, together with metaphors of death, light, and darkness. Job longs for darkness to seize the day of his birth and the night of his conception. Job cries out "That day, let it be darkness!" which echoes God's word "Let it be light!" on the first day of creation. Job laments his birth, and asks why the doors of the womb were not closed at birth so that he had never seen the light. Job wishes that he was a stillborn and that he would be among the dead. My metaphor analysis will primarily concern how the domain of BIRTH is blended with the domains of CREATION and DEATH, but also the interaction with metaphors and motifs of light, chaos, and parental care. However, before my metaphorical analysis, I present a translation of Job 3 and provide an overview of earlier interpretations of it.

Text and Translation of Job 3

1	אַחֲרֵי־כֵן פָּתַח אִיּוֹב אֶת־פִּיהוּ	After this, Job opened his mouth
	וַיְקַלֵּל אֶת־יוֹמוֹ׃	and cursed his day,
2	וַיַּעַן אִיּוֹב וַיֹּאמַר׃	and Job answered and said:
3	יֹאבַד יוֹם אִוָּלֶד בּוֹ	"Let the day I was born be destroyed,
	וְהַלַּיְלָה אָמַר הֹרָה גָבֶר	and the night that said: 'A man is conceived!'
4	הַיּוֹם הַהוּא יְהִי חֹשֶׁךְ	That day, let it be darkness!
	אַל־יִדְרְשֵׁהוּ אֱלוֹהַּ מִמָּעַל	Let God above, not seek it,
	וְאַל־תּוֹפַע עָלָיו נְהָרָה	and let no light shine upon it.
5	יִגְאָלֻהוּ חֹשֶׁךְ וְצַלְמָוֶת	Let darkness and the deep darkness reclaim it,
	תִּשְׁכָּן־עָלָיו עֲנָנָה	Let clouds dwell over it.
	יְבַעֲתֻהוּ כִּמְרִירֵי יוֹם׃	Let the blackness of the day terrify it.

6	הַלַּיְלָה הַהוּא יִקָּחֵהוּ אֹפֶל	That night, let the darkness seize it.
	אַל־יִחַדְּ בִּימֵי שָׁנָה	Let it not rejoice among the days of the year
	בְּמִסְפַּר יְרָחִים אַל־יָבֹא׃	and not come into the number of months.
7	הִנֵּה הַלַּיְלָה הַהוּא יְהִי גַלְמוּד	Yes, that night, let it be barren!
	אַל־תָּבֹא רְנָנָה בוֹ׃	Let no joyful cries come in it.
8	יִקְּבֻהוּ אֹרְרֵי־יוֹם	Let the ones who curse the day curse it.
	הָעֲתִידִים עֹרֵר לִוְיָתָן׃	The ones who are ready to awaken Leviathan.
9	יֶחְשְׁכוּ כּוֹכְבֵי נִשְׁפּוֹ	Let its twilight stars be dark.
	יְקַו־לְאוֹר וָאַיִן	Let it wait for light but not get it
	וְאַל־יִרְאֶה בְּעַפְעַפֵּי־שָׁחַר׃	and let it not see the eyelashes of the dawn
10	כִּי לֹא סָגַר דַּלְתֵי בִטְנִי	Because he did not shut the doors of the womb
	וַיַּסְתֵּר עָמָל מֵעֵינָי׃	and hide misery from my eyes.
11	לָמָּה לֹא מֵרֶחֶם אָמוּת	Why did I not die from the womb,
	מִבֶּטֶן יָצָאתִי וְאֶגְוָע	perish when I went out from the belly?
12	מַדּוּעַ קִדְּמוּנִי בִרְכָּיִם	Why were there knees to meet me,
	וּמַה־שָּׁדַיִם כִּי אִינָק׃	or breasts for me to suck?
13	כִּי־עַתָּה שָׁכַבְתִּי וְאֶשְׁקוֹט	Then I now would be lying down and be quiet.
	יָשַׁנְתִּי אָז יָנוּחַ לִי	I would be asleep, then I would have rest,
14	עִם־מְלָכִים וְיֹעֲצֵי אָרֶץ	with kings and counsellors of the earth,
	הַבֹּנִים חֳרָבוֹת לָמוֹ	who built ruins for themselves.
15	אוֹ עִם־שָׂרִים זָהָב לָהֶם	or with princes who owned gold,
	הַמְמַלְאִים בָּתֵּיהֶם כָּסֶף	who filled their houses with silver.
16	אוֹ כְנֵפֶל טָמוּן לֹא אֶהְיֶה	Or (why) was I not hidden like a miscarriage,
	כְּעֹלְלִים לֹא־רָאוּ אוֹר	like infants who never see the light?
17	שָׁם רְשָׁעִים חָדְלוּ רֹגֶז	There, the wicked cease to turmoil,
	וְשָׁם יָנוּחוּ יְגִיעֵי כֹחַ	and there the weary of power are at rest.
18	יַחַד אֲסִירִים שַׁאֲנָנוּ	Prisoners are wholly at ease,
	לֹא שָׁמְעוּ קוֹל נֹגֵשׂ	they do not hear the voice of the oppressor.
19	קָטֹן וְגָדוֹל שָׁם הוּא	Small and great are there,
	וְעֶבֶד חָפְשִׁי מֵאֲדֹנָיו	and the slave is free from his lord.
20	לָמָּה יִתֵּן לְעָמֵל אוֹר	Why is light given to the one in misery,
	וְחַיִּים לְמָרֵי נָפֶשׁ	and life to those with bitter souls,
21	הַמְחַכִּים לַמָּוֶת וְאֵינֶנּוּ	who wait for death, but it is not for them,
	וַיַּחְפְּרֻהוּ מִמַּטְמוֹנִים	and dig for it more than after hidden treasures,
22	הַשְּׂמֵחִים אֱלֵי־גִיל	who rejoice greatly over it,
	יָשִׂישׂוּ כִּי יִמְצְאוּ־קָבֶר	rejoice when they find their grave

23	לְגֶ֭בֶר אֲשֶׁר־דַּרְכּ֣וֹ נִסְתָּ֑רָה	to a man whose way is hidden,
	וַיָּ֖סֶךְ אֱל֣וֹהַּ בַּעֲדֽוֹ	and who God has shut in?
24	כִּֽי־לִפְנֵ֣י לַ֭חְמִי אַנְחָתִ֣י תָבֹ֑א	Because my sighs come to me like bread,
	וַֽיִּתְּכ֥וּ כַ֝מַּ֗יִם שַׁאֲגֹתָֽי	and my roars are poured out like water,
25	כִּ֤י פַ֣חַד פָּ֭חַדְתִּי וַיֶּאֱתָיֵ֑נִי	Because the dread I dreaded has happened to me,
	וַאֲשֶׁ֥ר יָ֝גֹ֗רְתִּי יָ֣בֹא לִֽי	and what I have feared comes to me.
26	לֹ֤א שָׁלַ֨וְתִּי ׀ וְלֹ֖א שָׁקַ֥טְתִּי	I am not at ease. I am not at peace,
	וְֽלֹא־נָ֗חְתִּי וַיָּ֥בֹא רֹֽגֶז	I am not at rest, but turmoil comes."

Literary Structure and Genre

Job's speech in Job 3 is structured in three parts. The first part (vv. 3–10) is formulated as a curse of Job's day of birth and the night of his conception. Job wishes that he had never been conceived or born. In this section, we find an interaction between the domains of CREATION and BIRTH. In the next section (vv. 11–19), Job wishes that he had died in the womb and imagines himself among the dead. It contains explicit references to the womb and blends the domain of WOMB and the domain of GRAVE. In the third section, Job describes how those who suffer long for death, portraying his own life as filled with misery, fear, and turmoil (vv. 20–26). There are no references to Job's birth in the third section, but it is important to the interpretation of how Job imagines death and the blend of the domains of WOMB and GRAVE. The structure is displayed in the table below.

1–2	Introduction saying that Job opened his mouth to curse his day.
	Job's speech
3	Serves as a heading to verse 3–10. Job wishes that both *the day of his birth* and the *night of conception* should be destroyed.
4–5	Job wishes that "that day" should be turned into darkness.
6–7	Job wishes that "that night" should be barren and seized by darkness.
8	Job wishes that "it" (presumably the day) should be cursed by the enchanters capable of awakening Leviathan.
9	Job wishes that "it" (presumably the day) should stay in darkness.
10	Gives the reason of why that day and night are cursed: Because he (presumably God) did not shut the doors of the womb (Verse 10 both explains the reason for the curse and shifts the focus to Job's birth.)
11–12	Job asks why he did not die at birth?
13–15	Expresses the implications of a death from the womb Then would Job be laying down and be at rest together with kings.

16	Job asks why he did not become like a miscarriage?
17–19	Expresses the implications of a death in the womb. Then Job would be where the oppressed and the imprisoned are free and where the small and the great are equal.
20–23	Job asks why life is given to the ones who suffer?
24–26	Gives the reason of why Job wishes he was unborn and longs for death: because Job is in pain and has no rest.

The curse begins in verse 3, with a wish to first annihilate the day of birth and then the night of conception, and ends in verse 10 with the reason for the curse. The references to Job's birth in verses 3 and 10 form an *inclusio* of the curse. The verbs יָלֹד (Niph), "be born," and הרה (pass Qal), "be conceived," in verse 3, referring to Job's coming into existence, are paired with the standard contrasting word pair of night and day.[1] Verse 3 sets the theme for Job 3:1–10, which continues to refer to the day of Job's birth and the night of his conception. Verses 4–5 express how the day of Job's birth is cursed by darkness, and express a wish that God should not seek it. Verses 6–7 are directed towards that night, which is cursed with darkness, by being wiped away from the days of the year, and by becoming barren. Verses 8–9 could either concern the night or the day, it is not clear, but I suggest that it is the day, which is wished to be cursed and to be held in darkness. Verse 10 starts with the causal conjunction כִּי and states the reason why Job wants to curse the night and day, namely that the doors of the womb were not shut at birth. Here it is not clear if it is God, the day, or the night that Job accuses for not having closed the doors, but I suggest that it is God.

The second part shifts the focus from a wish of never being born or conceived to a wish that he had died at birth, describing how much better it would be for Job if he was dead. Two descriptions of the existence of the dead follow two exclamations wishing that he had died at birth. First, kings and princes are described as resting in peace (vv. 13–15), followed by prisoners and the oppressed finding release in the land of the dead (vv. 17–18). The passage concludes by stating that in death, both the small and the great are united (v. 19).

The third part of Job 3 does not have any explicit references to Job's birth, but it shares metaphors with the descriptions of birth. The third section starts in verse 20 with the question of why the one in misery is given light and life. This parallels Job's question of why he was not like a miscarriage that never had to see daylight

---

[1] *HALOT*, s.v. "יָלֹד," "הרה." For further discussion of יָלֹד and הרה, see Chapter 3, page 90.

(v. 16). Verses 21–23 describe the sufferer's longing for death. Verse 23 implies the question "why is light and life given..." from verse 20 and adds "to a man whose way is hidden..." Verses 24–26 conclude Job 3 with a depiction of Job's misery. They describe his tears, fears, and how he cannot find rest or peace. These are terms opposite to those describing the existence in the land of the dead (vv. 11–19).

These three sections together ask why Job and all the ones who suffer are given life. Job contrasts his life with how it would be if he had died at birth. His wish that he had not been born corresponds to his longing to be dead. Job 3 displays Job's existence starting at conception, continuing with his state in the womb and at birth, and ending with the miseries of his life. Crucial to the poetry of Job 3 is the use of contrasting motifs such as day and night, light and darkness, womb and grave, being unborn and dead, silence and turmoil, and oppression and release.

The genre of Job 3 has been the subject of much discussion. Both the genres of curse and lament can be applied to verses 3–10, and lament is appropriate for verses 11–26. The curse has been interpreted as a parody rather than a real curse. I would argue that the genre of lament is the best way of understanding the curse, and Job 3 as a whole. The parallel texts from ancient West Asia (see below) show that curses of a day in the past are expressions of despair and grief. It is a feature which belongs to laments. A lament usually concerns experienced sufferings in the past and a hope that the gods will restore the lamenter. In Job 3, there is no hope, and Job does not express that God could help him or restore him from his suffering. The only way God could help him is if God changes the past and prohibits his birth, or if God would let him die. The powerful language of a curse intensifies Job's lament and makes it more critical. A curse of something that cannot be changed reduces all hope. The genre of lament has been questioned since Job is not addressing God directly. However, Breitkopf argues that the use of the לָמָּה, "why," implies an address to God, even if it is indirect. Job's complaint is a lament that is overheard by God and his friends, and Job's wish to die serves as an indirect petition to God to let him die.[2] The birth metaphors are used in Job 3 as part of this lament to God, to accentuate Job's despair.

---

[2] Breitkopf discusses the definition of prayer, and whether it must include a direct address to God, but concludes that an indirect complaint, as Job 3, also should be regarded as a prayer (Breitkopf 2020, 39–43).

Earlier Interpretations of Job 3

Former research on Job 3 is abundant. Many studies focus on the relationship between the domains of CREATION and JOB'S BIRTH, arguing that Job not only curses his own day of birth but also expresses a curse against creation itself. This interpretation presupposes a relationship between Job 3 and Gen 1–2:4a, and the discussion of Job 3 primarily focuses on whether, and to what extent, such a relationship exists. Another discussion revolves around whether Job 3 should be viewed as a curse or a parody of curses. The general argument is that it functions as a parody, primarily because it is impossible to curse an event that has already occurred. Job 3 has also been described as a parody of birth incantations. Metaphors have been studied, and it has been argued that conventional metaphors are inverted in Job 3. The womb and the wish to be unborn are important motifs in Job 3, and these have been studied from both a psychoanalytic perspective and in terms of how they interact with other motifs and metaphors. I will provide an overview of the major issues discussed in previous research, as well as of earlier studies on intertexts related to Job 3. These intertexts are relevant because they illuminate the genre of Job 3, which influences the interpretation of the metaphors.

Inversion of Creation

It has been argued that Job 3 expresses Job's wish to destroy not only his day of birth but also the whole of creation; in this interpretation, Job 3 refers to the destruction of the order of creation and intends to reverse God's creative acts in Gen 1–2:4a. This discussion presupposes two things. First, that there are intertextual links between Job 3 and Gen 1–2:4a. Second, as my metaphorical analysis will demonstrate, it also assumes that Job speaks of creation when he speaks about his birth, and does not merely use the motifs of creation to discuss his birth. The first presupposition is discussed in former research, but how Job 3 blends the language of birth with the language of creation has not been sufficiently explored. This analysis is crucial for understanding Job 3, as examining the birth metaphors will reveal whether and how the domains of BIRTH and CREATION are blended in Job 3.

Intertextual links between Gen 1–2:4a and Job 3:3–13 were recognized by Fishbane in 1971. He argues that Job's curse does not only concern Job's birth but is also a cosmic act of inverting creation back into chaos.[3] Fishbane divides Job 3 in

---

[3] Fishbane 1971. Fishbane uses the word "reversal," but I refer to it as an "inversion" to avoid a mix-up with how I use the term "reversed metaphors" to explain metaphors that switch the target and source domains of conventional metaphors.

seven curses, which he suggests reflect each day in the Gen 1–2:4a creation account.[4] The most obvious link is the linguistic parallel between God's word יְהִי אוֹר, "let it be light!" (Gen 1:3) and Job's words יְהִי חֹשֶׁךְ, "let it be darkness!" (Job 3:4), but Fishbane and others identify several additional links.[5]

Genesis 1–2:4a	Job 3
יְהִי אוֹר, "let it be light!" (1:3)	יְהִי חֹשֶׁךְ, "let it be darkness!" (3:4)
מַעַל, "above" in "waters above" (1:7)	מַעַל, "above," in "God above" (3:4)
Separation between day and night (1:14)	Job's wish that the night should not be counted among the days (3:6)
Creation of humankind in (1:26)	References to Job's womb and birth (3:11)
Sea creatures (1:21)	Leviathan (3:8)
Sabbath on the seventh day (2:2)	References to rest (3:13)

Fishbane argues that the links between Gen 1–2:4 and Job 3 show that Job's curse aims to reverse the whole creation. He claims that Job 3 belongs to a magical context, resembling Akkadian incantations. He states that these incantations begin with an invocation of the creator god referring to its cosmological power of ordering the universe and then asking the gods to redo these creative acts. Job 3, he argues, uses this pattern, but instead Job asks God to invert creation and to destroy the day of Job's birth. Furthermore, the reference to Leviathan in Job 3:8 would imply that Job's curse is an anti-cosmological act, since Leviathan is an "anti-cosmological force."[6] Fishbane connects Job's wish to bring darkness into creation with his wish of awakening Leviathan, as it was believed to cause eclipses and bring darkness over the world. He argues that the battle between cosmos and chaos needs to be repeated through history, and is used in images of the eschaton.[7]

Fishbane's interpretation of Job 3 as a curse to destroy creation has become the dominant one.[8] Perdue adopts Fishbane's view of the inversion of creation and his comparison to Akkadian curses, arguing that Job 3 highlights the battle between

---

[4] Fishbane 1971, 153–55.
[5] See also Habel 1985, 104.
[6] Fishbane 1971, 158.
[7] Fishbane 1971, 155–59.
[8] Many biblical scholars follow Fishbane's main arguments, such as Habel 1985, 104–10; Tönsing 1996, 438–40; Pettys 2002; Pyeon 2003, 88–93; Balentine 2006, 83–88; Balentine 2013, 45–48; Seow 2013, 319–28; Leonard 2019; Grant 2019; Breitkopf 2020, 48–52. They modify Fishbane's theories in different directions, but maintain that it is an anti-cosmological curse.

God and chaos through Job's wish to let Leviathan loose. He claims that Job 3 is an attack on P's language of creation and an assault on creation itself.[9] Seow recognizes the inversion of creation and relates the expression "that day" in Job 3:3 to eschatological ideas of the dark day of the Lord. He interprets Job's misery as a cosmic chaos and suggests that Job 3 depicts a "cosmological birth." He interprets Job 3:10 in the light of Job 38:8, and argues that verse 10 refers to God's failure to subdue chaos and to shut the doors for the cosmic sea. The womb in Job 3 is then the lower cosmos, where Sheol is located.[10]

Although interpreting Job 3 as an inversion of creation is the dominant view, there are other voices. Clines argues that Job 3 only concerns the destruction of Job's day of birth. He contends that the only genuine textual connection between Job 3 that refers to an inversion of God's creative acts are the expressions יְהִי חֹשֶׁךְ "let it be darkness!" and יְהִי אוֹר, "let it be light!" However, according to Clines, this is a parodic reversal of God's word.[11] Pelham claims that Fishbane never addresses why Job would wish to invert creation and turn order into chaos. She holds that Job is already experiencing chaos, and that his goal is to escape this disorder and restore order to his life. Pelham suggests that the new order Job seeks is actually the order of death.[12] Schmid also argues that Job wants to escape chaos and to erase his day of birth to maintain the order presented by P in Gen 1–2:4a.[13]

Häner explains that the contrast of Job 3 and Gen 1–2:4 should be interpreted as a critique of the "optimistic creation theology" of Gen 1–2:4a. He opposes the interpretation of Job 3 as a curse which inverts creation and brings chaos to order. He offers the most thorough investigation of shared lexemes, themes, and structure in Job 3 and Gen 1–2:4a, identifying twelve lexical elements that occur in both texts. However, he argues that these elements are very common in the HB, and that they do not appear in the same syntagma in the two texts except for "let it be light" and "let it be darkness." He examines both the shared and contrasting motifs between the texts, noting that there are many themes they do not have in common.[14] He argues that the shared motifs mainly occur in Job 3:3–11, while verses

---

[9] Perdue 1986; Perdue 1991, 91–110.
[10] Seow 2013, 327–28.
[11] Clines 1989, 81–84.
[12] Pelham 2012, 227–28.
[13] Schmid 2007, 4–5.
[14] Shared motifs: day/night, light/darkness, sea dwellers, and measuring of time. Contrasting motifs: blessing (Gen)/curse (Job), becoming (Gen)/perishing (Job), bring light (Gen)/bring darkness (Job), order (Gen)/disorder (Job) and rest (Gen)/unrest (Job). Themes they do not share: Genesis refers to humans and animals and Job 3 to birth and death (Häner 2020, 270–73).

12–25 introduce the motifs of birth and death which are not shared with Genesis. He concludes that the intertextual connections between Job 3 and Gen 1–2:4a can be "termed as subtle allusion" which he interprets as part of the irony in Job 3.[15]

Inverted Metaphors

It is not only the inversion of creation that is discussed. It has also been suggested that Job 3 inverts conventional metaphors so that they propose the opposite to their original meaning.

Perdue argues that Job 3 inverts the creation metaphors of fertility, artistry, myths, and language.[16] In his discussion on fertility metaphors he holds that conventional metaphors of the womb in the HB associate it with God's providential care, but in Job 3, Job rejects this view through his wish to have died at birth.[17] Wälchli discusses the inversion of light and darkness, and life and death metaphors in Job 3.[18] He maintains that Job 3 inverts the light and darkness metaphors because Job cries for darkness while the psalmists who suffer call for light. Van Loon discusses metaphors of suffering and analyzes Job 3:20–26.[19] She shows how Job uses conventional associations of the metaphors of life and light, but that Job's suffering makes him question the goodness of light and life.[20] Burnight investigates links between Job 3 and Israel's *Heilsgeschichte* instead of the creation story.[21] By the term *Heilsgeschichte* he refers to God's salvific acts toward Israel and Judah in order to liberate them from Egypt and the exile. Even if the name of his article is "The 'Reversal' of Heilsgeschichte," he claims that many motifs of the exile are inverted in Job 3, rather than arguing that Job's curse reverses God's liberation from exile.[22]

These examples demonstrate that Job 3 employs conventional metaphors in unconventional ways. The question that arises is whether Job truly inverts these metaphors, or if he uses them in their conventional forms to express unusual wishes, such as a longing for death and darkness.

---

[15] Häner 2020, 273.
[16] Perdue 1986, 305–13; Perdue 1991, 98–110.
[17] Perdue 1986, 309–10; Perdue 1991, 102–3.
[18] Wälchli 2013.
[19] van Loon 2018.
[20] van Loon 2018, 65–66.
[21] Burnight 2013.
[22] Burnight 2013, 30–31.

Interaction between Metaphors

Alter gives a short overview of the interaction of the metaphors in Job 3 and explores how different metaphors are intensified, and trigger each other. This accentuates the importance of discussing the relationship between birth metaphors and other metaphors, and never studying metaphors as isolated expressions. He shows how the darkness is intensified in Job 3:3–10. It starts to destroy Job's day of birth. That a day is destroyed by darkness is apparent, as a day is defined by its light, but the curse continues by expressing how the darkness may also capture the night. Darkness is an inherent characteristic of the night, but the blackness seizing the night is a deep darkness that would extinguish both day and night from the calendar. The climax is in verse 9, which depicts a hopeless waiting for light. The image of being enveloped by darkness transitions into the image of the darkness of the womb, which in turn evokes motifs of the grave and death. Alter suggests that the womb and the grave have an archetypal connection. In Job 3, Job is depicted as being hedged in, trapped between the womb, which he cannot return to, and the grave, which remains out of reach.[23]

Job 3 as a Parody

The fact that Job's curse in Job 3 concerns a day in the past has raised discussions regarding whether it should be interpreted as a curse or something else. Clines argues that Job 3 is not a genuine curse but rather a parody of curses. He contends that Job, having been stripped of all social power, lacks the authority to issue a real curse. Clines' main argument is that Job's curse is futile because the past cannot be altered. However, Clines also suggests that even if the curse is a parody, its purpose may be to express grief.[24] Other scholars also claim that Job is a parody, but they differ on what it parodies. Seow understands Job 3 as a parody of the lament form, while Häner and Pettys argue that the curse parodies the order of creation, and Langton sees it as a parody of Akkadian birth incantations.[25] The argument they all use is that Job's curse concerns events in the past which cannot be changed. This argument is only valid if there are no other possible explanations to why someone curses something in the past.

---

[23] Alter 2011, 98–100.
[24] Clines 1989, 78–81.
[25] Seow 2013, 335–36; Pettys 2002, 92; Häner 2020, 276–78; Langton 2012.

Birth Motif in Job 3

The womb and the birth motifs in Job 3 have been discussed from different perspectives. Langton argues that Job 3 should be seen as a parody of Akkadian birth incantations by means of inverting them. She claims that Akkadian birth incantations and Job 3 share several features, and refers to the descriptions of the darkness in the womb, the doors of the womb, and the light at birth. Job 3 would then be a counter-birth incantation to invert Job's birth and change the fact that he was born. It would enable Job to return to the safe darkness of the womb. By trying to change the past, Job tries to regain control over his destiny. She also argues that Job 3 challenges God's involvement in births, because it depicts the day and night as responsible for Job's conception and birth rather than God.[26]

Van der Zwan analyzes images of the womb in the Book of Job by using psychoanalytic theories. He interprets Job's wish to stay in the womb as regression. It is a reaction to a crisis, a way to hide from the attacks he experiences in life. He refers to psychoanalytic theories that suggest that a wish to return to the womb and the comfort of amniotic fluid symbolizes a desire to return to the origin of life and the sea. Van der Zwan adds that in Job it also symbolizes a return to God.[27] The wish to stay in the womb of one's mother is a wish to become part of the mother's body in a "seemingly eternal sleep."[28] Van der Zwan points out that this is exactly what is described in Job 3:13 where Job imagines death as an eternal sleep, and he concludes that Job's death-wish is linked to the womb. He argues that Job merges the womb and death to "sugar-coat death."[29] It is better to be united with God than to die and be separated from God. The womb becomes a protective shelter. He refers to Freud, who argues that fantasies of the grave are more anxiety-provoking than fantasies of the womb.[30] Van der Zwan also refers to theories which describe the womb in negative terms. Humans have negative memories of the womb as experiences of loneliness and claustrophobia. These negative feelings are related to the archetype of a devouring mother who consumes her children psychologically and emotionally. Van der Zwan argues that most references to the womb in the Book of Job carry negative connotations, citing Job 3:11, as well as Job 10:18 and 24:20, as examples. However, he does not explore in detail how these

---

[26] Langton 2012.
[27] van der Zwan 2019a, 1–5, 10–15.
[28] van der Zwan 2019a, 10.
[29] van der Zwan 2019a, 10.
[30] van der Zwan 2019a, 10–11.

negative connotations are utilized in Job 3:11. He simply notes that Job 3:10–11 merges the womb with death.[31]

Eckstein discusses Job 3:12a in terms of birth. She interprets the expression "knees to receive me" as a birth and not, as it is commonly assumed, as an act of a parent caring or acknowledging the child.[32] Vall contrasts Job 3 with Job 1:21 and argues that birth is a tragedy in Job 3, rather than a gift from God as it is in Job 1:21. Vall points out the similarity in how the womb and the tomb are depicted as places of rest and peace in contrast to life, but that it is done in a parodic and hyperbolic way.[33]

Parallels to Job 3: Cursing of Days in the Past

There are parallels to Job 3 in texts from ancient West Asia. These parallels help us to understand Job's curse and his wish that he had died in the womb in Job 3. Much of the discussion has been concerned with how Job can curse a day in the past and how to interpret the fact that Job wants darkness to seize his day of birth. This has led to the conclusion that Job 3 is a parody of curses and that Job does not only want to annihilate his day of birth but also the whole of creation. Jacobsen and Nielsen give several examples of curses from ancient West Asia which also curse a particular event or day in the past.[34] These help us realize that Job does not need to be ironic when he curses his day of birth, nor does he intend to invert creation. Instead, it is an expression of despair.

Jacobsen and Nielsen refer to a Sumerian text, in which a mother mourns her son, the god Tammuz (here called Damu), who has been killed in a battle.

> I am the mother who gave birth!
> Woe to that day, that day! Woe to that night! ...
> The day that dawned for my provider,
> that dawned for the lad, my Damu!
> A day to be wiped out,
> that I would I could forget,
> You night [...] that should [never]
> have let it go forth ...
> The lad! Woe!

---

[31] van der Zwan 2019a, 5–6.
[32] Eckstein 2019. See Chapter 6, pages 163–65.
[33] Vall 1993, 209–12.
[34] Jacobsen and Nielsen 1992.

The day destroyed him
lost me a son!³⁵

In this text, the woe is not only directed at the day and night of her son's birth, but also to the day when he was killed. Just as Job, the mother wants the day to be wiped out (cf. Job 3:6) and that the day never had dawned (cf. Job 3:9). Another Sumerian text contains a curse of the day of the destruction of Ur. The day of destruction is referred to as the day of storm.

> May that day of storm
> like rain rained down from the sky
> [seep into] the earth and not recur. ...
> May that day of storm be destroyed, all of it.
> May, as with great city gates at night, the doors be barred against it!
> May that day of storm
> not be put into the rosters,
> may its accounts be taken down
> from the peg in Enlil's temple.³⁶

This text describes how the day should be dissolved in the rain. That the thing being cursed should return to clay or dissolve as clay in water was a common motif in curses from ancient West Asia.³⁷ Another image, closer to the description in Job 3, is that the day should "not be put into the rosters," meaning that the day should not be called or signed up to serve the gods (cf. Job 3:4; 38:12).

In Atraḫasis there is a reference to cursing the day. The mother goddess, Mami, mourns the death of humankind in the flood and curses the day when the gods decided to let the flood overflow the earth.

> The goddess saw it as she wept,
> The midwife of the gods, the wise Mami,
> (She spoke) 'Let the day become dark,
> Let it become gloom again.
> In the assembly of the gods
> How did I, with them, command total destruction? ... '³⁸

Mami wishes that darkness should seize the day of the decision to destroy humankind, just as Job repeatedly asks for darkness to overwhelm his day of birth and his

---

³⁵ K 5208, translation from Jacobsen and Nielsen 1992, 188–89. It is a translation of an Old Babylonian copy of the lament from 1700 BCE. The lament is probably much older, according to Jacobsen and Nielsen.
³⁶ "Lamentation over the Destruction of Ur," (trans. from Jacobsen and Nielsen 1992, 191).
³⁷ Kitz 2014, 440–48.
³⁸ "Atraḫasis" III iii 32–37 (trans. Lambert, et al. 1999, 94–95).

night of conception. The expression "Let the day become dark" corresponds to the expression "let it be darkness!" in Job 3:4.

Burns investigates parallels with the laments in Job and Jeremiah. He discusses the Poem of Erra as a parallel to Job 3. In the Poem of Erra, the governor of a destroyed city says to his mother:

> On the day when you gave birth to me, would that I had remained in your womb, would that our (li)ves had perished, and we had died together.[39]

This is not a curse but a wish to change the past, the fact that he was born. It expresses that staying in the womb will lead to the death of both the child and the mother. This is a close parallel to Job 3:10, 11, 16.

The closest parallel to Job 3 is Jer 20:14–18. Jeremiah also expresses his despair and complaint by cursing the day on which he was born.

> Cursed be the day on which I was born!
> The day when my mother bore me, let it not be blessed!
> Cursed be the man who brought the news to my father, saying,
> "A child is born to you, a son," making him very glad.
> Let that man be like the cities that the LORD overthrew without pity;
> let him hear a cry in the morning and an alarm at noon,
> because he did not kill me in the womb;
> so my mother would have been my grave, and her womb forever great.
> Why did I come forth from the womb to see toil and sorrow,
> and spend my days in shame?[40]

Jeremiah's curse is part of a lament in which he wrestles with his identity as a prophet. The similarity between Job and Jeremiah has led to discussions regarding whether there is an intertextual dependence between them. Many scholars concludes that Job is a development of Jeremiah, others that they go back to a common source.[41] Job 3 is a longer and more elaborated lament than Jer 20:14–18. McKane notes that both texts share a similar structure, as each opens with a curse directed at the day of birth. Both Jeremiah and Job include references to the announcement of the birth, the thought of dying in the womb, and the question of why they were born to misery (עָמָל).[42] Jeremiah curses the day of his birth only in verse 14, then he turns his curse onto the messenger. In Job it is the night of conception that is cursed and functions as a messenger announcing the pregnancy. Jeremiah wishes that he had been killed in the womb and that the womb had

---

[39] Burns 1993, 15.
[40] NRSV.
[41] McKane 2014, 482; Greenstein 2004, 102.
[42] McKane 2014, 484–90.

become his grave. This is never explicitly stated in Job 3; however, the concepts of the womb and grave overlap and are blended.

These examples of various texts containing curses of days in the past illustrate that they are used to express deep despair, rather than to parody curses. I am not arguing that there are intertextual dependencies between these texts, but rather that the words of cursing or darkening a day in the past are shared expressions of grief in ancient West Asia. The wish to undo one's birth has the same function, because no one can change the fact that they are born. These parallels are important for determining the genre of Job 3. As argued above, Job 3 is best understood as a lament. The curse of Job's birth in the past and his wish that he had never been born underscore his deep despair and the sense that God cannot help him. It is too late for Job; he is already born to misery, and there is no hope for relief.

Open Questions from Earlier Interpretations

My investigation of the birth metaphors in Job 3 will engage in the major questions raised by former research. One dominant argument suggests that Job 3 is an inversion of the creation narrative and creation itself, relying on intertextual links between Gen 1–2:4a and Job 3, and presupposing that creation is a topic in Job 3. Blending theory is a good tool to examine how two domains are blended. I will, in my metaphorical analysis, show how Job 3 uses elements of creation to depict birth and not the other way around. This analysis challenges the notion that Job's curse aims to invert creation itself.

Both van der Zwan and Langton argue that Job wishes to return to the protective darkness of the womb. Van der Zwan also proposes that the associations with the womb may carry negative connotations. My examination of the birth metaphors will explore in detail which characteristics of the womb are emphasized in Job 3, and how these may be blended with motifs of death.

Alter is the only one who discusses the birth metaphors in Job 3 as metaphors, and their interactions with other motifs. My analysis will continue the discussion of how birth metaphors relate to other metaphors and motifs in Job 3 and whether they invert conventional metaphors.

Metaphors in Job 3

Job's curse in Job 3:3–10 begins and ends with references to his birth. In the second part of the speech, 3:11–19, birth metaphors are central, expressing Job's wish to die and leading to two descriptions of death. The third part, 3:20–26, contains no references to Job's birth, but uses the metaphor LIFE IS LIGHT and the domains of ENCLOSED SPACE, HIDDENNESS, DEATH, and HARDSHIP, which are also used in the metaphors of birth in the first two parts of Job 3. The birth metaphors interact with domains and metaphors of life, death, hardship, darkness, and light, and this interaction influences their interpretation. I will begin by discussing these related domains and metaphors before turning to the birth metaphors in Job 3.

Metaphors of Light and Darkness

The light and darkness metaphors are used throughout the whole speech, and dominate the first part of the speech, the curse. The day needs light to exist, and Job asks God not to shine light on it (Job 3:4, 9) and cries "let it be darkness!" The curse invokes darkness as a destructive force intended to extinguish Job's birth and conception. Even if darkness is an inherit characteristics of the night, the darkness Job asks for is something else, a deep darkness which destroys even the night itself (Job 3:6–9).[43] The metaphors depicting death, destruction, and fear as darkness are grounded in embodied experience of darkness. The night is a time of danger, and even more so, we may remind ourselves, in a premodern culture without electric light. The darkness hid predators and criminals, and it was easy to get lost in it. Death is associated with darkness due to the similarity between death and sleeping. The ones who shut their eyes and sleep experience darkness. The grave is also an enclosed dark room. Light is, on the other hand, associated with the day, when we are active, safe, and able to see the world around us.[44] Job 3 does not explicitly refer to the darkness of the womb, but it is a logical contrast to the description of the light outside the womb (3:16). Verse 9 describes how darkness overwhelms the day and night so that light never will arrive. This transitions into verse 10, where Job wishes to remain enclosed in the womb, which presumably is as dark as the night and day described in verse 9.

The metaphors of light and darkness in Job 3 are used in conventional ways, in which LIFE AND HEALTH ARE LIGHT and DESTRUCTION AND DEATH ARE DARKNESS. They are not inverted, as Wälchli argues.[45] Instead, Job wants something else, different than the common lamenter in the psalms. Job's wish is not for light and life but for death and darkness.

---

[43] Alter 2011, 95–98.
[44] Reece 1989, 129–30; Van Hecke 2011, 96–97.
[45] Wälchli 2013.

Metaphors of Death and Exile

Metaphors of death and hardship dominate the second and the third part of the speech. Job wishes he had never been born or had died at birth; but there are no explicit references to Sheol, the land of the dead, or the grave in Job 3. Instead, Job describes how it would have been if he had died in or from the womb. The descriptions of being dead use conventional metaphors when describing the physical state of the dead. The dead are sleeping (יָשֵׁן), lying down (שׁכב), and hidden (טמן) (Job 3:13, 16). The metaphors DEATH IS LYING DOWN and DEATH IS SLEEPING are universal metaphors to describe the physical state of the dead.[46] The dead cannot rise or be awakened. These metaphors are based on our physical experiences of dead people. The dead cannot move, they are still, and when we bury them, they are laid down in the grave and hidden within the soil. Our experience of sleeping also forms our ideas of death. When we sleep, we cannot move, we face darkness, and lay down.[47]

Job 3 also contains other metaphors of death, which are based on experiences of hardship and release from hardship. The conventional metaphors in the HB connect hardship with death in the metaphor DEATH IS OPPRESSION, TURMOIL, BONDAGE, AND IMPRISONMENT.[48] In the western culture of today, rest and peace are common associations of death, but these are not conventional metaphors in the HB. DEATH and EXILE are often described in the same terms of hardship as darkness, oppression, and imprisonment. They are also blended into metaphors describing either DEATH or EXILE, where death becomes the antipode to liberation.[49] In contrast, in Job 3, death is portrayed as liberation (vv. 17–19), while life is

---

[46] Lakoff and Turner 1989, 18–19.

[47] Reece 1989, 129–30.

[48] For further reading regarding connotations of death in the HB, see Tromp 1969. Clines summarizes: "The idea of the underworld as a place of rest by comparison with the turmoil of life seems an obvious one, but it is in fact rather hard to parallel in the HB. A quick overview of N. H. Tromp's *Primitive Conceptions of Death and the Nether World in the Old Testament* [...] shows no section in a most comprehensive study allotted to this aspect, despite very many sections on Sheol as a hidden place, the depths, waters, pit, corruption and ruin, destruction, silence, dust, forgetfulness, darkness, as a city, prison, river, mountains, with a personal god, his terrors and demons, and so on" (Clines 1989, 91). When Abraham is promised that he will be buried at old age, it is said that he will go to his ancestors "in peace"(בְּשָׁלוֹם) (Gen 15:15). However, it then rather describes that Abraham will go in peace after a fulfilled life, than that the state of death is described as peace.

[49] DEATH and EXILE are blended, for example, in Isa 51:14 and Jer 31: 15–16. Both Isa 26:16–19. and Hos 13:13–14 describe the exile in terms of Sheol and in metaphors of birth. For further reading on metaphors of exile and death, see Halvorson-Taylor 2010, 127–35.

instead described in terms of hardship. Burnight discusses how Job 3 inverts metaphors of the exile.[50] It is correct that in Job 3, we find many expressions commonly used to describe the hardship of exile and the liberation from it. These expressions are used to depict the hardships of Job's life and his wish for liberation from his misery. This does not mean that Job 3 refers to the exile, but rather that it uses terms of hardship also found in descriptions of exile.

Job 3 uses the conventional associations of the domain of HARDSHIP, but HARDSHIP is not the source domain for DEATH. Job applies common expressions and metaphors of hardship to depict his life. Job's experience of his life is what others associate with death. Death in the womb will be portrayed as a release from hardship and as a counter-image of his life, as a state of rest and freedom. The birth metaphors are, therefore, connected with descriptions of the hardship of Job's life.

Birth Metaphors in Job 3:1–9

The curse in Job 3:1–10 contains descriptions of how Job's day of birth and night of conception could have been extinguished. These descriptions mix light and darkness metaphors and creation language with references to Job's wish that he had not been conceived or born. I will begin by investigating the relationship between the domain of CREATION and the domain of BIRTH, and then proceed to discuss the references to Job's conception.

JOB'S DAY OF BIRTH and CREATION

Fishbane's identification of Job 3 as an inversion of creation has become a standard interpretation, but it has also faced criticism, and the presumed textual links have been challenged. The expression יְהִי חֹשֶׁךְ, "let it be darkness!" in verse 4 is probably an allusion to the expression יְהִי אוֹר, "let it be light!" in the creation story. The other links are more uncertain, as Clines and Häner argue.[51] Fishbane uses the links between Job 3 and Gen 1–2:4a to conclude that Job wants to curse not only his birth but also the entire creation by inverting God's actions of creation. This is achieved, even though Job 3 does not explicitly refer to God's creative acts nor the primeval creation. The problem is that the only topic explicitly stated is the day of Job's birth and the night of his conception. The only part of creation at stake is Job's life. In his wish to destroy that day and night he uses a language which resembles the language used in Gen 1–2:4. Descriptions of creation and birth often use

---

[50] Burnight 2013.
[51] Clines 1989, 81; Häner 2020.

the same expressions, and it is therefore not surprising that Job's curse of his birth also utilizes language used to describe the creation in Gen 1–2:4a.[52] Fishbane interprets Job 3:8 and the phrase "awaken Leviathan" as part of an anti-cosmological curse which will bring chaos into the world and destroy creation. In my metaphorical analysis, I will evaluate Fishbane's conclusions and discuss verses 4 and 8 and how they express wishes to destroy Job's day of birth.

Let It Be Darkness!

The expression "let it be darkness!" resembles God's exclamation "let it be light!" at the first day of creation in Gen 1:3. It is therefore possible to interpret Job 3:4 as a blend between CREATION and BIRTH. There are also other ways to interpret this expression which do not imply such a metaphorical blend, as I will discuss below. I start with the interpretation that understands "let it be darkness!" as an expression from the domain of CREATION.

The recognition of "let it be darkness!" as belonging to the domain of CREATION leads to an interpretation of Job 3:4 in which the expression from the domain of CREATION is used to describe the destruction of Job's day of birth. This would lead to a blending process where CREATION is the source, and JOB'S DAY OF BIRTH is the target of the blend. Fishbane argues that the phrase "let it be darkness!" signals that Job wants to destroy the whole of creation. If we follow his interpretation, then we would need to make JOB'S DAY OF BIRTH the source and CREATION the target; however, this is not stated in the text. The references to birth are not used to explain or depict creation, but rather the other way around. A close reading of the different parts of Job 3 will make this clear. Already, verse 1 states "Job opened his mouth and cursed his day." Verse 3 works as a heading for the whole curse, and refers to the destruction of the day of Job's birth and the night of his conception. Job 3:4 includes two expressions; "let it be darkness!" and "above" which Fishbane links to Gen 1, but the topic is clear: Job refers to the day he was born. The expression "let it be darkness!" refers to his day, that God above is asked not to seek. In my overview of the structure of verses 3–10, I show how verses 5–9 continue to refer to the day of Job's birth and to the night of his conception. Verse 10 concludes that the reason behind Job's wish for his day of birth to be overwhelmed with darkness is that the womb was not shut and his birth was not prevented. Verses 11–12 and 16 also refer to the day of his birth. The topic is Job's birth and never the primeval creation.

---

[52] Simkins 2014. See also Chapter 3, "BIRTH and CREATION," pages 82–83.

Job's day of birth is the topic of Job's curse and Job 3:4 and therefore JOB'S DAY OF BIRTH must be the target in an assumed blend between JOB'S DAY OF BIRTH and THE FIRST DAY OF CREATION. This blend would use the language of its source domain CREATION to describe the destruction of Job's first day, his birth (Figure 6.1). The expression of Gen 1:3 is negated into the words "let it be darkness!" If these words had been applied to the first day of creation, it would have led to the destruction of creation itself.

Before I map out the assumed blend between CREATION and JOB'S BIRTH, it is necessary to sort out how the language of creation and language of procreation cohere in Job 3. Procreation and creation share expressions and images, and it is not strange if expressions used to depict the primeval creation are used in descriptions of birth. The expression "let it be darkness!" works well within both the domains of BIRTH and CREATION, because both use the metaphors of light and darkness. The motif of the newborn seeing light when born refers to the metaphor LIFE IS LIGHT. This metaphor is also behind the expression "Let it be light!" in Gen 1:3. Langton suggests that Job 3:4 refers to Job's emerging from the womb and that Job wishes to return to the darkness of the womb.[53] Her interpretation of Job 3:4 is coherent with how birth is depicted in Job 3:10–11, 16. Verses 10–11 and verse 16 use the metaphor LIFE IS LIGHT in their depictions of Job's birth, and express his wish that he had stayed in the darkness of the womb. The first line of verse 4, "That day 'let it be darkness!'" would work well in the context of a birth as a wish of not being born to see the light. However, the continuation "Let God above, not seek it, let no light shine upon it," as well as verses 5–9, imply a context of preventing the day of Job's birth coming into existence. The seeking of the day implies God's actions of seeking and calling the day into existence. It is not coherent with the description of a baby who is born to light. Job 3:4 refers to the day of Job's birth, wishing it to be extinguished by darkness, as if it had never begun, because God did not seek it or allow light to shine upon it. It does not say that God should hinder the baby Job being born. It is, therefore, THE DAY OF JOB'S BIRTH that is the target of the language of creation in Job 3:4, not Job's birth out of the womb. The metaphor in Job 3:4 can be expressed in the metaphor JOB'S DAY OF BIRTH IS THE FIRST DAY OF CREATION with focus on the destruction of Job's day of birth.

---

[53] Langton 2012, 465–66.

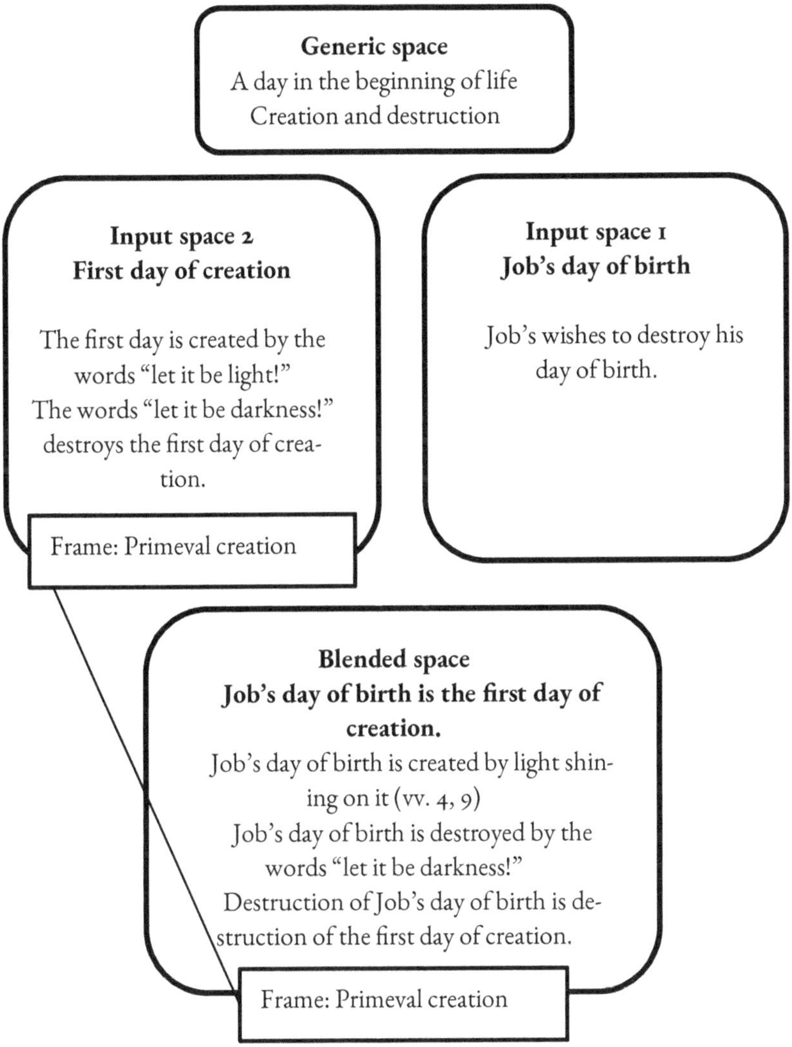

```
                    ┌─────────────────────────────┐
                    │      Generic space          │
                    │ A day in the beginning of life│
                    │  Creation and destruction   │
                    └─────────────────────────────┘
```

Input space 2
First day of creation

The first day is created by the words "let it be light!"
The words "let it be darkness!" destroys the first day of creation.

Frame: Primeval creation

Input space 1
Job's day of birth

Job's wishes to destroy his day of birth.

Blended space
Job's day of birth is the first day of creation.

Job's day of birth is created by light shining on it (vv. 4, 9)
Job's day of birth is destroyed by the words "let it be darkness!"
Destruction of Job's day of birth is destruction of the first day of creation.

Frame: Primeval creation

Figure 6.1 *The metaphor (DESTRUCTION OF) JOB'S DAY OF BIRTH IS (DESTRUCTION OF) THE FIRST DAY OF CREATION. Target: JOB'S DAY OF BIRTH. Source: THE FIRST DAY OF CREATION.*

If the phrases "let it be darkness!" and "let no light shine upon it" refer to undoing the first day of creation and are used in the description of the destruction of Job's day of birth, then the network would be mapped as in Figure 6.1. It depicts the metaphor JOB'S DAY OF BIRTH IS THE FIRST DAY OF CREATION, which includes the metaphor DESTRUCTION OF JOB'S DAY OF BIRTH IS DESTRUCTION OF THE FIRST DAY OF CREATION. The target is JOB'S DAY OF BIRTH, and the source is the FIRST DAY OF CREATION. The source, THE FIRST DAY OF CREATION, projects its frame to the blend regarding how days are created and destroyed. Job's day is then seen as the first day of creation, which would be created by the words "let it be light!" and correspondingly destroyed by the words "let it be darkness!"

The blending schema in Figure 6.1 explains our interpretation of Job 3:4 if the expression "let it be light!" triggers allusions to the first day of creation. However, it is not necessary to interpret Job 3 in terms of this blend or as referring to the primeval creation. There are other ways to interpret the expression "let it be darkness!" in Job 3:4. It could, as well as "let it be light!" in Gen 1:3, refer to how all days need light to exist. Both JOB'S DAY OF BIRTH and the FIRST DAY OF CREATION are part of the domain of DAYS. The same language used to describe the first day of creation could be applied to Job's day of birth, without necessarily blending them. Parallel texts from ancient West Asia reflect the belief that every day is called into service and needs the light of dawn to begin.[54] Job 3:9 describes how the day awaits the light of dawn in vain. This idea is also echoed in Job 38:12, where Job is questioned about whether he has commanded the morning and instructed the dawn about its place. Similarly, in Job 3:6, Job wishes that his night of conception never had rejoiced among the days or entered the number of months. The expressions "let it be light!" and "let it be darkness!" could therefore also belong to the language of how God calls each day into service. The first day of creation was the first day to be called by the words "let it be light!" but it is not necessarily unique. Light is an essential feature of all days, not only the first day of creation. God therefore needs to give light to all days, just as God did the first day of creation. Job's use of the words "let it be darkness!" expresses that he wants to keep his day of birth in the darkness and not call it to begin. This view explains why both Job 3:4 and Gen 1:3 use similar expressions. It is also congruent with the continuation of Job 3:4, where Job asks God not to seek his day and let no light shine upon it, and Job 3:6, where the night of Job's conception should not enter the numbers of months.

It is more difficult to describe how the night of conception is destroyed by the deep darkness. Darkness is an inherent characteristic of a night and does not threaten its existence the way it threatens the day. The metaphors DANGER IS DARKNESS and DESTRUCTION IS DARKNESS are crucial to understanding these descriptions. These metaphors can explain Job 3:4 without references to the primeval

---

[54] See pages 144–46.

creation or to how God calls the day to service. Darkness in itself is seen as a destructive power, which can be used to destroy Job's day of birth and the night of his conception.

The process of understanding Job 3:4 and the darkness as destroying Job's day of birth depends on what associations that come to our minds when we read it. If the phrase "let it be darkness!" triggers ideas of the first day of creation, then it is interpreted as the metaphor THE DESTRUCTION OF JOB'S DAY OF BIRTH IS DESTRUCTION OF THE FIRST DAY OF CREATION. If it instead activates associations of how all days are called into service by the light of dawn, then would it refer to Job's wish to prohibit his day from beginning. Finally, if it triggers ideas of darkness as a destructive force then the expression "let it be darkness!" would simply be a wish to bring destruction on Job's day of birth.

To summarize: The only targets of the curse in Job 3:3–10 are Job's day of birth and the night of his conception. The expression "let it be darkness!" is similar to the expression "let it be light!" in Gen 1:3. It can be explained as a blend between JOB'S DAY OF BIRTH and THE FIRST DAY OF CREATION and the metaphor DESTRUCTION OF JOB'S DAY OF BIRTH IS DESTRUCTION OF THE FIRST DAY OF CREATION. If so, and the day of Job's birth is depicted in terms of creation, it would not imply, as Fishbane argues, that the destruction of creation is described through the language of Job's birth. The expression "let it be darkness!" can also be understood from the background that God calls all days into existence with light, or as an expression of the metaphor DESTRUCTION IS DARKNESS.

Cursers of the Day and Leviathan

Fishbane and others use the references to Leviathan in Job 3:8 as an argument for interpreting Job 3 as an anti-cosmological curse that refers to the destruction of creation. The expression "awaken Leviathan" in Job 3:8 is then seen as a wish to cancel God's subjugation of Leviathan and bring chaos into creation.[55] This interpretation of Job 3:8 is not self-evident. Job asks the enchanters of the day and of Leviathan to curse "it." "It" presumably refers to the day of Job's birth, but it might also be the night of his conception. I argue that verse 8 is not a request to awaken Leviathan, but a call for help from the ones who have power to curse Leviathan. Verse 8 contains a wordplay: the standard word pair "Leviathan and the

---

[55] Fishbane 1971, 158–66. See also Kubina 1979, 59–61; Perdue 1991, 104–6.

sea (יָם)" is changed to "Leviathan and the day (יוֹם)."⁵⁶ It has been suggested that the text in Job 3:8 is corrupted, and that יוֹם, "day," should be emended to יָם, "sea," to form a better parallel to Leviathan in verse 8b.⁵⁷ However, the recognition of the standard word pair "the sea and Leviathan" does not imply that the author did not intend to refer to the day. Rather, it suggests that verse 8 deliberately changes the standard word pair "the sea and Leviathan" to "the day and Leviathan" for rhetorical effect.⁵⁸ Fishbane discusses how paronomasia and homonyms are used in magical contexts, and that the word יוֹם generates associations of יָם, and therefore brings another anti-cosmological force into Job's curse.⁵⁹ I agree that יוֹם should be retained, even though I argue that Job's words do not constitute an anti-cosmological curse. The standard word pair "the sea and Leviathan" evokes associations of the sea. The wordplay transfers associations of the danger of the sea, to the day of Job's birth as depicted in Figure 6.2.

Figure 6.2 displays the blend of the input spaces DAY and SEA. They are blended, and even though a day and a sea hardly resemble each other, the blending process creates certain similarities. The search for similarities is induced by the context, which declares that Job is accusing the day of his birth to be the cause of his suffering. The blend highlights the day as a powerful and dangerous enemy that causes destruction and suffering. Job's day of birth is Job's enemy, and Job needs someone powerful to curse it.⁶⁰

---

⁵⁶ The sea and Leviathan appear together in a mythological Aramaic formula from an inscription in Nippur: "I enchant you with the adjuration of Yam, and the spell of Leviathan the serpent" (Habel 1985, 108).

⁵⁷ This was first suggested by Gunkel in 1921, based on a suggestion by Gottfried Schmidt in 1895 (Gunkel and Zimmern 2006, 37–39, 306 n.101). However, this interpretation is not found in any early manuscripts. LXX uses ἡμέραν, "day." Dahood suggests that יוֹם reflects a Phoenician pronunciation of יָם (Dahood 1974, 24). Greenstein argues for this interpretation, but that יוֹם conveys a double entendre (Greenstein 2003, 654–55). Wikander argues against Phoenician origin, although he also interprets it as "sea" (Wikander 2010, 265). The interpretation of יוֹם as the sea is used by Horst 1968, 46–47; Pope 1973, 26, 30; Gordis 1978, 34–35; NRSV; Bibel 2000. Fohrer, however, contends that the change suggested by Gunkel cannot be justified. (Fohrer 1963, 110). It appears that most commentaries from the late 20th century are more inclined to translate it as "day" (Dhorme 1984, 29–30; Habel 1985, 99, 101; Clines 1989, 68, 86; Newsom 1996, 368; Seow 2013, 312, 349–50).

⁵⁸ Habel 1985, 101; Seow 2013, 349–50.

⁵⁹ Fishbane 1971, 161–65.

⁶⁰ Similarly, Seow suggests that the night "is depicted as an evil chaos monster" (Seow 2013, 325).

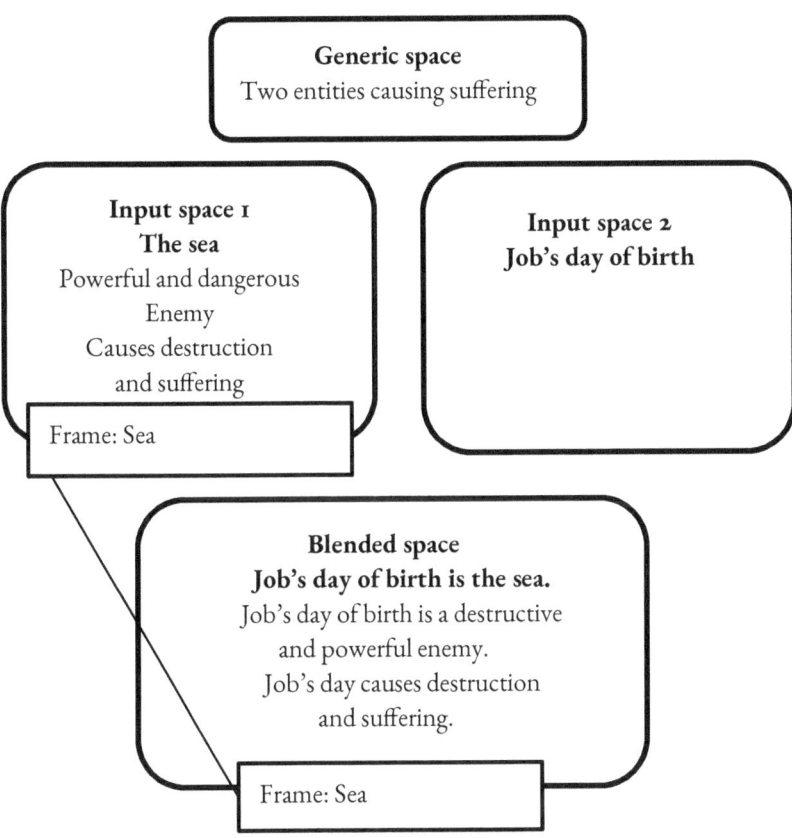

Figure 6.2 The metaphor JOB'S DAY OF BIRTH IS THE SEA.

The wordplay also brings out other associations with the ones who curse days: they become as strong as the enchanters of the sea. Wikander discusses who those who curse Leviathan and the sea might be.[61] He argues that such spells were not practiced, asserting that such spells only occur in mythological texts such as the Enuma Elish, where Marduk and Tiamat use spells as weapons in their battle. References to magicians' power to bind Leviathan and the sea are instead used to threaten enemies. It is not the sea or Leviathan themselves that are used to threaten the enemies, but the power of the magicians.[62] The ones who have the power to bind such a force as Leviathan are the most powerful magicians that could be imagined. Job's

---

[61] Wikander 2010.
[62] Wikander 2010, 266–67.

request for help from such powerful enchanters accentuates how deeply he wants to destroy his day of birth. It is not a request to stir up Leviathan, but a plea for those who control Leviathan to curse Job's day of birth. The expression "ready to awaken Leviathan" has often been interpreted as Job's desire for Leviathan to be unleashed.[63] However, the ones who are said to be ready or skilled to awaken Leviathan in verse 8 are the same people who curse the day. The one who has the power to curse the chaotic forces also has the power to stir them up. Verse 8 can be compared to Job 26:12, where God is said to both stir up (רגע) the sea and crush Rahab (cf. Isa 51:15). Job's goal is not awakening Leviathan but to curse his day of birth with help from the most supreme enchanters. The intention behind Job's fight against his day is not to bring chaos into creation but to defeat it. The day and Leviathan are both seen as destructive forces in Job 3.

My interpretation of verses 4 and 8 aligns with the conclusions of Clines, Pelham, and Schmid: that Job does not wish to destroy all of creation, but only his own existence.[64] Job wants to delete the chaos, misery, and turmoil which are brought upon him. Newsom highlights the word רגז, "turmoil" (vv. 17, 26) in her discussion of Job 3 and claims that the turmoil in Job's life corresponds to chaos in creation. She argues that Job's experience of turmoil in his life leads to his desire to unleash chaos and set Leviathan loose.[65] I would argue the opposite: the turmoil in Job's life makes it clearer that he wants to escape chaos, not unleash it. He believes he can only escape it by erasing the day of his birth from the calendar or through death.

To summarize: Job 3:8 reflects Job's desire to destroy the day of his birth. The word pun between the day and the sea projects associations of the dangerous and destructive sea onto the day of Job's birth, and those who curse the day are seen as the powerful enchanters capable of controlling the sea. Job does not express a desire to unleash Leviathan or chaos, but rather wishes for the enchanters, who are powerful enough to control Leviathan, to curse the day of his birth.

The Night of Job's Conception

Job 3:1 starts by stating that Job opens his mouth and curses his day. In verse 3 we understand that the curse also includes the night he was conceived. Verse 3–9 continues to refer to Job's day of birth and the night of his conception.

---

[63] Fishbane 1971, 158–61; Habel 1985, 108–9; Perdue 1991, 104–6.
[64] Clines 1989, 81; Schmid 2007, 4–5; Pelham 2012, 227–28.
[65] Newsom 2003, 93–96.

Verse 3 describes the announcement of Job's conception. The one who speaks is commonly identified as a personified night.[66] The speaker could also be an indefinite subject, and the verse could be translated as, "The night in which one said, 'A man is conceived.'"[67] In Jer 20:15, a messenger announces the birth, and Jeremiah curses the messenger. Similarly, Job curses the night of his conception, which might also be identified as the messenger that announces the pregnancy. By personifying the night and day, Job can indirectly curse God. Although the explicit targets of the curse are the night and the day, the implicit target is God.

The announcement of the conception in verse 3 is "A man (גֶּבֶר) is conceived!" The word גֶּבֶר, "man," has puzzled interpreters.[68] It is a term never applied to children, only to adult men. Greenstein argues that the expected word should be "a son," but the use of "a man" reflects the depersonalization of the humans involved in Job's birth. Greenstein contrasts Job 3 with Jer 20:14–18, where Jeremiah's mother and father are mentioned, and the unborn Jeremiah is referred to as a son. In contrast, Job is depicted as isolated, with no references to relatives. By using "a man," Job's relationships with a mother, father, or anyone else are obscured. Job 3 refers to the fetus as a man and does not explicitly mention Job's father or mother. Instead, the main characters in Job 3:3–10 are the night of Job's conception and the day of his birth.[69] Seow interprets "a man" as an expression that refers to "any man," and interprets it synonymous with אֱנוֹשׁ, and אָדָם, meaning "human being," and "mortal. He connects this expression with the creation of humans and claims that it refers to an unidentified person or humanity in general.[70] I would argue the opposite, that the word גֶּבֶר, "a man," clearly points out that the embryo is Job. The word גֶּבֶר, "a man" is also used in verse 23 to refer to a man whose way God has hidden. In this context, "a man" refers to Job himself, as it is linked to the explicit mentions of his tears, sighs, and sufferings in verses 24–26. The word גֶּבֶר is used because Job identifies the conceived embryo he once was (v. 3) with the miserable grown man he has become (v. 23). He sees his identity as consistent since the

---

[66] Habel 1985, 107; Clines 1989, 82; Seow 2013, 319; Leonard 2019, 249–50.

[67] LXX: η νυξ, εν η ειπαν, "the night in which they said"; Vulgate: "et nox in qua dictum," "and the night in which it was said."

[68] Dhorme argues that the word גֶּבֶר should be understood as "a male" or "male son," which implies that Job does not identify himself with the embryo because "he is only the embryo which will become גֶּבֶר 'a male' or a בֵּן גֶּבֶר 'male son' (Jer 20:15)" (Dhorme 1984, 25).

[69] Greenstein 2004, 102–3.

[70] Seow 2013, 339–40. Tur-Sinai interprets also גֶּבֶר as "human being" or "person" (Tur-Sinai 1957, 49).

time of conception. To annihilate the embryo would be to annihilate his adult self.[71]

To call the newly conceived embryo "a man" reflects a blend between Job as a grown man who suffers and Job as a fetus. The link, the vital relation, between the two spaces is IDENTITY. Other vital relationships such as TIME and CHANGE are overlooked, and the fetus and the adult Job are seen as the same person.[72] To identify oneself with a younger self is not to create a metaphor per se. Job's identification of the embryo with himself can be seen as a blend with the same organizing frame, the frame THE IDENTITY OF JOB.[73] Job then wants to annihilate the night of his conception so that he never had lived and never became the miserable man he is. Because the newly conceived embryo is explicitly called "a man," it is also possible to interpret the expression "A man is conceived!" as a metaphorical expression in which the target EMBRYO is structured by the source MAN in the metaphor THE EMBRYO IS A MAN. This would highlight that the embryo is seen as a man with life experiences and as a reference to Job as a man who has experienced suffering. The difference if we interpret verse 7 as a blend of identity or as a metaphor is small. Both identify the embryo with Job as a grown miserable man, which causes Job's wish to annihilate the night of his conception. This is coherent with Job's wish in verse 10 that God had shut the doors of the womb at his birth, as well as his question in verse 23 about why God has given life to a man whose way is hidden.

Verse 6 refers to the night of Job's conception and Job's wishes to annihilate this night with darkness. This image is, as discussed above, grounded in the metaphor that displays darkness as a destructive power. Verse 6 continues with the wish: "Let it not rejoice among the days of the year, and let it not come into the number of months." This reflects the idea, discussed earlier, that days and nights are summoned into service and integrated into the already existing calendar of days, nights, months, and years.[74]

Verse 7 expresses the wish that the night of conception had never taken place. It describes the night as barren with no joyful cries associated with it. The cries have been interpreted as cries of sexual pleasure or as the joy typically associated with the announcement of a pregnancy, in accordance with Job 3:3.[75] In either

---

[71] For a discussion of the formation of a fetus in the womb in ancient West Asia and ancient Greece, see chapter 7, pages 191–93.

[72] Fauconnier and Turner 2002, 95–96.

[73] A blend with input spaces with the same organizing frame is called mirror network, see Fauconnier and Turner 2002, 122–26.

[74] See page 151.

[75] See discussion of the joyful cries in Clines 1989, 86.

case, the verse reflects Job's desire to have never been conceived. The wish for a barren night coheres with the wish for the absence of joy, as barrenness is linked to sadness while fertility and childbearing are associated with joy. The shame of infertility in the HB is commonly attributed to women and is often explained as a barren or closed womb.[76] Job does not long for the time he was an embryo, or to the time in a sheltered womb; he wishes instead that he had never been conceived, that his mother's womb had been barren, so that he would never have existed.

To summarize: Job wishes that he had never been conceived and that his conception had never been announced. The night is personified as the messenger who declares "A man (גֶּבֶר) is conceived!" The word גֶּבֶר, "a man," which is typically not used for children, here marks that Job identifies himself with the newly conceived embryo. He desires to undo his conception so that he would never have lived and avoided becoming the grown, miserable man whose path God has hidden (v. 23). Job wants his night to be barren; he never longs to be sheltered in the womb because he sees himself as a miserable man already present in the newly conceived embryo.

Birth Metaphors in Job 3:10–19

In the second part of Job 3, we find explicit references to the womb, and descriptions of Job's wish that he had died in the womb so that his birth had never taken place. Verse 12 also mentions the care of the newborn. These images of the womb and the newborn interact with the imagery of the existence of the dead. The domain of WOMB is blended with the domains of GRAVE and LAND OF THE DEAD. The birth metaphors in Job 3:10–19 also interact with the metaphors of darkness in Job 3:3–9 and the descriptions of Job's life in Job 3:20–26.

Literary Comments

Verse 10 ends the first part of Job's speech, providing the reason for his curse, and introduces the second section, which expresses Job's wish that he had stayed and died in the womb. Verses 10–12 and 16 are exclamations of Job's pain, asking why he did not die at birth, and contain several references to the womb and Job's birth. These verses are followed by descriptions of the existence of the dead (vv. 13–15, 17–19).[77]

---

[76] Gen 30:22–23; 1 Sam 1:5–6.
[77] See above "Literary Structure and Genre," pages 135–37.

Job wishes that he had died "from the womb" in verse 11. The expressions מֵרֶחֶם and מִבֶּטֶן have been understood either as referring to a death "*in* the womb" or "*from* the womb." LXX uses ἐν κοιλίᾳ, "in the womb," in 11a and as ἐκ γαστρὸς, "from the womb," in 11b.[78] Eckstein points out that מֵרֶחֶם in Jer 20:17 is usually translated as "in the womb," depicting Jeremiah's wish that he had died in the womb so that his mother would have been his grave. Here, the intention must be a death in the womb, depicting the womb as enclosing the dead body like a grave. Therefore, Eckstein argues that Job 3:11a also refers to death "in the womb" rather than neonatal death.[79] I would instead suggest that the expression "die from the womb" (מֵרֶחֶם and מִבֶּטֶן) refers to birth complications which can take place before or during birth. It does not necessarily imply that death occurs outside the mother's belly nor exclusively inside the womb before birth. The most dreaded birth complication was the baby being stuck in the birth canal during delivery, described as if the doors of the womb were closed at the time of birth. This type of death is presumably implied in verse 11. The verb in 11b is יצא "go out," which together with מִבֶּטֶן indicates the baby perishing when it *goes out from* the womb, implying death as the baby is being born. This coheres with the description in verse 10, where Job laments that God did not close the doors of the womb when he was born.

In verse 11, two synonymous words for "die" are used, the common מות and the more uncommon גוע. Verse 16 refers to the dead child as נֵפֶל, from the root נפל, "fall." The noun נֵפֶל refers to miscarriages in Ps 58:9 and Eccl 6:3.[80] The verb טמן, "hide," used to describe the hiddenness of the stillborn in verse 16, can also mean "bury," as in Exod 2:12, referring to the act of hiding a dead body in the ground. It is also used in descriptions of hiding valuables or snares in the ground (Josh 7:21; Job 18:10). Verse 21 describes those who long for death with the image of someone digging for "hidden treasures" (מַטְמוֹן), presumably alluding to them digging their own grave. The verb טמן in verse 16 can either refer to the womb or the grave. However, since a grave is never mentioned in Job 3, it likely refers to a stillborn hidden in the womb. This interpretation would also be coherent with

---

[78] Vulgate follows LXX and translates מרחם in 11a "in vulva." LXX uses the synonyms κοιλία and γαστήρ for רֶחֶם and בֶּטֶן. Both Greek words are more general than רֶחֶם, referring to the belly as well as the womb. *LSJ* s.v. "γαστήρ"; "κοιλία."

[79] Eckstein 2019, 388.

[80] The verb נפל is also used in Isa 26:18 with the meaning giving birth.

16b, which describes the baby as dying before it sees the light, before it is born. As I will discuss below, it can also refer to a womb that is blended with the grave.[81]

The term עָמָל, "misery," in verse 10 has connotations of oppression, toil, suffering, anguish, destruction, and mischief.[82] The expression of being born to misery is also used in Jer 20:18, where עָמָל is paralleled with יָגוֹן, "grief." Job 7:3 uses עָמָל to describe Job's life as servitude and his sleeplessness at night. Similarly, Job 3:10 and 20 use עָמָל to describe Job's life.

Knees to Meet Me

Verse 12 describes the care of the newborn Job. Job asks: "Why were there knees to meet me, or breasts for me to suck?" This verse continues Job's wish to have died at birth. He either wishes that no one had cared for him, allowing him to die from neglect as a newborn, or that he had been stillborn, never placed on a lap or at the breast.[83] Given the context of Job's wish to have died from the womb, it is more likely that verse 12 continues this wish rather than expressing a desire to have died from neglect.

It is not specified whose knees and breasts verse 12 refers to. The Hebrew text omits the definite article here, a common feature in poetic texts in the HB. In this context, it may also underscore that it does not matter whose breasts or knees they are: the issue is that Job did not die. The breasts are often seen as an implicit reference to Job's mother, but there have been many suggestions about the interpretation of "knees to meet me." The act of placing a child on one's knees has mainly been interpreted either as an act of care or as a legal act in which the parent legitimizes the child. It has been discussed whether the knees belong to the mother, father, or a midwife, but all of these are speculations.[84] We cannot know if the knees

---

[81] See pages 167–72.

[82] Otzen, "עָמָל," *TDOT* 11:196–201.

[83] Clines argues that it refers to a wish of dying from neglect while, other commentaries only discuss the content of the image but not why Job refers to it (Clines 1989, 90).

[84] Many commentators present the suggestions that it could be either a welcoming act or an act of care, but do not take a stand (Pope 1973, 31; Habel 1985, 110; Seow 2013, 356–57), Fohrer, Horst, Dhorme, and Clines claim that v. 12 most likely refers to the care of the mother who has the child on her knees while breastfeeding (Fohrer 1963, 121; Horst 1968, 49–50; Dhorme 1984, 32; Clines 1989, 90). Hartley argues that it is the father, but that the text is unclear (Hartley 1988, 95). For an investigation of the legal act of putting a child on one's knees in the HB and texts from ancient West Asia, see Viberg 1992, 166–76. Worth noting is that a newborn usually is held close to one's chest rather than placed on one's knees, which could speak in favor of the interpretation of some sort of ritual. It has also been speculated that the knees in v. 12 belong to a midwife who receives the baby (see discussions in Clines 1989, 90; Eckstein 2019, 384).

refer to a symbolic act or an act of care and compassion, or if it is the knees of the mother, the father, or someone else. The act of placing a baby on one's knees was a symbolic act of adoption or legitimizing a child as one's own, as described in texts from ancient West Asia, and possibly reflected in Gen 50:23 and Ruth 4:16. But we cannot be certain whether Job 3:12 portrays such a legal act or not. It is more important to acknowledge that the knees and breasts are unspecified than to speculate who they belong to. For Job, it does not matter who took care of him; the tragedy is that he was born alive, allowing someone to care for him.

Eckstein suggests that verse 12a refers to Job's birth and that the knees are the knees of the mother, which the baby sees during their birth.[85] She argues that if the mother stands in a kneeling position, then the mother's knees would be the first thing the baby sees when it is pushed out of the womb. She points out that the verb קדם implies movement and that this movement was done between delivery and breastfeeding. However, the literary support for the motif of a baby seeing the knees at birth is weak. Her only example is from Hesiod's *Theogony*, where the movement from the womb to the knees is described, but even there it is not clear whose knees the text refers to. Eckstein's interpretation of verse 12a is in line with Job's wishes that he had been enclosed in the womb in verse 10, died at birth in verse 12, and not seen the light at birth in verse 16. Even so, it seems more likely that verse 12 describes someone caring for Job by placing him in the lap and at the breast. It must be noted that metaphors are created from adult experiences at birth, making the idea of imagining a baby seeing their mother's knees at birth a far-fetched association. It is hard to explain how this metaphor would be grounded in actual experiences of childbirth. Furthermore, the image of a baby seeing the knees as a metaphor for birth contradicts the fact that during birth, a baby's face typically faces backward, towards the mother's spine, making it unlikely that the baby would see the knees at that moment. It is less likely that the idea of a baby seeing the knees would be used as a metaphor or a synecdoche for birth than the thought of a baby seeing the light. The light is a strong metaphor of life, and the contrast between a dark enclosed room and the bright daylight is evident. Moreover, there is a shift in the syntax of verse 12 compared to verses 11 and 13–16. In these other verses, Job describes his own birth using the first-person singular, indicating that he is the subject who imagines himself dying in the womb or at birth and lying dead alongside princes. In verse 12, it is instead the knees that are the subject who meet Job. Job is then the object of the clause. This shifts the perspective from Job

---

[85] Eckstein 2019.

as an active subject to the one being cared for. Therefore, I argue that the knees who meet Job in verse 12 are knees of a caring parent who might put him on the knees as a symbolic act.

Job's exclamations in verse 12 echo his overall question of why he did not die at birth. Both Eckstein's interpretation and the more common view of the "knees to meet me" express that Job survived his birth. Verse 12 refers to acts that signify Job's survival: if the baby survives birth, it needs to be breastfed and cared for by parents who acknowledge it as their child. The mentions of the knees and breast-feeding form a counter-image to the death Job longs for. In a late Babylonian incantation, a stillborn is described as someone who never nurses at their mother's breast: "Just as a child of a miscarrying woman does not persist, just as an abortion does not take its mother breast."[86] This line shows that a stillborn child is thought of as a child who never was breastfed. This is also expressed in verse 12, which is a continuation of the question of why Job did not die in the womb (vv. 10–11), because if he had been stillborn, then he would not have been placed at the breast nor had any knees received him. This implies that verse 12 expresses Job's wish that he had died at birth rather than from neglect. Job wishes that he had been dead at birth and thus never breastfed or welcomed into a family. For Job, it does not seem to matter whose breast or whose knees they were. He loathes the fact that he survived and was cared for.

To summarize: Verse 12 presents the care of the newborn Job. The expression "knees to receive me" has been debated. It has mainly been argued that it refers to a legal or welcoming act. It has also been suggested that it depicts a successful birth. Job's exclamation in this verse either expresses a wish that he had died of neglect or that he had died at birth and therefore never been cared for. I argue for the latter.

THE WOMB IS A ROOM OF DARKNESS

In Job 3 there are three references to the womb, one to רֶחֶם and two to בֶּטֶן. In verse 10, the womb is said to be an enclosed space with doors. Job wishes that the doors had been closed at his birth so that he had stayed in the womb. In verse 10a, it is unclear whether Job is blaming God, the night, or the day for not closing these doors. Langton argues that God's involvement in births is challenged in Job 3 and suggests that the night of conception and the day of birth are responsible for Job's existence.[87] However, even if Job is cautious enough not to curse God (2:9), only

---

[86] Stol 2000, 29. Stol's translation based on Hunger's transliteration and German translation of *SpbTU* I no. 44:67.

[87] Langton 2012, 465–66.

the day and the night, he refers to God in verses 20–23, where he asks why life is given to those in misery and to the man whom "God has shut in." It is likely that verse 10 is an implicit accusation of God for not closing the doors, consistent with the way God's role in birth is depicted elsewhere in Job (10:18; 38:8–11, 28–29).

It is also not apparent whether the failure to close the doors in verse 10 takes place at the time of Job's conception or at his birth. In Akkadian birth descriptions, gods and goddesses are depicted as the ones who open the doors of the womb at the time of birth, whereas in the HB, God is generally said to open and close the wombs at the time of conception. However, in Job 38:8–10, God is explicitly described as closing the doors of the womb at birth, and Job 3:10b–12 continues to discuss his death at birth. Therefore, it is likely that the closing of doors in verse 10 also refers to the time of birth.

The contrast between the darkness in the womb and the light outside the womb is used in Job 3. The newborn meets the light when it is born, and Job wishes that he had died at birth and not seen the light (v. 16). Akkadian birth incantations often end their descriptions of births with the images of the baby seeing daylight. This is an expression of the universal metaphor LIFE IS LIGHT, which also is used in verse 20 when Job asks why light and life are given to the one in misery. In verse 10, however, Job says that he saw misery. This changes the expected expression—that the newborn sees light—and instead states that Job saw misery. It implies the metaphor MISERY IS LIGHT. Light is commonly associated with goodness, happiness, and life. For Job, light is associated with misery because his life is misery. Job still equates life with light, but he changes the conventional metaphor HAPPINESS IS LIGHT to MISERY IS LIGHT. The darkness of the womb as a destructive darkness is underscored by how verse 9 and 10 correspond to each other. The night or the day is imagined to be left in the dark and not seeing the light of dawn in verse 9, and Job wishes he had been kept in the darkness of the womb and not born to see misery in verse 10.[88] The references to the night or the day as seeing and the eyelashes of the dawn in verse 9 correlate to Job's eyes in verse 10. Thus, verses 9–10 function as a transition from focusing on the darkness that would destroy the day and night to Job's wish to be enclosed by the destructive darkness of the womb and death (vv. 10–23).

Verses 10–12 and 16 use conventional descriptions of the womb and birth. Greenstein has pointed out that the metaphor THE WOMB IS A ROOM WITH DOORS

---

[88] In verse 9, it is unclear whether "it" refers to the night or the day. It could describe a pitch-dark, never-ending night without stars, or a day perpetually stuck in darkness, never able to begin.

also is found in Akkadian birth incantation.⁸⁹ Langton refers to the motif of being born to the light in Akkadian birth metaphors as an argument for her conclusion that Job 3 is a parodic inversion of an Akkadian birth incantation.⁹⁰ However, the shared metaphors do not necessarily mean that Job 3 imitates and inverts Akkadian birth incantations or that there is a textual dependency between them. Rather, they are shared because they are common conceptualizations of birth, midwifery, and the gods' power to help at birth. If it was a supposed parody or imitation of Akkadian birth incantations, it would have used more specific images from these incantations, such as references to the moon god Sîn, the journey on the sea, or a cow giving birth. I also disagree with Langton's view that Job searches for control and not for death by cursing the day of his birth. The wish for dying in the womb in verses 10–12 is paired with the descriptions of death in verses 13–15 and 17–19. The longing for death is also stated in verse 21, which is preceded by the exclamation of why life is given to the ones living in misery (v. 20). Job's life is misery and only death can release him from his suffering.

To summarize: The womb is depicted as a dark room with doors that could be opened and closed at birth. This is a conventional way of describing the womb in Akkadian birth metaphors. Furthermore, the motif of the newborn seeing the light is part of the image in verses 10, 16, and 20, which are grounded in the metaphor LIFE IS LIGHT. However, neither light nor life are valued as good to Job and in verse 10, the conventional metaphor HAPPINESS IS LIGHT is changed to MISERY IS LIGHT. Job longs for the destructive darkness in the womb. His wishes that he had stayed in the womb reflect the birth complication of being stuck in the womb, which would have killed him.

The Womb and Death

The womb and the grave, the unborn and the dead, are linked together by being contrasts to one another. Therefore, we easily associate one of the concepts with its counterpart, as I have discussed in my previous chapter "Birth Metaphors in Job 1."⁹¹ There is a strong connection between the womb an death in Job 3. Job wants to stay in the womb and die there, and the domain of the WOMB is blended with the domains of GRAVE and LAND OF THE DEAD.

---

[89] Greenstein 2017, 148–49. In my chapter on Job 38, I also demonstrate how Job 38 employs other metaphors that appear in these incantations.

[90] Langton 2012.

[91] See pages 119–24.

The Womb and the Grave of a Stillborn

Job expresses a wish that he had been a miscarriage or died at birth. He describes his thoughts of how he then would be among the dead. In Job 10:19, Job wishes that he had been carried immediately from the womb to the grave. Ecclesiastes 6:3 states that a stillborn baby is better off than an old man who is not buried, which may imply that stillborn babies are buried. These are the only references in the HB that suggest that stillborn babies were buried. In Mesopotamia, stillborn babies, particularly those who were full-term and died late in pregnancy, were buried with the belief that these infants entered the land of the dead. Flynn refers to the belief in Mesopotamia that an unburied preborn or newborn child could turn into an evil demon. Therefore, a stillborn baby was buried rather than simply discarded. She also gives an example from Gilgamesh, Enkidu and Netherworld, which depicts a stillborn in the land of dead. This example is from Stol, who explains that the infants in the land of the dead are full term babies.[92] Archaeologists have discovered that in Canaan, dead infants were commonly placed in household pots and buried under the family house. The pots could also be buried in graves, caves, or tombs. The jars were not special burial jars but common household pots.[93] The infants were laid in a fetal position in the jars, and the similarities between the womb with a child and the pot with a dead infant have led to suggestions that this custom reflects a belief that the baby, at death, returns to a womb and is reborn.[94] Pots are used as metaphors for wombs in ancient West Asian texts, and infants buried in pots were laid in the fetal position, though it remains unclear whether this burial practice directly reflects a belief in rebirth or the idea of the baby returning to a womb. In my chapter on birth metaphors in the HB, I discussed how the domain of WOMB can be blended with the domains of GRAVE and DEATH in the HB. These images do not portray the womb at death as a comforting place for rebirth.[95]

---

[92] Flynn 2018, 124; Stol 2000, 32.

[93] Garroway 2014, 218–44; Flynn 2018, 133–34.

[94] Garroway suggests this as a probable conclusion, arguing that many cultures perceive a connection between the tomb and the womb. She also points out that it is a cross-cultural phenomenon to bury infants under the floor to encourage them to be reborn and return to the family (Garroway 2014, 239–44).

[95] See chapter 3, pages 85–88.

THE WOMB IS A GRAVE AND THE LAND OF THE DEAD

Job 3:11, 16 depicts the womb as a container for a dead body. Death is the implication of verse 10, as a baby stuck in the womb will die. Job's first wish is that he had never been conceived or born at all (vv. 3–9); his second, that he had died in or from the womb (vv. 10–19); and his third, that as a grown man, he might find his grave to escape the miseries of life (vv. 20–26). Job never expresses a desire to return to the womb, as suggested by van der Zwan and Langton.[96] Instead, Job wishes that he had never left the womb. However, since he was born, his suffering now makes him long for death as the only escape from his miseries (v. 21–22). Job's wish that he had stayed in the womb is not a longing for unification with his mother or God, but a wish that he had been dead and out of reach of God (cf. Job 14:13).

The womb and death are undoubtedly associated with each other in Job 3. Verse 10 imagines Job being stuck in the womb. Verse 11 expresses a wish to die "from the womb." Verse 16 describes a miscarriage as hidden, presumably in the womb, but with associations of a grave. Job 3:10–19 uses the womb as the space where death takes place, and the dead body is hidden. The womb and the grave share the image schema CONTAINMENT. The womb is an enclosed space just as the grave, they both are imagined as dark, and both hide bodies inside them. In Job 3, the womb is described as a grave, but the grave is not described as a womb. The grave is not even mentioned in verses 10–19. The images of Job's death in the womb (vv. 10–12 and 16) are followed by descriptions of the existence of the dead. The expression כִּי־עַתָּה, "then now" or "surely then," which introduces the description of the existence of the dead in the grave in verses 13–15, refers back to the references of the death in or from the womb in verses 10–12. The adverb שָׁם, "there" or "then," in the beginning of verse 17, refers back to the description of the hidden stillborn who never sees light in verse 16. The womb is the only place where the dead bodies are enclosed in Job 3:10–19. The metaphor THE WOMB IS A GRAVE is described below in Figure 6.3. Shared characteristics between the input spaces are marked in red, while conflicting ones are marked in blue and italicized.

---

[96] van der Zwan 2019a, 1–5, 9–13; Langton 2012, 466–67.

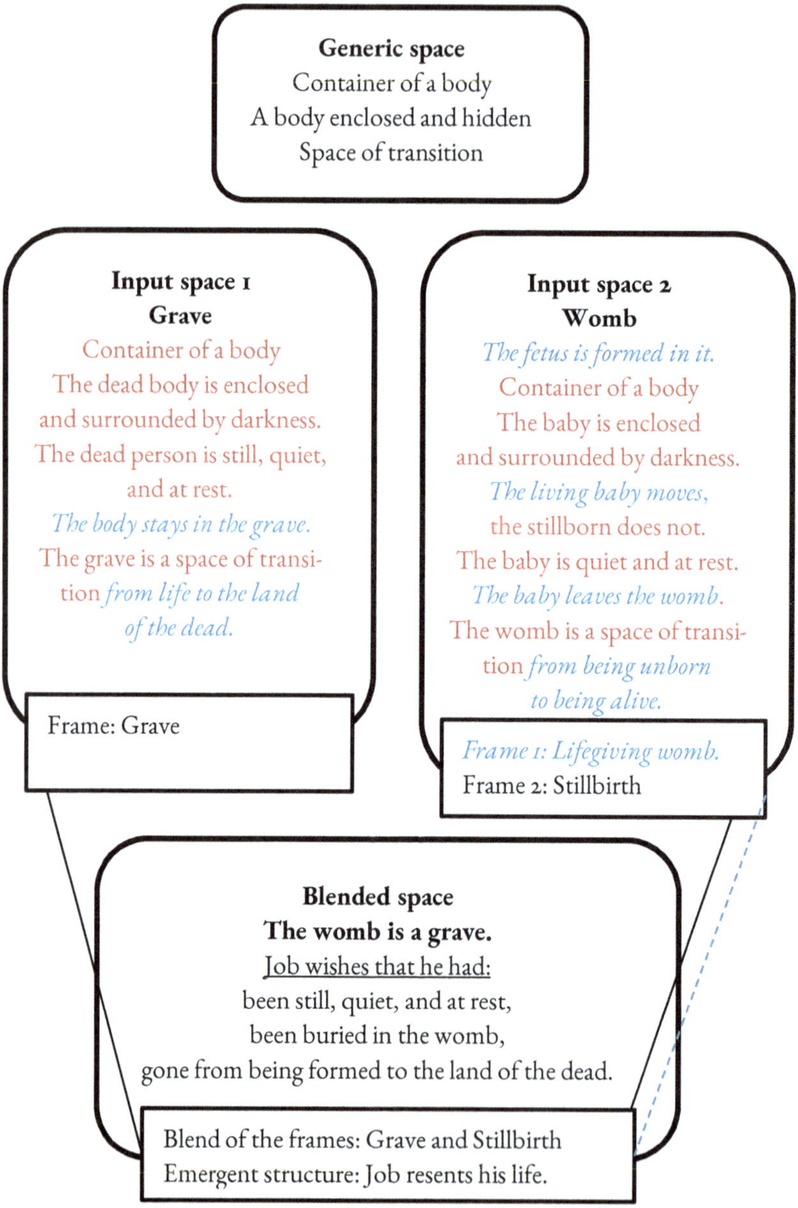

Generic space
Container of a body
A body enclosed and hidden
Space of transition

Input space 1
Grave
Container of a body
The dead body is enclosed
and surrounded by darkness.
The dead person is still, quiet,
and at rest.
The body stays in the grave.
The grave is a space of transition *from life to the land of the dead.*

Frame: Grave

Input space 2
Womb
The fetus is formed in it.
Container of a body
The baby is enclosed
and surrounded by darkness.
*The living baby moves,
the stillborn does not.*
The baby is quiet and at rest.
The baby leaves the womb.
The womb is a space of transition *from being unborn to being alive.*

Frame 1: Lifegiving womb.
Frame 2: Stillbirth

Blended space
The womb is a grave.
<u>Job wishes that he had:</u>
been still, quiet, and at rest,
been buried in the womb,
gone from being formed to the land of the dead.

Blend of the frames: Grave and Stillbirth
Emergent structure: Job resents his life.

Figure 6.3 The metaphor THE WOMB IS A GRAVE. Shared characteristics are in red and colliding ones in blue and italicized.

Birth Metaphors in Job 3:10–19   171

The metaphor WOMB IS A GRAVE in Job 3 is constructed as a double-scope network where the input space WOMB is the target, and the input space GRAVE is the source. They share the structure of a body enclosed and hidden in a container. WOMB has two different organizing frames. Frame 1 describes a healthy pregnancy, where the baby is formed, grows inside the womb, and is eventually born into life. This frame represents Job's (and the typical) experience of birth. Frame 2 is the frame of a stillborn child, which matches Job's wish that he had died hidden in the womb and never been brought into the world. The frame GRAVE depicts someone who dies, and how the body then is placed in a grave from where the dead never return. The grave is also seen as a place of transition to the land of the dead. The frame GRAVE dominates the blend. It corresponds and highlights the frame STILLBIRTH and projects the idea that Job never has to leave the womb (not even as a dead fetus) and how he wants the womb to serve as a transition to the land of the dead. Parts of the frame STILLBIRTH are also projected to the blend. This frame contains both the formation of a fetus inside the womb and their death. This is important in Job's arguments. Job wishes that he had died in the womb, remaining in the same space where he was formed, and that he had never been born or lived. These features of the frame of STILLBIRTH are projected to the frame of the blend. The frame A LIFE-GIVING WOMB also plays a role in the blend, even if it is the frame of the womb STILLBIRTH that is blended with the frame GRAVE in the blend. The collision between the frames A LIFE-GIVING WOMB and GRAVE leads to the emergent structure of the blend. The womb is supposed to be lifegiving and the antonym of the grave, but Job wishes it to be the space of death. This collision accentuates the despair of Job, and that Job resents his life. It forms an emergent structure of the blend which uses our intuition of wishing for a healthy pregnancy and successful birth. When someone wishes for the opposite, something must be terribly wrong.

The blending schema of the metaphor THE WOMB IS A GRAVE in Figure 6.3 refers to how the womb is depicted in Job 3:10–19. The descriptions in verses 10–11, 16 refer explicitly to the womb; however, verse 13 may also be explained within the domain of WOMB. If verse 13 is interpreted as derived from the domain of WOMB it depicts the baby as sleeping, being quiet, and at rest inside the womb. However, these terms are also conventional metaphors of the dead who are buried in graves, so verse 13 is also applicable to a dead person. Verse 13 can then describe both the dead body in the grave and baby in the womb. It serves as a literary transition from describing Job's death in the womb to describing the dead in the grave. Verses 14–15 continue the description of verse 13 and add that kings and princes will also be at rest together with Job in the womb-grave. Verses 17–19 describe an existence of the dead that is more applicable to the land of the dead than to the grave. The features of rest and quietness in verse 13 may trigger these descriptions of the land of the dead in verses 17–19, which focus on a manifestation of what the rest and quietness may be: no slavery, not hearing the voice of the oppressor, and no turmoil. Verses 10–15 refer then to the domains of WOMB and GRAVE and the metaphor THE WOMB IS A GRAVE, while verses 16–19 rather refer to the domains of WOMB and THE LAND OF THE DEAD and the metaphor THE WOMB IS THE LAND OF THE DEAD. The metaphor THE WOMB IS THE LAND OF THE DEAD is an elaboration of the metaphor THE WOMB IS A GRAVE. As I point out in Figure 6.3, the grave is a transitory place, where the dead are laid, but at the same time the dead are believed to be in the netherworld, in Sheol. This corresponds to the fact that humans are said to be created in both the womb and in the depths of the earth (Ps 139:13–15). The idea that fetuses are formed in the netherworld where Sheol is also situated supports the blend between the womb and the grave, and between the womb and the land of the dead. The description of the grave and the land of the dead underscores the belief that all humans are equal in death. Job would be alongside kings and princes in verses 14–15, and verse 19 highlights the equality between the small and the great, servants and masters. This is a shared characteristic with the womb in the Book of Job. In Job 31:13–15, Job declares that all humans are created in a womb by the same Creator, using this as a reason to express solidarity with others (cf. Prov 22:2). Therefore, the description of equality easily fits in a blend of the womb and the land of the dead.

To summarize: Job 3:10–15 contains the metaphor THE WOMB IS A GRAVE. It is a double-scope blend, but it is mainly structured by the frame GRAVE, which also corresponds to the frame STILLBIRTH. Job wishes that he would remain in the womb where he was created, and that it would have transferred him directly to the land of the dead. The description of Job in the womb-grave describes him as sleeping, at rest, and silent (vv. 10–15). Job also describes his death in the womb as a release from oppression (vv. 16–19). Verses 16–19 are best understood as a blend of THE WOMB and the LAND OF THE DEAD into the metaphor THE WOMB IS THE LAND OF THE DEAD. Both this metaphor and the metaphor THE WOMB IS A GRAVE use the collision between the frames A LIFE-GIVING WOMB and DEATH to highlight Job's despair and that he resents life.

DEATH IS NEGATION OF LIFE

Job 3:10–19 describes both the womb (vv. 10–12, 16) and the existence of death (vv. 13–15, 17–19). The metaphors THE WOMB IS A GRAVE and THE WOMB IS THE LAND OF THE DEAD illustrate what Job's existence might have been if he had died in the womb. The descriptions of death in verses 13–15, 17–19 mirror the harsh reality of Job's life. They negate Job's experiences in a life of oppression, hardship, and turmoil (vv. 20–26). The final verse of Job 3, verse 26, summarizes what Job's life has turned out to be: "I am not at ease. I am not at peace. I am not at rest, but turmoil comes." The antonymic state of Job's life in verses 13–15, 17–19 can be explained by a counterfactual blend in which the existence of the dead is understood as NEGATION OF JOB'S LIFE. Below follows an overview of how verses 10–26 depict Job's life, and how they correspond to the description of Job's existence if he died in the womb.

Job's life	Description of death
Misery (עָמָל,) (vv. 10, 20)	No misery (implied in v. 10)
God has shut in Job (v. 23)	Prisoners are at ease (v. 18)
	Slaves are free (v.19)
Sigh (אֲנָחָה) and screaming (שְׁאָגָה) (v. 24)	Rejoicing (גִּיל, שָׂמֵחַ) (v. 22)
Turmoil (רֹגֶז) (v. 26)	The wicked cease to turmoil (רֹגֶז) (v. 17)
Shake of fear (פַּחַד) (v. 25)	At ease, no anxiety (שַׁאֲנָן) (v. 18))
Not at ease (לֹא+שׁלה) (v. 26)	
No rest (לֹא+נוח) (v. 26)	Rest (נוח) (vv. 13, 17)
Not quiet, not at peace (לֹא+שׁקט) (v. 26)	Quiet, at peace (שׁקט) (v. 13);
	Not hearing one's oppressor's voice (v.18).

Many of the characteristics of Job's life are explicitly negated in descriptions of death. Job refers to his life as רֹגֶז, "turmoil" (v. 26) and in the description of death it has ceased (v. 17). The verbs שׁקט, "be quiet," "at peace" (vv. 13, 26) and נוח, "rest" (vv. 17, 26) are used in the description of death and with negations in references to Job's life. Rest and to be at ease are also described in other terms, such as שַׁאֲנָן and שׁלה. The verb שַׁאֲנָן refers to the prisoners at ease and שׁלה is negated in the description of Job's miserable life in verse 26. Other contrasts are not explicitly stated but are implied, as in verse 10, which highlights the misery of being born and, by implication, suggests that there is no misery in the womb-grave. The use of contrasting word pairs and negations throughout Job 3 suggests that the womb-grave represents a place where all the hardships of life come to an end. It is envisioned as a refuge from all the difficulties of life.

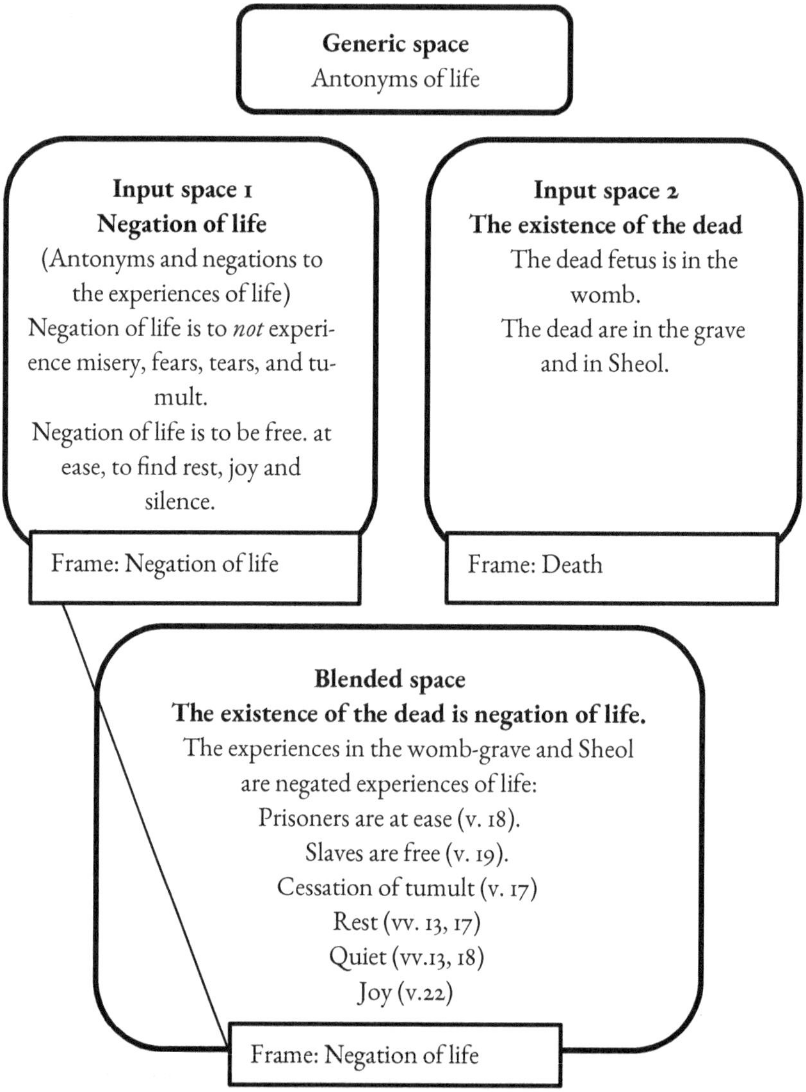

Generic space
Antonyms of life

Input space 1
Negation of life
(Antonyms and negations to the experiences of life)
Negation of life is to *not* experience misery, fears, tears, and tumult.
Negation of life is to be free. at ease, to find rest, joy and silence.

Frame: Negation of life

Input space 2
The existence of the dead
The dead fetus is in the womb.
The dead are in the grave and in Sheol.

Frame: Death

Blended space
The existence of the dead is negation of life.
The experiences in the womb-grave and Sheol are negated experiences of life:
Prisoners are at ease (v. 18).
Slaves are free (v. 19).
Cessation of tumult (v. 17)
Rest (vv. 13, 17)
Quiet (vv.13, 18)
Joy (v.22)

Frame: Negation of life

Figure 6.4 *The counterfactual blend* THE EXISTENCE OF THE DEAD IS NEGATION OF LIFE.

Figure 6.4 displays the counterfactual blend THE EXISTENCE OF THE DEAD IS NEGATION OF LIFE. Life experiences are negated and then projected to the blend. The content of what we may experience in death is unknown and must be filled and structured by experiences or negated experiences from life.[97] Similarly to how Figure 5.1 displays death as negation of birth, this blend presents death as the negation of life. The understanding of death in negated terms of life involves a metaphorical step, as death is not a literal negation of life. The metaphor DEATH IS NEGATION OF LIFE uses the NEGATED TERMS OF EXPERIENCES OF LIFE to structure the abstract domain of DEATH.

Job 3 switches the target domains of LIFE and DEATH compared to conventional metaphors of death and life. HARDSHIP is here linked with LIFE while LIBERATION is connected to DEATH. The description of life as hardship and death as liberation mirror Job's desire to escape the turmoil and misery in life.

To summarize: Death is described as a place of rest, silence, and liberation from hardship in Job 3: 13–15 and 17–19. The description of the existence of the dead is a counter-image to Job's life which contains misery, hardship, turmoil, and oppression. This is best understood by a counterfactual blend in which the domain of THE EXISTENCE OF THE DEAD is structured and filled with content from NEGATED EXPERIENCES OF LIFE.

Summary and Conclusions

This chapter presents a close investigation of the birth metaphors in Job 3. Blending theory has been used to evaluate former research and as a tool to explore how the domain of BIRTH interacts with other domains such as the domains of CREATION, LIGHT, LIFE, DARKNESS, DEATH, and HARDSHIP.

I have demonstrated that the target of the curse is Job's day of birth and night of conception. The curse does not intend to destroy creation itself. If associations of the order of creation are used, then it is to enforce the destruction of Job's day of birth. The assumed links between God's act of creation in Gen 1–2:4a and Job 3 are weak and rely primarily on the similarity between the expression "let it be darkness!" and "let it be light!" I have presented three ways to interpret the expression "let it be darkness!" The first interpretation is based on the presumption that the words "let it be darkness!" allude to the first day in creation and the words "let it be light!" and that Job 3:4 uses the language of creation to describe the

---

[97] Tromp's investigation into how death is conceptualized demonstrates that death is described in negative terms of life (Tromp 1969, 187–96).

destruction of Job's day of birth. This creates a blend where JOB'S DAY OF BIRTH is the target and THE FIRST DAY OF CREATION is the source in the metaphor DESTRUCTION OF JOB'S DAY OF BIRTH IS DESTRUCTION OF THE FIRST DAY OF CREATION. It is not that Job uses his day of birth to describe the destruction of creation as Fishbane and others have claimed. Second, the expression "let it be light!" and "let it be darkness!" are understood within the domain of DAYS, going back to the idea that all days are called into service by God and that God initiates every day by commanding light upon them. When Job instead says, "let it be darkness!" he wishes that his day of birth should be kept in darkness and God should not seek it. Third, the phrase "let it be darkness!" is understood through the metaphor DESTRUCTION IS DARKNESS, suggesting that the darkness is used as a destructive force to annihilate Job's day of birth.

Job's aversion to his day of birth is emphasized in Job 3:8 where he asks the ones who curse days and have the power to awaken Leviathan to curse his day of birth. The word pun that changes the standard word pair "the sea and Leviathan" to "the day and Leviathan" accentuates that Job sees in his day of birth characteristics of the sea such as a destructive, dangerous, and fear-inducing enemy. Job 3:8 implies that Job is seeking the ones capable of invoking the sea and Leviathan to curse his day of birth, rather than desiring to unleash Leviathan and chaos.

The metaphors of light, darkness, hardship, and death interact with the metaphors of the womb and birth. I have shown how Job 3 uses conventional metaphors such as LIFE IS LIGHT and DEATH AND DESTRUCTION ARE DARKNESS, but that Job longs for death and, therefore, he values death and darkness as good things while light and life relate to his misery. The reason why he wants to destroy his day of birth and be dead is that his life is filled with misery and turmoil.

Job does not wish to return to the womb; he wants to die. The womb is only a protective shelter from life because it causes death. Job identifies himself with the newly conceived embryo and calls it a man (גֶּבֶר). The metaphor THE EMBRYO IS A MAN implies that the embryo is already seen as the adult Job, who experiences suffering. Therefore, it would have been better if he never had been conceived. Verse 12 expresses Job's wish that he had died before any caretaker had placed him on their knees or breastfed him. This is coherent with his wish that he had died in the womb.

Several interpreters have pointed out that the womb and the tomb are merged in Job 3. I have shown how these networks are constructed. THE WOMB is depicted as A GRAVE in the metaphor THE WOMB IS A GRAVE. Both a grave and a womb are enclosed spaces containing bodies. The existence in the womb-grave is described in verses 10–15. It begins with Job's wish that he had died in the womb, continues by describing how he then would be at rest, sleeping, and being together with kings and princes. Verse 16 once again describes the death of Job inside the womb, which continues in verses 17–19 by describing a place beyond the womb and the grave, where the imprisoned are freed and the oppressed are liberated. The metaphor in verses 16–19 is best understood as THE WOMB IS THE LAND OF THE DEAD which can be said to be an elaboration of the metaphor the WOMB IS A GRAVE. The metaphors are double-scope blends where the contrast between the womb, as the source of life, and death, as the end of life, generates an emergent structure, underscoring Job's despair, and strong wish to not be alive.

Job 3 uses conventional metaphors when it comes to the physical state of the dead as sleeping and lying down, but the conventional metaphors which describe death as hardship and as exile are changed. The expressions used to describe Job's life are commonly used as depictions of hardship, exile, and death. The descriptions of death in Job 3 form a counter-image to Job's hardship in life. Job's life is filled with misery, fears, tears, and turmoil, and he refers to death in terms of being free, at ease, to find rest and silence. This can be explained in a blending schema of counterfactual blend displaying the metaphor DEATH IS NEGATION OF LIFE.

Job 3 is a lament. The curse of his birth in the past accentuates his hopelessness and pain. All the metaphors I have analyzed in this chapter underscore Job's misery and his wish of never having been born into life.

7. Birth Metaphors in Job 10

Job 10 is part of Job's third speech, in which he seeks to bring God to court. Job perceives his suffering as divine punishment for a crime he did not commit. He wishes that God would declare him innocent, and Job accuses God instead of being the true criminal. He appeals to God to remember that God has created him, and that Job only is a mortal. The birth metaphors are part of Job's dispute with God. In Job 10, two passages refer to the domain of BIRTH. In the first, Job describes how God once formed him and cared for him in the womb (vv. 8–12) in contrast to how God now crushes him. This passage questions why God destroys the work of God's hand. It contains the most extensive description in the HB of how a human is formed in the womb using several metaphors of craftsmanship. In the second passage, Job asks why God brought him out of the womb and wishes that he had died in the womb and been carried from the womb to the grave (vv. 18–19). These two passages are analyzed in this chapter, exploring the metaphors related to Job's formation and birth and the characteristics of Job and God they highlight. The exploration will both concern the details of the specific metaphors, and how they are used together to contribute to Job's overall argument in Job 10, and whether Job's attitude toward his birth has changed since Job 3.

Earlier Interpretations

Job 10:8–12 has commonly been interpreted as containing four different metaphors, displaying how God forms Job in the womb. The source domains of the metaphors have been identified as POTTERY MAKING, CHEESEMAKING, DRESSING, and WEAVING. The references to God as potter and humans as clay are conventional metaphors in the HB. The image of God as the one who has intertwined (סכך) a human is also present in Ps 139:13. The cheesemaking metaphor does not occur elsewhere in the HB. It is usually explained by referring to Aristotle (384–322 BCE), who uses the metaphor of cheesemaking in the depiction of fetal formation. Gordis argues that the metaphors in Job 10:9–11 describe fetal development in the womb: First the fetus is conceived (cheese metaphor, v. 10), then the fetus receives structure and the body parts are formed (dressing and weaving metaphors, v. 11), and at birth it receives life and the breath of God (v. 12).[1] Frevel discusses the analogy between cheesemaking and gestation, drawing parallels between semen and milk, and between cheese and a newborn baby.[2] Van Hecke challenges the common interpretation of verse 11b and the word סכך as referring to the domain of WEAVING and instead suggests it refers to the domain of CASTING METAL. This interpretation is integral to his discussion of metaphors in Job, where he argues that a "healthy existence" is depicted through metaphors of solidity, while the loss of strength is conveyed through metaphors of fluidification.[3] Vall claims that the description of Job's formation accentuates the idea that God has a purpose for Job. A vessel, cheese, and a human are not created for nothing. Vall argues that God's actions in destroying Job are inappropriate, as the futility of Job's destruction does not align with the purposeful nature of his formation.[4] Vall explains that Job prefers prenatal death over adult death, concluding that it is better not to have lived at all than to live a disrupted life. A complete life is marked by enjoying the fruits of one's labor.[5]

The relationship with Ps 139 illuminates how the formation of oneself in the womb can be employed in a plea to God. Both Brown and Kynes discuss how God's formation of a human implies intimate knowledge of the one created. The psalmist believes that God's omniscience and omnipresence will affirm the psalmist's righteousness and prompt God to listen to the appeal to kill the wicked (vv. 19–22). Similarly, the references to Job's formation are used to argue that God knows Job is innocent, thereby making God's punitive acts towards Job unjust. Kynes point out that the psalmist praises God's omnipresence and omniscience, whereas Job sees them as oppressive. Both Brown and Kynes argue that Job 10 alludes to Ps 139.[6]

Job 10:18–19 has not received as much attention as the formation metaphors in 10:8–12. Job's wish that he had died in the womb and been carried directly from the womb to the grave, as expressed in these verses, is often interpreted as a continuation of his lament in Job 3 and as an expression of the womb being imagined as a grave. Commentaries frequently note that Job now directly accuses God,

---

[1] Gordis 1978, 522 (special n. 12). Many commentators follow Gordis, including Habel 1985, 199; Hartley 1988, 187; Balentine 2006, 174.
[2] Frevel 2016, 303–4.
[3] Van Hecke 2010; Van Hecke 2011.
[4] Vall 1993, 229–32.
[5] Vall 1993, 250–56.
[6] Brown 2000, 107–24; Kynes 2012, 108–12.

holding God responsible for Job's birth. The expression מִבֶּטֶן לַקֶּבֶר, "from the womb to the grave," is often interpreted as linking, or even blending, the concepts of the grave and the womb together. Vall argues that there is a stronger connection between the womb and the grave in Job 10:18–19 than in Job 3, because they are explicitly linked by a linguistic expression.[7] Van der Zwan suggests that Job here regards the womb as a grave. He also argues that 10:18 is an example of how Job values the womb negatively.[8] Pelham contends that both the womb and the grave are seen as spaces where Job can hide from God.[9] These interpretations raise the question of whether and how the womb relates to death, and if there is a development of Job's arguments in Job 3.

Birth Metaphors in Job 10:8–12

The formation of Job is described by different metaphors in Job 10:8–12. Earlier interpretations have raised broader questions such as how these metaphors relate to gestation or how they are part of Job's defense of his innocence. Other questions have been more specific, such as which metaphors the particular word סכך, "intertwine," generates or the specific connection between cheesemaking and gestation. I will engage with these and similar questions throughout my detailed analysis, ending in a discussion on how the various metaphors interact.

Text and Translation of Job 10:8–12

8	יָדֶיךָ עִצְּבוּנִי	Your hands formed me
	וַיַּעֲשׂוּנִי יַחַד סָבִיב	and put me together all around,
	וַתְּבַלְּעֵנִי	but (now) you destroy me.
9	זְכָר־נָא כִּי־כַחֹמֶר עֲשִׂיתָנִי	Remember that you made me like clay,
	וְאֶל־עָפָר תְּשִׁיבֵנִי	and (now) you turn me back to dust again.
10	הֲלֹא כֶחָלָב תַּתִּיכֵנִי	Did you not pour me out like milk
	וְכַגְּבִנָּה תַּקְפִּיאֵנִי	and curdle me like cheese?
11	עוֹר וּבָשָׂר תַּלְבִּישֵׁנִי	With skin and flesh, you clothed me
	וּבַעֲצָמוֹת וְגִידִים תְּסֹכְכֵנִי	and with bones and sinews, you intertwined me.
12	חַיִּים וָחֶסֶד עָשִׂיתָ עִמָּדִי	Life and loyalty you made me with.
	וּפְקֻדָּתְךָ שָׁמְרָה רוּחִי	Your supervision protected my spirit.

---

[7] Vall 1993, 49–50.
[8] van der Zwan 2019a, 5.
[9] Pelham 2012, 158–59.

Literary Structure and Comments

Job 10:8–12 is part of Job's third speech in Job 9–10. In these chapters, Job expresses his wish to confront God in court for the first time, accusing God of being unreliable, a criminal, and a creator who has turned the order of creation upside down. Verse 8 introduces the section of verses 8–12 and sets the theme by stating that God's hands have formed Job, but now God destroys him. God's hands are emphasized, and they are also mentioned in Job 10:3, 7. Job questions why God oppresses "the toil of your hands" in verse 3, and in verse 7 he states that there is no one who can deliver from God's hands. Verses 8 and 9 refer to both the formation and the destruction of Job, while verses 10–12 focus solely on his formation. The metaphors of crafting pottery, cheesemaking, dressing, and intertwining offer various perspectives on how God made Job. The word עשׂה, "make," "create," is used in verses 8, 9, and 12, and the repetition accentuates that God is the maker of Job.[10]

The formation of Job is a work of shaping and putting him together. It is expressed by the metaphors, but also in the expression יַחַד סָבִיב, "together all around," in verse 8. This expression has various translations, and there are differing views on whether it belongs to the verb עשׂה or the verb בלע, or if סָבִיב should be emended to the verb סבב, "turn."[11] Dhorme and Habel link יַחַד סָבִיב to בלע and translate it "destroy me utterly/totally."[12] Clines points out that the expression יַחַד סָבִיב is separated from בלע with a *waw*. I agree with Clines that the *waw* indicates that it should not be linked with בלע, but not with his conclusion that it should be emended to the verb סבב "turn" and belong to verse 8b. Instead, I connect it with the verb עשׂה and translate וַיְעַשּׂוּנִי יַחַד סָבִיב, "put me together all around." A recurring idea in Job 10:8–11 is that God creates by bringing different parts together in a solidification process. The description of God putting Job together on all sides thus serves as an appropriate introduction to verses 9–12. It also corresponds to Job 1:10, which states that God protects Job from all sides (מִסָּבִיב). Verses 9–11 use various metaphors to develop the idea of how God's hands have created Job. These are contrasted by descriptions of God's destruction (vv. 8–9). Verses 13–17 further elaborate on Job's experience of how God destroys, watches, hunts, and attacks him. Job's intense misery culminates in his wish that he had died in the womb and been carried directly from the womb to the grave (vv. 18–19).

---

[10] *HALOT*, s.v. "עשׂה I."
[11] For various emendations of סָבִיב, see Clines 1989, 221.
[12] Dhorme 1984, 148; Habel 1985, 181.

GOD IS A HANDCRAFTER

The metaphors in Job 10:8–12 portray God as a handcrafter. They are introduced in verse 8, where God is said to have created Job with God's own hands. The expression "the work of God's hands" is used in the HB to both express the value of God's creation and to depict God's superiority over it (Pss 19:2; 95:5). References to the work of God's hand usually contain the general noun for work, מַעֲשֵׂה, but verse 3 uses the expression יְגִיעַ כַּפֶּיךָ, "the toil of your hands." The word יְגִיעַ, "toil," suggests that God's creation of a human is hard work, and the subsequent metaphors in verses 9–11 vividly depict this effort. The questions of whether God has eyes or is like a human in verses 4–5 are answered by the description of God as the creator in verses 8–12. These verses highlight the inequality between God and Job. God is not a human: God is the creator, intimately engaged in the creation of Job. Consequently, as argued by Kynes and Brown, God knows Job and that Job is innocent.[13] The questions asked are: If God knows that Job is blameless, then why is God bringing suffering upon him? Why does the creator destroy what has been created?

References to God's involvement in births and in the formation of humans are used in pleas to God (Pss 22:10–12; 71:2–6; Isa 64:7–8). God is often asked to remember God's mercy, former relationships, the transience of human life, and the covenant (Exod 32:13; Job 7:7; Pss 25:6; 89:48). Job asks God in Job 10:9 to remember that God has made Job like clay. Job's reference to how God formed him serves as a plea, with metaphors underscoring God's responsibility as Job's creator, emphasizing that God should therefore take care of him.

Formation in the Womb

There are no explicit references to the location of Job's formation in Job 10:8–12; the focus is on God's acts as the maker of Job. Nonetheless, I will argue that these descriptions implicitly refer to the womb as the location of Job's formation. Some of the metaphors used in Job 10:9–11 are used in the context of birth elsewhere in the HB. The metaphor of God as the potter is combined with metaphors of God as the begetter and as the one giving birth in Isa 45:9–10. Psalm 139:13 uses the intertwining metaphor to describe the formation in the womb. The metaphor of milk and cheese, as I will argue, depicts the formation of a fetus as a coagulation of semen, suggesting a formation process in the womb. This metaphor is similar to the imagery in Job 38:28–29, which describes a coagulation process in the womb

---

[13] Brown 2000, 107–24; Kynes 2012, 108–12.

to depict the solidification of water into ice. There are two references to the womb (רֶחֶם, בֶּטֶן) in Job 10:18–19, and it is said that Job would have avoided his misery if God had not brought him out of the womb or if he had never lived. This implies that Job's misery begins with his birth, contrasting his time in the womb with his life afterward. Verses 8–12 describe the time in the womb as a period when God treated Job well, associating it with protection, loyalty, and life.

FORMATION OF JOB IS POTTERY MAKING

Job 10:9 describes first the formation of Job and then his destruction. God is seen as the potter and Job as the clay, which is formed, dried, and destroyed. These are common metaphors in the HB, and the metaphor HUMANS ARE CREATED OF CLAY is a cross-cultural metaphor. Myths of gods creating humans or other gods out of clay are found worldwide. Metaphors of pottery are often combined with references to procreation. For instance, in the Atraḥasis epic, the mother goddess creates humans from a mixture of clay and blood, which she then places into a womb.[14] Isaiah 45:9–10 combines the metaphor of creation of clay with metaphors of begetting and birth. The clay metaphor in Job 10:9 refers to Job's formation pre-birth, but the exclamation that God turns him to dust refers to Job's sufferings as a grown man. The clay metaphor continues the arguments presented in verses 3–8, where Job highlights the disparity between God and himself, questioning what pleasure the creator finds in destroying what has been created and why the innocents are punished. The clay metaphor also coheres with the other descriptions in Job 9–10 that refer to the transience of humans (9:25–26; 10:5, 20).

My analysis of the clay metaphor in Job 10:9 begins with a background on how the domains of CLAY and DUST are represented in the HB. The exploration of the clay metaphor in Job 10:9 will consider the portrayal of God as a potter and how the clay metaphor encompasses both the formation and destruction of Job.

The Domains of CLAY and DUST

The craft of pottery has been known in the Levant since at least 6000 BCE. Objects such as vessels, spindles, figurines, and bricks have been made from clay. Archeological excavations of potters' workshops in Megiddo from the late Bronze and Iron Ages reveal that potters used tournette wheels and that they had water cisterns, firepits or kilns, spaces for fuel, and spaces for discarded work in their workshops. Vessels were crafted either using a wheel or by hand.[15]

---

[14] "Atraḥasis" I 202–214 (trans. Lambert, et al. 1999, 56–59).
[15] King and Stager 2001, 133–39.

The Hebrew noun for clay in verse 10a is חֹמֶר, which is more specific than עָפָר, "dust," and refers to clay as a construction material. This term is used for the clay used to build buildings (Exod 1:14), produce ceramic ware (Isa 29:16; Jer 18:6), the clay of the streets (Isa 10:6), and the formation of a human (Job 33:6). It is also used as a parallel with טִיט, "mud," (Isa 41:25; Nah 3:14), and with עָפָר, "dust," (Job 4:19; 27:16).[16] When humans are described as being formed from clay, they are typically not compared to specific objects like vessels; rather, they are simply described as being formed as humans (Gen 2:7; Isa 29:16; 64:7). It is more common to refer to humans as vessels in contexts involving their destruction (Ps 2:9; Jer 18:4; 22:28). Job 10:10 uses חֹמֶר in the description of the formation of Job, while עָפָר, "dust" is used in the reference to destruction. The word עָפָר, "dust," has various meanings, primarily referring to dry dust (Gen 13:16; Deut 28:24), but it can also refer to wet clay (Gen 2:6–7). The expression "turning something to dust (עָפָר)" can be combined with different expressions such as fire (Ezek 28:18), crushing things (Isa 25:12), and trampling (2 King 13:7; Isa 26:5–6). To say that humans return (שׁוּב) to dust (עָפָר) is a common expression for death and mortality (Gen 3:19; Pss 104:29; 146:4).

The metaphors FORMATION OF A HUMAN IS POTTERY MAKING, HUMANS ARE CLAY, and GOD IS A POTTER are common in the HB. They are employed not only in descriptions of the creation of individuals but also in imagery depicting how God has formed the people of Israel. The potter metaphor is apparent in Gen 2:7, in which God forms the human out of "the dust of the ground" and then breathes life into the nose. Isaiah 64:7 is an appeal to God, addressing God as both a father and a potter, asking God to remember that the people are clay, shaped by God's own hands. The combination of God as both a parent and a potter is even more evident in Isa 45:9–11.[17] In this passage, the potter metaphor emphasizes God's superiority over humans and highlights the absurdity of a created object arguing with its creator or questioning the creator's work (cf. Isa 29:16). The notion that humans are created from dust is often combined with other imagery that accentuates the transience of human life, such as the metaphor HUMANS ARE PLANTS (Pss 90:3–6; 103:14–15). Gen 3:19 describes the cycle of life which both relates to the plant and potter metaphors. Expressions describing how humans are turned to

---

[16] Ringgren, "חמר," *TDOT* 5:3.

[17] For details on the birth and pottery metaphors in Isa 45, see Dille 2004, 107–23.

dust both apply to an undisturbed cycle of life as well as to instances where life is abruptly ended, either by accident or by God's intervention.[18]

Jeremiah 18:1–11 describes God as a potter who shapes a vessel from clay. If displeased with the vessel, God destroys it and recreates another vessel from the same clay. Here, God does not crush the vessel as in Isa 30:14, but turns it back to a lump of clay. The vessel is still moldable, not yet hardened. The metaphor DESTRUCTION OF HUMANS IS DESTRUCTION OF CLAY can thus either refer to wet clay or dried ceramics, with destruction as either returning the clay to its unformed state or crushing the hardened vessel. The distinction between these forms of destruction lies in their finality: crushing a vessel is more definitive, while returning it to moldable clay allows for potential renewal. In Job 10:8–9, the destruction is depicted not as a natural part of the lifecycle but as a deliberate and destructive action of God. Verse 8 uses the word בלע, "swallow," "destroy," to describe God's action. This term accentuates the hostility of the act and carries associations of death and Sheol (Num 16:30; Ps 69:16). It is used in Job 2:3, where God says that the Accuser has turned against Job to destroy him (בלע). The expression אֶל־עָפָר תְּשִׁיבֵנִי, "you turn me into dust," should be understood as a parallel to בלע in Job 10:8, emphasizing God's act of total destruction. This implies that God's action in verse 9 refers to a breaking of Job as if he were hardened ceramic rather than reverting him to moldable clay.

JOB IS CLAY and GOD IS A POTTER

The clay metaphor in Job 10:10 includes the metaphors FORMATION OF JOB IS POTTERY MAKING and DESTRUCTION OF JOB IS DESTRUCTION OF CERAMIC WARE. The formation of Job will be accentuated and complemented by three other metaphors in verses 10–11, but the clay metaphor is the only one used to describe the destruction Job endures as an adult. The fact that the source domain of POTTERY offers images for both formation and destruction is a notable strength, and it is used in the HB to describe both the creation and destruction of people and individuals. I will first examine and display the construction of the metaphor depicting the formation of Job. Then, I will analyze the metaphor of destruction and how these metaphors interact to highlight the absurdity of God's actions.

---

[18] For further discussion on Gen 3:19 and the expression "returning to dust," see Chapter 5, pages 122–24.

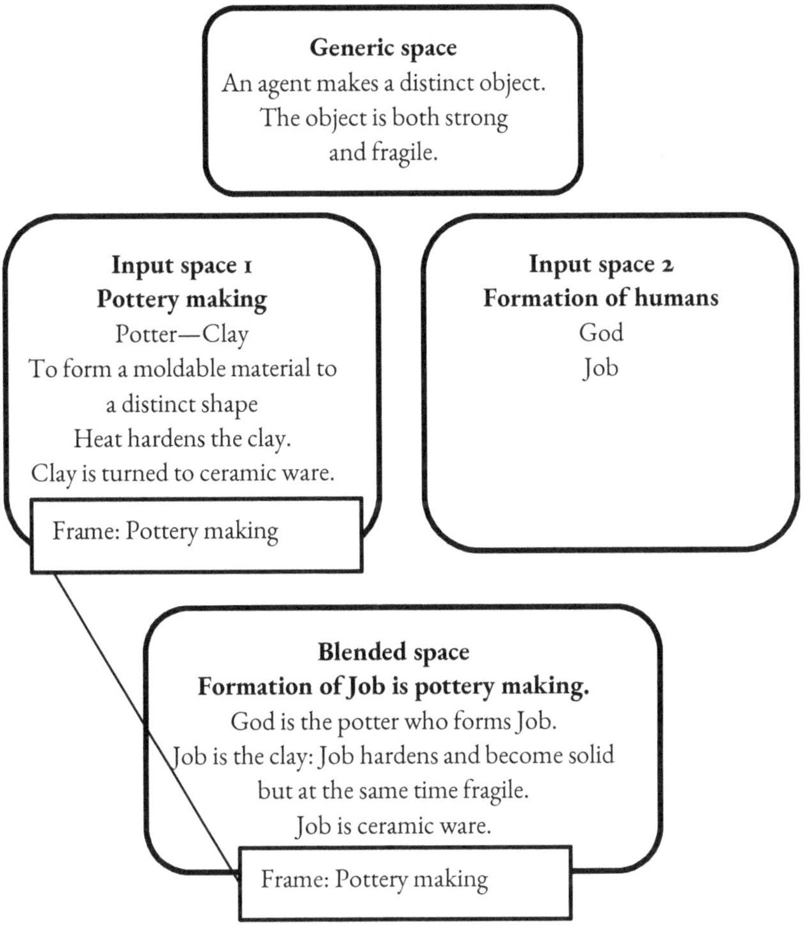

```
                    ┌─────────────────────────┐
                    │     Generic space       │
                    │ An agent makes a distinct object. │
                    │  The object is both strong │
                    │       and fragile.      │
                    └─────────────────────────┘

┌─────────────────────────────┐   ┌─────────────────────────┐
│       Input space 1         │   │      Input space 2      │
│      Pottery making         │   │   Formation of humans   │
│      Potter—Clay            │   │          God            │
│ To form a moldable material to │   │          Job            │
│      a distinct shape       │   │                         │
│   Heat hardens the clay.    │   │                         │
│ Clay is turned to ceramic ware. │   │                         │
│ ┌───────────────────────┐   │   │                         │
│ │ Frame: Pottery making │   │   └─────────────────────────┘
│ └───────────────────────┘   │
└─────────────────────────────┘

              ┌─────────────────────────────────┐
              │         Blended space           │
              │ Formation of Job is pottery making. │
              │  God is the potter who forms Job. │
              │ Job is the clay: Job hardens and become solid │
              │   but at the same time fragile. │
              │      Job is ceramic ware.       │
              │  ┌───────────────────────┐      │
              │  │ Frame: Pottery making │      │
              │  └───────────────────────┘      │
              └─────────────────────────────────┘
```

Figure 7.1 *The metaphors GOD IS A POTTER, FORMATION OF JOB IS POTTERY MAKING, and JOB IS CLAY.*

The organizing frame of the blend is from the input space POTTERY MAKING. It structures the blend and implies that God is the subject and Job is the object. Job is dependent on God. The frame POTTERY MAKING falls within the broader frame CRAFTSMANSHIP where skilled crafters produce products by using their special skills. Crafters, as potters, decide whether to create something and determine the shapes and characteristics of their creations. Vall is correct in his conclusion that the clay metaphor accentuates that God must have a purpose in creating Job.[19] Potters use their hands to shape the clay. Clay is the only material required, and the potter molds it into the desired form, and once the clay reaches the intended shape, it is left to harden. This process involves transforming the material through both shaping and the subsequent solidification in the kiln. Job 10:9 does not describe Job as being created as a specific vessel or type of ceramic ware. The shape of Job is not discussed; neither are specific body parts. The image of God forming Job out of formless clay accentuates that he is formed to a distinct object with a shape of its own, as a distinct individual. The solidification process adds the feature of stability. After a vessel is formed, the clay dries and hardens, allowing the ceramic ware to stand on its own. Although the organizing frame SOLIDIFICATION is not explicitly mentioned in verse 9, definitive destruction is commonly associated with the crushing of hardened ceramic ware. The frame of solidification is also repeated in verse 10, where Job's formation is described as the curdling of cheese.

The act of formation and destruction and the unequal relationship between Job and God is highlighted in this metaphor. The clay metaphor in verse 9 may also imply what is explicitly said in Isa 45:9–10, that the created cannot strive with its creator. Job knows that it is true that a mortal cannot question God, and that God can crush him if God pleases (Job 9:2–3, 12). Job still pleads his case, and uses the argument of the inequality between them to assert that it is inappropriate for God to attack him.

Van Hecke discusses the clay metaphor in Job 10:9. He argues that the potter and clay metaphors describe the formation of a human as a process from a soft shapeless lump of clay to a distinct solid object. According to van Hecke, Job's mental state is depicted through metaphors that express a loss of stability and individuality, illustrating a transformation into an unformed mass where the self dissolves. Consequently, he argues that verse 9b describes how Job is turned to wet clay, back to an unformed lump of clay.[20] I agree that the potter and clay metaphors in Job 10:9 describe the formation of Job as a process of transformation from formlessness to distinct form, and from soft clay to a hardened state. However, this implies that God has shaped Job into a hard ceramic, which is later crushed as a solid object. Once pottery has hardened, it cannot turn to wet mud again. The smashing of ceramic ware is definitive and Job's experience of destruction as being swallowed in verse 8 aligns more with being crushed into pieces than being turned back into unformed clay for reformation.

---

[19] Vall 1993, 229–32.
[20] Van Hecke 2011, 101–4.

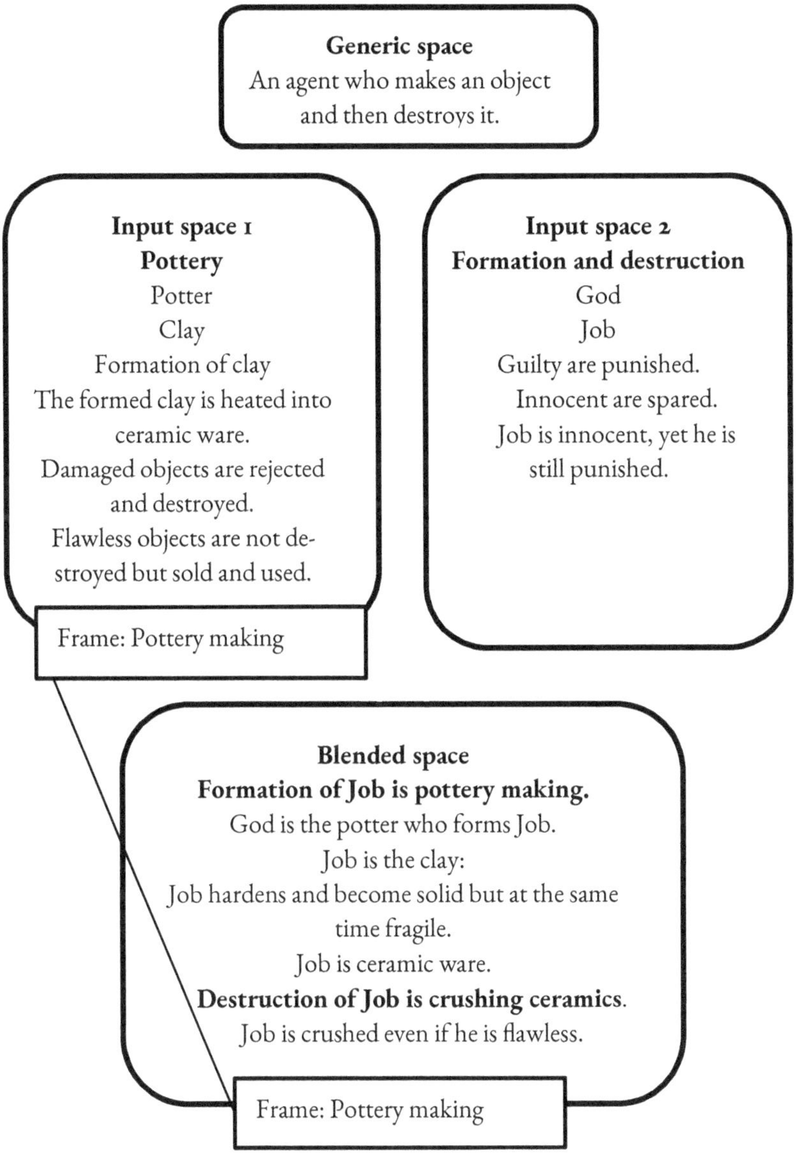

Generic space
An agent who makes an object and then destroys it.

Input space 1
Pottery
Potter
Clay
Formation of clay
The formed clay is heated into ceramic ware.
Damaged objects are rejected and destroyed.
Flawless objects are not destroyed but sold and used.

Frame: Pottery making

Input space 2
Formation and destruction
God
Job
Guilty are punished.
Innocent are spared.
Job is innocent, yet he is still punished.

Blended space
Formation of Job is pottery making.
God is the potter who forms Job.
Job is the clay:
Job hardens and become solid but at the same time fragile.
Job is ceramic ware.
Destruction of Job is crushing ceramics.
Job is crushed even if he is flawless.

Frame: Pottery making

Figure 7.2 *The metaphors* DESTRUCTION OF JOB IS CRUSHING CERAMICS, JOB IS CLAY AND CERAMIC WARE, *and* FORMATION OF JOB IS POTTERY MAKING.

The domain of POTTERY can be used to describe both God's formation and destruction of Job as disputed in Figure 7.2. The metaphor DESTRUCTION OF JOB IS CRUSHING HIM INTO PIECES is derived from the domain of POTTERY and from how hardened ceramic ware can be crushed into pieces. Job is the clay, which is formed and solidified into ceramic ware, and as such he can crack and be crushed into pieces. The fragility of ceramics corresponds to the vulnerability and mortality of humanity. The clay metaphor contains the duality of humans as both strong and fragile. While the solidification process emphasizes the individuality and the stability of Job, the destruction of Job as a ceramic ware underscores his fragility.

Job 10:9 can be understood as illustrating the absurdity of crafters destroying their own creations, similar to the imagery used in Isa 64:7. However, it can also be viewed as more specifically highlighting the absurdity of destroying items that are not damaged or deformed. A potter produces objects without the intention of destroying them, but if they are damaged, they will be rejected. Dumps of rejected pottery have been found in potters' workshops in archaeological excavations. The metaphor in Job 10:9 may emphasize the irrationality of destroying objects that are intact and well-formed. The clay metaphor then continues the arguments in 10:2–7 for why God destroys Job even if God knows that Job is innocent (cf. Job 9:20–23). The metaphor of God as the potter who crushes Job is used to emphasize that Job should be spared because he is not defective. The clay metaphor further underscores the question of why God would destroy Job when he is innocent, highlighting the injustice of his suffering.

To summarize: The clay metaphor in Job 10:9 communicates several perspectives. Firstly, it portrays God as the maker of Job, emphasizing that God is responsible for Job's existence and the effort invested in his creation. The metaphor questions why such effort should be in vain. Secondly, God and Job are unequal. Potters form and destroy their creations as they please. Job is not in position to argue with God; however, he does, and turns the argument of inequality against God, questioning the fairness of God's treatment. Thirdly, the formation of Job is a process of shaping a specific object from a formless mass and then letting it solidify to gain stability. God has given Job his individuality and stability. Fourthly, to be made of clay implies that Job is mortal. As ceramic ware, Job is fragile and can crack if treated violently. Finally, God destroys Job deliberately, even though he is innocent. Potters do not destroy the things they have created unless they are defective.

FORMATION OF JOB IS CURDLING MILK TO CHEESE

Job describes his formation using the metaphor of cheesemaking in Job 10:10. In this metaphor, God is seen as the cheesemaker who pours out milk and curdles it into cheese. The metaphor FORMATION OF A HUMAN IS CHEESEMAKING is not used elsewhere in the HB, but it is employed to describe fetal formation in later ancient texts and other cultures. These sources may offer insights into how this metaphor should be interpreted, though it cannot be proven that the associations of milk and cheese found in these later texts are also relevant to Job 10:10. The investigation of the cheesemaking metaphor will here begin with background information on how formation of a fetus can be understood as a process of coagulation, and what is known about dairy products and cheesemaking in ancient West Asia. Following this, the metaphor will be investigated in the context of Job 10, which will include discussions of how the domains of CHEESEMAKING, GESTATION, and GOD'S FORMATION OF HUMANS interact and what features of Job, God, and their relationship are highlighted.

Formation of a Fetus Is Coagulation of Fluids

Gestation as a process of coagulation is depicted in several ancient texts, describing how fluids come together or becoming hard.[21] For instance, the Sumerian text UM 29-15-367 describes gestation as coagulation: "He has poured the true seed of humanity in her innards; the seed that has been poured into the innards, is clotting (*ka.kešda,* gloss *ki-ší*), is giving a child (?) to the man."[22] Similarly, in the Enuma Elish, when Marduk initiates the creation of man, he says: "I shall compact [*kaṣāru*] blood, I shall cause bones to be, I shall make stand a human being."[23] The verbs *kaṣāru* and *kešda* may also mean "knot," "tie," as well as "gather," "organize," "go hard," "consolidate" (of ice), and "contract" (of a part of the body).[24] This may

---

[21] For a discussion of how solidification of water into ice is described in Job 38, see Chapter 8, pages 266–67.

[22] From UM 29-15-367, (trans. Stol 2000, 9). There is also another version of the text, VAT 8381. Van Dijk discusses both and he interprets the verb *kešda* as "coagulate": "[le sperme] déposé dans [le sein] étant coagulé" (van Dijk 1975, 57, 63). Cunningham translates the verb in UM 29-15-367 in more general terms as "The semen poured into the womb having taken form" (Cunningham 1997, 70–71).

[23] "Epic of Creation" ("Enuma Elish") VI 5–6, (trans. Foster *COS* 1.111:400). To use blood in the formation of a fetus is also seen Atraḫasis, and Enki and Ninmaḫ. In these narratives, a goddess creates the first humans by mixing blood and clay, forming them from this mixture ("Atraḫasis," I 202–214 (trans. Lambert, et al. 1999, 56–59); "Enki and Ninmaḫ" 30–34, (*COS* 1.159:517).

[24] *CDA*, s.v. "*kaṣāru(m)*."

imply that Marduk is depicted as tying the blood vessels together, as argued by Stol, but a more common interpretation is that it refers to an coagulation process.[25] The idea of a coagulation in the womb is also described by Hippocrates (ca. 460–370 BCE), who discusses how the male and female sperm mix at conception before solidifying.[26] Wis 7:1–2 depicts formation of a fetus as a coagulation of the blood of the semen:

> I am also mortal, like everyone else, a descendant of the first-formed child of earth; and in the womb of a mother I was molded into flesh, within the period of ten months, compacted [πήγνυμι, "to make solid"] with blood, from the seed of a man and the pleasure of marriage,[27]

Additionally, the birth metaphor in Job 38:28–29 refers to the creation of ice and hoarfrost as a process of the solidification of water in a womb.[28]

The Hebrew verb קפא (Hiphil) is used in Job 10:10 to describe milk curdling into cheese. The same verb is also used to describe how the water piles up in Exod 15:8, and may refer to frost in Zech 14:6. The Greek word for the coagulation of the fetus in Wis 7:2 is πήγνυμι, which means "fix," "make solid," "fasten together," "build," and "freeze."[29] It is also used in Sir 43:20 (LXX) in reference to how water freezes. Milk, water, and body fluids share the organizing frame COAGULATION. This makes them easy to combine in different metaphors.

Formation of a Fetus Is Cheesemaking

The idea that a fetus is formed in a coagulation process is specified in the metaphor FORMATION OF A FETUS IS CHEESEMAKING. Cheesemaking may be the experience behind the metaphor of formation of a fetus as coagulation. The oldest known text to explicitly describe the formation of a fetus as the curdling of cheese comes from Aristotle.

> The material secreted by the female in the uterus has been fixed by the semen of the male: this acts in the same way as rennet acts upon milk, for rennet is a kind of milk containing vital heat, which brings into one mass and fixes the similar material.[30]

---

[25] Stol 2000, 11.

[26] Hippocrates, *Nat. Puer.* VII 486 (trans. Potter 2012, 30–31).

[27] NRSV. Referring to semen as blood might seem strange today, but it corresponds with ancient views that both semen and breast milk were derived from heated, coagulated blood (Longrigg 1985).

[28] See chapter 8, pages 261–74.

[29] *LSJ*, s.v. "πήγνυμι."

[30] Aristotle, *Gen. An.* II, 4 739B, (trans. Stol 2000, 12). A similar description appears in *Gen. An.* II, 4 737A (trans. Peck 2014, 172–75, 188–93).

Aristotle states that semen resembles milk in its texture and color, and he argues that both become thicker and coagulate when heated. However, in his description of the coagulation of the fetus, he instead compares the semen with rennet, a milk-like substance which coagulates milk to cheese. The semen is seen as the substance that coagulates the fluids of the womb into an embryo. Aristotle argues that the body of a fetus is formed solely from the woman's secretions, and that the semen is not consumed in the process but instead brings the spirit to the fetus. The heat of the womb contributes to the coagulation of the fluids of the womb which react like milk and not like water.[31] The metaphor of fetal formation as cheesemaking is also used in later texts by Philo, Pliny the Elder, Tertullian, as well as in Leviticus Rabbah and the Quran.[32] It is also attested to in other various cultures.[33] The experience of how milk coagulates when heated is a universal experience. This experience is then used as a source domain to understand the more unknown process of a fetus being formed hidden in the womb. These examples from various contexts show that even though Job 10:10 is the only instance of this metaphor in the HB, it is a metaphor grounded in the cross-cultural experience of coagulation of fluids. However, different understandings of the source and target domains modify how the metaphor is used in different contexts. For the best interpretation of Job 10:10, we need to understand how the domains of CHEESEMAKING and GESTATION were conceptualized in ancient West Asia and within the HB.

The Domains of MILK and CHEESE

The metaphor in Job 10:10 uses cheesemaking as its source domain. To understand the metaphor, we need to comprehend not only how milk was processed into cheese in ancient West Asia but also how milk and cheese are used in other metaphors in the HB. There are no descriptions of how cheeses were made in extant texts from ancient West Asia or from Greek Hellenistic sources.[34] However, butter, ghee, and different kinds of cheeses are mentioned in many administrative Sumerian lists, with the earliest dating back to the late fourth millennium BCE.[35] The specific animal source of the milk is rarely mentioned in descriptions of cheese from ancient West Asia, but people kept cattle, goats, and sheep.[36] The oldest

---

[31] Aristotle, *Gen. An.* II, 4.735 A–B (trans. Peck 2014, 154–63).
[32] For a compilation and discussion of these texts, see Frevel 2016, 295–307.
[33] Stol 2000, 13.
[34] Curtis 2001, 237–38, 315.
[35] Kindstedt 2017, 7.
[36] Lev-Tov 2022, 83–84.

references to rennet are found in texts from the Hittite civilization in the mid-second millennium BCE.[37] Although there are no detailed sources describing the methods of cheesemaking, descriptions of different kinds of cheeses combined with modern methods suggest two different ways of producing cheese. The first involved drying fermented soured milk or buttermilk. Buttermilk is the liquid that remains after the fat of the milk has clotted together during butter churning. The sour milk or the buttermilk is dried in cloths and then used as soft cheese or baked into balls. Images of small round cheeses are found on seals from ancient West Asia.[38] Stol describes how dried cheeses, likely dried on a roof in the sun, would become as hard as chalk. They could be pulverized, and by adding water, a substitute for fresh milk was created.[39] The second method of making cheese involved adding rennet to speed up the coagulation of the milk. During this process, the whey is separated from the clotted mass. Salt is added, and the mass is pressed to remove more liquid, followed by a ripening period. This second method of making cheese is used in Aristotle's image of gestation, but the process was first described in detail by the Roman writers Varro and Columella in the first and second centuries CE.[40]

In the HB, there are many references to חָלָב, "milk," and חֶמְאָה, "cream," "butter," but the word גְּבִינָה, "cheese," is only used in Job 10:10.[41] The word חָלָב, "milk," probably also refers to other dairy products.[42] Judg 4:19 refers to fresh milk as a beverage, and 1 Sam 17:18 mentions חֲרִצֵי הֶחָלָב, which is best translated "slices of cheese." The word חָלָב, "milk," is also close to the word חֵלֶב, "fat." The meaning of the word חֶמְאָה is unclear, but it is probably some kind of processed milk such as cream, butter, or soft cheese. Proverbs 30:33 describes the production of חֶמְאָה as the squeezing of milk, which could refer to the making of soft cheese.

Milk and curd symbolize wealth, vitality, and prosperity in the HB. The expression זָבַת חָלָב "flowing of milk" is a standard description of the promised land and signifies that it was prosperous (Exod 3:8; Lev 20:24; Deut 6:3). Serving milk and curd was a sign of generosity (Gen 18:8). Job refers to his wealthy time as a time when his steps were washed in milk (Job 29:6). Job 21:24 describes the vitality of a

---

[37] Kindstedt 2017, 8.
[38] Stol 1993, 104.
[39] Stol 1993, 104.
[40] Curtis 2001, 400–402.
[41] It is attested to in imperial Aramaic and rabbinic Hebrew (Seow 2013, 588; Jastrow, s.v. "גְּבִינָה").
[42] Caquot, "חָלָב," *TDOT* 4:386–91.

man by referring to the milk of his olives, and in Song of Songs milk is used in descriptions of the beauty and taste of the loved one (Song 4:11; 5:1).

Analogies between GESTATION *and* CHEESEMAKING

The metaphor GESTATION IS CHEESEMAKING, found in texts from Aristotle to the Quran, highlights how the fetus is formed from fluids. There has been discussion regarding whether this metaphor also relates to other parts of pregnancy or to the newborn baby. A metaphor that combines two domains creates similarities between them, even if these were not intended by the person who originally formulated the metaphor. More analogies between the two domains strengthen the metaphor and make it more viable. However, the specific analogies used in a given metaphorical expression are always selective and determined by its context.

Frevel maps several analogies between CHEESEMAKING and GESTATION in his interpretation of the cheese metaphor in Job 10:10.[43] He points out the resemblance between milk and sperm, and argues that the milk in verse 10a refers to the sperm. He identifies analogies between soft white cheese and the amniotic sac, and between whey and amniotic fluid, noting their similar textures and colors. He also finds analogies between the salt used in cheese and the custom of rubbing newborns with salt, the maturation time of cheese and the duration of pregnancy, and the fact that both babies and cheeses are soft and wrapped in cloths. Although he highlights these different analogies, he does not discuss their relevance to Job 10:10. It is unlikely that all these analogies are in focus in Job 10:10. The context of Job 10:10 emphasizes the formation of Job in the womb, not the characteristics of a newborn. The metaphor of coagulation in the womb in Job 38:28–29 depicts the origin and formation of ice and hoarfrost through the metaphors of coagulation of a fetus and birth. This description may use the analogy between hoarfrost and birthing custard, the white waxy substance which covers the newborn.[44] Birthing custard has the same texture and color as cheese and snow, but in Job 10:10, the focus is on Job's formation before birth. Even if this analogy might be part of the background to the metaphor THE NEWBORN IS CHEESE, it is not used in Job 10:10.

Job probably refers to semen as milk in Job 21:24 in the expression עֲטִינָיו מָלְאוּ חָלָב, "his olives are filled with milk." Vall discusses this expression and argues that this verse should be interpreted as a euphemism for the semen of

---

[43] Frevel 2016, 303–4.

[44] For further discussion on similarities between hoarfrost and birthing custard see Chapter 8, pages 271–72.

the testicles.⁴⁵ However, this verse has been debated. The noun עֲטִין is a *hapax legomenon*. *HALOT* suggests עֲטִין refers to olives or to body parts such as the breast or thigh.⁴⁶ LXX uses ἔγκατα, "entrails," NRSV "loin," and the Swedish translation Bibel 2000 "pung" ("scrotum"). It has been argued that חָלָב, "milk," should be emended to חֵלֶב, "fat."⁴⁷ However, the simplest way to understand the verse is when it is not emended but taken as a metaphor, a euphemism, in which the milk represents the semen of the loins, or the testicles.

These two examples, Job 21:24 and 38:28–29, show that the author of Job was aware of the metaphors FORMATION OF A FETUS IS COAGULATION and SEMEN IS MILK, and it is likely that they are also used in Job 10:10. The cheese metaphor in Job 10:10 serves as a parallel to the clay metaphor in verse 9. This highlights the aspect of solidification in the cheesemaking process and that Job's formation is the work of a maker. The focus on the cheesemaker in Job 10:10 differs from Aristotle's presentation of the cheese metaphor and how the coagulation of the fetus in the womb is used in the metaphor of the formation of ice in Job 38:28–29.

GOD IS A CHEESEMAKER *and* JOB IS CHEESE

Job 10:10 may very well be understood independently of other texts that use the metaphor of cheese to describe gestation of a fetus. It can be interpreted in accordance with the general metaphor GOD IS A HANDCRAFTER. It would highlight God as the crafter, with the specific product being secondary. However, it is more likely that the product, cheese, is chosen because it shares the frame COAGULATION with the believed process of fetal formation in the womb. Here, I will first discuss the cheesemaking metaphor in Job 10:10 as a metaphor of a crafter, and then examine its connection to the domain of GESTATION.

In Job 10:10, milk is the raw material from which cheese is produced, and rennet is not part of the description. This is not problematic, as cheese can be produced without rennet. Coagulation is used in the refining process of making cheese, but it can also destroy fresh milk, though this frame is not employed here. The association of milk and cheese as valuable products might contribute to the metaphor describing Job as milk and cheese, emphasizing that Job was once created as a healthy, vital, and valuable person who should not be destroyed. God is

---

⁴⁵ Vall 1993, 247–49.

⁴⁶ *HALOT*, s.v. "עֲטִין."

⁴⁷ For an overview of different interpretations of Job 21:24, see Clines 2006, 514, 531. He argues that it refers to Job as having his buckets full of milk but also that "milk" and "fat" signify physical health.

explicitly described as the one who makes Job by pouring him out and curdling him into cheese. The emphasis on God as the agent coheres with the other metaphors in Job 10:9–11.

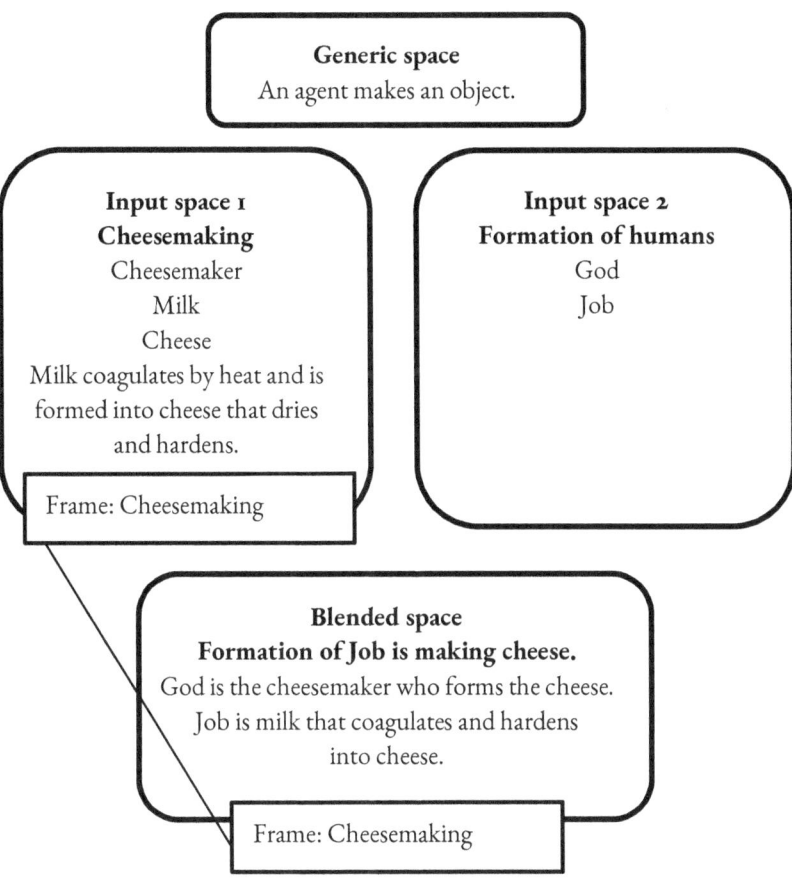

Figure 7.3 The metaphors GOD IS A CHEESEMAKER, FORMATION OF JOB IS CHEESEMAKING, and JOB IS MILK AND CHEESE.

The organizing frame of the input space CHEESEMAKING structures the blend. The metaphor of cheesemaking is a natural parallel to the metaphors of pottery. The frames POTTERY MAKING and CHEESEMAKING both entail the process of solidification, and they are both derived from the general frame CRAFTSMANSHIP. God is depicted as the crafter and the agent who takes the initiative to form objects, having a purpose for the things crafted. Both the cheesemaker and the potter transform raw material into something new. They shape the product by modeling the mass with their hands and then allow it to solidify. Both cheese and clay undergo a process of hardening through heat. Stol describes cheese as hard as chalk, which parallels the way clay becomes hard ceramic.[48]

Is Gestation Implied in Job 10:10?

In Job 10:10, the metaphor explicitly refers to the domains of CHEESEMAKING and FORMATION OF A HUMAN. It does not explicitly refer to the domain of GESTATION. The blending schema above depicts the explicit metaphors of Job 10:10: GOD IS THE CHEESEMAKER and JOB IS THE MILK AND CHEESE. It has been discussed whether the domain of GESTATION is implied in Job 10:10 and, if so, how this would impact the interpretation of Job 10:10. Rancour-Laferriere and Meyer argue that God is depicted as the begetter who ejaculates his semen into the womb.[49] Van Hecke rejects the idea that Job 10:10 refers to sperm and the domain of GESTATION. He claims that the cheese metaphor, just as the clay metaphor, only refers to the solidification of Job and not to gestation. He argues that the semen is never compared to milk in the HB.[50] A common interpretation is to recognize the parallel between gestation and coagulation, as well as between milk and semen, with God being described as the creator who oversees the process of coagulation.[51] Even if not many would go as far to call God the begetter in this image, it is often suggested that the reference to gestation expresses God's intimate relationship with the one created.[52]

I argue that the domain of GESTATION is implied in Job 10:10, and that the metaphor GESTATION IS CHEESEMAKING is involved in verse 10. It explains why cheesemaking is a fitting metaphor for the formation of Job. The metaphor FORMATION OF JOB IS CHEESEMAKING entails the metaphor GESTATION IS CHEESEMAKING and its metaphors SEMEN IS MILK and FETUS IS CHEESE, and the under-

---

[48] Stol 1993, 104.

[49] Rancour-Laferriere 2021, 18; Meyer 2021, 141–42.

[50] Van Hecke rejects the interpretation of the metaphor in terms of gestation in Van Hecke 2011, 102–3. In Van Hecke 2010, 106 he instead states that associations with the domain of GESTATION should be minimalistic and only concern the coagulation. In both works, he asserts that the metaphors in verses 9, 10, and 11b refer to the domain of AGGREGATION.

[51] Clines 1989, 248; Habel 1985, 199; Balentine 2006, 174. Others only mention the image but do not discuss God's role in the metaphor of cheesemaking (Pope 1973, 80; Seow 2013, 580–81, 588; Gordis 1978, 113, 522; Dhorme 1984, 149–50; Hartley 1988, 187).

[52] Fisch 1988, 31–32; Habel 1985, 199; Balentine 2006, 174.

standing that formation of a fetus is coagulation of body fluids. The cheesemaking metaphor in Job 10 is used in a context which describes Job's formation before birth, which implies the time from conception to birth. That a metaphor can entail other metaphors and imply characteristics from domains not explicitly mentioned in the text is certainly possible. For example, in Ps 23, the metaphor GOD IS A SHEPHERD entails the metaphor THE KING IS A SHEPHERD and the references to God as a shepherd also imply the metaphor GOD IS A KING.

The interpretation that Job 10:10 implies that the milk represents semen, and that the coagulation of cheese refers to Job's formation from body fluids in the womb, is supported by the context, but it is harder to know if God's role as a cheesemaker also implies that God is the begetter of Job. In Isa 45:9–10, the metaphor of God as a potter is combined with the metaphor of God as a begetter, which shows that these metaphors can complement each other. On the other hand, Ps 139:13–15 describes how God forms the fetus in the womb without implying that God is the father or the mother of the fetus.

The input spaces GESTATION and CHEESEMAKING do not need to project all their characteristics to the metaphor, even if there are elements in them that correspond. The metaphor GESTATION IS CHEESEMAKING may only highlight the semen as milk and the fetus as cheese without any references to the begetter and the cheesemaker. This metaphor was probably first invented from the need to explain how a fetus is formed in the hidden womb. This follows the common pattern of metaphors, where a more concrete source domain structures a more abstract target domain. The metaphor would then be concerned only with the formation of the fetus and not with portraying the begetter or the impregnated woman. This is how Aristotle constructs the metaphor.

In the image of Job 10:10, the metaphor is extended to also include the cheesemaker and not only the milk and cheese. This step is induced by the purpose: to portray God as the maker of Job. This extension can take place within the implicit metaphor GESTATION IS CHEESEMAKING so that it also includes a blend of THE CHEESEMAKER and THE BEGETTER.[53] However, it is more likely that it is done in the explicit metaphor FORMATION OF JOB IS CHEESEMAKING. The purpose of the extension is to describe God as the one who formed Job. The surrounding metaphors of pottery and intertwining also depict God as a crafter. The cheesemaking metaphor in Job 10 is used because it effectively addresses both the formation of a

---

[53] Job 38:28–29 refers to both the begetter and the birth mother in describing the solidification of water. The purpose of this imagery is to highlight the mystery of the origin of ice by referring to unknown parents. See discussion in Chapter 8, page 270.

fetus and the portrayal of God as a crafter. There are no indications in Job 10 that the cheese metaphor is used to describe God as the begetter of Job.

To *summarize:* Job 10:10 describes how God creates Job through the metaphors FORMATION OF JOB IS CHEESEMAKING, GOD IS A CHEESEMAKER, and JOB IS MILK AND CHEESE. These metaphors highlight God as the crafter and Job as a valuable product which should not be wasted. The use of the cheese metaphor in the context of the fetal formation of Job implies the metaphor GESTATION IS CHEESEMAKING, where the semen is milk, and the fetus is cheese. Even so, it is unlikely that God's role as a cheesemaker implies that God is the begetter of Job. The metaphors of Job 10:8–12 refer to different kinds of craftsmanship. The cheesemaking metaphor is suitable because it can both portray God as a cheesemaker and give a more concrete organizing frame to the abstract domain of GESTATION.

FORMATION OF JOB IS DRESSING AND INTERTWINING

Verse 11 continues to describe the formation of Job. This time it is not by transforming or shaping a substance as in the clay and cheese metaphors. Instead, verse 11 describes how God assembles Job by putting body parts together. The material in verses 9–10 is from the source domains of the metaphors and Job is formed from clay and milk. In verse 11, the material used in the formation is from the target domain of JOB'S BODY. In verse 11a, Job is dressed in skin and flesh, and in verse 11b the sinews and bones are brought together. The verbs of verse 11 refer to the source domain of DRESSING and to a less unclear source domain of the verb סכך, which traditionally has been interpreted as the domain of WEAVING A FABRIC; however, it is not clear, and I will discuss some other suggestions as well.[54]

The clay and cheese metaphors contain the entailment of solidification: the clay solidifies, and the milk coagulates into cheese. In the discussion above in "Formation of a Fetus is Coagulating of Fluids," I discuss how coagulating was perceived in ancient text as the fluids gather, come together, or are bound together. The dressing and intertwining metaphors describe how body parts come together. It is the same process, but instead of fluids, it is body parts that are brought together. This coheres with verse 8, where God is said to put Job together all around.

---

[54] The commentaries typically do not elaborate on the imagery in 11b, often simply describing it as an act of weaving or knitting. When they do provide further explanation, they interpret it as referring to the production of a weaved fabric, with God depicted as a weaver (Dhorme 1984, 150; Newsom 2003, 147; Seow 2013, 581). This is also how the use of the word סכך in Ps 139:13 is usually interpreted (Grogan 2008, 217; Hossfeld, et al. 2011, 541). Gray, however, translates סכך in Job 10:10 as "constructing a framework" (Gray 2010, 203).

The analyses of the dressing metaphor will begin with an overview of how the domains of DRESSING, SKIN, and FLESH are expressed in the HB and the Book of Job. Following this, the metaphor of God dressing Job will be examined within the context of Job 10. Special attention will be given to how this metaphor relates to other metaphors in Job 10:9–11, and to other descriptions of flesh and skin in Job. The analysis of the intertwining metaphor will start with a discussion of the meaning of the verb סכך and an overview of the domains of SINEWS and BONES. I will then propose three different metaphors that can explain the intertwining of sinews and bones and discuss the different characteristics they highlight.

The Domains of DRESSING, SKIN, and FLESH

Job says that God dresses him with skin (עוֹר) and flesh (בָּשָׂר). The association between clothing and skin is illustrated in Gen 3:21, where God makes garments of skin (עוֹר) and dresses the first humans before expelling them from Eden. In this context, the term עוֹר refers to animal hides used to make clothing.

The act of God dressing someone occurs in several texts in the HB. God dresses his appointed priest with holy clothes (Exod 28:41; 40:13) and kings with royal dresses (Isa 22:21). The clothes signify the status and the office of a person. A change of clothes is part of the ritual when the power is transferred to a new priest or prophet (Num 20:26; 2 King 2:14). In Ezek 16:10, God clothes the orphan Jerusalem in beautifully embroidered clothes. God may dress the ones God favors with salvation and righteousness (Ps 132:9, 16; Isa 61:10). Psalms also express wishes that God would clothe enemies in dishonor and shame (Pss 109:29; 132:18, cf. Job 8:22). Before his suffering, Job describes himself as a man whom God has clothed in righteousness and justice (Job 29:14). In contrast, during his affliction, Job laments that his flesh is covered with worms and dirt (Job 7:5). Job 1:21 implies the metaphors of God dressing and undressing Job.[55]

The destruction of Job's skin (עוֹר) and flesh (בָּשָׂר) are recurring motifs in the Book of Job.[56] The Accuser breaks down God's protective shelters around Job, and God allows him to go so far as to the skin, flesh, and bone, as long as he spares Job's life (Job 2:4–5). There are several descriptions of how Job's skin shrivels, hardens, turns black, and falls off (Job 7:5; 16:8; 30:30). The skin is put in parallel with the flesh several times in the Book of Job. For instance, Job 7:5 depicts how Job's flesh is clothed with worms and his skin has hardened and melted.[57] In Job 19:20–26,

---

[55] See Chapter 5, pages 127–30
[56] For further discussion of Job's flesh and skin, see van der Zwan 2017; Erickson 2013.
[57] For the metaphor referring to the destruction of skin as melting, see Erickson 2013, 303.

skin and flesh are mentioned repeatedly, with the assertion that, despite being stripped of his skin, Job will see God in his flesh. Both skin and flesh are used in parallel with bones (עֲצָמִים), and these body parts may also serve as synecdoche for Job's whole body. His physical appearance, marked by wounds and shriveled skin, is seen as a witness of his guilt and leads to rejection by his family and friends (Job 16:8; 19:13–19).

God Dresses Job with Skin and Flesh

Job 10:11 is unique in the HB for describing the formation of a human in the womb as an act of dressing. God's act of dressing humans in other contexts often signifies the conferral of a specific status, which can be either degrading or exalting, depending on the situation. The act of dressing Job with skin and flesh in verse 11 should be viewed as a positive act of God, cohering with Job 10:12, where Job acknowledges that he was made with "life and loyalty" (חַיִּים וָחֶסֶד). The dressing metaphor is used to accentuate Job's worth, just as the cheese and clay metaphors.

The metaphor of God dressing Job with skin and flesh is a double-scope blend, where both input spaces contribute to the organizing frame of the blend (Figure 7.4). The act of dressing comes from input space 1, while the sinews and bones come from input space 2. The topic in Job 10:8–12 focuses on God's formation of Job, and earlier metaphors of God as a potter and cheesemaker, with Job as clay and cheese, affect the interpretation of this image. This influences us to visualize flesh and skin as clothes, just as the material of the source domain is visualized in the former metaphors. However, while the sinews and flesh are explicitly mentioned as part of this blend, the clothes are not ordinary clothes, but rather ones that remain to be and appear like skin and flesh.

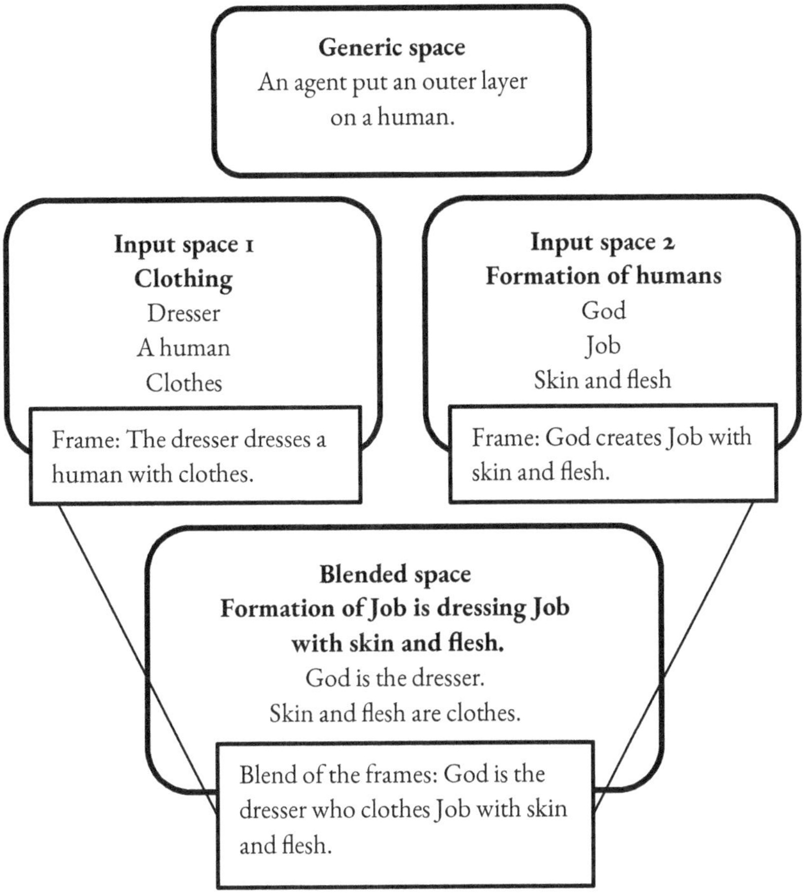

Birth Metaphors in Job 10:8–12 203

```
                    ┌─────────────────────────┐
                    │     Generic space       │
                    │ An agent put an outer   │
                    │   layer on a human.     │
                    └─────────────────────────┘
```

Generic space
An agent put an outer layer on a human.

Input space 1
Clothing
Dresser
A human
Clothes

Frame: The dresser dresses a human with clothes.

Input space 2
Formation of humans
God
Job
Skin and flesh

Frame: God creates Job with skin and flesh.

Blended space
Formation of Job is dressing Job with skin and flesh.
God is the dresser.
Skin and flesh are clothes.

Blend of the frames: God is the dresser who clothes Job with skin and flesh.

Figure 7.4 The metaphors GOD IS A DRESSER, FORMATION OF JOB IS DRESSING, and FLESH AND SKIN ARE CLOTHES.

The skin and flesh serve as the outer layer of the body, which covers the bones and the inner parts of the body. The metaphor SKIN IS CLOTHES is a universal metaphor and is grounded in the universal experience of wearing clothes to protect the body. The skin and clothes share characteristics: the skin resembles thin leather or fabric, and both serve as protective surfaces for the body. The metaphor of clothes highlights that the body is protected and covered all around (cf. v. 8), but the shaping of the human is not highlighted as in the clay metaphor. The skin and flesh protect the inward parts just as the clothes protect the body. Clothes are just an extra protective layer added to the flesh and skin. The metaphor of God as the one who clothes Job in skin and flesh is a counter-image to how Job experiences his life. Job describes how his flesh is clothed with worms and dirt (not skin) in Job 7:5, and how his wounded skin has become a witness against him in Job 16:8. The skin that was meant to protect him has instead become his enemy. Job describes his exposure in the metaphor of nakedness in Job 1:21, inferring that God has taken his clothes from him. In Job 10:11, Job wants God to realize that as Job's creator, God should dress him and not unclothe him.

To summarize: The dressing metaphor coheres with the clay and cheese metaphor because it highlights the value of the one dressed. The act of dressing is an act of giving someone protection. The skin and flesh are here depicted as clothes. The association of protection complements the previous metaphors in verse 9–10, and coheres with other images of Job's destruction, in which his skin and flesh are afflicted.

The Domains of BONES and SINEWS

Job says that God has intertwined his bones and sinews. The word עֶצֶם, "bone," is common in the HB, while the word גִּיד, "sinew," is rare.[58] Bones in the HB can refer to separate bones, to the whole person, or a whole skeleton. The bones are the strongest part and the core of a human.[59] *HALOT* refers to two other roots of עצם, the root עָצַם which means strength and might, and another which also is vocalized עֹצֶם, with the meaning "frame" or "bone structure" (Ps 139:15).[60] These meanings show that references to bones are associated with strength and the bones as the load-bearing structure in the body. The word sinew is also associated with strength. Isaiah 48:4 refers to sinews of iron. Job 40:17 describes the thighs of Behemoth as plaited or knitted (שׂרג) sinews.[61]

References to damaged or trembling bones are often used in laments to depict the lamenter's poor condition (Isa 38:1; Jer 23:9; Hab 3:16). Conversely, the strength and refreshment of bones are used to describe health and vitality (Job 20:11; Ps 34:21; Isa 58:11). There are several references to bone(s) (עֶצֶם) in Job.[62] The Accuser is allowed to touch Job's bone as well as his skin and flesh in Job 2:4–5.

---

[58] *HALOT*, s.v. "עֶצֶם I," "גִּיד."
[59] Beyse, "עֶצֶם," *TDOT* 11:305.
[60] *HALOT*, s.v. "עֶצֶם I," "עֹצֶם I," "עֹצֶם II."
[61] The verb שׂרג is only used twice in the HB (*HALOT*, s.v. "שׂרג").
[62] For an overview of how the words עֶצֶם and עֹצֶם are used in the book of Job, see van der Zwan 2019b, 7.

The expression עַצְמִי, "my bone," in Job 19:20 seems to refer to Job's whole skeleton. It describes how his bones cling to his skin and flesh, as a description of how Job dissolves from within. Normally, the skin clings to the bones, not the other way around. Other expressions of Job's despair also refer to his bones, such as in Job 30:17, 30, where his bones are described as being pierced or burning with heat. Fear is depicted as trembling, with bones shaking (Job 4:14). Job 20:11 and 21:23–24 refer to a person's strength and vitality by mentioning their bones. Behemoth's body parts are depicted to accentuate his strength, and his bones are said to be like tubes of iron or bronze (Job 40:18).

An important text to understand how sinews and bones come together with flesh and skin is Ezek 37:6–9. The dry, dead bones first come together; then the sinews are laid upon them, followed by the flesh. Finally, the skin is applied over the flesh and God gives the body breath. Ecclesiastes 11:5 discusses the formation of a fetus in the womb and the mysterious process by which breath enters the bones. In this context, "bones" appears to represent the entire body of the fetus.

God Intertwines Job with Sinews and Bones

Verse 11b refers to God's creating act with the verb סָכַךְ. The same verb is used in a similar context in Ps 139:13. The exact meaning of סָכַךְ in these passages is hard to define. In my translation I have used "intertwine." Sinews and bones are intertwined and fastened to each other. This verse may simply refer to how God shapes Job by intertwining his bones and sinews. However, it is more likely that it contains a metaphor as a continuation of the previous metaphors and as a parallel to the dressing metaphor. Before I discuss the meaning of the verb סָכַךְ, I want to point out the syntax of this verse. It refers to God as the subject of the verb and Job as the object. The preposition בְּ in 11b designates the material used in the formation process.[63] If verses 11a and 11b are seen as parallel expressions, and the sinews and bones serve the same function as the skin and flesh, then they should be understood as the materials God assembles in the act of creating Job. The traditional interpretation of סָכַךְ as weaving or knitting implies that the sinews and bones represent the materials used in this textile process.[64] However, this translation has been challenged, and alternative interpretations suggest other metaphors. The

---

[63] Arnold and Choi 2018, 118.

[64] NRSV: "and knit me together"; Bibel 2000: "vävde mig samman"; Gordis: "knitted me together" (Gordis 1978, 98); Habel: "knitted me" (Habel 1985, 181); Clines: "knit me together" (Clines 1989, 215).

interpretation of the verb סכך is crucial for understanding how sinews and bones are used in the formation of Job.

HALOT distinguishes between three roots of סכך.[65] The first and most common is "shut off for protection," which has the by-forms שׂוּךְ, שׂכךְ. It is used to describe how the cherubim protect the ark, how the psalmist is protected under God's wing, and how a tree shades from the sun (Exod 25:20; Ps 91:4; Job 40:22). The second root is interpreted as "weave," "shape," "intertwine" (Ps 139:13; Job 10:11). It must be noted that this second root is not used in the HB non-metaphorically, in reference to the act of weaving a fabric. It is first attested in Middle Hebrew and Jewish Aramaic. The meaning of the third root is "cover with" and "veil" (Lam 3:42) and *HALOT* notes that in Middle Hebrew and Jewish Aramaic, this root is used to mean "bedeck a roof with twigs or matting." The meanings of the three roots of the verb סכך are overlapping. *BDB* only referred to two roots of סכך: root I, "cover," "screen," and root II, "weave."[66] The nouns derived from סכך are סֻכָּה and סֹךְ, "booth," "thicket."[67]

According to *HALOT,* there are two or possibly four occurrences of root II in the HB. It depends on how נסכתי is vocalized and interpreted in Prov 8:23 and Ps 2:6. It can either be derived from the verb נסך, "pour out," "be consecrated," or from the verb סכך.[68] The verb נסך commonly refers to "pour out," but *HALOT* also suggests that it may be understood as a by-form of סכך with the meaning "intertwine," "weave," or "shape." All these presumed four occurrences of root II of סכך would then describe the formation of a being; a human in Ps 139:13, Job in Job 10:11, Wisdom in Prov 8:23, and a king in Ps 2:6.[69] Jastrow Dictionary shows how סכך is used in later Hebrew and Aramaic texts. It provides examples from Mishna and Talmud where the term describes threads being intertwined either to create a woven fabric or to make a thicker thread out of thinner ones. It is also used to describe intertwining branches and creeper plants to construct a booth. In these examples, the Hiphil form of סכך primarily refers to the act of weaving, while the Piel form is used to describe covering with boughs or constructing a festive

---

[65] *HALOT*, s.v. "סכך I, II, III."
[66] *BDB*, s.v. "סכך I, II."
[67] *HALOT*, s.v. "סֹךְ," "סֻכָּה."
[68] *HALOT*, s.v. "נסך I, II," "נסך II," "סכך II."
[69] Ps 2:6–7 combines the formation of the king with a metaphor of giving birth to the king and Prov 8:23–24 describes wisdom as both formed and born.

booth.⁷⁰ In Job 10:11, the word is used in Poel, which opens up for the interpretation that it refers to the act of intertwining Job's bones and sinews as a booth builder intertwines branches and plants to build a booth.

Van Hecke rejects the interpretation of סכך as meaning "weave," instead positing that it has a single root meaning "cover." He suggests that verse 11 can be translated as, "You dressed me with skin and flesh, you covered me with sinews and bones." While this translation is syntactically correct, he argues that bones and sinews cannot be used to cover Job in this context because they constitute the inner structure of the body. Instead, he interprets תְּסֹכְכֵנִי in verse 11 as derived from נסך and interprets verse 11b as "you cast me with sinews and bones."⁷¹ I agree with Van Hecke that the interpretation of the word סכך as weaving is not evident, but not with his conclusion that verse 11b should be understood in terms of casting, suggesting that Job is "cast" with bones and sinews. Metaphors depicting body parts in terms of cast metal are used in Job 6:12 and 40:18. However, the direct object of סכך in verse 11b is Job, not the sinews and bones; they are the material used in the formation of Job, just as the skin and flesh in 11a. While the metaphor of casting coheres with the clay and cheese metaphor, as well as with the idea of Job's solidification, it is less appropriate as a parallel to the metaphor of God dressing Job in verse 11a. The image of casting might be suitable in Ps 139:13, Prov 8:23, and Ps 2:6, where there are no specific materials mentioned for the formation of the human.

The different meanings of סכך described in Jastrow Dictionary and *HALOT* would lead to different metaphors with the source domains of WEAVING A FABRIC, PLAITING ROPES, and BUILDING BOOTHS. Although these interpretations are speculative due to the verb סכך not being used non-metaphorically in these specific domains in biblical Hebrew, I will examine these three options. I find it plausible that verse 11b contains a metaphor coherent with the dressing metaphor in verse 11a, and thus exploring these alternatives is warranted. The source domains of WEAVING A FABRIC, PLAITING ROPES, and BUILDING BOOTHS offer suitable parallels to the act of dressing Job with skin and flesh, as well as to the image of God as a crafter in verses 9–10. The bones and sinews correspond to the threads

---

⁷⁰ Jastrow, s.v. "סכך." Intertwined threads: m. Shabb. 7:2; y. Shabb. 7:2, 10c. Creeper plants intertwined to cover the booth (m. Sukkah 1:4, metaphorically in b. Ber. 62b). The showbread is also said to be interwoven with rods when laid crosswise to prevent molding (b. Menah. 97a). *CDCH*, s.v. "סכך II," also mentions 4QapLamA 2:7, where all the paths of the city are described as intertwined.

⁷¹ Van Hecke 2010, 106–8. He argues that סכך and נסך should be understood according to the first root of נסך, "pour out," "cast."

and branches in these images. They would be used as materials in the formation of Job's inner parts, paralleling how verse 11a describes Job's skin and flesh as the material for the formation of Job's protective surface. I will discuss these different metaphors and the perspectives they bring to the overall image of Job 10:8–12. These three interpretations present metaphors constructed as double-scope blends, where God's act comes from the source domain, and the material used in the formation, such as sinews and bones, comes from the target domain.

GOD IS A WEAVER AND A ROPE PLAITER

The most common interpretation of Job 10:11b is to imagine that God is a weaver who weaves or knits the sinews and bones together into a woven fabric. Spinning and weaving were daily crafts in ancient Israel, typically carried out by women (Judg 16:13–14; Prov 31:19). Spindle whorls, looms, loom weights, and needle shuttles have been excavated and there are images of looms on artifacts from ancient Israel. Both portable horizontal looms and vertical looms with loom weights have been used in weaving practices. The basic technique of weaving is to let weft threads go over and under the threads of the warp.[72]

Psalm 139:13 uses סכך without any references to the material used in the formation of the human. There is a reference to the creation of the human as an act of embroidering in Ps 139:15. The participle of the verb, רקם, "embroid," is used to describe the crafter and the products of weaving or embroidery in Exodus (Exod 26:36; 38:23). The noun רִקְמָה refers to colorful weaving or clothes with colorful embroidery (Ps 45:15; Ezek. 26:16).[73] This can support interpreting סכך in Ps 139:13 and Job 10:11 as referring to an act of weaving, with sinews and bones as the textiles and Job as the woven fabric. However, it cannot be taken for granted that verse 13 and verse 15 of Ps 139 take the same perspective on the formation of the fetus. They can also complement each other by presenting two different images of God's formation of a human. In Job 10 there are no other descriptions to the formation of a human as embroidering or weaving a fabric, but the metaphor LIFE IS WEAVING illustrates the transience of life in Job 7:6 (cf. Isa 38:12). The images of Job as a woven fabric and God as the weaver are possible interpretations of Job 10:11b.

---

[72] King and Stager 2001, 152–58.
[73] *HALOT*, s.v. "רקם," "רִקְמָה."

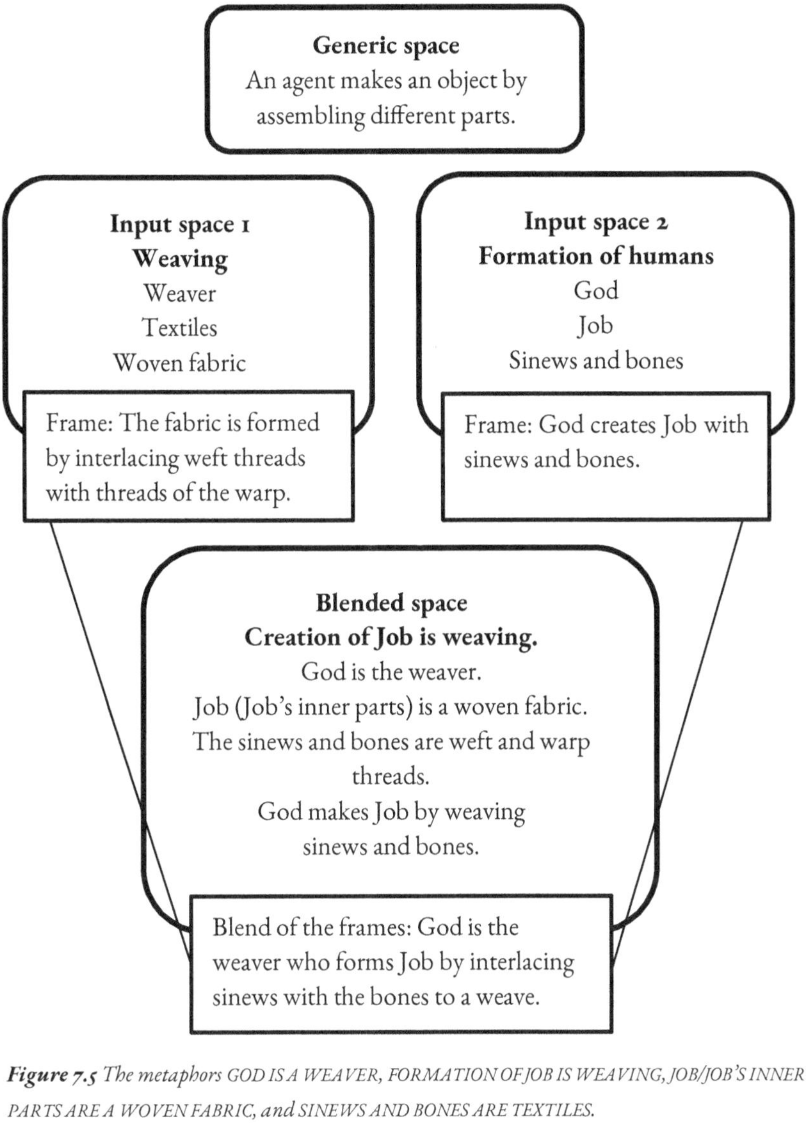

```
                    ┌─────────────────────────────┐
                    │      Generic space          │
                    │ An agent makes an object by │
                    │  assembling different parts.│
                    └─────────────────────────────┘
```

Input space 1
Weaving
Weaver
Textiles
Woven fabric

Frame: The fabric is formed by interlacing weft threads with threads of the warp.

Input space 2
Formation of humans
God
Job
Sinews and bones

Frame: God creates Job with sinews and bones.

Blended space
Creation of Job is weaving.
God is the weaver.
Job (Job's inner parts) is a woven fabric.
The sinews and bones are weft and warp threads.
God makes Job by weaving sinews and bones.

Blend of the frames: God is the weaver who forms Job by interlacing sinews with the bones to a weave.

Figure 7.5 *The metaphors GOD IS A WEAVER, FORMATION OF JOB IS WEAVING, JOB/JOB'S INNER PARTS ARE A WOVEN FABRIC, and SINEWS AND BONES ARE TEXTILES.*

The organizing frame WEAVING goes back to the same general frame CRAFTSMANSHIP as the metaphors of pottery making and cheesemaking. The assembling of threads into a piece of cloth corresponds to the coagulation in the clay and cheese metaphors, but it diverges from them because the material of the product is not solidified by heat but is instead assembled into a new unit. This is coherent with 11a, which describes how God adds the skin and flesh to Job. The body parts in both 11a and 11b are then viewed as textiles. Verse 11a includes the SKIN AND FLESH ARE CLOTHES which corresponds to the metaphor BONES AND SINEWS ARE TEXTILES. The weaving metaphor departs from the dressing metaphor because it does not describe an act of covering Job, but an act of shaping the inside of the body. The image of a woven fabric corresponds to the image of how sinews are attached to the bones. Just as a weave is formed by threads that together create a unified fabric, the body takes shape and becomes a visible, cohesive unit.

Another way of understanding intertwining, which also uses the metaphor SINEWS AND BONES ARE TEXTILES, is that God plaits them into more stable units. The sinews and bones are then intertwined as threads are plaited to thicker and stronger ropes. Job 40:17 describes the sinews of Behemoth as plaited (שׂרג) and continues on to describe his bones as tubes of metal. Habel suggests that Job 40:17 is an allusion to the formation of Job in Job 10:11.[74] The best way to understand Job 40:17 is that his sinews are entwined to thicker and stronger chunks of sinews. This could also be the image in Job 10:11b.

The metaphor FORMATION OF JOB IS PLAITING ROPES implies the metaphor JOB'S SINEWS AND BONES ARE THREADS INTERTWINED TO STRONG ROPES as depicted in Figure 7.6. Job's inner parts are described as strong ropes made of intertwined sinews and bones. Verse 11b complements verse 11a, which describes the formation of Job's outer layer, and the entire verse then refers to the complete formation of Job. The image of Job as plaited highlights the stability and strength of Job. If the skin and clothes are used to give a protective cover, then the intertwining of the bones and sinews highlight the inner strength. This is in accordance with how the bones are usually depicted in the Book of Job and the HB. As the rope plaiter, God is a crafter who, by uniting different treads, makes a new unit with new characteristics. If God has plaited Job's sinews and bones, then God has deliberately made Job strong and robust. It accentuates the question of why God would now want to tear down the strength of Job.

---

[74] Habel 1985, 566.

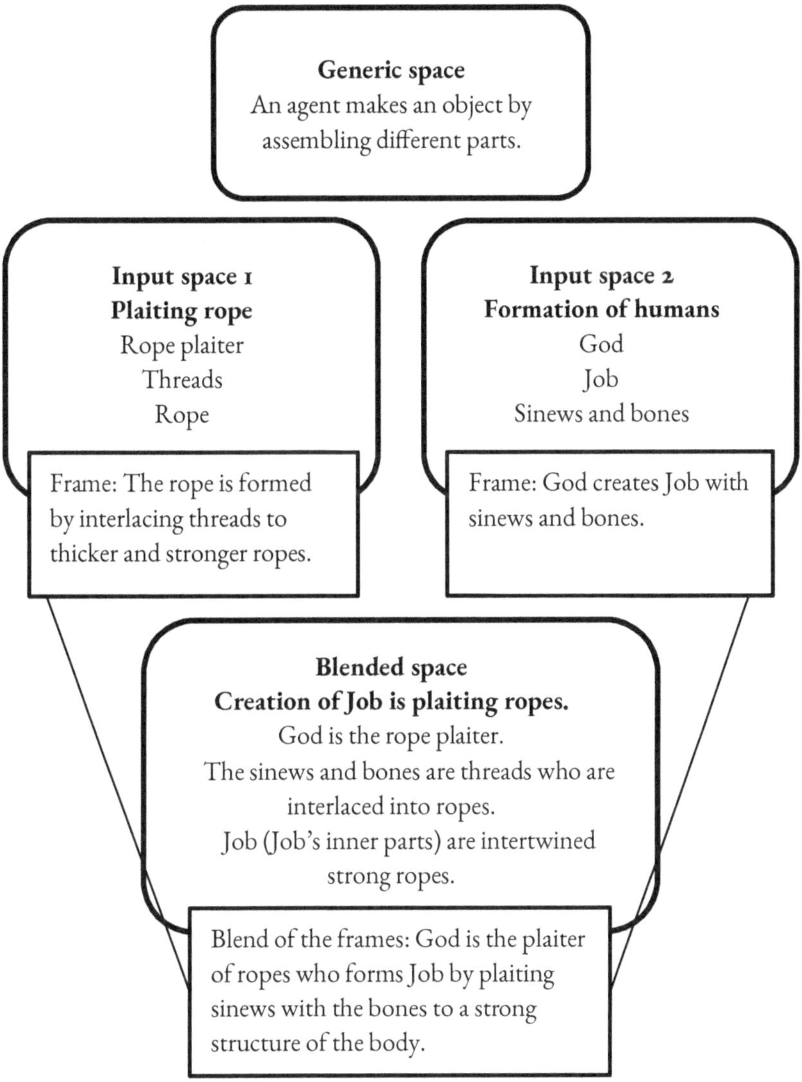

```
                    ┌─────────────────────────┐
                    │    Generic space        │
                    │ An agent makes an object by │
                    │ assembling different parts. │
                    └─────────────────────────┘

┌──────────────────────────┐      ┌──────────────────────────┐
│      Input space 1       │      │      Input space 2       │
│      Plaiting rope       │      │   Formation of humans    │
│       Rope plaiter       │      │           God            │
│         Threads          │      │           Job            │
│          Rope            │      │     Sinews and bones     │
│                          │      │                          │
│ Frame: The rope is formed│      │ Frame: God creates Job with│
│ by interlacing threads to│      │ sinews and bones.        │
│ thicker and stronger ropes.│    │                          │
└──────────────────────────┘      └──────────────────────────┘

              ┌──────────────────────────────────┐
              │         Blended space            │
              │ Creation of Job is plaiting ropes.│
              │     God is the rope plaiter.     │
              │ The sinews and bones are threads who are │
              │        interlaced into ropes.    │
              │ Job (Job's inner parts) are intertwined │
              │           strong ropes.          │
              │                                  │
              │ Blend of the frames: God is the plaiter │
              │ of ropes who forms Job by plaiting │
              │ sinews with the bones to a strong │
              │      structure of the body.      │
              └──────────────────────────────────┘
```

Figure 7.6 *The metaphors: GOD IS A ROPE PLAITER, FORMATION OF JOB IS PLAITING ROPES, JOB/JOB'S INNER PARTS ARE INTERTWINED STRONG ROPES, and SINEWS AND BONES ARE TEXTILES.*

These two interpretations, where Job's interior is a woven fabric and strong ropes, are coherent: both a woven fabric and a rope consist of intertwined threads which together form a larger and more fixed unit. The characteristics of stability and being a fixed unit are coherent with the coagulation metaphors.

To summarize: One possible interpretation of 11b is that it depicts the metaphor FORMATION OF JOB IS WEAVING A FABRIC. It would cohere with the clay and cheese metaphors by depicting God as a crafter, and to some extent, also with the solidification process. The woven fabric coheres with the image of skin and flesh as clothes, yet it refers to an inner structure of the body rather than its covering. The weaving metaphor downplays the strength of the bones and sinews. These characteristics are instead highlighted if the bones and sinews are imagined as being plaited as ropes, interpreting 11b as the metaphor FORMATION OF JOB IS PLAITING ROPES.

God Is a Builder of a Booth

Verse 11b may also be interpreted as God intertwining Job's bones and sinews as branches and creeping plants to make a booth. This would correspond to the third root of סכך in *HALOT* meaning "covering," and how it is used in Mishna and Talmud in descriptions of building a booth by intertwining branches. The image of building a booth would be suitable to describe the formation of a body. The branches and the creeping plants are intertwined to become stronger, much like a rope gains its strength from many threads being plaited together. In a booth constructed from branches and plants, the intertwined branches and creeper plants form the load-bearing structure, but also the roof, which provides protection from the sun and rain. Van Hecke rejects the image that God covers Job with bones and sinews, due to the fact that the bones and sinews are the inner structure of the body and not the outer layer which can be said to cover Job.[75] However, if the word סכך refers to a covering with branches as in the constructing of a booth, then the covering would be part of the metaphor. The bones and sinews refer to the bearing structure of the body which holds the body together as the branches do in a leaf booth, but they are also a protective shelter which covers Job's innards. The thorax and the skull bone are examples of how bones shelter vital organs. The image of the bones and sinews as protecting the inner body would be a close parallel to verse 11a, which describes the outer layer of protection.

---

[75] Van Hecke 2010, 108.

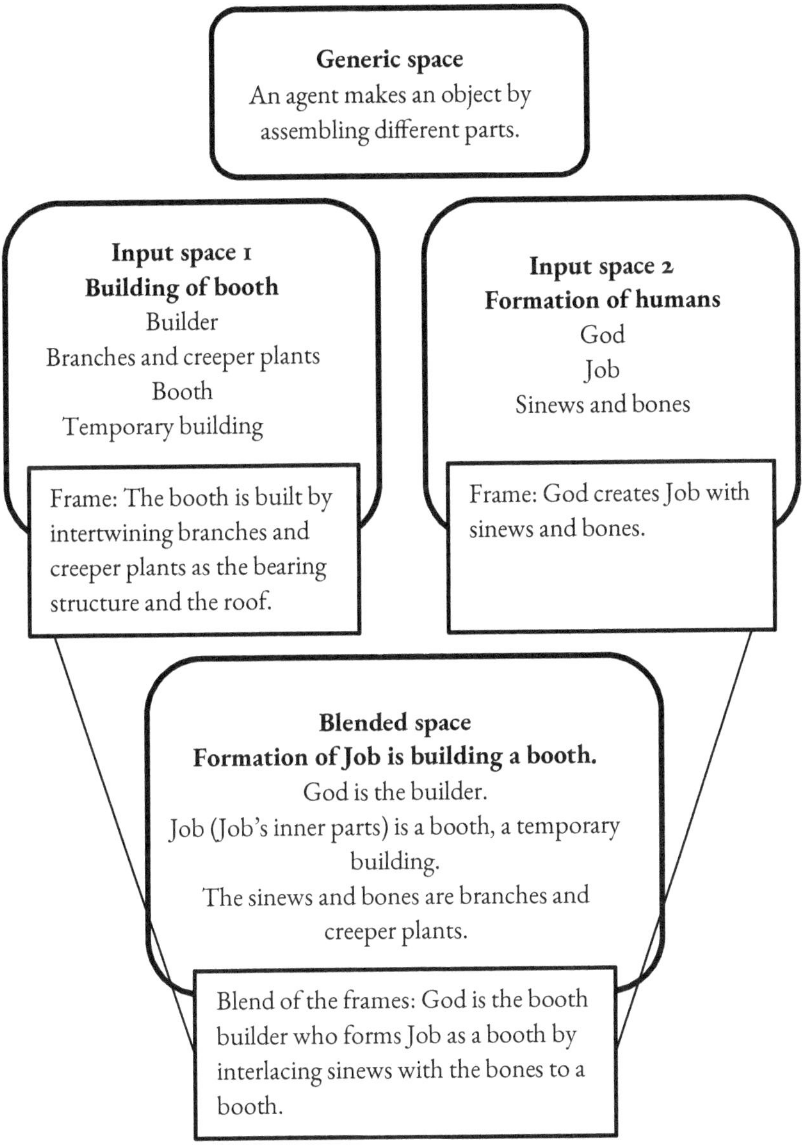

Birth Metaphors in Job 10:8–12   213

Generic space
An agent makes an object by assembling different parts.

Input space 1
Building of booth
Builder
Branches and creeper plants
Booth
Temporary building

Frame: The booth is built by intertwining branches and creeper plants as the bearing structure and the roof.

Input space 2
Formation of humans
God
Job
Sinews and bones

Frame: God creates Job with sinews and bones.

Blended space
Formation of Job is building a booth.
God is the builder.
Job (Job's inner parts) is a booth, a temporary building.
The sinews and bones are branches and creeper plants.

Blend of the frames: God is the booth builder who forms Job as a booth by interlacing sinews with the bones to a booth.

Figure 7.7 *The metaphors GOD IS A BUILDER, FORMATION OF JOB IS BUILDING A BOOTH, JOB/JOB'S INNER PARTS ARE A BOOTH, and SINEWS AND BONES ARE BRANCHES.*

The metaphor GOD IS A BUILDER OF A BOOTH, displayed in Figure 7.7, is also derived from the more general frame CRAFTMANSHIP, just as the metaphors of the potter, cheesemaker, weaver and rope plaiter. Just as the weaving and plaiting metaphors, it diverges from the cheese and clay metaphors because Job is not formed by solidification through heat but by assembling parts together. The bones and sinews are in this blend seen as branches and creeper plants, which both cover Job's inwards and form the bearing structure of Job's body. The bones are, as I have shown, often used to describe the health and strength of a person, which corresponds well to how the branches are used in the construction of a booth. This way of constructing a booth may also highlight that the building is temporary. Such booths were used in the feast of the tabernacle, and they should resemble the temporary booths used in the wandering in the wilderness (Lev 23:43; 1 King 20:12; Jonah 4:5). The metaphor JOB IS A BOOTH, then, just as the clay metaphor, refers to the transience of Job's life. Like the dressing metaphor, it also accentuates God's protection of Job. God's covering of Job with bones and sinews is an act of protection which can be compared with how God shelters the psalmists under God's wing (Ps 91:4) or in a booth (Ps 27:5).

Even if the intertwining of Job's bones and sinews highlights Job's inner structure, it also corresponds to Job's whole body. The metaphor JOB IS A BOOTH is a more specific metaphor of the general metaphor THE BODY IS A BUILDING. The metaphor BODY IS A BUILDING is a universal metaphor, but it is modified by how the specific culture conceptualizes bodies and buildings.[76] The metaphor JOB IS A BOOTH is explained above by how a booth was said to be constructed in the HB, Mishna, and Talmud. The metaphor BODY IS A BUILDING is rarely used in the HB. Instead, the house metaphor is applied to groups of humans, such as family, lineage, or nation (Exod 2:1; Deut 25:9; Jer 35:2). This is also seen in the expression of David's dynasty as "the house of David" (2 Sam 7:11; 1 King 12:26). Humans, as a group, and nations are referred to as houses that God can destroy and rebuild (Ps 28:5; Jer 42:10). The metaphor BODY IS A BUILDING may be implied in Gen 2:22 and in metaphors referring to the body as a tent or house of clay. The image of God building a human from bones may be implied in Gen 2:22, when God takes

---

[76] In English, the conceptual metaphor BODY IS A BUILDING is behind expressions such as "Eyes are windows to the soul," and "There's not much going on upstairs," (Lakoff, et al. 1991, 192). Chilton and Lakoff discuss the importance of recognizing cultural differences in how houses are conceptualized to understand how house metaphors are used. They compare Russia and the USA, noting that these differences also affect political discourse, where nations are often likened to houses (Chilton and Lakoff 1995, 54–55).

a "rib" (צֵלָע) from the first human and builds (בנה) a woman from it. The verb בנה, "build," is primarily used for constructing buildings, but also appears metaphorically in contexts such as building a family or receiving a child (Gen 16:2; 30:3; Deut 25:9).[77] The destruction of a house or a tent is used in descriptions of death and threats to someone's life (Job 4:19; Ps 52:7, Isa 38:12; Jer 10:20). In such descriptions, the metaphor THE BODY IS A BUILDING could be implied. However, it could also refer to the house as the building that provides protection, and when destroyed it leaves the residents homeless and vulnerable. The metaphor BODY IS A TENT is used in Wis 9:15, which refers to the body with the Greek word σκῆνος, "tent."[78] Isaiah 38:12 uses both the metaphor of removing a tent and that of cutting a loom to describe death. This implies both the metaphor of a human as a tent and as a woven fabric. The tent is made of woven cloths and can therefore be seen as an extension of the weaving metaphor, and does not need to be grounded in the general metaphor THE BODY IS A BUILDING.

To summarize: The intertwining of sinews and bones can also be interpreted in the metaphor FORMATION OF JOB IS BUILDING A BOOTH. The bones and sinews would then correspond to the branches and creeper plants used to build the bearing structure as well as the protective roof. It underscores the strength of the bones and sinews as well as protecting vital organs. God is also here described as a crafter who makes something. A booth is a temporary building and thereby depicts the transience of life. JOB IS A BOOTH is a specific metaphor of the universal metaphor BODY IS A BUILDING, which is, however, rarely used in the HB:

Weaving, Plaiting, or Booth Construction?

Verse 11 describes God assembling Job's body by uniting its parts. The dressing metaphor and the intertwining of sinews and bones entail bringing parts together. The verb סכך can be interpreted metaphorically as weaving a fabric, plaiting a rope, or building a booth, or as a literal act of intertwining bones and sinews. All four, like the coagulation metaphors, describe the process of the body coming together into a more solid unit. Because verse 11b is part of a cluster of metaphors in verses 9–11, it is most likely that סכך refers to a metaphor. These metaphors share some features, as God is depicted as a handcrafter who makes a product by assembling parts to a unity. The weaving and rope plaiting metaphor refer to Job's body as a textile, which corresponds to the clothing metaphor. The booth metaphor and

---

[77] *HALOT*, s.v. "בנה." The Akkadian verb *banû* means both "build" and "create," and so also the same root in Ugaritic. (Wagner, "בנה," *TDOT* 2:166).
[78] *LSJ*, s.v. "σκῆνος."

the dressing metaphor share the act of covering someone with a protective surface. I would argue that the rope and booth metaphors more closely correspond to the strength of the bones and sinews, which is an important characteristic of bones and sinews elsewhere in Job and the HB. The act of plaiting rope easily applies to other forms of intertwining and is a simpler technique than weaving or booth-building. As a double-scope metaphor, with ropes visualized as sinews and bones, it effectively portrays God as the one intertwining them. The advantage of the booth metaphor is that it describes the bones and sinews as both a bearing structure and as a protective surface of the inward organs. The analogy between bones and sinews and branches and creeper plants are more compelling than between them and fabrics used to make a woven fabric or a rope.

The metaphors of humans as woven fabrics, buildings, and ropes are not common in the HB. The transience of life is depicted through metaphors suggesting that humans are like woven fabrics, as seen in Isa 38:12 and Job 7:6. The metaphor BODY IS A BUILDING is not explicitly stated in the HB, but may be implied in Gen 2:22 and the tent metaphor in Isa 38:12. The image of plaited sinews only occurs in Job 40:17. Psalm 139:13 also uses the word סכך and its proximity to Ps 139:15, which describes the formation of a human as embroidery, supports the interpretation that סכך refers to a needleworker tying parts together or to weaving.

To conclude, there are arguments supporting all three interpretations. The booth building metaphor corresponds better to the construction of the body, where the sinews and bones form the strong bearing structure. The metaphor of rope plaiting makes it easier to visualize how God intertwines sinews and bones, as it is a simpler technique than the others. The weaving metaphor would better correspond to the description of fetal formation as embroidery in Ps 139:15.

Interaction of the Metaphors in Job 10:8–12

The metaphors in Job 10:8–12 both strengthen and complement each other. Collectively, they emphasize Job's value and highlight God's role as a handcrafter, underlining the expectation that God should not destroy what God has created.

God is the agent in all four metaphors and is the handcrafter who works as a potter, cheesemaker, and as either a weaver, a plaiter, or a booth builder. God is the dresser who puts Job together by dressing him. These metaphors highlight God as the creator, and that God worked hard in the formation of Job. Job should therefore not be wasted. God is the potter, and potters should not destroy their artifacts unless they are flawed and damaged. Job insists on his innocence, and the clay metaphor emphasizes that if Job is indeed innocent, then God should not destroy him.

Similarly, the other metaphors reinforce the idea that God should refrain from destroying Job. The value of the product is emphasized in the metaphor JOB IS MILK AND CHEESE, as milk and cheese were valuable products not to be wasted. The dressing metaphor suggests God granted Job special status by dressing him. The interaction between the metaphors shapes the interpretation of God's role in the cheesemaking metaphor. Even though the formation of Job as cheese relates to the domain of GESTATION, God's role will be interpreted, in line with other metaphors, as a handcrafter rather than a begetter.

Only the clay metaphor unites both the formation and destruction of Job and encompasses both Job's strength and fragility. The material clay also signals transience and mortality. The transience of Job's life may also be described in the metaphor JOB IS A WOVEN FABRIC or in JOB IS A TEMPORARY BOOTH. The clothing metaphor does not express the destruction in its immediate context, but it coheres with other descriptions in Job in which the destruction of Job is made by destroying his skin. The dressing metaphor in Job 10:11 is a counter-image to these descriptions.

The clay and cheese metaphors obtain the craft and the material from the source domain. The dressing and intertwining metaphors instead combine the acts of the source domain with the material from the target domain, as they refer to body parts. The clay and milk metaphors describe the process of shaping something soft that then solidifies through heat. The acts of dressing and intertwining are instead acts of creating by assembling parts into one new unit. This implies that the clay and cheese metaphors describe the shape and formation of Job's whole body, while the dressing and intertwining metaphors highlight specific features of Job, his protective outer layer, and his strong inner structure.

The metaphors in Job 10:8–12 display Job as a distinct object with boundaries. The clay is formed from formless clay to a specific object with a specific form. The cheeses are formed from a coagulated mass of milk to distinct cheeses. The metaphor SKIN ARE CLOTHES coheres with many metaphors in the Book of Job that describe protection as setting boundaries, especially God's protection of Job in the prologue (Job 1:10). The intertwined bones and sinews are both the inner structure and a protective shelter of internal organs. This characteristic of a skeleton is best displayed if the word סכך refers to the action of building a booth of intertwined branches and creeper plants. The metaphor JOB IS A BOOTH is a specific metaphor of the general metaphor THE BODY IS A BUILDING, which highlights the construction of the body and the way different body parts fit together. The body and the building share the image schema of CONTAINMENT, having DISTINCT SURFACES and BEARING STRUCTURE. The booth metaphor is the only metaphor in Job 10:9–11 that entails that the body is a container, though this aspect is downplayed in this context, while the bearing structure is highlighted. The distinct surfaces are highlighted by the dressing metaphor, while the metaphor depicting Job as hardened clay further emphasizes Job's stability. Hardened ceramic ware and a raised booth with a proper bearing structure can each stand on their own. These metaphors go back to the primary metaphor PERSISTENCE IS REMAINING UPRIGHT.[79] The intertwining of bones and sinews enhances their strength and structure. This is implied in the metaphor of weaving, but is even more pronounced in the metaphors of rope plaiting and building a booth. Job is created as a human with both boundaries and stability. God's act of giving him boundaries and inner strength is an act of protection and forming Job as a self-reliable individual. Furthermore, verse 12 refers to God's protection.

It is not explicitly said that the formation described in verses 8–12 takes place in the womb, but this is implied by the cheese metaphor. It contains several associations with the domain of GESTATION. Milk shares entailments with semen, and formation of a fetus was understood as a coagulation of body fluids. The cheese metaphor is suitable in Job 10 because it both entails associations with how a fetus is formed by coagulation and is able to depict God as the crafter making the cheese. Associations between procreation and the clay metaphor are also well-established in the HB and ancient West Asia.

The description of Job's formation in Job 10:8–12 coheres with the description of the formation of a fetus in in Ps 139. They share the metaphor of God as the crafter who intertwines the fetus in the womb. Both Job and the psalmists use the fact that God has formed them as evidence of God's omniscience, asserting that God is aware of their innocence. The metaphors of the psalm are not distorted in Job but rather adapted to fit another context. While both Job 10 and Ps 139 portray the formation of a fetus as a positive act, in Job, this positive imagery is used as a counter-image to Job's sufferings. As previously noted, the same metaphors used to describe the formation of Job are employed elsewhere to describe his destruction. The Accuser destroys Job's protective boundaries, even the skin. There are several descriptions of Job losing his skin, and how his body is pierced. Just as the expression in Job 1:21 uses negation of birth to describe death, the metaphors in Job 10:9–11 can be negated and used to depict death and destruction.

---

[79] For discussion on PERSISTENCE IS REMAINING UPRIGHT, see Grady 1997b, 273–279.

Birth Metaphors in Job 10:18–19

Job expresses once again his wish that he had died in the womb, and he blames God for his birth saying, "Why did you bring me out of the womb?" Job 10:18–19 can be mistaken for a simple repetition of Job's words in Job 3. However, the context of an imagined court turns Job's complaint of God's involvement in his birth into a direct accusation against God. The midwife metaphor is used together with the metaphor depicting God as a watcher to accentuate the absurdity of how God delivers Job from the womb only to later destroy him. This parallels the metaphors of formation and destruction found in Job 10:8–12. My investigation of the birth metaphors in Job 10:18–19 focuses on God's role in Job's birth and discusses how the domains of WOMB and DEATH relate to each other and how the birth metaphors in Job 10:18–19 differ from Job 3.

Text and Translation of Job 10:18–19

18	וְלָמָּה מֵרֶחֶם הֹצֵאתָנִי	And why did you bring me out from the womb?
	אֶגְוַע	I should have died,
	וְעַיִן לֹא־תִרְאֵנִי׃	so that no eyes would have seen me.
19	כַּאֲשֶׁר לֹא־הָיִיתִי אֶהְיֶה	Then it would have been as if I never had lived,
	מִבֶּטֶן לַקֶּבֶר אוּבָל׃	carried from the belly to the grave.

Literary Structure and Comments

Job 10:8–12 expresses the belief that God should protect and care for the ones God has created. This is rejected in verses 13–17, which state what is really in God's heart: not care, but anger and condemnation. Verse 12 says that God has preserved (שמר) Job's spirit, and verse 14 uses the same verb to describe how God watches Job to see if he sins (cf. Job 7:17–21; 14:3). Job asserts that God will not absolve him of his sin; instead, God continually renews the testimony against him and intensifies God's anger towards him. God is said to hunt Job like a lion, and to repeat God's wonders against him (v. 16).[80] The tone is ironic: this is not the way God, the creator, should treat humans, especially not innocent ones. Job's sense of being watched and hunted by God leads to his complaint in verses 18–19, where he wishes that God had never brought him out of the womb or that he had died before any eyes would have seen him. The eyes must here belong to God, in accordance with

---

[80] Whether God or Job is being compared to a lion in this verse is ambiguous. In the Psalms, enemies are often compared to lions (Pss 7:3; 10:9; 17:12; 22:14; 35:17; 57:5), and God is depicted as an attacking lion in Hos 5:14; 13:7.

how God is described as a watcher in verse 14. Following this complaint, Job pleads with God to leave him alone, before he goes to the land of no return.

Verse 18 starts with וְלָ֣מָּה, "and why," and is a parallel to the complaint in Job 3:11, 16, 20. The difference is that Job now directly accuses God of being responsible for his birth. Job's explicit accusations against God begin in Job 6–7, and by Job 9–10 he seeks to summon God to court. Job focuses on what he sees as irrational and unjust actions by God. The birth metaphors are used in Job's accusation, claiming that God delivers Job with the intent to bring sufferings upon him.

GOD IS A MIDWIFE AND A WATCHER

Job asks, "And why did you bring me out (הֹצֵאתָ֑נִי) from the womb?" The verb יצא (Qal), "go out," is used in several references to birth in Job (Job 1:21; 38:8, 29), describing the one born as going out from the womb. The Hiphil of יצא, "bring out," is not commonly used in descriptions of birth or in references to the midwives. However, the act of God as the one who brings Job out of the womb is similar to the descriptions of God as a midwife in Pss 22:10–11; 71:6; Isa 66:9, and when the sea goes out of the womb in Job 38:8–10.[81] Therefore, it most likely that the metaphor GOD IS A MIDWIFE is behind the expression "Why did you bring me out from the womb?" This is the first time in the Book of Job that God is explicitly said to be the one who delivered Job. This image is implied in Job 3:10 when God implicitly is accused not to have closed the doors of the womb.

Figure 7.8 displays the metaphor GOD IS AN UNMERCIFUL MIDWIFE as it is used in Job 10:18–19. The metaphor does not use the caring associations of a midwife as the one who protects and cares for the child and the mother. The references to God's act of delivering babies in Psalms and Isaiah are used to portray God's mercy and ability to save the ones who suffer. These associations of a midwife are absent in Job 10:18–19. Instead, God is described as unmerciful, watching Job, attacking him, and bringing suffering upon him. The disanalogy between the care typically associated with a midwife and God's destructive actions toward Job is used to emphasize the perceived injustice and cruelty of God's acts. The notion of the absurdity of God's actions is the emergent structure of the blend.

---

[81] See Chapter 3, pages 81–82.

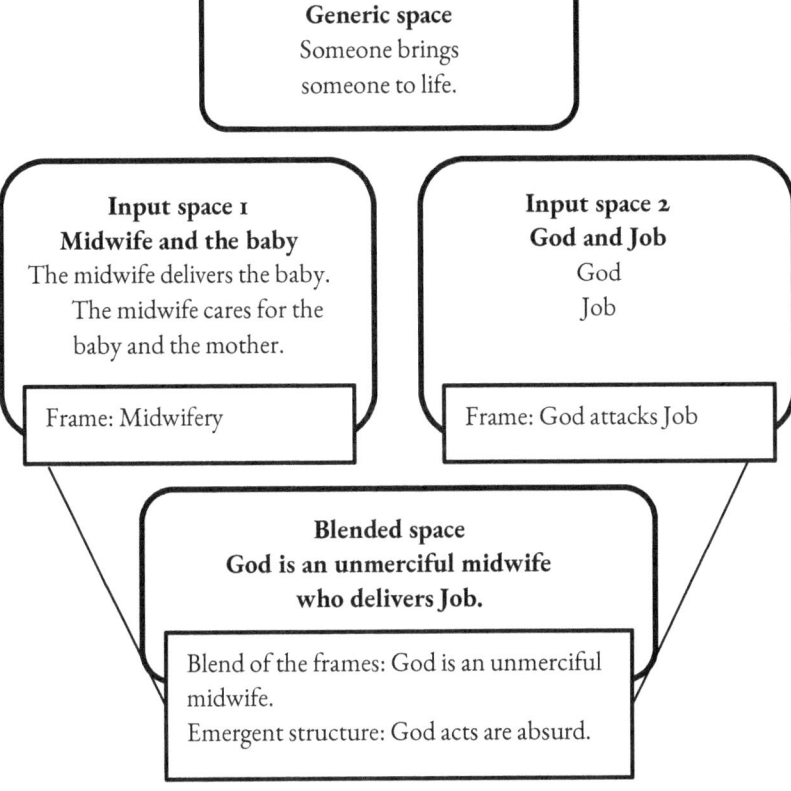

Figure 7.8 The metaphor GOD IS AN UNMERCIFUL MIDWIFE WHO DELIVERS JOB.

The fact that God has brought Job out of the womb does not prevent God from destroying him. God does not care for Job, despite being his creator and midwife. This is the same clash as in Job 10:8–12 where God is both described as the one forming Job in the womb and as the one who later destroys him. When the reader integrates the metaphor of God as a midwife with the context which also depicts God in other images such as a watcher who destroys Job, it leads to a clash between the frames of these different metaphors and to an emergent structure which underscores the absurdity of Job's situation and God's actions. The mental process of integrating these two roles could be depicted in the blending schema in Figure 7.9.

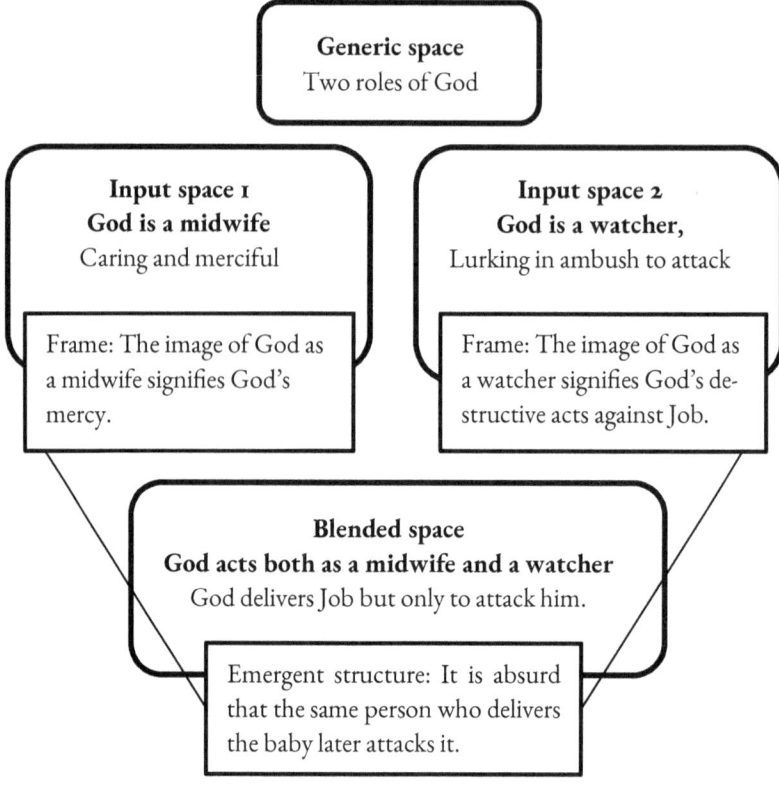

Figure 7.9 Blending schema of the integration of God's double roles as a midwife and a watcher.

The emergent structure is that God's acts are absurd, and it strengthens Job's accusation that God acts unjustly. The absence of God's mercy as a characteristic of God's midwifery makes Job wish that he had not been delivered at all. The images of God as a cruel watcher influence the image of God as a midwife and God is not portrayed as a merciful midwife associated with God's protection and care. The portrayal of God's supervision of Job is ambiguous in Job 10. God's supervision should include God's loyalty as is stated in Job 10:12, but in Job 10:14–19 it rather portrays God as lurking in ambush to attack Job, punishing him for his sins.[82] The psalmist of Ps 139 praises God's supervision, but in Job 10:14–19 it is the reason

---

[82] As Habel points out, this theme already starts with the Accuser who is portrayed as an observer or supervisor of the humans in Job 1:7–8 (Habel 1985, 200–201).

behind the complaint and Job's wish that he had died at birth instead of being delivered from the womb.

In Job 10:8–12, Job asks why God created him only to destroy him, but also refers to the womb as a place where God showed him protection and loyalty. This idea is completed in Job 10:18–19 with Job's question of why God brought him out of the womb. In the womb he would have been hidden from his watcher. Nevertheless, Job does not express a wish to stay in the womb, only that he had never been delivered from it, as he prefers death to being harassed by God. This contrast between the usual appeal for divine protection during birth and Job's wish that he had died at birth underscores Job's resentment towards his life and, more specifically, towards God's actions in his life.

To summarize: God is depicted as a midwife in Job 10:18–19 who has brought Job out of the womb. The context makes it clear that God is not acting as a merciful midwife once Job is delivered. Job 10 contains metaphors of God as a lion who hunts Job and a watcher that waits for him to sin. The expected associations of a midwife as caring and merciful clash with the associations of an evil watcher, underscoring the absurdity of God's actions. God acts unjustly and not as a creator, nor with the care of a midwife. Job regrets his birth because when he was born God, as a watcher, started to attack him.

WOMB and DEATH

Job 3 describes death in positive terms. The existences of the womb and death were blended in the metaphor THE WOMB IS A GRAVE, and the existence in the womb-grave was seen as a counter-image to the misery of life. The darkness of the womb was preferred to the light of life (Job 3:16, 20) and death was described as a liberation from hardship (Job 3:13–19). Job 10 presents another view of death in Job 10, describing it as darkness and a place of no order (vv. 21–22). The womb, on the other hand, is a place of God's loyalty. Death and the womb are not blended into the same place. In Job 3, the grave and Sheol are not mentioned as specific places but blended with the womb. Job 10:18 expresses Job's wish that he had died in the womb, but this womb is not implied to be the grave as in Job 3. Instead, verse 19 expresses that if Job had died, he would be carried from the womb to the grave. The womb and the grave are presented as distinct places in Job 10:19. They are not blended, because the stillborn who dies in the womb or at birth is carried to the grave. There is a time between the womb and the grave, and Job wishes this time could be eliminated, making it as if he had never lived. Even though the linguistic expression מִבֶּטֶן לַקֶּבֶר, "from the womb to the grave," links the womb to the grave, they are not thought of as the same place. It is not, as Vall and others claim, that the expression links the grave and the womb more closely together compared to Job 3.[83]

In Job 3, Job wishes that he had never left the womb, so that the misery would be hidden from his eyes. He regrets that he saw the light of life as a newborn. In 10:18, he instead wishes that no eyes had seen him. The eyes in verse 19 belong to God who is described as Job's watcher in Job 10:14. This is a thought shift. Job 3 equates birth and life with his misery. In Job 10, Job also wishes he had not been born, not because he would have immediately experienced misery, but because the watcher would see him and then bring misery upon him. In this chapter, Job does not view misery as an inherent characteristic of light and life; instead, he blames his watcher, God. Unfortunately, he does not know how he would be able to escape from his watcher. Therefore, it would be better if he had died and gone straight from the womb to the grave.

Verse 19 explains the reason behind Job's wish to have been carried from the womb to the grave. He says, "then it would have been as if I had never lived." Job does not want to live, but he does not say that he longs for death. In verse 20, he asks God to turn away from him, so that he might cheer up a little before he dies. Job 10:22 describes death as the land of deep darkness and no order. It is a different description than that of rest, liberation from oppression, and equality between slaves and masters presented in Job 3. Mathewson concludes that Job cannot long for death and at the same time try to bring God to court. He argues that death would then be the ultimate proof of Job's guilt, and that the legal language brings bad connotations to death.[84] I agree, and it is also clear that Job's argument and mood shift when the idea of bringing God to court is introduced. It empowers Job, as if Job realizes that he cannot bring God to court if he is dead. Job's hope is not the grave (Job 17:15) but the court. The legal procedure makes Job challenge God's actions. The accusation of God being an unmerciful midwife and a destructive watcher are part of Job's indictment against God. The legal language articulates the tension between how God should act and how God acts. God is a criminal who does not act righteously (Job 9:24) and God is a midwife who does not care for the wellbeing of the newborn.

To summarize: Job does not long for death in Job 10, but sees death as a way to escape life. The womb and the grave are not blended in Job 10 but seen as different places. The womb is depicted in positive terms while death in negative. In Job 3,

---

[83] Vall 1993, 49–50; van der Zwan 2019a, 5.
[84] Mathewson 2006, 107–10.

Job complains about having to see the light of life as a newborn, whereas in Job 10, he laments that God, his watcher, has laid eyes upon him. Job does not wish to die but, due to God's attacks, he wishes he had never lived.

Summary and Conclusions

The birth metaphors in Job 10 are used as counter-images to the misery of Job's life, and serve as part of Job's accusation against God. These metaphors highlight how God has worked hard to form him, giving him strength and protection, which contrasts sharply with how God then destroys him. Job's lament about why God brought him out of the womb implies that he was better off in the womb than outside it.

Job 10:8–12 depicts God's formation of Job in metaphors, depicting God as a handcrafter and Job as a valuable product, or God as a dresser who dresses Job with protective clothes. The different metaphors complement and strengthen each other. The clay metaphor can unite the theme of God's work of forming Job with the notion of waste in destroying him if he is innocent; a potter does not destroy undamaged goods. The cheese metaphor can both refer to God as a handcrafter and to the formation of a fetus as coagulation. The dressing metaphor highlights God's act of giving Job a protective shelter. The description of God intertwining Job's bones and sinews can be explained by the metaphors displaying God as a weaver, rope plaiter, or a builder of a booth. These metaphors refer to the inner structure of Job, and the rope plaiting and both building metaphors accentuate the strength of the bearing structure. All these metaphors refer to God as the agent, and imply that Job is created as a valuable person with vitality, inner strength, and clear boundaries. However, they also suggest Job's fragility: a ceramic vessel can be shattered, a woven fabric can be cut from its loom, and a booth built of branches is only temporary. Correspondingly, Job is made of flesh and is mortal, subordinate to God, who is not made of flesh. The question arises: why does God, who has formed Job, now seek to destroy him?

The metaphors describing Job's formation are used to force God to treat Job better, to behave as a creator instead of a destructor. The request to "remember" in verse 9 explains the purpose of these metaphors. They are used to make God remember God's creative act, serving as an appeal for God to continue treating Job with loyalty and respect. God needs to respect Job's constitution as being both strong and fragile, valuable and mortal. Brown and Kynes emphasize that the description of the formation of Job is used to show that God knows that Job is innocent.[85] This is accentuated by the clay metaphor. The description of Job's formation is used both as an accusation against God and as an appeal to make God change and start treating Job justly.

The disanalogy between how God behaves and should behave is accentuated by the clash between the metaphors GOD IS A MIDWIFE and GOD IS A WATCHER. God has, just as a midwife, brought Job from the womb, but in Job 10 God is not a midwife who protects and cares for the one she has delivered, as in Ps 22:10–11 and Isa 66:9–10. Instead, the midwife metaphor is used in a context describing how God hunts Job as a lion, bring sufferings upon him, and acts as a watcher. It is irrational that the one who acts as a midwife and brings the baby out of the womb later hunts and destroys the one born. God's act of formation and bringing Job to life are not followed up by a caring God. Job 10 describes the womb and the realm of death differently. The formation of Job is valued as good, while death is described as darkness and no order. The womb and the grave are not blended. Job does not long for death or the grave. He wishes he had not been born and thus escaped the attacks of his watcher.

In Job 10, God does not act as a creator should, but Job begins to regain some of the characteristics given to him at his creation. He regains some strength and wants to force God to court to hear his accusation. The birth metaphors help him to argue his case.

---

[85] Brown 2000, 107–24; Kynes 2012, 108–12.

8. Birth Metaphors in Job 38

God answers Job from the whirlwind in Job 38–39, first reprimanding him for darkening God's counsel without knowledge, and then asking Job to prepare himself for an interrogation. God proceeds to ask questions about creation and takes Job on a tour of its different parts. The tour begins with the primeval creation and the depths of the world, continues to the sources of precipitation by asking who delivers the snow and rain, and ends with God showing Job the life of wild animals. Each of these three parts of God's first speech contains a birth scene, two of them are in Job 38. The first one, in Job 38:8–11, describes the birth of the sea, and the second, in Job 38:28–29, refers to the birth of ice and hoarfrost.

In this chapter, I will explore the birth metaphors in Job 38, and how the domain of BIRTH is used as a source domain in metaphors referring to the domain of CREATION. The birth scenes in God's first speech share metaphors with Akkadian birth incantations, and I will examine how Job 38 creatively uses these presumed standard metaphors. Traditionally, Job 38–39 is interpreted as an expression of God's control over creation, with the birth of the sea mainly viewed from the perspective of the combat motif, where God subjugates the sea. The birth metaphors are rarely acknowledged, and when they are, they are often considered subordinate to the combat motif or the order of creation. In this chapter and the next, I will demonstrate what insights emerge when the birth metaphors are recognized on their own terms rather than as subordinate to other motifs.[1]

Earlier Interpretations of God's Speeches

Earlier interpretations of God's speeches primarily focused on how God relates to the wild parts of creation. There are two main perspectives on interpreting these speeches. The traditional view suggests that they describe a well-ordered world where God triumphs over evil forces. This view has been challenged by those who argue that the speeches depict creation as both awe-inspiring and terrifying,

---

[1] A preliminary and condensed version of this chapter will be published in Plantin Forthcoming-a.

containing elements of both chaos and order, with God delighting in all creatures, including the wild beasts. These two perspectives are not necessarily in conflict. It is not unusual to assert that Job 38 portrays a well-ordered creation, while Job 39 and God's second speech highlight the disorder within this ordered creation.[2]

Other perspectives on God's speeches have also been explored in previous research. One important insight is that these speeches challenge an anthropocentric worldview. Neither Job 38 nor Job 39 mentions humans or settled areas; they focus solely on the wilderness. The depiction of wild animals in Job 39 underscores the non-human perspective, which I will explore further in the next chapter, "Birth Metaphors in Job 39." Another angle examined in previous research is how God's speeches relate to legal language and Job's quest for justice.[3] However, these interpretations do not engage with the birth metaphors, and will not be discussed further here.

I will present how the speeches are interpreted as describing either a well-ordered world where God combats chaos, or a sublime world that embodies both beauty and danger. The birth metaphors, especially the birth of the sea, are considered in both approaches. Understanding these two major approaches provides essential background for discussing how the birth metaphors interact with conventional beliefs and affect the overall interpretation of God's speeches. A more detailed analysis of existing interpretations of specific birth metaphors will accompany the metaphor analyses.

A Well-Ordered Creation

Job has accused God of failing to preserve the order of creation and not providing for those created (Job 3:10–26; 9:4–12; 10:8–17). Job 38–41 has been viewed as a response to these accusations, illustrating how God is involved in creation, gives it order, and has not abandoned it. It has been argued that Job 38 provides an overview of the order of creation, its foundation, and boundaries. The sea in Job 38, the wild animals in Job 39, and Behemoth and Leviathan in Job 40–41 are commonly interpreted as chaotic forces, although interpretations of how God deals with them vary. These forces have been viewed according to the combat motif, as known from other texts such as the Baal Cycle, the Enuma Elish, and the Egyptian

---

[2] Newsom 2003, 244, 252; Brown 2010, 129.
[3] For this perspective, see Scholnick 1976; Scholnick 1992. She discusses how Job's speeches refer to מִשְׁפָּט as concerning only legal justice, whereas in God's speeches, it takes on a broader meaning as "rule" or "govern." God's speeches emphasize how God governs creation, portraying God as the sovereign ruler of the universe.

myth of Horus and Seth, where the hero god combats the sea and the sea monsters.[4] Consequently, the sea, wild animals, Behemoth, and Leviathan have been regarded as evil and as enemies of God.[5] Keel argues that they represent evil, but that God keeps them bridled and controls them, so they do not pose a threat to God's order of the world.[6] Mettinger contends that God's speeches demonstrate how God protects creation from chaotic waters (38:8–11), emphasizing God's power over chaotic forces that are considered enemies. The depiction of the sea as a baby and Leviathan as a pet are interpreted as humorous representations of God's supremacy over them. Mettinger concludes that God is not a criminal, as Job accuses, because God combats chaotic evil forces.[7]

Levenson discusses the absence of a battle between the sea and God, calling the sea a "sinister" chaotic force. He argues that Job 38:8–11 highlights this by depicting how God encloses and sets limits to the sea. He claims that Job 38 references both the tradition of creation through confinement of water (Gen 1) and the tradition of the flood that threatens the inhabited world (Gen 9). He also notes that to tame Leviathan, God needs a fishhook, arrows, and harpoons. Leviathan is not eliminated; God continues to overpower him. Levenson argues that God's speeches diverge from the traditional combat motif by not describing the sea as a monster but as a baby, and by not portraying Leviathan as defeated in battle, only restricted.[8]

Interpretations that acknowledge the sea, Behemoth, and Leviathan as integral parts of God's creation offer a more nuanced view of God's control over them. These forces may still be viewed as chaotic, but not evil or enemies. Newsom claims that God limits their power but rejects the notion that they are evil. Instead, she argues that God identifies with these chaotic forces. She discusses how the scene of God delivering the sea transforms the image of it: the sea remains a chaotic force, but God cares for and restricts it by swaddling it as a baby.[9] Habel emphasizes the order of God's design, asserting that God gives chaotic forces their place

---

[4] For a discussion of how the sea is portrayed in other texts in the HB, see pages 234–37.

[5] Gordon 1966, 1–3; Keel 1978, 85–86, 125, 156–58; Kubina 1979, 68–76; Lindström 1983, 153–57; Day 1985, 38–49, 65–72; Mettinger 1987, 182–91; Mettinger 1988, 190–200; Gibson 1988, 415–19; Mettinger 1992, 44–47.

[6] Keel 1978, 85–86, 125, 156–58.

[7] Mettinger 1987, 182–91; Mettinger 1988, 190–200; Mettinger 1992, 44–47. The text from 1992 summarizes his more extensive presentation in *Namnet och närvaron* from 1987 (English translation: *In the Search of God* 1988).

[8] Levenson 1988, 15–18.

[9] Newsom 2003, 244–52. Brenner also argues that Leviathan and Behemoth represent God's dark side (Brenner 1981, 134–35).

within creation. God's design contains the sea, the wicked, and alien forces, but God has limited their space for maneuver. God is in control over these chaotic forces, rejoices over them and the paradoxes of creation. Habel suggests that God balances light with darkness, order with chaos, and life with death.[10] Schifferdecker also claims that the sea is not depicted as an enemy and that God grants the chaotic forces a certain degree of freedom.[11]

God's first speech has been seen as a response to Job's first speech in Job 3. Job 3 is often interpreted as Job's wish to destroy the order of creation and to unleash chaos. The description of how God sustains the order of the world in Job 38 is then viewed as a response to Job's wish. Alter articulates this view thoroughly, presenting God's speeches, especially Job 38, as a reversal of Job 3, with God rebuilding the order of creation that Job tried to destroy.[12] Job 3 and 38 share motifs such as paths, water, light, darkness, and (which Alter accentuates) birth. Job wishes the twilight stars had remained dark and that no one had rejoiced over his birth, while God describes how the morning stars sang and rejoiced at the beginning of creation. Job wishes his day had been seized by darkness and clouds, while Job 38 describes how God uses darkness and clouds to swaddle the baby sea. Job says it would have been better if he had stayed in the womb, and wishes the doors of the womb had been closed. God refers to the womb containing the sea and how the doors are closed when the sea gushes out. The sea is restricted, but still allowed to be born and active within certain borders. Alter points out that the image of the sea does not describe a battle; instead, God is said to hold back the sea as an act of protection. God restrains the destructive parts of creation but still values them as "forces of life."[13] Alter also argues that the two other birth scenes in God's first speech are antitheses to Job 3. The birth of the hoarfrost and ice in Job 38:28–29 embraces contrasts in creation, such as rain and ice or father and mother, and connects rain with the life-giving characteristics of birth.[14] Alter's interpretation that Job 38 rebuilds the structure destroyed in Job 3 can, however, be criticized by questioning whether Job 3 contains a wish to destroy all of creation, and whether the order of creation is emphasized in Job 38. In my chapter on birth metaphors in Job 3, I argue that Job 3 only describes the disorder in Job's life, and that he does not

---

[10] Habel 1985, 533–34. Clines also emphasizes the order of creation, and that there is nothing wrong with the order which needs to be corrected (Clines 2011, 1089–90).
[11] Schifferdecker 2008, 124–25.
[12] Alter 2011, 111–12, 117–32.
[13] Alter 2011, 121–24.
[14] Alter 2011, 123–28.

wish to destroy the order of creation. Even so, Alter's recognition of the shared motifs between Job 3 and God's speeches cannot be overlooked in interpreting God's speeches.

A Sublime World with Beauty and Danger

Job poses cognitive questions, but receives answers that immerse him in the magnificence of creation, highlighting both its beauty and danger. Gordis focuses on how the speeches highlight the beauty of nature. He argues that while humans may never fully comprehend the moral or cosmic order, they can experience its beauty. In the face of the world's beauty, personal sufferings diminish and become relatively insignificant compared to the greatness of nature. He suggests that the "beauty of the world becomes an anodyne to human suffering."[15] Following Gordis, several scholars have explored the beauty of creation presented in God's speeches. However, instead of viewing beauty as merely an anodyne to suffering, these interpretations show how it also cherishes the wildness within creation. Patton argues that the beauty in creation challenges traditional interpretations that focus on God's power to control chaos. She suggests that the beauty of the beasts, like Leviathan and Behemoth, are manifestations of God's glory, created for God's enjoyment. They embody human experiences of the divine as both a beautiful and terrifying power.[16] O'Connor contends that Job is transformed by beauty, changing from self-centeredness to being open to the world.[17] This transformation makes him more compassionate, inviting him to replicate the beauty of the world, which he does by giving his daughters names that celebrate their beauty. According to her, God is not the god of order but a deity who is "wild, beautiful, free, and deeply unsettling."[18]

Newsom discusses the divine speeches from the perspective of the sublime, presenting Job with the vastness of creation.[19] Job experiences the wilderness and destructive forces beyond his control, offering him an experience that transcends human comprehension. Through God's answer, Job encounters divine power and his own powerlessness. The speeches subtly show that God cherishes and nurtures the wild, even identifying with chaotic forces like the sea, Behemoth, and Leviathan. Newsom refers to the experience of the sublime, that "evokes fear through a

---

[15] Gordis 1969, 84–85.
[16] Patton 2001, 155–59, 162.
[17] O'Connor 2003.
[18] O'Connor 2003, 173.
[19] Newsom 2003, 241–56.

dynamic of terror."[20] The wild animals and Leviathan evoke fear, but encountering them also brings about a sense of "elation."[21] This elation comes from surviving a threat, leading to a sense of unity and acceptance of the world as both tragic and beautiful. God's speeches address the presence of tragedy in the world, which Newsom describes as an experience of the tragic sublime.[22] Job attempts to shield himself from tragedy by clinging to his moral order, struggling to accept that violence, suffering, pain, and loss are natural parts of life. God's identification with chaotic forces highlights the non-moral and non-rational sides of God, clashing with Job's belief in a moral order. The tragic sublime is a clash between the moral and non-moral, the rational and non-rational, violence and security. Job's response to this experience is silence; he is overwhelmed, but he also finds consolation. The consolation of the tragic sublime is not an anodyne to suffering but an ability to live in a tragically structured world. Newsom also notes that in the epilogue, Job starts anew, brings children into the world, and regains his capacity to enjoy life and beauty.[23]

Following Newsom, several scholars have continued exploring how God's speeches present creation as sublime.[24] Drawing on Newsom's discussion of the sublime, Brown describes Job's experience of God's speeches as a movement from security to sublime danger. He argues that creation described in God's speeches is a polycentric world where different life forms have distinct centers, yet are interconnected. According to Brown, the world God presents is not cozy but one of wild beauty. God engages with it not as a warrior, but "with a word of admiration and an open hand," relating to the wild like a mother admiring her children.[25] God's speeches allow Job to identify himself with both the fragile parts of creation that cry out to God and the strong, alien monsters. Brown concludes that Job finds comfort, and his place, in creation.[26] Hankins discusses the sublime, using Newsom's definition and Brown's description of a polycentric world as starting points. He questions whether the speeches truly invoke fear and reverence in Job, suggesting instead that they broaden Job's vision, forcing him to confront unfamiliar, alien parts of creation. God's speeches incorporate these elements, which are seen as alien and chaotic, into the rest of God's creation, even if they cannot be fully

---

[20] Newsom 2003, 242.
[21] Newsom 2003, 253.
[22] Newsom 2003, 252–56.
[23] Newsom 2003, 258.
[24] Linafelt 2006; Brown 2010.
[25] Brown 2010, 129.
[26] Brown 2010, 126–31.

comprehended. According to Hankins, creation cannot be unified or comprehended as a whole; it includes confrontation and can only be understood in part. God's and Job's speeches are from opposing perspectives that cannot be unified. Hankins rejects the notion that God controls chaotic forces by limiting them. He argues that creation relies on violence and segmentation, and the sea is not an adversary to creation but essential for its existence.[27]

Open Questions from Earlier Interpretations

I have presented two different approaches to interpreting how God relates to the wild parts of creation in God's speeches. These two different approaches lead to different readings of the birth of the sea. At the same time, our understanding of the birth of the sea can also shape our interpretation of God's entire speech and relationship with the wild. The birth of the sea has been interpreted either as a parodic way of diminishing its danger by depicting the sea as an infant, or as a sign of God's affection for the wild aspects of creation. The interpretation depends on whether the birth of the sea is seen as an expression of the combat motif or as an indication that wild forces are integral part of God's creation, where chaos and order coexist. I will explore these interpretations further and what insights emerge when the birth metaphors are studied on their own terms, without being forced into the combat motif. I will also examine whether, and in what way, the birth of the sea depicts a closeness between God and the sea.

The birth of ice and hoarfrost in Job 38:28–29 has received less attention than the birth of the sea. Ice and hoarfrost do not, like the sea, personify enmity, even though snow is associated with God's punishment in Job 38:23. The birth of ice and hoarfrost has primarily been studied as an isolated scene, which has not significantly influenced the interpretation of God's first speech. The focus has been on whether it is plausible that God's creative acts are depicted through metaphors of begetting and birth in the HB. This birth scene has also been interpreted as an example of the alien, mysterious, and beautiful aspects of creation that Job cannot comprehend. Alter acknowledges the importance of the birth metaphors in God's first speech, noting that the repetition of the birth motif in the description of three parts of God's creation suggests that they are central to understanding the first speech.[28] This chapter and the next, "Birth Metaphors in Job 39," will discuss how the birth metaphors interact with each other, and how they together influence the portrayal of creation and God.

---

[27] Hankins 2015, 178–203.
[28] Alter 2011, 123–28.

The Domains of BIRTH and WATER

The two birth scenes in Job 38 describe the origins of different forms of water. The first concerns the sea, while the second addresses various forms of precipitation, including dew, rain, hoarfrost, and ice. My metaphorical analysis will investigate how the domains BIRTH and WATER OF CREATION are blended. I will first give an overview of these domains.

The Domain of BIRTH

Chapters 3 and 4 of this study provide a detailed presentation of how the domain of BIRTH is expressed in the HB and ancient West Asia. Here, I will only briefly mention the birth metaphors used in the HB and Akkadian birth incantations, which are also central to Job 38. The metaphor THE WOMB IS AN ENCLOSED ROOM WITH DOORS is used in Job 3, and it reappears in Job 38. This metaphor also entails the metaphors describing birth as an act of breaking and opening the doors. It is paired with the metaphors MIDWIVES ARE OPENERS OF THE DOORS OF THE WOMB and GODS ARE MIDWIVES. The discussion of the metaphors in Job 10 recognized the metaphor FORMATION OF A FETUS IS COAGULATION, which will be reversed in Job 38. Two other metaphors elaborated in Job 38 are THE AMNIOTIC FLUID IS A SEA, and THE BABY WHO COMES FORTH IS A RUSHING RAINFALL.

The Domain of WATER OF CREATION

Water, and metaphors of water, play a prominent role in the Book of Job. Nõmmik argues that water in its various forms is mentioned throughout the poetic sections of Job and is primarily used metaphorically. They are often employed in metaphors concerning existential and divine issues and to express God's supremacy.[29] The birth metaphors in Job 38 contribute to a broader depiction of the primeval creation and how God sustains the world. They refer to various forms of water, including the sea, rain, dew, hoarfrost, and ice. Other descriptions of God's interaction with water in creation in the HB provide essential background to the water metaphors in Job 38.

Psalm 147 contains the most vivid description of frozen precipitation in the HB. It describes snow as wool, hoarfrost as dust, and hail as crumbs. God commands the water to stream, and by God's breath, water transforms into ice. Elihu's speech describes both the sea and precipitation, using metaphors of storms enclosed in storehouses and water coagulating by God's breath (Job 36:27–37:22).

---

[29] Nõmmik 2014, 284–91.

Psalm 104 shares many motifs with Job 38–39 by referring to cosmogony, meteorology, and zoology.[30] It describes both how the sea was rebuked and restrained during creation and how God sustains the world, its vegetation, animals, and humans by providing rain and letting water flow from springs.

The various forms of precipitation in the HB carry different symbolic meanings and associations. During the long, dry summers, morning dew often served as the only source of water for vegetation, making it a cherished and renewing gift, seen as a blessing (Gen 27:28; Ps 110:3). Hail, on the other hand, is primarily depicted as a destructive force, used by God to devastate harvests and strike down cattle and humans (Exod 9:25; Pss 78:48; 105:32–33). Rain is generally valued as a blessing, nourishing the earth and allowing it to flourish (Deut 11:14; Ps 65:10; Isa 55:10). However, God may withhold rain as a form of punishment, while excessive rain can lead to destructive floods (Gen 7:4; Deut 11:17; Ezek 13:11). Snow is mentioned less frequently, but is portrayed as both lifegiving and destructive (Job 38:23; Isa 55:10). Hoarfrost and ice are rarely referenced and not valued as good or bad (Ps 147:16–17). However, the comparison of manna to the flaky hoarfrost in Exod 16:14 might suggest a positive association with hoarfrost.

God's relationship with the sea is portrayed ambiguously in the HB, as the sea is depicted both as a powerful enemy and an ally to God. The motif of a god combating the sea is present in both the Baal Cycle and the Enuma Elish. In the Enuma Elish, Marduk battles Tiamat, creating the world from her cleaved carcass, and is then proclaimed king among the gods. Similarly, in the Baal Cycle, Baal fights Yam and the sea dragon Leviathan, gaining authority as king and building his palace after his victory. In the HB, the sea and its monsters are powerful forces depicted as either chaotic enemies or God's creations. The sea monsters are referred to as dragons (תַּנִּין), Leviathan, and Rahab. The motif of God overpowering the sea is often used in descriptions of the primeval creation. In Pss 74:12–14; 89:10–11, and Job 26:10–13, the sea is described as being defeated as part of God's creative act. In Prov 8:27–29 and Jer 5:22, however, the sea is not depicted as defeated but as restricted within set boundaries. The sea needs to be restricted by God, for if it is not, it might flood and overwhelm all of creation. The story of creation in Gen 1 may allude to the combat myth, but does not describe a creation through combat. The waters are instead divided by God's word. Gen 1 also portrays God's creation

---

[30] Psalm 104 refers to the foundation of earth and the restriction of the sea (Ps 104:2–9; cf. Job 38:4–11) watering of the earth (Ps 104:10–13; cf. Job 38:22–38) and God's provision for the humans, cattle, and the wild animals (Ps 104:11–30; cf. Job 38:39–39:30).

of the sea monsters (תַּנִּינִם) and how God blesses them. Psalm 104:6–9 describes how God covers the earth's foundation with the sea, flooding even the mountains, and then God rebukes the sea, restricting it to specific areas. Psalm 104 refers to Leviathan, who is not depicted as a monster but alongside other wild animals, as a creature that plays in the sea (104:26).[31]

There are several examples where God is described as a divine warrior who crushes the sea and the rivers (Job 26:12–13; Pss 74:12–14; 89:10–11). The sea and its monsters often symbolize the enemies of the Israelites. King Nebuchadnezzar of Babylon is depicted as a dragon in Jer 51:34–37, and Egypt is identified with Rahab in Ps 87:4 and Isa 51:9. The purpose of depicting the enemy as a monster is both to invoke God's intervention and to demonstrate that the enemy is destined for defeat. Isaiah 27:1 describes the battle and God's victory on the day of the Lord. It is the closest verbal parallel to how the Baal Cycle depicts Leviathan (*KTU* 1.3 iii 38–42; 1.5 i 1–8). Leviathan is described as a fleeing, twisting serpent or a dragon that God defeats with a sword in both in Isa 27:1 and the Baal Cycle. Rahab is also referred to as a fleeing serpent (Job 26:12–13). There may also be a parallel between the Enuma Elish, where Marduk pierces the sea dragon (IV 101), and descriptions of Leviathan in Job 40:26.[32]

Descriptions of God's power over the sea are combined with images of God as king (Pss 74:12–14; 93:1–4; 96; 98). In Ps 93, God's power is proclaimed to be greater than the sea, and in Pss 96 and 98, the sea rejoices and praises God as king, along with the rest of creation. The sea is also part of images of God as a refuge that stands strong when the sea roars (Pss 46:4; 65:8). The motif of God subjugating the sea is used in combinations with the exodus motif. God is described as a divine warrior fighting the Egyptians by using the sea in Exod 15:1–18. Here God cleaves the sea and makes it rush back to cover the enemies. The combination of the exodus motif and God's control over the sea is also present in several psalms (Pss 77:15–21; 106:7–12; 114:3–8). God also here uses the sea to drown the Egyptians and to rescue the Israelites. God is not depicted as being in opposition to the sea.

---

[31] For an overview of different interpretations regarding how Psalms and Gen 1 allude to combat myths, see Cho 2019, 69–87. Cho argues that the absence of a combat in Gen 1 and the descriptions of the sea monsters in Gen 1:21 and Leviathan in Ps 104:26 subvert the combat myth, and that they emphasize that the God of Israel does not need to combat the sea monsters because God has created them

[32] The weapons mentioned in Job 41 resemble those of Marduk—such as the arrow, bow, quiver, club, and net (Enuma Elish IV 36–38, 95). However, these were also commonly used weapons in ancient West Asia. For a discussion of how these weapons were used to hunt and control animals and human captives, see Watson 2005, 355–56.

These various descriptions of God's relationship with the sea demonstrate that the sea is a strong powerful force, which can be seen as either an ally or an enemy of God. God's control over the sea is accentuated in descriptions of the primeval creation, but the sea is also depicted as an integral part of God's creation, celebrating God, and as being on God's side when God fights enemies.

Birth Metaphors in Job 38:8–11

Job 38:8–11 portrays God as a midwife delivering the sea at the beginning of creation. In this scene the water breaks, the sea rushes out from the womb, and God is holding back the sea in its out-bursting, breaking the limit for it, and welcoming it into the world.

Interpretations of the birth of the sea have often been influenced by the combat motif. These interpretations may describe God as battling the sea, or they may portray the sea as a hostile or dangerous force that, under all circumstances, God must restrain or enclose. I will explore how this scene can be understood if it is interpreted from the domain of BIRTH and discuss whether the birth metaphors challenge conventional metaphors, how the birth metaphors are grounded in embodied experience, how they use standard metaphors in new creative ways, and most importantly how the scene portrays the sea, God, and God's relationship with the sea.

Text and Translation of Job 38:8–11

8	וַיָּסֶךְ בִּדְלָתַיִם יָם	And who shut in the sea behind doors,
	בְּגִיחוֹ	when it burst out,
	מֵרֶחֶם יֵצֵא	from the womb it went out,
9	בְּשׂוּמִי עָנָן לְבֻשׁוֹ	when I made the clouds its garment,
	וַעֲרָפֶל חֲתֻלָּתוֹ׃	and the thick darkness its swaddling band,
10	וָאֶשְׁבֹּר עָלָיו חֻקִּי	and I broke my limit for it,
	וָאָשִׂים בְּרִיחַ וּדְלָתָיִם	and I set the bar and the doors,
11	וָאֹמַר עַד־פֹּה תָבוֹא	and I said: "As far as here shall you come,
	וְלֹא תֹסִיף	but no further,
	וּפֹא־יָשִׁית בִּגְאוֹן גַּלֶּיךָ	and here shall your high waves be put down"?

Literary Structure and Comments

God's first speech (Job 38:2–39:30) can be divided into an introduction and three main sections. Job 38:2–3 serves as an introduction to the speech, in which God asks Job to prepare himself to answer God. The first section, 38:4–21, concerns the primeval creation and the depths of the world. The second section, 38:22–38, depicts the maintenance of precipitation and stars. The third section, 38:39–39:30, describes the wild animals and God's relationship to them. The birth of the sea in Job 38:8–11 belongs to the part of God's first speech which discusses the primeval times, when God laid the foundation of the earth. Verses 8–11 continue the reasoning of verses 4–7, where God asks where Job was when God founded the earth and who set the earth's measurements and laid its base? Verse 8 implies a question, but does not contain an interrogative pronoun. The pronoun מִי from the question "who threw (ירה Qal pf) its cornerstone?" in verse 6b is implied in verse 8. The verbs in verses 8–11 are wayyiqtol verbs, which may mark the logical succession of thought from verse 6b.[33] They also unite verses 8–11 and contrast with the description in verses 5–6, which uses perfect in the "who"-questions. Verse 12 starts a new section with the interrogative particle הֲ and the use of the perfect. Verses 4–11 are structured as follows:

4	Serves as a heading both to vv. 4–11 and to its first part vv. 4–6.
	"Where were you (Job) when I (God) founded the earth?"
5	Asks questions about who set the measurements of the earth.
6	Asks questions about the foundation of the earth:
	"who threw the cornerstone?"
7	Is a temporal clause to v. 6: "when the stars rejoiced!"
8a	Is initiated by a wayyiqtol and continues the who-questions in v. 6 by adding:
	"and (who) shut the sea behind doors?"
8b	Is a temporal clause to v. 8a: "when it burst out."
9	continues the temporal clause to v. 8a: "and I clothed the sea."
	(Vv. 10a, b, 11 continue the temporal clause but also serve as answers to the questions asked in v. 8.)
10a	"and I broke my limit for it."
10b	"and I set the bar and the doors,"
11	"and I said: 'As far as here … but no further …'"

The structure of verses 4–11 shows that they should be considered as a single unit describing God's creative act in primeval times. This unit is divided into two parts: the first part contains architectural metaphors (vv. 4–7), and the second uses birth metaphors (vv. 8–11). The sea is born at the same time as the foundations of the

---

[33] Arnold and Choi 2018, 97–101.

earth are established, contrasting with Gen 1, where the sea preexists God's creation of the earth.

The verb סכך, which is used in the description of Job's formation in Job 10, is employed here to describe God shutting the doors to the sea. According to *HALOT*, root 1 of סכך means "shut off (as a protection)," which would fit the context here.[34] Job 1:10 uses the by-form שׂוּךְ when God is said to protect Job by hedging him in. Verse 8 is the only instance where סכך refers to the closing of doors, but it is used in the context of birth, describing the formation of a fetus in Job 10:11 and Ps 139:13. It is possibly also used also in Prov 8:23 and Ps 2:6, where it then would refer to the formation of the wisdom and the king. The choice of the word סכך indicates that God's act of shutting the doors is an act of protection.[35]

The sea is not only said to go out (יצא) from the womb but also to "burst out" (גיח). The verb גיח, meaning "burst out," is used in various contexts in the HB. It refers to a woman in labor in Mic 4:10, a river in Job 40:23, a military attack in Judg 20:33, and a dragon in the sea in Ezek 32:2.[36] These different uses of גיח contribute to the image of the sea as a powerful, moving force.

God swaddles the sea in clouds (עָנָן) and thick darkness (עֲרָפֶל) in Job 38:9. In the HB, "clouds" and "thick darkness" are primarily used in theophanic language to describe God's presence, both separately and as a pair. At Mount Sinai and the tabernacle, clouds and thick darkness signify God's presence (Exod 24:15–16; 40:34; Deut 4:11; 5:22). This imagery is also present in the Psalms (Pss 18:10–12; 97:2) and in descriptions of the day of the Lord (Ezek 34:12; Joel 2:2; Zeph 1:15). Meteorological occurrences of עָנָן are relatively rare compared to its use in theophanic descriptions.[37] Verse 9 could therefore be interpreted as God dressing the sea with God's own garment, highlighting the closeness between the sea and God.[38] The noun חֲתֻלָּה, "swaddling band," is a *hapax legomenon* derived from the verb חתל, "swaddle," used in Ezek 16:4 to describe the care of a newborn.

---

[34] *HALOT*, s.v. "סכך I."

[35] For a thorough examination of the word סכך, see Chapter 7, page 206.

[36] Two similar verbs to גיח are used in a description of birth and God acting as a midwife: גחה in Ps 22:10 and גזה in Ps 71:6. For more on these verbs, see Chapter 3, pages 81–83.

[37] The noun עָנָן as meteorological phenomena: Gen 9:13–16; Job 26:8. It also carries the meaning of "cloud" in metaphors of transience (Isa 44:22; Hos 6:4) and opacity (Lam 3:44; Ezek 38:9, 16) (Freedman—Willoughby, "ענן," *TDOT* 11:254–55).

[38] Baal Cycle may narrate how Baal clothes his baby in KTU 1.5 v 2–6, 23–26. The text is damaged but de Moor interprets it as if Baal clothes his baby with his own garment, a cloak of his sovereignty and strength (de Moor 1987, 77, 79).

Verse 10 states that God breaks the limit for the sea, but also sets a bar and doors for it. This can be interpreted as an ambiguous attitude toward the sea. The expression וָאֶשְׁבֹּר עָלָיו חֻקִּי, "and I broke my limit for it," has been questioned. It is difficult to explain why God would break the limit rather than set it. The conventional expression in the HB is that God sets the limit for the waters and the sea (Job 26:10; Ps 104:9; Jer 5:22). Therefore, the word וָאֶשְׁבֹּר, "I broke," has often been emended to words meaning "set" or "shut." I will explain below how "I broke my limit for it" fits within the context of birth.[39]

I translate חֹק in verse 10 as "limit." The noun חֹק is used in the context of enclosing water in Job 26:10, which uses חָג־חֹק, "bound-circle," and in Jer 5:22, which uses חָק־עוֹלָם, "an everlasting limit." A synonym is גְּבוּל, "boundary," used in descriptions of containing water in Ps 104:9 and Jer 5:22. The noun חֹק can also mean statute, decree, and regulation, and God gives his חֹק to the people as well as to creation (Gen 26:5; Ps 148:6; Ezek 36:27).[40]

In verse 11, the waves of the sea are described as גָּאוֹן, which is used in the HB to describe something high, proud, or majestic.[41] The feature of height serves as the physical basis from which the meanings of "proud" and "majestic" are derived. The waves of the sea can embody all these characteristics, particularly the feature of height. This physical description of the sea is also reflected in verse 8, where the sea is depicted as bursting out (גיח) of the womb, emphasizing its powerful and impressive appearance. Whether the description in verse 11 also refers to the moral height of the sea as being "proud" is uncertain. If it does, it is not necessarily a negative description. Job 41:26 describes Leviathan as the king of all proud (שַׁחַץ) who knows or inspects all the proud/high (גָּבֹהַּ) beings. In God's speeches, height and pride are not negative traits per se, but part of the description of God's admiration of these strong beings.

Earlier Interpretations of Job 38:8–11

Job 38:8–11 has often been interpreted through the lens of the combat motif. Verses 8–9 have been explained as depicting the birth of the sea, while verses 10–11 are typically viewed as God subduing the sea. Perdue argues that there is a shift from birth to conflict between verses 9 and 10.[42] Hartley suggests that the doors in verse 8 refer to the doors of the womb of the universe, whereas the doors in verse

---

[39] See pages 248–49.
[40] *HALOT*, s.v. "חֹק."
[41] Kellermann, "גָּאָה," *TDOT* 2:344–50.
[42] Perdue 1991, 207.

10 are bolted defense doors.⁴³ Clines contends that verse 9 adds a caring aspect to God's act of restraining the sea, but claims that the bar and doors in verse 10 are evidence enough to state that verses 10–11 belong to a combat scenario rather than to a birth scene.⁴⁴ Greenstein was the first to discuss the generic similarities between the image of the womb as a room with doors in Job (3:10; 38:8, 10) and those in Akkadian birth incantations, noting how the sea, like a fetus, is enclosed behind the doors of the womb.⁴⁵ However, he also compares Job 38:8–11 to Enuma Elish IV 137–139, which describes Marduk splitting Tiamat and confining her waters. Greenstein interprets line 139 as Marduk enclosing Tiamat behind a bar and argues that God restricts the sea similarly in Job 38:10. This line can also be understood as Marduk "stretched the skin" instead of "setting a bar" ⁴⁶ Speiser's translation of Marduk "pulled down the bar" in *ANET* has influenced interpretations of Job 38:10, as seen in the work of Pope, Habel, and Clines.⁴⁷ A common view is that verse 8 describes the birth of the sea, while verses 9–11 describe how the monstrous baby is restricted.⁴⁸ Habel and Mettinger point out that the ironic description of the sea as an infant accentuates God's power over the sea.⁴⁹ Tur-Sinai relates both verses 8 and 10 to the birth of the sea, and verses 9 and 11 to the parents' tender restriction of the baby. Some of his interpretations are speculative, such as suggesting that the doors are swaddling sheets, and the bar is a straight board for the infant's back. However, Tur-Sinai should be recognized as the only one to explain how the verb שבר fits the birth context, arguing that it refers to the act of opening the womb, as in Isa 66:9.⁵⁰

Newsom discusses how the birth metaphor transforms the image of the sea, arguing that it is not hostile but aggressive, requiring restrictions while also being an object of care. The swaddling in verse 9 restrains the baby sea, but is also an act of care and protection.⁵¹ Keller, Balentine, and Schifferdecker share this view, suggesting that the sea is not hostile and is restrained out of care to protect it from

---

⁴³ Hartley 1988, 496.
⁴⁴ Clines 2011, 1055.
⁴⁵ Greenstein 2017, 148–50.
⁴⁶ Greenstein explains how both the word "bar" (*parka*) and the word "skin" (*maška*) are depicted with the same cuneiform sign (Greenstein 2017, 148). Lambert understands it as Marduk "stretched the skin" in Lambert 2013, 94–95.
⁴⁷ *ANET*, 67; Pope 1973, 293; Habel 1985, 538; Clines 2011, 1102.
⁴⁸ Newsom 2003, 244; Clines 2011, 1054–55, 1101–2; Balentine 2006, 647.
⁴⁹ Habel 1985, 538; Mettinger 1992, 44–47.
⁵⁰ Tur-Sinai 1957, 525–26.
⁵¹ Newsom 2003, 244.

harming itself and others.⁵² Balentine highlights God's care for the sea and suggest that this implies that the sea and God are "something like family."⁵³ Keller concludes that the womb of the deep, from which she believes the sea is born, is God's womb.⁵⁴ Newsom, Schifferdecker, Doak, and Keller describe God as the midwife of the sea who delivers and swaddles it in verses 8–9, though they do not discuss whether God is also seen as the midwife in verses 10–11.⁵⁵

THE SEA IS AMNIOTIC FLUID AND A BABY

The sea can be seen both as the amniotic fluid and the baby in Job 38:8–11. In verse 8, the sea seems to be the amniotic fluid, while in verse 9, it is clear that the sea is a baby. Akkadian birth descriptions are valuable for interpreting these verses, helping us identify the role of the sea. When the sea bursts out of the womb, it resembles amniotic fluid rushing out during childbirth. The image of amniotic fluid as a sea is present in both Akkadian and Sumerian texts. The Akkadian birth metaphor THE AMNIOTIC FLUID IS A SEA, highlights the dangers of pregnancy. The baby or mother is said to travel on the sea as a boat that departs from the quay of death, and at birth it reaches the quay of well-being.⁵⁶ The sea surrounding the baby is described as fearsome and raging in the Old Babylonian incantation YBC 4603.⁵⁷

The Akkadian metaphor THE AMNIOTIC FLUID IS A DANGEROUS SEA is displayed in Figure 8.1. The organizing frame of the blend is the frame of the source, THE SEA, which highlights its danger. It also uses associations of dangerous boat journeys on the sea to depict the birth, where the baby or the mother is a boat.

---

⁵² Keller 2002, 130–31; Balentine 2006, 646–47; Schifferdecker 2008, 76–77.
⁵³ Balentine 2006, 647.
⁵⁴ Keller 2002, 131.
⁵⁵ Newsom 2003, 244; Schifferdecker 2008, 77; Doak 2014, 194. Habel refers to God as a nursemaid (Habel 1985, 534).
⁵⁶ VAT 8869 (Stol 2000, 65; Ebeling 1923). UM 29-15-367; VAT 8381 (van Dijk 1975, 53–65; Stol 2000, 60–61).
⁵⁷ van Dijk 1973, 503; Stol 2000, 11.

Birth Metaphors in Job 38:8-11 243

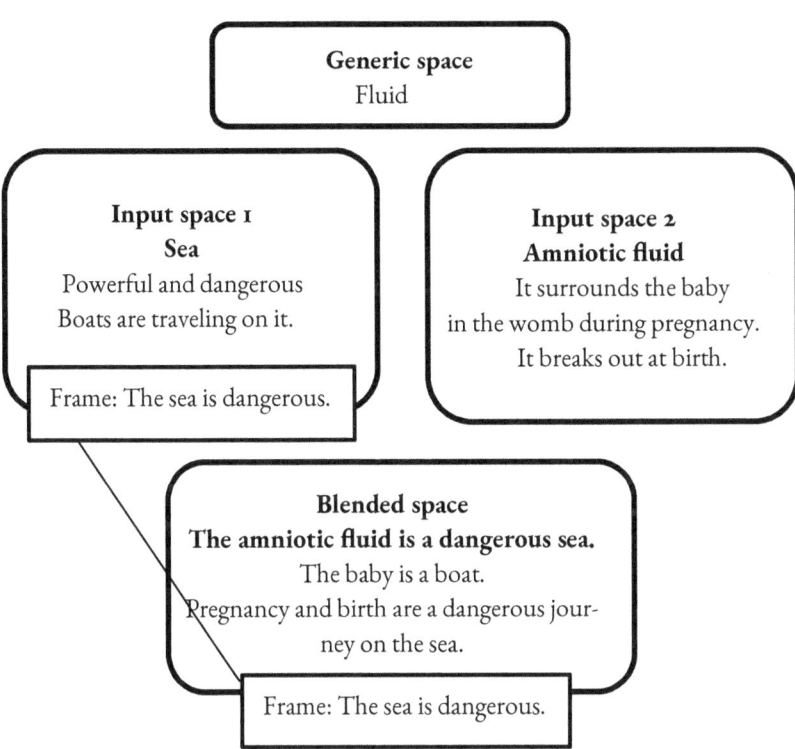

Figure 8.1 *The Akkadian metaphor* THE AMNIOTIC FLUID IS A DANGEROUS SEA.

The metaphor THE SEA IS THE AMNIOTIC FLUID in Job 38:8 is a reversed metaphor of the Akkadian metaphor THE AMNIOTIC FLUID IS A SEA. The target has become the source, and the source has turned into the target (see Figure 8.3). Job 38 personifies the sea as a baby who is born and swaddled by God. In the compendium from Assur and older Sumerian texts, the baby is imagined as rushing out of the womb like a streaming gutter or rainfall.[58] The Akkadian metaphor THE BABY WHO COMES FORTH OF THE WOMB IS A RUSHING RAINFALL emphasizes the movement, speed, and gushing of water. Although it is the baby that is wished to emerge like rainfall, not the amniotic fluid, this description is likely grounded in the experienced similarities between the streaming of amniotic fluid from the womb and the flow of rain.

---

[58] VAT 8869 (Ebeling 1923; Stol 2000, 65). UM 29-15-367; VAT 8381 (van Dijk 1975, 53–65; Stol 2000, 60–61).

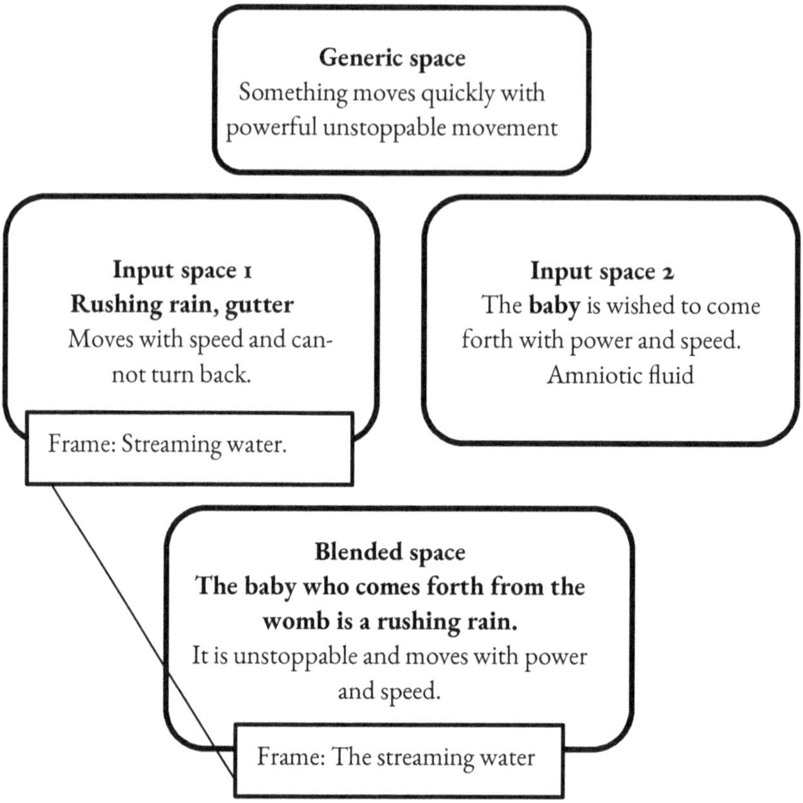

```
┌─────────────────────────────────┐
│        Generic space            │
│  Something moves quickly with   │
│  powerful unstoppable movement  │
└─────────────────────────────────┘

┌──────────────────────┐    ┌──────────────────────────┐
│    Input space 1     │    │      Input space 2       │
│  Rushing rain, gutter│    │  The baby is wished to   │
│  Moves with speed    │    │  come forth with power   │
│  and cannot turn back│    │  and speed. Amniotic     │
│                      │    │  fluid                   │
└──────────────────────┘    └──────────────────────────┘
  │ Frame: Streaming water. │
  └─────────────────────────┘

         ┌─────────────────────────────────┐
         │        Blended space            │
         │  The baby who comes forth from  │
         │     the womb is a rushing rain. │
         │  It is unstoppable and moves    │
         │        with power and speed.    │
         └─────────────────────────────────┘
              │ Frame: The streaming water │
```

Figure 8.2 *The Akkadian metaphor* THE BABY WHO COMES FORTH FROM THE WOMB IS A RUSHING RAINFALL

The blending schema above in Figure 8.2 displays how the movement of rainfall is used in the incantation to depict an ideal birth, where the baby easily slips out of the womb. Like rain that rushes forward, unable to turn back or be stopped, amniotic fluid rushes out of the womb and cannot return. The Akkadian metaphor THE BABY WHO COMES FORTH FROM THE WOMB IS A RUSHING RAINFALL provides a useful background for interpreting the metaphor of the sea rushing out of the womb in Job 38:8. In this passage, the sea is depicted both as water streaming from the womb and as the baby being born. The sea serves as the target in the metaphor THE SEA IS A BABY, while also corresponding to the source, the streaming rainfall, in the Akkadian metaphor, which portrays a safe birth as a baby emerging with the force of streaming water. The rushing water symbolizes a safe birth in the Akkadian metaphor, and depicting the sea as rushing out of the womb suggests the birth of the baby sea as a successful and safe birth.

It is important to recognize that when metaphors are elaborated and reversed, there is a shift in the entire metaphorical network. Different associations and structures are projected onto the metaphor, and different characteristics are highlighted or downplayed, when the target and source are reversed. Thus, the metaphors THE SEA IS THE AMNIOTIC FLUID, and THE SEA IS A BABY need to be examined on their own terms. The metaphor THE AMNIOTIC FLUID IS A SEA highlights the danger of pregnancy by using associations of danger of the sea in its construction. However, when this metaphor is reversed to THE SEA IS THE AMNIOTIC FLUID, the dangerous associations of the sea are downplayed, as the sea is described as amniotic fluid.[59] Amniotic fluid is less threatening than the sea, and the breaking of the water is associated with the progression of labor rather than a risky aspect of childbirth.

The birth scene relates to the domain of MIDWIFERY and portrays God in the metaphor GOD IS A MIDWIFE. The interaction between the midwife metaphor and the baby metaphor also influences the interpretation of THE SEA IS AMNIOTIC FLUID, and THE SEA IS A BABY. God's role as a midwife will be discussed later in this chapter, but the blending schema for the metaphor THE SEA IS A BABY in Figure 8.3, highlights how the baby sea is cared for, as seen in God's act of wrapping the sea.

---

[59] See discussion of reversed metaphors in Chapter 2, page 66. For the examples THE SURGEON IS A BUTCHER, which highlight the incompetence of the surgeon, while the reversed metaphor THE BUTCHER IS A SURGEON implies competence, see pages 49–51, 56.

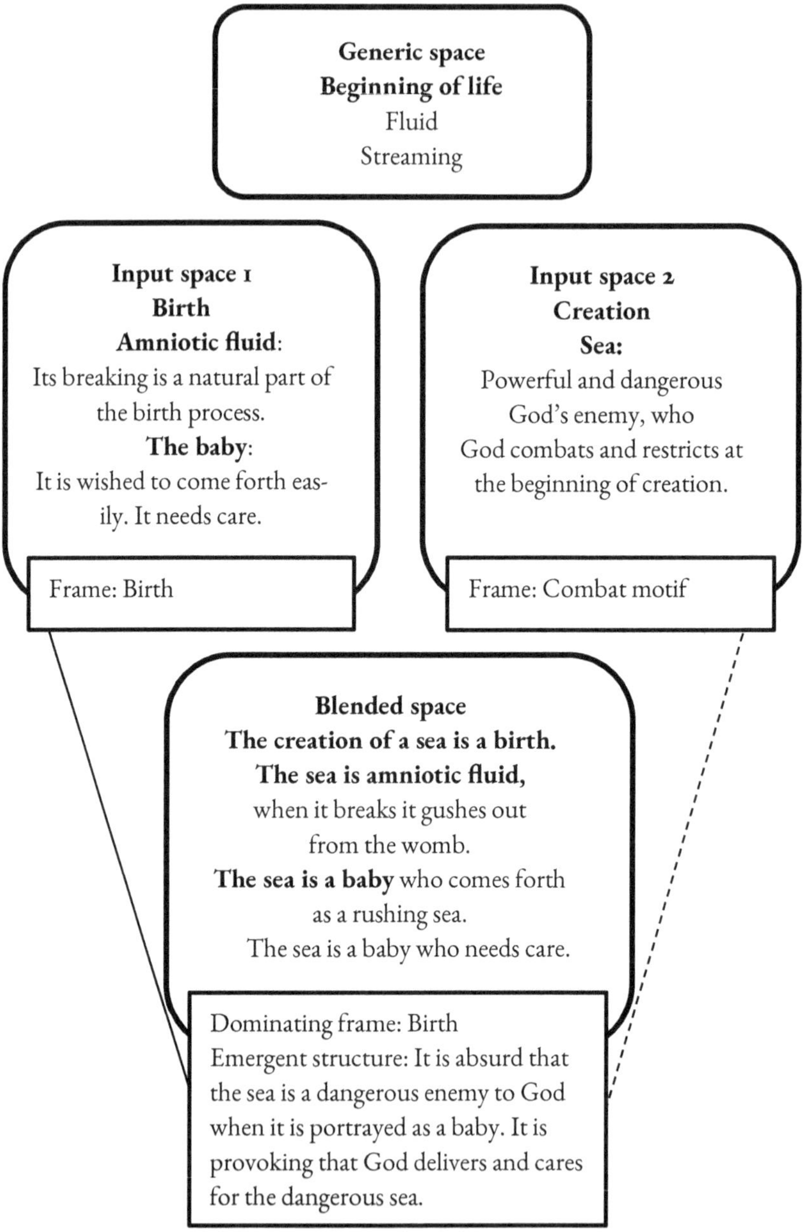

Generic space
Beginning of life
Fluid
Streaming

Input space 1
Birth
Amniotic fluid:
Its breaking is a natural part of the birth process.
The baby:
It is wished to come forth easily. It needs care.

Frame: Birth

Input space 2
Creation
Sea:
Powerful and dangerous
God's enemy, who
God combats and restricts at the beginning of creation.

Frame: Combat motif

Blended space
The creation of a sea is a birth.
The sea is amniotic fluid,
when it breaks it gushes out from the womb.
The sea is a baby who comes forth as a rushing sea.
The sea is a baby who needs care.

Dominating frame: Birth
Emergent structure: It is absurd that the sea is a dangerous enemy to God when it is portrayed as a baby. It is provoking that God delivers and cares for the dangerous sea.

Figure 8.3 The metaphors CREATION IS A BIRTH, THE SEA IS AMNIOTIC FLUID, and THE SEA IS A BABY.

Job 38:8–11 blends the sea with both amniotic fluid and a baby. The sea is described as gushing out of the womb, and the verb גיח, meaning "burst out," in verse 8 emphasizes the powerful movement and the strength of the sea. While the sea retains its power in the description of birth, its dangerous aspects are downplayed. The sea is neither defeated at the beginning of creation nor dangerous to God. Its gushing out represents a healthy birth, where the amniotic fluid and the baby emerge like rushing water. This blend highlights that the gushing of the sea is a desired and healthy characteristic. The birth of the sea also relates to the broader domain of CREATION, which is blended with the domain of BIRTH in the metaphor CREATION IS A BIRTH. This is one of the few instances in the HB where the creation of a specific element of nature is depicted as a birth.

The portrait of the dangerous sea as a newborn is an absurd or comical image, as noted by several scholars.[60] The frame BIRTH is the dominant frame, which mainly structures the blend, but the COMBAT MOTIF is also involved in the blend. The comical effect comes from the emergent structure of the blend, which arises from the collision between the conventional frame COMBAT MOTIF and frame BIRTH. Ridiculing an enemy or belittling danger to reduce fear is often used in satire, as it undermines the seriousness or respectability of the subject. The absurdity of the metaphor THE SEA IS AN INFANT strips the sea of its danger and ability to oppose God, and therefore alters the power dynamic between the sea and God. The baby sea cannot harm or threaten God, effectively dismissing the combat motif as an interpretive frame for the relationship between God and the sea in Job 38:8–11. It is important to note that the ancient reader would certainly have brought associations of the sea as a dangerous and powerful force to the encounter with this birth scene. These presumptions make the image of the sea as an infant cared for by God both comical and provocative. It is provocative that God delivers the sea, allows it to gush out, and cares for it as a newborn, despite the dangers the sea poses to humans.[61] God's delivery of the sea expresses that it is a wanted part of God's creation, and the birth scene highlights God's care for it. The blending schema in Figure 8.3 displays how the sea is portrayed in Job 38:8–11, and briefly notes God's role as the caretaker of the newborn sea. I will now turn to discuss God's role in the birth of the sea.

---

[60] Habel 1985, 538; Mettinger 1992, 47.

[61] Cho similarly discusses how the description of the sea creatures in Gen 1 and Leviathan in Ps 104 must have shocked ancient readers (Cho 2019, 75, 81–82).

God Swaddles the Sea

The act of swaddling the sea helps to identify God's role in the birth scene. Verse 9 interrupts the image of the birth of the sea by describing how it is cared for as a newborn. This highlights that God's role is to nurture the sea rather than combat it. The common purpose of swaddling a baby is not to restrict its movements but to calm the baby, warm it, and help it sleep better.[62] Wrapping is also used in descriptions of God making clouds out of water (Job 26:8; Prov 30:4). In Prov 30:4, water is described as wrapped in a cloak (שִׂמְלָה), whereas in Job 38:9, it is the sea that is wrapped in clouds and thick darkness. The terms "clouds" (עָנָן) and "thick darkness" (עֲרָפֶל) are primarily used in the HB in theophanic language to describe God's presence. The image of God wrapping the sea thus implies that God gives the sea God's own garments, signifying a close relationship rather than an adversarial one. This act of dressing the sea is reminiscent of Job 10:11, where God is said to have clothed Job with skin and flesh during his formation in the womb, at a time when God showed Job love and loyalty. Similarly, in Ezek 16:10, God dresses the abandoned orphan Israel, symbolizing divine love and care for the people. Thus, the symbolism of swaddling the sea is an act of love.

God Breaks the Water

Job 38:8–11 uses the conventional metaphor THE WOMB IS A HOUSE WITH DOORS, which is also found in Akkadian incantations. In these incantations, the gods are said to open the doors of the womb at birth, which may involve unlocking locks and throwing the doors aside.[63] Job 38:8–11 depicts the sea streaming out of the womb, with God breaking the water by breaking the limit to the sea. God is also said to set a bar and shut the doors to the sea when it is born. The Akkadian metaphor GODS OPENS THE DOORS OF THE WOMB is extended to include the act of shutting the doors, and becomes GOD OPENS AND SHUTS THE DOORS OF THE WOMB.

Recognizing the Akkadian metaphors THE WOMB IS A ROOM WITH DOORS and GODS ARE MIDWIVES WHO OPEN THE DOORS helps us understand God's actions when the sea is born. Verses 10–11 have typically been interpreted as a scene where God subdues the sea, similar to Baal's struggle with Yam or Marduk's battle with Tiamat, including interpretations where Marduk sets a bar against Tiamat.[64] When Job 38:8–11 is understood according to the combat motif, verse 10a becomes

---

[62] Pease, et al. 2016.
[63] See Chapter 4, pages 95–99.
[64] See pages 240–41.

problematic. It is then difficult to explain how the word וָאֶשְׁבֹּר, "I broke," fits the context, and why God would break the limit (חֹק) to the sea. The word וָאֶשְׁבֹּר has been emended to וָאָשִׁית, "I set," and other verbs such as שִׂים, "set," סגר, "shut," שׁמר, "keep," שׂכר, "shut," or שׂבר, "inspect."[65] These interpretations follow the LXX, which uses the verb τίθημι, "set," in Job 38:10a. Interpreting God as setting, shutting, or inspecting the limit aligns with the combat motif, where God restrains the sea. However, if verse 10 is viewed in the light of Akkadian birth descriptions, the word שׁבר, "break," makes sense. In these descriptions, gods unlock and break the bolts and doors. The limit (חֹק) in verse 10a corresponds to the bars and doors of the source domain of the metaphor THE WOMB IS A ROOM WITH DOORS. These elements are cross-mapped with the opening of the womb in the WOMB domain, either as a general term for the opening of the womb or as a more specific part as the cervix. The noun חֹק, "limit" or "boundary," is often used for water enclosures and could here refer to the membrane of amniotic sac. When the sac breaks, the amniotic fluid rushes out, aligning with the description of the sea bursting forth in verse 8. God acting as a midwife and breaking something to open the womb is not foreign to the HB. Tur-Sinai notes that both Isa 66:9 and Job 38:10 use the word שׁבר in a birth context, although he does not explain how opening the womb can involve breaking.[66] This parallel shows that the breaking the limit or the womb is part of the metaphor of God acting as a midwife. Recognizing that "I broke my limit for it" in verse 10 describes the act of a midwife at birth implies that the entire passage (8–11) should be read as a birth scene, with God as the midwife and the sea as amniotic fluid and a baby.

A detail in this description of God's breaking of the water is that God says, "I broke *my* limit (חֻקִּי) to the sea." The pronoun "my" indicates that God has the authority to establish or break it.

The Dual Act of Opening and Holding Back

The strange aspect of Job 38:8–11, compared to Akkadian birth incantations, is not that God breaks the limit for the baby sea, but that God shuts the doors of the womb at birth. The swaddling of the sea implies that God is a caring midwife, and a good midwife only opens the womb at birth. In Mesopotamian myths, only evil

---

[65] Pinker gives an extensive review of earlier emendations of וָאֶשְׁבֹּר. He argues that וָאֶשְׁבֹּר, "I broke," contains a scribal corruption of a שׂ instead of a שׁ and claims it should be understood as שׂבר , "inspect" (Pinker 2020).

[66] Tur-Sinai 1957, 524.

demons close the wombs to prevent babies from being born.[67] Therefore, God's act of shutting the doors would typically be seen as an attempt to stop the sea from being born. This is coherent with the interpretations derived from the combat motif. These interpretations instead only recognize that God shuts the doors in Job 38:8–11, not that God opens them or breaks the limit. Nevertheless, if God wants to stop the birth, then God is not successful; the sea rushes out even when God shuts the doors. Job 38:8–11 describes a dual act of restricting and releasing the sea into the world. In verse 8, God shuts the doors, but not so tightly as to not allow the sea to rush out. Verse 10 depicts how God both breaks the limit and barricades the doors. Furthermore, verse 11 refers to God's dual action of first guiding the sea to move forward and then telling it to stop. This can be described as an extension of the metaphor GOD IS THE OPENER OF THE DOORS OF THE WOMB to include additional elements of the domains of DOORS and MIDWIFERY. Akkadian birth incantations emphasize the act of opening the womb, but doors can be both opened and closed, and a midwife must regulate a birth by both opening the womb and holding the baby back, both hastening and slowing the birth, and both advising the mother when to push and when to relax. Metaphors are derived from experience, and the dual role of a midwife, who both helps the baby move forward and slows down the birth, may be the background for how the birth of the sea is depicted in Job 38:8, 10–11.

One reason to slow down the birth process is to prevent perineal tears, a common complication during labor. These occur mainly when the baby's head breaks through. The birth of Perez in Gen 38:27–30 probably refers to such a complication.[68] A Neo-Assyrian text prescribes a salve made of cowrie shell or acacia to heal such tears.[69] Various methods exist to prevent perineum tears, such as massaging the perineum with oil before birth, a practice described in Akkadian birth texts

---

[67] The demon Lamaštu was believed to complicate births. Among other things, she could block the opening of the womb at birth (Foster 2005, 173–74). Finkel discusses several Sumerian texts (CBS 10489+10756, YBC 5636, CBS 1509) and a later Neo-Assyrian text (VAS 10 189), which may describe the need to block the womb in order to stop rushing water. The Sumerian texts are very difficult to interpret, and it is unclear whether they refer to opening or shutting the womb, and whether the water refers to amniotic fluid or blood. Finkel concludes that these texts most likely refer to the need to shut the womb to stop a woman from bleeding during childbirth (Finkel 1980, 37–46). Butz, on the other hand, argues that these texts concern the release of the amniotic fluid (Butz 1982, 221–26). Johandi interprets the Neo-Assyrian text as depicting Asalluḫi being unable to stop a bleed (Johandi 2019, 94).

[68] See chapter 3, page 74.

[69] *BAM* 240. Scurlock, 1991, 150, 176 (n. 139).

and still recommended today.⁷⁰ The most effective way to minimize severe ruptures is for the midwife to press her hand on both the perineum and the baby's head during the delivery of the head, while instructing the mother not to push too hard when the head crowns.⁷¹ The first known written midwifery instruction was by the physician Soranus of Ephesus (98–138 CE), who explains the importance of supporting the perineum, and instructs midwives to press a warm linen cloth against it as the head advances.⁷² Although written records of midwifery practices are scarce, this technique is spread worldwide and was likely shared knowledge among those assisting births long before Soranus. The practice of holding the baby back to protect the perineum may explain how Job 38:8–11 can extend the standard metaphor of breaking the doors of the womb with an unused part of the domain of MIDWIFERY, the act of holding the baby back. In this context, God shuts the doors to slow down the movement of the sea.

This blending schema in Figure 8.4 illustrates how Job 38:8–11 can be interpreted from the frame MIDWIFERY. It reveals the same collision between the organizing frames of COMBAT MOTIF and BIRTH as seen in Figure 8.3. The disanalogy between the COMBAT MOTIF and the BIRTH OF THE SEA is expressed in the blend by references to the limit, which is set as a border to the sea according to the combat motif, but is broken as an act of opening the womb according to the frame of midwifery. In Job 38:8–11, the closing of doors and breaking the limit of the sea refer to God's role as a midwife, regulating the birth to protect both the baby and the mother. In verse 11, God also guides the baby sea, saying how far the baby sea should be pushed, and when to stop. While it might seem strange for God to speak to the unborn sea rather than to the mother, the motif of gods speaking to unborn babies and urging them to move forward and to be born is also present in Akkadian incantations. Additionally, it is not uncommon for parents and others to speak to their unborn children during pregnancy.⁷³

---

⁷⁰ See discussion in Scurlock 1991, 145–46, 169 (n. 74). Akkadian texts also refer to the use of the pure fat of a cow, presumably ghee or cream, to smear the vulva (Finkel, 1980, 47–48; Stol, 2000, 61, 63.)

⁷¹ Dahlen, et al. 2010; WHO 2018, 5, 139–49.

⁷² Dahlen, et al. 2010, 106.

⁷³ See Chapter 4, pages 95–96, 100(n.23).

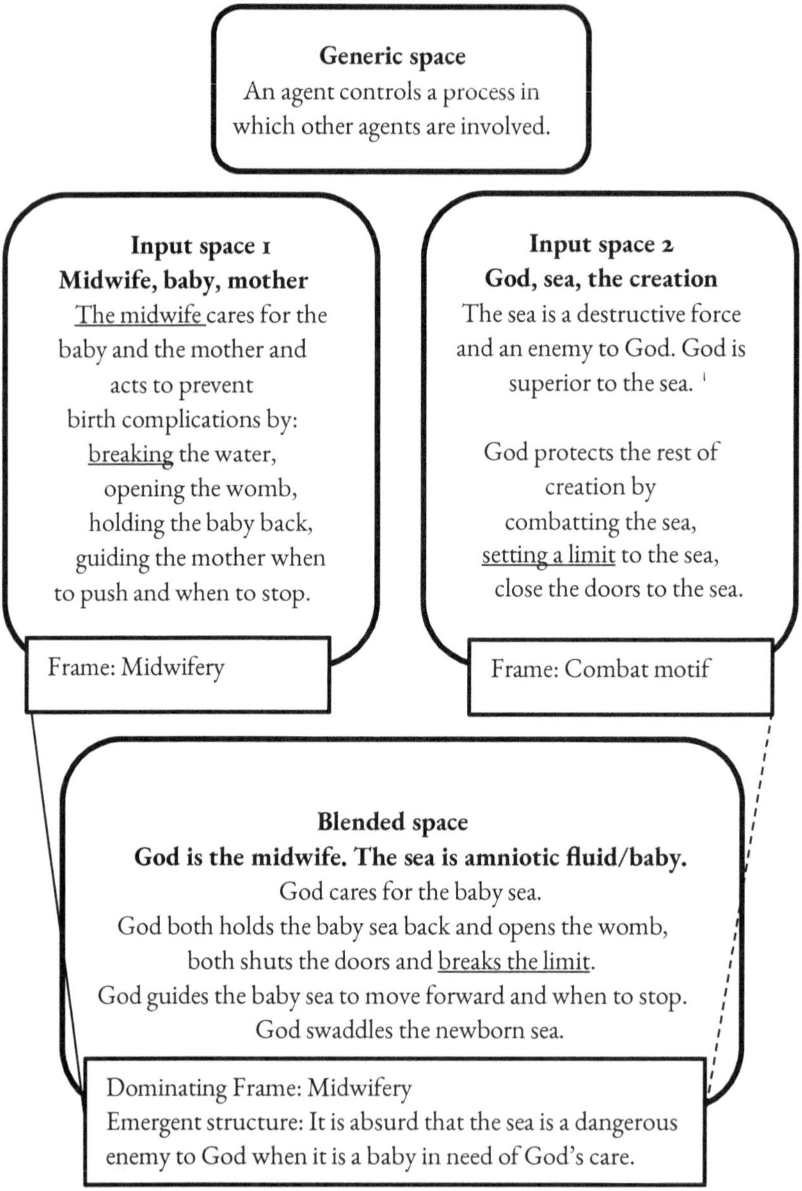

Generic space
An agent controls a process in which other agents are involved.

Input space 1
Midwife, baby, mother
The midwife cares for the baby and the mother and acts to prevent birth complications by:
breaking the water,
opening the womb,
holding the baby back,
guiding the mother when to push and when to stop.

Frame: Midwifery

Input space 2
God, sea, the creation
The sea is a destructive force and an enemy to God. God is superior to the sea.[1]

God protects the rest of creation by
combatting the sea,
setting a limit to the sea,
close the doors to the sea.

Frame: Combat motif

Blended space
God is the midwife. The sea is amniotic fluid/baby.
God cares for the baby sea.
God both holds the baby sea back and opens the womb, both shuts the doors and breaks the limit.
God guides the baby sea to move forward and when to stop.
God swaddles the newborn sea.

Dominating Frame: Midwifery
Emergent structure: It is absurd that the sea is a dangerous enemy to God when it is a baby in need of God's care.

Figure 8.4 The metaphors GOD IS A MIDWIFE and THE SEA IS AMNIOTIC FLUID/BABY.

A striking feature of the description in Job 38:8–11 is the absence of any reference to a mother. The image focuses solely on the baby sea and God as a midwife. While the springs of the sea are mentioned in Job 38:16, they are absent from the birth scene. A midwife's concern typically extends beyond the baby to the mother, aiming to minimize any injuries the baby may cause during birth. Similarly, God's concern as a midwife involves not only the baby sea but also minimizing the potential damage the sea could cause when it gushes out, achieved by holding the sea back and shutting the doors. The act of holding back the sea to protect others aligns with the combat motif, where God subjugates and restricts the sea to protect the rest of creation. Although the birth scene does not mention the mother of the sea or God's concern for her, it includes mention of how the baby is slowed down to not cause damage. The restriction of the sea is a crucial element in the worldview of ancient West Asia; if God does not restrain the sea, the world would be flooded and uninhabitable. By describing God's actions during the birth of the sea as both breaking the limit and barricading the doors, the passage includes the essential act of restricting the sea to protect creation, even as it is delivered and allowed to rush out.

References to God's dual action of enclosing water and letting it flow appear in descriptions of precipitation in the Book of Job (Job 38:22–30; 12:14–15), while the sea is elsewhere only described as guarded or restricted (Job 7:12; 26:10–12). As previously argued, the release of the sea, along with the care of the sea, wild animals, Behemoth, and Leviathan, would have been provocative. The mention of God also holding back the sea mitigates the image of its release. At the same time, the birth scene reframes the purpose of God's restraint of the sea—not as restriction to dominate the sea but to ensure a safe birth for both the sea and the rest of creation.

Birth Replaces the Combat Motif

Job 38:8–11 is a birth scene that also contains allusions to the combat motif. In the Book of Job, it is common to reshape conventional images and fill them with new meanings. By using expressions typically associated with the combat motif and changing them, the author encourages readers to rethink and reimagine how God relates to the sea. For instance, changing the action from setting a limit to breaking it would provoke a reaction from the reader. Reshaping, negating, or replacing old metaphors with new ones are poetic tools used to influence readers to reflect on the implications of conventional metaphors and beliefs.[74]

The care highlighted in God's actions as a midwife alters the perception of God's relationship with the sea. The sea remains powerful but is no longer an enemy or a threat to God. Newsom argues that the combat motif is transformed, referring to the swaddling of the sea as an image showing God's restriction of the chaotic sea for the purpose of care.[75] She does not acknowledge that God opens the womb to let the sea out, nor that closing the doors is also part of the midwife's role. According to her, God only restricts the sea, as described in God's setting the limit and doors and in the act of swaddling. If all four verses, 8–11, are viewed as a birth scene, with the shutting of doors and swaddling interpreted as acts of care, and the dual act of the breaking and the closing as that of a midwife, then the combat motif is replaced rather than transformed by the birth scene.[76] The combat motif would only explain why God shut the doors, not why the sea gushes out or why God breaks the limit. Only the birth metaphor can explain the dual role of God as the one who both restrains the sea and helps it gush out, and acknowledge that both these acts are done to ensure a safe birth.

Reading Job 38:8–11 as a birth scene without the lens of God combating or restricting an evil, chaotic sea provides new images of God, the sea, and their relationship. It changes the purpose of why God restricts the sea; the birth metaphor turns the sea and its outburst into natural elements of creation, rather than portraying the sea as an alien, chaotic force. God's speeches continue to describe God's concern for the wild in the depictions of wild animals, Behemoth, and Leviathan. No restrictions are imposed on wild animals; instead, they are released from their bonds (39:6).

How Can BIRTH Replace the Combat Motif?

In my presentation of birth metaphors in the HB and in Akkadian texts, I have shown that the domains of BIRTH and COMBAT are blended into metaphors that describe struggling mothers in labor or frightened warriors. If BIRTH can serve as a source domain for combat, is it then necessary to exclude the combat motif when

---

[74] See Chapter 2, 64–67.
[75] Newsom 2003, 244.
[76] Similarly, Cho discusses how Gen 1 alludes to various elements of the combat myth, but intentionally modifies and negates them. In doing so, Gen 1 presents a new myth that replaces the traditional combat myth (Cho 2019, 79–87).

interpreting the birth of the sea in Job 38? Could it be possible that the sea is intended to be both a combatant and a baby in this birth scene?

As previously argued, the notion of the sea as a combatant contributes to the absurdity of depicting the sea as an infant and amniotic fluid. However, the birth scene does not portray the baby as fighting or capable of opposing God. Additionally, it does not employ the conventional associations between the domains of COMBAT and BIRTH, which are used when blending combatants and women in labor. Neither the midwife nor the baby is depicted as a combatant in the conventional metaphors that blend BIRTH and COMBAT in the HB or in Akkadian texts. Only the mother giving birth is depicted in this manner, and she is absent in Job 38:8–11. Her absence further underscores that the author does not aim to highlight the conflict between the sea and God. The implications of the shift from the combat motif to birth in Job 38:8–11 can be explained by examining how the domains of COMBAT and BIRTH usually interact in the metaphor THE WOMAN GIVING BIRTH IS A WARRIOR or in its reversed counterpart THE WARRIOR IS A WOMAN IN LABOR. The reversed metaphor is often used ironically to humiliate the warrior or the enemy. Both these metaphors are depicted in Figure 8.5. The domains of BIRTH and COMBAT are linked through these metaphors of women in labor and warriors. Both domains are associated with danger, death, struggle, and physical exertion, as well as reactions such as tears, screaming, and trembling. The physical reactions are highlighted in the metaphors of the blending schema below. In the HB, warriors who are likened to women in labor are depicted as afraid, in pain, shaking, and screaming.[77] Similarly, the Ligabue tablets focus on the struggle and blood in the description of a woman in labor, sprawling in her own blood.[78]

---

[77] Bergmann discusses shared associations between warriors and women in labor in Bergmann 2010, 45–49.

[78] Lambert 1969, 31–32; Foster 2005, 1006.

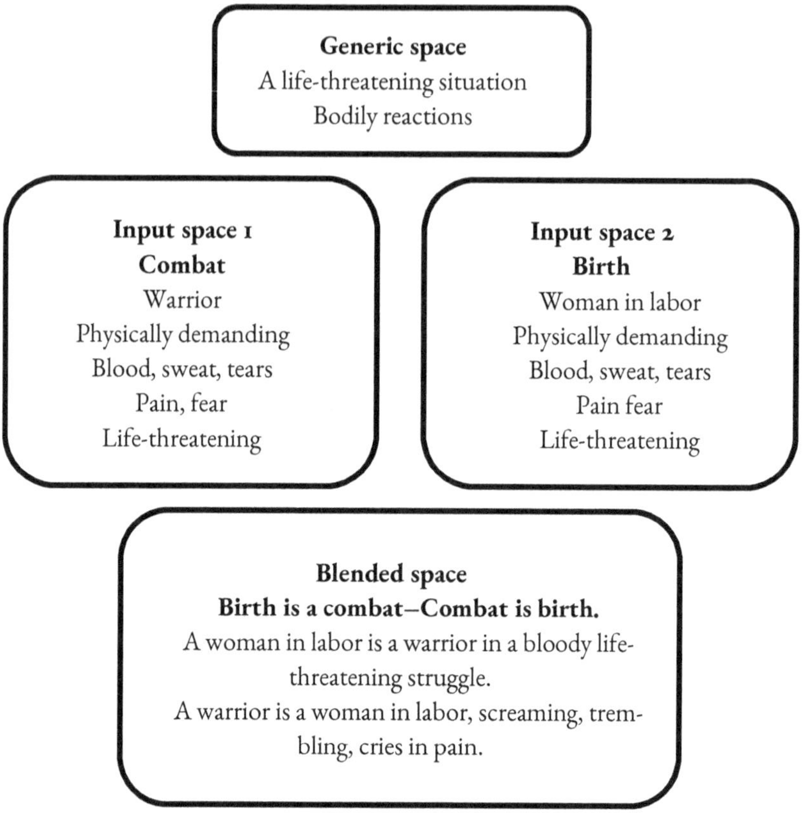

```
                    ┌─────────────────────────────────┐
                    │       Generic space             │
                    │  A life-threatening situation   │
                    │       Bodily reactions          │
                    └─────────────────────────────────┘

  ┌───────────────────────────┐     ┌───────────────────────────┐
  │      Input space 1        │     │      Input space 2        │
  │         Combat            │     │          Birth            │
  │         Warrior           │     │     Woman in labor        │
  │   Physically demanding    │     │   Physically demanding    │
  │    Blood, sweat, tears    │     │    Blood, sweat, tears    │
  │        Pain, fear         │     │        Pain fear          │
  │      Life-threatening     │     │      Life-threatening     │
  └───────────────────────────┘     └───────────────────────────┘

            ┌─────────────────────────────────────────────┐
            │              Blended space                  │
            │  Birth is a combat–Combat is birth.         │
            │ A woman in labor is a warrior in a bloody   │
            │   life-threatening struggle.                │
            │ A warrior is a woman in labor, screaming,   │
            │   trembling, cries in pain.                 │
            └─────────────────────────────────────────────┘
```

Figure 8.5 *The metaphors BIRTH IS A COMBAT and THE WOMAN GIVING BIRTH IS A WARRIOR with the organizing frame COMBAT, and their reversed counterparts COMBAT IS BIRTH and THE WARRIOR IS A WOMAN IN LABOR with the organizing frame BIRTH.*

When the relationship between the sea and God is depicted as combat, it draws on other associations from the COMBAT domain than used in the blend above. The metaphor GOD'S RELATIONSHIP TO THE SEA IS A COMBAT highlights associations of opposition, enmity, danger, and struggle.

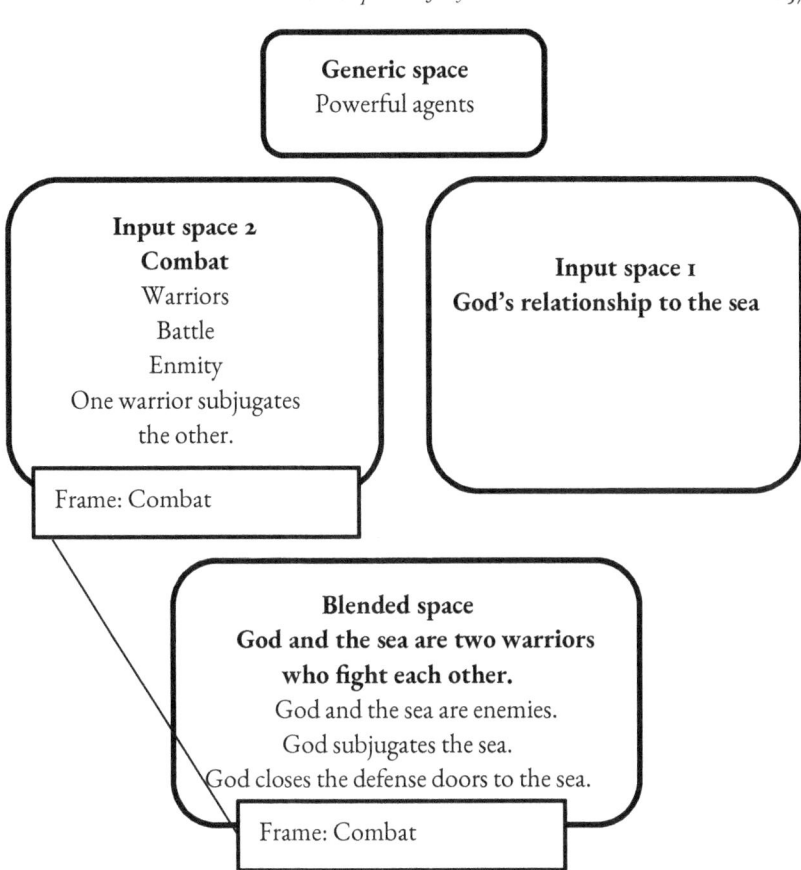

Figure 8.6 *The standard metaphor of God's relationship to the sea in the HB:* GOD'S RELATIONSHIP TO THE SEA IS A COMBAT.

In the blend of the input space GOD'S RELATIONSHIP TO THE SEA and the input space COMBAT, depicted in Figure 8.6, we do not find the physical reactions that are significant when BIRTH is blended with COMBAT. Likewise, the blend of BIRTH and COMBAT lacks associations of enmity and subjugation, which are crucial in the blend of COMBAT and GOD'S RELATIONSHIP TO THE SEA.

The numerous associations between the domains of BIRTH and COMBAT might lead a reader of Job 38:8–11 to expect that the birth scene also implies combat, even though it is a birth scene. However, God is not fighting, nor is God portrayed as a struggling mother, and the sea is not depicted as an enemy. The metaphorical description in Job 38:8–11 uses other associations from the domain of BIRTH than those used in the metaphors COMBAT IS BIRTH or BIRTH IS COMBAT. It uses associations of midwifery, release, and care, which are not shared by the domain of COMBAT and cannot be used to describe a battle scene. However, these associations are applicable to describe the relationship between God and a personified sea. In Job 38:8–11, the only shared conventional association between COMBAT and BIRTH is that they both are life-threatening situations, but the domain of BIRTH does not attribute the danger to an enemy. The primary reason for assistance during birth is to prevent complications and ensure the safety of the mother and child. In this context, God's role shifts from being a warrior protecting the world from the sea to a midwife protecting both the sea and the world. God is not threatened by the sea, just as the baby poses no danger to the midwife; only the mother and baby face risks during birth. In this birth scene, the work of the midwife is emphasized, particularly the dual act of both opening and shutting the womb, breaking the limit, and setting the bar and doors, guiding the sea on how far it can go and when to stop. This passage depicts God as the midwife. The domain of COMBAT is replaced with the domain of BIRTH and specifically the domain of MIDWIFERY, where restricting the sea is redefined as an act of managing birth. The imagery in Job 38:8–11 twists the reader's expectations: the dreaded enemy is portrayed as an infant, and God's role is to release and care for the sea.

The description in Job 38:8–11 still contains expressions that can apply to both the domains of BIRTH and COMBAT: the doors and the limit. In military language, doors would refer to the defensive gates of a city, but in the domain of BIRTH they symbolize the opening of the womb. Similarly, "the limit" (חק) is significant in expressions of how God restricts the sea according to the combat motif, yet here it describes how God releases the sea. These shared expressions are used to connect the domains of BIRTH and COMBAT while simultaneously questioning the combat motif.

Summary: Birth Metaphors in Job 38:8–11

Job 38:8–11 depicts the birth of the sea and how God swaddles it. Verses 8 and 10–11 refer to the midwife's act of delivering the sea, while verse 9 focuses on swaddling. This passage shares the metaphors THE WOMB IS A ROOM WITH DOORS and GOD IS A MIDWIFE with Akkadian birth incantations. Other Akkadian birth metaphors are used in new ways; for example, the metaphor THE AMNIOTIC FLUID IS A SEA is reversed to THE SEA IS AMNIOTIC FLUID, and the metaphor concerning the necessity of opening the doors is extended to include shutting them as well. The metaphor THE BABY COMES FORTH AS A RUSHING RAINFALL explains an entrenched structure depicting a baby's birth as water rushing out, and that the out bursting depicts a healthy birth. An extension or reversal of a metaphor changes the associations projected onto it: while describing the amniotic fluid as a sea highlights the danger of birth, this danger is downplayed when the sea is seen as amniotic fluid. The depiction of the sea as an infant in need of care also downplays its danger, and shows that the sea cannot oppose God.

The birth of the sea portrays God as a midwife and the sea as the baby that God cares for. Breaking the limit to the sea is part of the midwife's work in opening the womb at birth. Traditional interpretations based on the combat motif can explain why God shuts the doors but not why God breaks the limit and cares for the sea. God's dual action of both closing and opening the doors can be seen as the work of a midwife who must regulate birth by both helping the baby to move forward and holding it back. The birth scene uses terms commonly associated with the combat motif, but places them in a new context, the domain of BIRTH, and more specifically, the domain of MIDWIFERY. This shifts the meaning of these terms. Job 38:8–11 emphasizes the care of the sea and infuses the sea with positive associations, even regarding its outburst. God prevents the damage caused by the sea, not as a combatant but as a caring midwife. The swaddling of the sea in God's garments, the clouds and thick darkness, also expresses this care and God's closeness to the sea. The birth scene is a comical image that belittles the powerful, dangerous sea by portraying it as an infant. This portrayal is also provocative because it depicts the feared sea as bursting out and being intimately close to God, with God being the one who cares for it and helps it burst out.

Precipitation and Birth Metaphors

Metaphors should not be studied in isolation; their interaction with other metaphors is crucial to understanding their full meaning. When multiple metaphors depict the same target domain, they either reinforce each other by highlighting the same aspects of the target or complement each other by focusing on different features. In Job 38, the metaphor of the birth of the sea is combined with metaphors of precipitation to underscore God's dual role in both releasing and withholding water. The womb also serves as a source domain for precipitation in Job 38:28–29.

The breaking of the limit and the rushing sea in Job 38:8–11 find parallels later in the chapter, where metaphors describe how precipitation is managed by God. Snow and hail are stored in storerooms to be released on the day of war (vv. 22–23), channels are cut in heaven for the rain (vv. 25–26), clouds are commanded to empty themselves (v. 34), and the waterskins of heaven are tilted (v. 37).[79] These images emphasize the opening of these containers of water rather than the closing. The metaphors of the womb and the sources of precipitation are coherent and share the image schema of CONTAINMENT. In ancient West Asia, it was common to conceptualize meteorological phenomena as stored in containers such as storerooms and pots, or behind doors in heaven. These are opened by gods at the appropriate time.[80] These weather metaphors also share the same source domains as the conventional womb metaphors. Both babies and precipitation are imagined as being stored in rooms or pots that need to be opened or broken when it is time for them to be released.[81] In Job 38, the womb is depicted as a container, first for the sea and then for rain, dew, ice, and hoarfrost.

Job 38 not only describes how precipitation is released from heaven, but also includes descriptions of how water solidifies. Verses 28–29 depict the solidification of water in terms of fetal formation inside the womb. The domain of WOMB also includes the function of being a space of transformation, making it a suitable source domain for precipitation. It encompasses the image schemas of both CONTAINMENT and TRANSFORMATION and can therefore depict both how frozen precipitation is formed and how precipitation is released from heaven. The birth scene of the sea emphasizes the water streaming out of the womb, focusing on the womb as a container. In contrast, the subsequent birth scene highlights the womb's role as a space of transformation. Job 38:25–27 describes how God brings rain to the wilderness, highlighting the transformative effect of rain that causes the wilderness to sprout. This is followed by the depiction of the transformation of water into ice. By being placed side by side, these two images strengthen the notion of transformation. The birth of ice and hoarfrost is followed by the depiction of solid ice, which also highlights the solidification of water.

---

[79] The description of the star constellations Hyades, Pleiades, and Orion refers to God as the one who opens the bonds of the stars, allowing them to rise in the sky (vv. 31–33). Stars were associated with rain and dew, as expressed in *KTU* 1.3 ii 40–41; iv 43–44, and Amos 5:8. These constellations appeared in the sky during the winter rains. Hesiod's calendar also describes the winds and rains of winter that follow when the Pleiades and Orion are visible in the sky. See Hesiod, *Op.* 609–614 (trans. Most 2018, 136–37).

[80] Storerooms: Ugaritic texts: *KTU* 1.101 3–4 and according to de Moor also in *KTU* 1.4 vii 59–60 (de Moor 1987, 65). HB: Job 37:9; Ps 135:7; Jer 10:13. Open fissures or windows: Ugaritic texts: *KTU* 1.4 vii 17–19, 25–28. HB: Gen 7:11; 8:2; Isa 24:18.

[81] Womb as a house with doors, see above. For the womb as a pot, see UM 29-15-367 (van Dijk 1975, 57–61).

The interaction between birth and precipitation metaphors in Job 38 underscores the importance of context in metaphor studies. It strengthens the argument that God breaks the limit to the sea even if God also shuts its doors. This also explains why the womb is a suitable metaphor for the origin of ice and hoarfrost and offers insights into God's role in the birth of these phenomena. This serves as a valuable starting point for exploring the birth metaphors in Job 38:28–29.

Birth Metaphors in Job 38:28–29

Job 38 presents a second birth scene in verses 28–29, where God asks Job if he knows whether the rain has a father or from whose womb the hoarfrost goes out. While some biblical scholars have debated whether God should be viewed as the father or mother of precipitation, I question whether the issue here is really the parenthood of precipitation. I will explore this further, by investigating what these birth metaphors emphasize, the embodied experiences underlying them, and whether God plays a specific role in this description.

Text and Translation of Job 38:28–30

28	הֲיֵשׁ־לַמָּטָר אָב	Is there a father of the rain?
	אוֹ מִי־הוֹלִיד אֶגְלֵי־טָל	Or who begets the drops of dew?
29	מִבֶּטֶן מִי יָצָא הַקָּרַח	From whose womb comes the ice?
	וּכְפֹר שָׁמַיִם מִי יְלָדוֹ	Who gives birth to the hoarfrost of heaven?
30	כָּאֶבֶן מַיִם יִתְחַבָּאוּ	When the water hides itself, it becomes like stone,
	וּפְנֵי תְהוֹם יִתְלַכָּדוּ	and the surface of the deep comes together.

Literary Structure and Comments

Job 38:28–29 continues the description of precipitation that began in verse 22, drawing attention to its origins. These verses describe the solidification of water through the metaphors of begetting and giving birth, forming a parallelism in which the father's role in verse 28 complements the mother's role in verse 29. The different states of water in these verses correspond well with each other: rain (28a) and dew (28b) are paralleled by their frozen counterparts, ice (29a) and hoarfrost (29b). The verb ילד in Hiphil refers to the man who begets a child (28b), while in Qal (29b) it refers to the woman who bears the child.[82] The noun אֶגֶל, meaning

---

[82] Schreiner, "ילד," *TDOT* 6:77.

"drop," is a *hapax legomenon* and may be related to אגר, meaning "gather," leading to the interpretation of אֶגְלֵי־טָל as "a gathering of dew" or "drops of dew."[83]

The parallel between the birth metaphor in verses 28–29 and the description of ice in verse 30 further illuminates the process of solidification. It describes the solidification of water with the simile "like a stone," and by depicting how the surface of the water comes together and freezes into ice.

Earlier Interpretations of Job 38:28–29

Many attempts have been made to answer the rhetorical questions in verse 28a with either a yes or no, and to respond to the questions in verses 28–29 by identifying God as the parent to precipitation or by rejecting the idea of such parenthood altogether. These assumed answers have often shaped the understanding of the birth metaphors, particularly regarding God's role in this birth scene.

Two main arguments have been presented in earlier interpretations to support negative answers to these questions, concluding that there is no father of the rain and that no-one begets or gives birth to precipitation.[84] The first is a linguistic argument, most clearly articulated by Vall.[85] Vall refers to syntactical rules for rhetorical questions, where the expected yes or no answer is indicated by the phrasing of the question. The general syntactic rule for rhetorical questions suggests that a positive question with הֲ yields a negative answer (as seen in Job 38:12, 16, 17, 22). Vall demonstrates that other rhetorical questions with הֲיֵשׁ in the HB typically receive a negative answer. He argues that if the author had intended to imply that God is the father and mother of precipitation, then הֲלֹא would have been used instead.[86] He also asserts that a negative answer to the first question in verses 28–29 would logically lead to the conclusion that "no one" is the answer to the subsequent three questions. Fox similarly advocates negative answers based on his understanding of rhetorical questions. He explains that the purpose of these questions is to evoke "awe and gratitude, not a feeling of stupidity."[87]

---

[83] Clines 2011, 1061–62.

[84] Tsevat, Hartley, Cooper, van Wolde, Alter, Clines, and Fox answer the question in 28a with a "no!" and the others "no one!" (Tsevat 1966, 87; Hartley 1988, 502; Cooper 1997, 240–41; van Wolde 2006, 367; Alter 2011, 126; Clines 2011, 1111; Fox 2013, 5; Hartley 2013, 42).

[85] Vall 1995b, 512–13. Van Wolde, Clines, and Hartley use Vall's linguistic arguments in their interpretation of verses 28–29 (van Wolde 2006, 367; Clines 2011, 1111; Hartley 2013, 42; Clines 2021, 236–37).

[86] Vall 1995b, 512.

[87] Fox 2013, 5.

The second main argument for negative answers is that these questions are polemical, countering other myths from ancient West Asia that describe precipitation in terms of procreation. The description of dew and mist as Baal's daughters Tallay and Pidray in the Baal Cycle is cited as an example of how precipitation is conceptualized as children of gods.[88] Vall and Tsevat stress that Job 39:28–29 is polemical against other myths that claim that rain has a father.[89] It has been argued that imagining God as both the father and mother of precipitation is too anthropomorphic and shocking, leading to the conclusion that the obvious answers to these questions must be negative.[90] Vall refers to the images as too "graphic" to be appropriate for describing God, and that the purpose of these lines is to show that human procreation cannot "do justice to God's creation of the hydrous forms."[91] Others, however, claim that these lines present a deliberately provocative image, serving as a rhetorical device to encourage readers to think critically or to teach a lesson regarding the transcendence of God.[92] Trible contends that these verses are ironic, teaching Job that God transcends the metaphors used to describe God. According to her, these questions should be interpreted affirmatively, recognizing God as the father and mother of precipitation, while also acknowledging the inherent ambiguity of metaphors. She contends that they express that God is the father and mother of the rain, but at the same time, it is also true to say that God is not the father or mother of the rain.[93] Alter, who favors negative answers, suggests that the figurative language here reveals the limitations of figuration itself, describing the passage as a riddling paradox: "no one is the father of the rain, but the rain is the father of life."[94]

When the question of fatherhood in verse 28a is answered affirmatively, the identities of the father and mother are most often seen as God.[95] God is the obvious answer to other "who"-questions in Job 38 (38:5, 6, 25, 36, 37), making it easy to

---

[88] *KTU* 1.3 i 22–27; 1.4 iv.54–57.

[89] Tsevat 1966, 86–87; Vall 1995b, 512–13.

[90] Vall 1995b, 510, 513. Clines rejects the affirmative answers to these questions by arguing that God is never spoken of in terms of procreation and motherhood (Clines 2021, 236–37).

[91] Vall 1995b, 513.

[92] Gibson 1985, 229; Trible 1978, 68.

[93] Trible explains: "On the one hand, divine creation is not comparable to human procreation. On the other hand, it is through human comparisons that the transcendence of Yahweh is understood" (Trible 1978, 68).

[94] Alter 2011, 126.

[95] Mettinger, Trible, Gibson, Perdue, Wilson, and Ham identify the father and the mother as God (Mettinger 1976, 264; Trible 1978, 68; Gibson 1985, 229; Perdue 1991, 211; Wilson 2007, 434; Ham 2013, 538–39).

conclude that God is also the answer to the questions in verses 28–29. The identification of the birth parents as God is often combined with the explanation that God's parenthood must be understood figuratively, not as a mythical belief. Gibson holds that the poet of the Book of Job uses these "extremely daring" questions to provoke thought and to describe God as the sole originator of precipitation. Mettinger refers to these verses in a discussion of Ps 110:3, which he regards as a figurative description, similar to Job 38:28–29. He claims that Job 38:28–29 expresses God's production of precipitation "in the figure of paternity."[96] Anderson also asserts that the poetic description of birth serves only to emphasize that "the Lord made them all," not to affirm belief in precipitation as small gods.[97] Lévêque appears to be the only one who believes the these verses states that rain has a father and is born from a womb and yet maintains that neither the father nor the mother is God. He also contends that these birth metaphors are inappropriate and too extreme for describing God.[98] In contrast, Perdue argues that these verses portray God as both mother and father of moisture, similar to how Baal is the father of Pidray, the mist. He does not view verses 28–29 as polemical but instead uses these myths to support affirmative answers.[99]

A third interpretive approach is to argue that these questions have no answers.[100] De Regt suggests that rhetorical questions can operate on different levels. The syntactical form implies a negative answer to the question in Job 38:28a, but the rhetorical level implies the lack of an answer. He believes the lack of an answer is purposeful, reflecting "God's humor, which is subtle beyond words."[101] Newsom and Habel also refrain answering the rhetorical questions, arguing that the birth metaphors are used to illuminate the mystery of the origin and transformation of rain, ice, dew, and frost.[102] Newsom, in particular, argues that these verses emphasize the transformation of water into ice and claims that "it is unlikely that one should search for mythological identities for a father of rain or mother of ice. The questions identify wondrous and mysterious phenomena."

---

[96] Mettinger 1976, 264.
[97] Andersen 1976, 278.
[98] Lévêque 1970, 516–20. See especially n. 3 on p. 519.
[99] Perdue 1991, 211.
[100] Tur-Sinai, Pope, Rowley, Dhorme, Gray, and Wilson (Lindsay) do not give answers to the rhetorical questions but do not discuss why (Tur-Sinai 1957, 530; Pope 1973, 299; Rowley 1981, 245; Dhorme 1984, 587–88; Gray 2010, 464; Wilson 2015, 186).
[101] de Regt 1996, 51–52.
[102] Habel 1985, 542–43; Newsom 1996, 604.

Open Questions from Earlier Interpretations

Earlier interpretations of Job 38:28–29, whether dismissing the idea of divine parenthood or identifying God as the birth parent, often fail to consider the broader context of the birth scene. Job 38 emphasizes God's wisdom and Job's lack of knowledge, and Job is confronted with several rhetorical questions, to which the most common answers must be, "I do not know," or "No, I have not been there or seen that!" Someone who was not present when God laid the foundation pf the earth, or who has not witnessed the sources of precipitation, cannot claim knowledge about them. Thus, Job cannot know whether the rain has a father or from whose womb the frost is born. He cannot simply answer "yes" or "no" to these questions; his only possible response is, "I do not know!" This answer applies to all four questions in verses 28–29. De Regt's analysis of different levels of meaning can also be used to argue for the answer "I do not know," aligning with his understanding that the implied meaning at the rhetorical level is the absence of definitive answers.

Another key to understanding the rhetorical questions in verses 28–29 lies in examining the structure of the birth metaphor. Unlike other metaphors in Job 38 that describe the sources of snow and hail, or the earlier birth metaphor in verses 8–11, God's role is not explicitly expressed in verses 28–29. However, in these other metaphors, God is depicted as the one who opens and closes the womb, the storehouses of snow, and most certainly also the heavenly containers of rain. The birth metaphor in verses 28–29 should be interpreted in agreement with these other metaphors. Therefore, the womb in Job 38:28–29 must be understood as a container of precipitation that God opens and closes. Just as the birth parents are unknown in 38:8–11, they remain unknown in verses 28–29, with God's role being more akin to that of a midwife who delivers the sea and precipitation. Therefore, God is not portrayed as the parent in verses 28–29.

The two main arguments supporting the answers "no" and "no one" have several weaknesses. A problem with the syntactical argument is that it only addresses the first question in verse 28a and not the other questions in verses 28b–29. As Vall's interpretation demonstrates, the argument for negative answers based on syntactical grounds must be supported by either showing that these verses are polemical against other myths or that procreation is an inappropriate way to depict God's creative acts. I challenge the conclusion that procreative language should be rejected on the grounds that it is considered inappropriate or overly graphic. There are three birth scenes in God's first speech. In the first and third, God is involved as a midwife, and when it comes to the birth and care of wild animals, God also acts as a mother goddess. The birth metaphors are used to depict God's closeness to creation. The centrality of birth metaphors in God's first speech contradicts the argument that the purpose of Job 38:28–29 is to reject that God is associated with procreation. Furthermore, it is not clear that these verses are polemical against other myths in ancient West Asia, such as the Baal Cycle. The birth of the sea may be seen as polemical against Baal through its rejection of the image of a warrior defeating the sea, but the descriptions of God as concerned with precipitation and the fertility of the wilderness are features shared with Baal and other storm gods in ancient West Asia.[103]

Habel's and Newsom's arguments that the purpose of the birth metaphor is to illuminate the mystery of the origin and transformation of precipitation fit the context well. The questions of parenthood draw attention to the unknown origin of precipitation. The transformation of water is further described in verse 30, underscoring the focus on water's transformation into ice. The investigation below will explain how the construction of the birth metaphors visualizes the mystery of the origin and transformation of precipitation.

Formation of Precipitation and Fetuses

The frozen precipitation, snow and hail, is stored in storehouses (vv. 22–23). The womb serves a similar function as these storehouses, acting as a chamber to contain frozen precipitation. The birth metaphor in verses 28–29 further illustrates the solidification of water into ice, offering an additional perspective on precipitation. Verse 28 refers to the father of rain and the begetter of dew, but the forms of precipitation that emerge from the womb are the frozen varieties: ice and hoarfrost. The womb is depicted as a space where solidification occurs, leading to the metaphor SOLIDIFICATION OF WATER INTO ICE IS FORMATION OF A FETUS. Understanding this metaphor requires insights into the processes by which both frozen precipitation and fetuses are formed.

Solidification of Precipitation

Job's knowledge of creation is questioned in Job 38. He has not ventured to the underworld, or ascended to heaven; he has seen neither the springs of the sea nor the source of precipitation. In Job 36:29, Elihu asks if anyone can comprehend the spreading of God's clouds, and Job 5:9–10 describes the release of rain as an unsearchable act of God. The metaphors for the sources of precipitation in Job 38

---

[103] For a discussion of the characteristics of storm gods, see Green 2003, 281–92.

highlight God's control over meteorological phenomena, each offering a unique perspective on how God exercises that power.

The solidification of water into ice is mentioned in Elihu's speech. Job 37:10 states that ice is given, and broad waters solidify (מַיִם בְּמוּצָק), by God's breath. Similarly, Ps 147:16–18 describes how God gives snow like wool, scatters frost like dust (אֶפֶר), and melts them by God's word. In Sir 43:19–20, God pours out frost (כפור) like salt (מלח), and the north wind freezes (קפא) the water, with the ice described as a breastplate or armor (שריון).[104] The Hebrew word used for freezing קפא, "coagulate," is also used to describe the formation of Job in Job 10:10. The noun מוּצָק is used to describe solidified ice in Job 37:10. *HALOT* identifies two roots for מוּצָק, relating Job 37:10 to the second root, translating it as "narrowing (of a stretch of water)." The first root means "cast metal," which also aptly describes hard ice.[105]

Job 38:30 uses different expressions to describe ice and the process of solidification. It first employs the simile of water becoming like a stone when it freezes, combined with the description of water hiding itself (חבא, Hithpael), which can be interpreted as the frozen surface concealing the water beneath. Some scholars suggest that חבא is a textual corruption of חמא, which presumably means "become hard," "coagulate," though this verb does not appear in the HB, only the noun חֶמְאָה, "curd," "cream," "butter" (Gen 18:8; Job 20:17).[106] While this interpretation might simplify the text, I agree with Habel that in poetic language, חבא, "hide," works well to describe the freezing of water.[107] Verse 30b continues the depiction of solidification with the verb לכד (Hithpael), meaning "cling together," to describe how the surface of the deep freezes. The same verb is used in Job 41:9 to describe how Leviathan's scales are joined together. In Job 38:30, it appears that the solidification of water is envisioned as water drops clinging onto each other, or as a lake freezing from the shores toward the center.[108] The expressions of solidification in Job 38:30 convey the idea of ice as water joined together into a solid mass.

---

[104] Hebrew fragments of Sir 43:19–20: Mas 6:13 (=Sir 43:19a); SirB 13r:3 (=Sir 43:19b); Mas 6:14 (=Sir 43:20a); SirB 13r:4–5 (=Sir 43:20b).

[105] *HALOT*, s.v. "מוּצָק I, II."

[106] Pope 1973, 299–300; Dhorme 1984, 588; Clines 2011, 1062.

[107] Habel 1985, 522.

[108] The verbs לכד (Hithpael) and דבק (Pual) are used synonymously in Job 41:9.

Formation of a Fetus

The chapter "Birth Metaphors in Job 10" discusses how the formation of a human being is described in several ancient texts as the coagulation of body fluids, providing a background to the metaphor FORMATION OF A FETUS IS MILK COAGULATING TO CHEESE, used in Job 10:10.[109] This understanding is also crucial for interpreting the metaphors in Job 38:28–29. Metaphors are essential tools for grasping abstract or unknown concepts, such as the formation of a fetus, which remains beyond human understanding. Ps 139:13–16, for instance, describes God's creation of the fetus as taking place in secret (בַּסֵּתֶר), with the unformed fetus (גָּלְמִי) being known to God but hidden from human sight. An important association of the domain of FORMATION OF A FETUS is secrecy.

SOLIDIFICATION OF WATER INTO ICE IS FORMATION OF A FETUS

Job 38:28–29 uses the understanding of the formation of a fetus as coagulation of fluids to depict the solidification of dew into hoarfrost and rain into ice. It is a reversal of the metaphor FORMATION OF A FETUS IS COAGULATION OF FLUIDS into the image COAGULATION OF FLUIDS IS FORMATION OF A FETUS (Figure 8.7). This description of ice and hoarfrost is unique and, to my knowledge, does not appear in any other text from ancient West Asia.

The formation of precipitation is highlighted in the metaphor COAGULATION OF FLUIDS IS FORMATION OF A FETUS (Figure 8.2). The organizing frames of the input spaces FORMATION OF A FETUS and FORMATION OF ICE go back to the same general frame, the frame COAGULATION. The ice and hoarfrost are formed as a baby in the hidden womb. Verse 30 continues to describe the solidification of water, supporting the idea that the primary purpose of the birth metaphor in verses 28–29 is to illustrate solidification of water. While the release of precipitation is part of the metaphorical image, it is not highlighted. Unlike the explicit mention of God's role in the birth of the sea, God's role here remains implicit.

---

[109] See chapter 7, pages, 191–93.

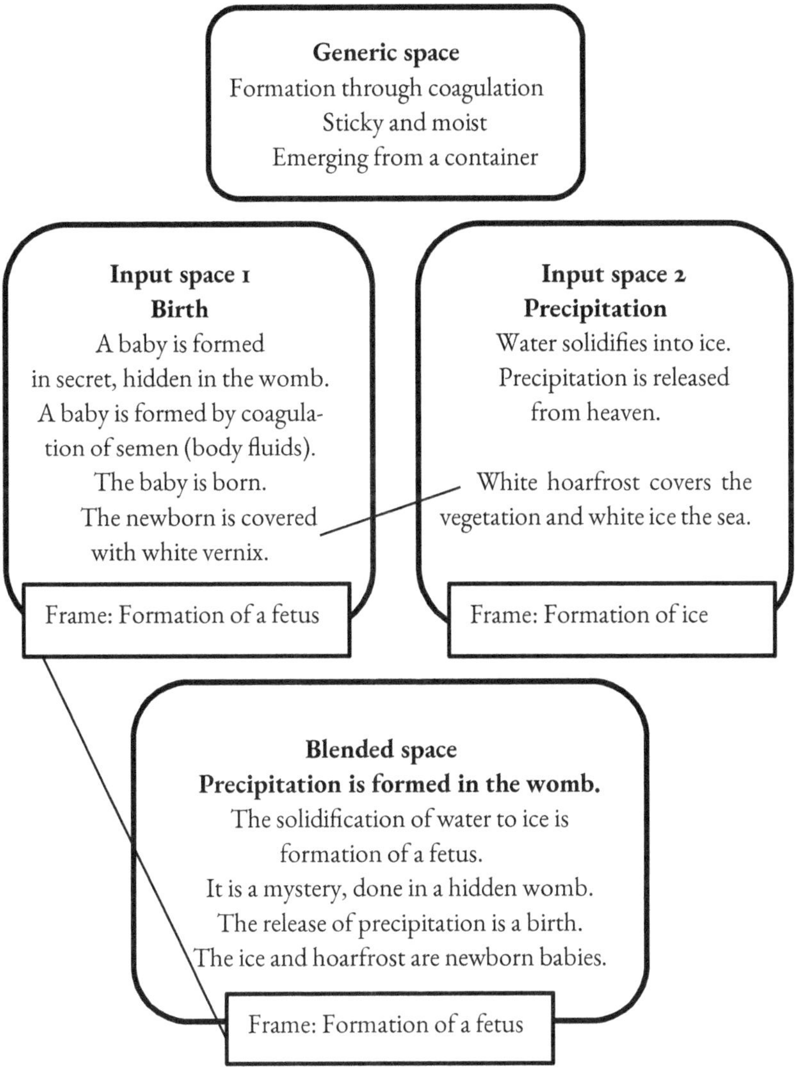

```
                    ┌─────────────────────────────────┐
                    │        Generic space            │
                    │  Formation through coagulation  │
                    │        Sticky and moist         │
                    │   Emerging from a container     │
                    └─────────────────────────────────┘
```

Input space 1
Birth
A baby is formed in secret, hidden in the womb. A baby is formed by coagulation of semen (body fluids). The baby is born. The newborn is covered with white vernix.

Frame: Formation of a fetus

Input space 2
Precipitation
Water solidifies into ice. Precipitation is released from heaven.

White hoarfrost covers the vegetation and white ice the sea.

Frame: Formation of ice

Blended space
Precipitation is formed in the womb.
The solidification of water to ice is formation of a fetus.
It is a mystery, done in a hidden womb.
The release of precipitation is a birth.
The ice and hoarfrost are newborn babies.

Frame: Formation of a fetus

Figure 8.7 The metaphors SOLIDIFICATION OF WATER INTO ICE IS FORMATION OF A FETUS, THE DELIVERY OF FROZEN PRECIPITATION IS A BIRTH, and THE ICE AND HOARFROST ARE NEWBORN BABIES.

The metaphor of the hoarfrost and ice being born implies not only their formation within a womb but also that they emerge from the womb as babies being born.

Although this aspect is an entailment of the metaphor, it is not emphasized in verses 28–29. This can be compared to the imagery of the birth of the sea, where the sea is portrayed as a baby that is cared for and swaddled. However, the image of hoarfrost and ice as babies might reveal an analogy, an experienced similarity between the frozen precipitation and a newborn. Specifically, hoarfrost covers vegetation with a sticky, moist layer, much like how newborns are born with a sticky, creamy layer of vernix. This analogy will be discussed further below.

A common feature of reversed metaphors is that a more abstract domain is used as the source for a more concrete target domain, as seen in this case. While the solidification of water into ice is observable, the formation of a fetus is not. God's speeches challenge Job's understanding of various aspects of creation, and by using THE FORMATION OF A FETUS as the source domain for FORMATION OF PRECIPITATION, the mystery of creation is highlighted. This is consistent with the other rhetorical questions regarding the unseen sources of precipitation in Job 38. The mention of unknown parents in verses 28–29 further accentuates the secrecy surrounding the origin of precipitation.

Precipitation Emanating from the Womb

The birth metaphors in Job 38:28–29, where ice and hoarfrost are described as being born from the womb, are reinforced by other ancient descriptions that link precipitation to the womb. Such metaphors are not uncommon in ancient West Asia and can be found in Akkadian birth incantations and medical texts. Psalm 110:3 also uses a similar metaphor, describing how dew is born from the "womb of the dawn." These descriptions use the associations between bodily fluids emanating from the womb and the waters of precipitation. There are also examples in ancient texts where bodily fluids from the womb, such as blood, amniotic fluid, or female semen, are referred to as water.[110] Akkadian birth incantations use the image of streaming rainfall to represent a healthy birth.[111] Psalm 110:3 reverses the image, changes the streaming rain into dew, and uses this to describe how the dew covers the ground in the morning. Unlike the Akkadian metaphor, which emphasizes the speed and power of water, this one focuses on the mystery of its formation and its appearance in the morning.

The metaphor in Job 38:28–29 similarly reverses the traditional imagery of fluids emerging from the womb as precipitation. However, these verses take the metaphor even further than Ps 110:3 by describing not a fluid, neither rain nor dew,

---

[110] See discussion note 67, page 250, and Chapter 3, pages 95–99.
[111] VAT 8869 (Ebeling 1923; Stol 2000, 65).

but ice and hoarfrost as emerging from the womb. Ice and hoarfrost are elements of the domain of PRECIPITATION that are not typically used in metaphors depicting precipitation as coming from the womb. This, however, coheres with the metaphor FORMATION OF A FETUS IS SOLIDIFICATION, which implies that it is the solidified mass, the baby that is born, not the fluids. In Job 38:28–29, dew and rain are not portrayed as streaming out of the womb; instead, they are linked to the father and correspond with semen in the image of the coagulation of a fetus. This can be seen as an extension of metaphors describing rain and dew as emerging from the womb because concepts like FATHER, BEGETTING and SEMEN refer to another part of the domain of BIRTH that is less commonly used in these metaphors, which typically focus on the womb, birth mother, and body fluids from the womb. If the metaphor in Job 38:28–29 is meant to emphasize the formation rather than the delivery of precipitation, it is logical to link rain and dew to the body fluids involved in the formation process.

Job 38:28–29 uses a familiar link between the water streaming out of the womb and precipitation. However, because the purpose is to describe how the precipitation is formed not how it is released, it needs to combine the domains of PRECIPITATION and BIRTH differently. The dew and rain become the semen which coagulates in the womb, and then it is the solidified water, the ice and hoarfrost, which eventually are born.

Experiential Similarities between a Newborn and Hoarfrost

The metaphor of fetal formation as coagulation is primarily rooted in the concrete experiences of water solidifying into ice or milk curdling into cheese. These are tangible processes that can serve as concrete source domains for the hidden process of fetal formation. The birth metaphor in Job 38:28–29 may also use the association between hoarfrost and the white substance that covers a newborn. In Num 12:10–12, there is a connection between snow and a stillborn. Miriam's skin disease causes her skin to become like snow, and she fears that she might become like a stillborn whose skin is half consumed. The textures of something half rotten and snow can be described in the same terms, as sticky, creamy, and moist.

The idea that the skin of an unborn or newborn baby might be conceptualized as snow or as sticky and moist is not surprising, given that newborns are covered with vernix, a white, cheesy substance also known as "birthing custard." Vernix is formed during the last trimester and is believed to protect the baby's delicate skin. The texture and color of snow and vernix bear a strong resemblance, as does the texture of soft cheese, which might explain the metaphor of fetal formation as the coagulation of cheese (Job 10:10). Hoarfrost covers trees and grass with a thin layer of ice, similar to how vernix covers a newborn. In Ps 147:16, hoarfrost is compared to אֶפֶר, "dust." In Exodus 16:14, manna is described as a fine, soft (דַּק), flaky substance, likened to the frost covering the ground. These descriptions imply that כְּפוֹר is more like soft snow than solid ice. The vernix does not correspond to the hardness of the ice as it is expressed in the simile "hard like stone" in verse 30; it shares the characteristics of hiding or covering, which is also conveyed in verse 30. Frevel suggests several analogies between cheese and a baby that is formed and born, but apart from coagulation, these analogies are not easily applied to the domain of FROZEN PRECIPITATION. He does not mention the whiteness of the newborn, but its softness, which he compares to the softness of cheese.[112] This association with softness might apply to snow, but the resemblance between vernix and sticky, moist snow is particularly striking. I would suggest that the experienced similarities between hoarfrost and vernix are one of the reasons why the hoarfrost is thought of as a newborn or why a newborn is depicted in the metaphor of cheese.

God's Role in Job 38:28–29

It has been speculated as to whether God should be seen as the begetter or the birth mother of the hoarfrost and ice in these verses.[113] Even though it is not explicitly stated, God's role seems to be that of the opener of the womb rather than that of a parent. The surrounding context, including the scene of God delivering the sea and the various metaphors of storing and releasing precipitation, portrays God as the one who opens the containers of precipitation. The implied role of God in the description of the birth of ice and hoarfrost is that of a midwife who opens the womb, though this role is downplayed. Job 38:23 explicitly refers to God as the one who has stored frozen precipitation, snow and hail, for the day of battle. These negative associations are not part of the description in Job 38:28–29, as ice and hoarfrost are not associated with destruction in the same way as hail and snow.[114] The emphasis is on the mystery of how ice and hoarfrost are formed. The birth metaphor highlights that Job does not know anything about the containers of snow or how water is transformed into ice; this is a mystery only known to God. The preceding verses, 25–27, describe how God gives rain to make the wilderness sprout, illustrating God's role in transforming the barren into the fertile. Similarly,

---

[112] Frevel 2016, 303–4.
[113] See pages 262–64.
[114] For discussion of associations of different kinds of precipitation, see page 235.

in Job 10, God is depicted as the crafter behind Job's formation, showing that God can be the agent of a formation of a fetus without necessarily being the one who begets or gives birth. It is likely that God is seen as both the midwife and the agent behind the coagulation process in this birth scene. The idea that God is the one who makes the waters solidify is also present in Job 37:10, where God's breath causes the water to freeze.

The metaphor of God as a midwife fits well within the context of God's speeches, which emphasize God's wisdom and the mystery of creation. The domain of MIDWIFE entails associations with wisdom. Many cultures, modern as well as ancient, refer to the midwives as wise women. The Akkadian word for midwife is *šabsutu*, which originates from the Sumerian *šá.zu*, "knowing the inside (of the body)." Its extended form *šabsutu remim* means "midwife of the womb," implying that she knows the inside of the womb.[115] In Atraḥasis, "the wise" is an epithet for Mama, the midwife of the gods.[116] In Job 38, God is portrayed as the wise midwife with the knowledge of the inside of creation, as the hidden womb where rain turns into ice and dew into hoarfrost. This motif of God as an all-knowing midwife continues in Job 39, where verses 1–3 imply that God oversees the birth of wild animals, counts the days of their pregnancies, and knows when it is time for them to give birth.

Summary: Birth Metaphors in Job 38:28–29

Job 38:28–29 highlights the mystery of how ice and hoarfrost are formed. This mystery is described by using the more abstract source domain of FORMATION OF A FETUS to describe a more concrete target domain of THE SOLIDIFICATION OF WATER INTO ICE. The metaphor THE SOLIDIFICATION OF WATER INTO ICE IS FORMATION OF A FETUS relies on the belief that a fetus is formed through the coagulation of body fluids. The idea of precipitation being born from a womb is utilized in both metaphors depicting births and those depicting releases of precipitation. The metaphor of ice and hoarfrost being a newborn may use the analogy between hoarfrost and the sticky white birthing custard. God's role is downplayed in these verses, but the surrounding metaphors imply that God is the one who opens the containers of precipitation, acting as a midwife who opens the womb. God is presumably both the midwife and the one who causes the water to solidify in the womb. The midwife metaphor coheres with the portrayal of God as the wise one who understands and regulates creation.

---

[115] Stol 2000, 171.
[116] "Atraḥasis" III iii 33 (trans. Lambert, et al. 1999, 94–95).

Birth in Job 38 and Job's Speeches

As noted throughout this chapter, there are connections between Job 38 and Job's speeches in Job 3 and 10. For instance, God shutting the doors to the sea in Job 38 parallels Job's wish in Job 3 that God had shut the doors at his birth. In Job 3, the closing of the doors would have resulted in Job's death, whereas in Job 38, it is part of God's protective act over the sea and creation. The sea is born despite the closing of the doors, underscoring God's role as a midwife who both opens and closes the doors to the womb.

Both Job 10 and Job 38:28–29 use metaphors with the domain of FORMATION OF A FETUS IS COAGULATION. In Job 10, God is described as the agent forming Job, while in Job 38, it is implied that God is the one who transforms water into ice. Job 10:11 portrays God as forming Job by dressing Job with skin and flesh, whereas in Job 38:9, God clothes the newborn sea. The care that Job recalls God showing him in the womb is, in Job 38, extended to the newborn sea. The care Job claims God showed him in the womb is, in Job 38, directed toward the newborn sea.

In Job's speeches, he accuses God of being a midwife who delivers him only to later become a watcher who destroys and confines him. In Job 38 God's role as a midwife includes caring for the sea and the wild animals after they are born. The birth is described in positive terms in Job 38, whereas Job never speaks of his own birth positively, only his formation. The birth metaphors in Job 38 are part of God's display of the wild nature unknown to Job, which makes him to consider other births beyond his own. God is involved in these births, and God's responsibility as a midwife is to bring them forth, including the powerful sea. Job 38 may not directly respond to Job's lament over his birth, but it offers another perspective on God's relationship with creation. In this view, God does not combat or confine the strong forces within creation; instead, God releases them and cares for them.

Summary and Conclusions

Job 38:8–11 depicts the birth of the sea, with God portrayed as the midwife who delivers and swaddles it at birth. Verses 10–11, often interpreted as an expression of the combat motif where God restricts the sea, actually reflect the same dual action as verse 8, where God both holds the sea back and lets it rush out. Therefore, all four verses, Job 38:8–11, are best understood together as metaphors of birth rather than as expressions of the combat motif. Using associations of old conventional metaphors to highlight their flaws, limitations, or inappropriateness, as well as creating new metaphors, are poetic tools employed by poets to challenge conventional metaphors. The birth scene is an example of this.

The birth scene employs several birth metaphors also found in Akkadian texts. The metaphors GODS ARE MIDWIVES and THE WOMB IS A ROOM WITH DOORS are used in conventional ways, but they are extended to include the act of closing the doors. The metaphor THE AMNIOTIC FLUID IS A SEA is reversed into the metaphor THE SEA IS AMNIOTIC FLUID. The Akkadian metaphor THE BABY WHO COMES FORTH FROM THE WOMB IS A RUSHING RAINFALL, depicting an ideal birth, may also explain the choice of depicting the creation of the sea in the metaphor THE SEA IS A BABY WHO RUSHES OUT OF THE WOMB. In this way, the sea is described as either rushing amniotic fluid or a baby moving quickly and smoothly out of the womb, emphasizing that the bursting forth of the sea is a positive event. The swaddling of the sea makes clear that it is a baby who is cared for. Depicting the dreadful sea as an infant strips it of its power in relation to God, portraying the sea not as a chaotic, evil force, but as a cherished part of God's creation, which God lovingly tends to. The sea is swaddled in clouds and thick darkness, both of which are used in theophanies to signal God's presence. This implies that the sea is clothed in God's own garments, further strengthening the connection between the sea and God.

While there are associations between COMBAT and BIRTH in Job 38:8–11, these associations serve to question the combat motif. The birth scene refers to the limit to the sea, but instead of setting the limit, God breaks it. It refers to an act of enclosing the sea, yet the sea rushes out. Both births and combats are life-threatening situations, and this shared association is still part of the scene. However, while the danger in war is associated with an enemy and reduced by overpowering the foe, the danger in birth is alleviated by the work of a midwife who assists at birth. God does not combat the sea; instead, God delivers it by both shutting and opening the doors of the womb. God's act of shutting the doors is an act of protection, as the verb סכך, "shut off for protection," suggests. The breaking of the limit corresponds to the act of opening the womb during birth, which may refer to the breaking of the doors of the womb, as expressed in Akkadian metaphors, or to the actual breaking of the amniotic fluid. The dual act of shutting and breaking corresponds to the midwife's role in regulating birth by both holding the baby back at times and helping it move forward at others, asking the mother to push, and telling her when to stop. The image of God as a midwife who both restrains the baby and opens the way for it accentuates God's desire to protect the sea while also preventing it from causing harm when it gushes out. It also articulates that God wants the sea to gush out, and that the release of the sea is, in God's eyes, something good. The midwife metaphor offers a new perspective on God's relationship with the wild sea. The shift from the combat motif to the birth metaphor is intentional and integral to a broader description of God's relationship with the wild forces of nature, including lions, vultures, and Leviathan. In Job 39, God oversees the birth of wild animals, providing for their young, and granting them freedom. God's delight in the wild is also portrayed in Job 40–41, where God takes pride in the awe-inspiring creatures Behemoth and Leviathan that God has created.

The conclusion, that the birth scene in Job 38:8–11 challenges the combat motif, aligns with interpretations that view God's speeches as highlighting the sublime nature of the sublime nature of both creation and God's relationship with it. These interpretations suggest that God embraces and nurtures the wild parts of creation. However, I question the interpretation that Job 38 illustrates the order of creation, while Job 39–41 depicts its disorder and wildness. The birth of the sea shows that God allowed the sea to rush out at the same time as God laid the foundations of earth. Both Job 38 and 39 mix references to God's power and order with God's role in granting freedom and caring for the wilderness. There is no significant break between these chapters; rather, they together illustrate the dynamic interplay between divine control and the freedom given also to the wild and dangerous parts of creation. Nevertheless, the sea and Leviathan are portrayed differently. Leviathan is described as an awe-inspiring and terrifying beast (as well as a pet), while the depiction of the sea does not emphasize its dangers or chaotic nature, though readers may still perceive it as threatening. The birth scene suggests that, while the infant sea may seem fearsome, it cannot overpower God, who manages its potential dangers. This image is both frightening and comforting, depending on whether the reader focuses on the sea's capacity to threaten humans or its inability to challenge God's supremacy.

In Job 38, precipitation and birth metaphors interact, with a recurring motif of God opening containers of water. The womb is both used as a source domain describing the storage of water and as a source domain for the transformation of water to ice. These two perspectives of birth highlight two important characteristics in God's relationship to creation: God's role in releasing and granting freedom to the inhabitants of the earth and God's transformative power. God controls both the opening and closing of containers, including those holding destructive forces like the sea, snow, and hail. The birth metaphors in Job 38:28–29 depict the mysterious formation of ice and hoarfrost. The abstract domain of THE FORMATION OF A FETUS serves as the source domain to the more concrete target domain of

SOLIDIFICATION OF WATERS. The metaphor of precipitation emanating from the womb is a familiar metaphor in ancient West Asia. It is used in texts that describe either births or precipitation and is grounded in the experience of fluids flowing from the womb, such as amniotic fluid and blood. The depiction of ice and hoarfrost as being born may also relate to the experience of a newborn, drawing an analogy between hoarfrost covering vegetation and the white, creamy vernix covering a baby's skin.

The portrayal of God as a midwife coheres with the central motif in God's first speeches: God's wisdom with respect to creation, that Job cannot fathom. God knows how the fetus is formed in the secret room of the womb and how precipitation is stored in hidden realms of heaven.

9. Birth Metaphors in Job 39

The second part of God's first speech, Job 38:39–39:30, concerns ten wild animals and their young ones.[1] It includes one birth scene in Job 39:1–4, depicting births among mountain goats and deer, and one description of how the ostrich treats its eggs and offspring. The birth scene contains metaphors describing birth as an act of breaking and loosening bonds. These metaphors are best understood through similar metaphors found in Akkadian birth incantations. The question of parenthood is highlighted in the odd description of the ostrich and in the questions of how animals feed their young. It is implied that both God and the parents provide for them.

Job 38:39–39:30 gives special attention to young wild animals. God's role at their birth is linked to how God meets their needs. This chapter will therefore not only analyze birth metaphors, but also how they are combined and overlap with God's care for the young. It will investigate how God's relationship with wild animals relates to the domains of PARENTHOOD, FREEDOM, and HUNTING. This chapter explores how God's care for young wild animals offers a different image of God's relationship with the wild than the traditional combat or "lord of the animals" motifs. I will argue that God shares characteristics with the mother goddesses of ancient West Asia, as well as with wild animal parents, creating an image of God as both parent and midwife.[2]

Earlier Interpretations of the Wild Animals

The wild animals in Job 38:39–39:30 have mainly been discussed from two different perspectives and surveying these will form an introduction of this chapter. The

---

[1] The description of the animals starts in Job 38:39, according to the BHS. The descriptions of the various animals constitute the third section of God's first speech and need to be studied together; therefore, I will also include the descriptions of the animals in Job 38:39–41 in my discussion on metaphors in Job 39.

[2] A condensed version of this chapter, focusing on God's relationship to the young animals, will be published in Plantin Forthcoming-b.

first concerns how the description of the animals transforms the worldview of Job and undercuts standard metaphors such as HUMANS ARE KINGS and WILD ANIMALS ARE DESTRUCTION. The other perspective relates to the "lord of the animals" motif and discusses whether the wild animals in Job 38–39 represent chaos, and if and how God controls them. This is closely related to the larger discussion of earlier interpretations of God's speeches presented in the previous chapter "Birth Metaphors in Job 38." The descriptions of birth and procreation in Job 39 have not been particularly examined in these two perspectives. However, they concern God's role in creation, and the study of the birth metaphors will provide crucial insights into how God relates to the wild animals in Job 38–39. This overview of earlier interpretations ends with presentation of previous research on how animals are used in metaphorical descriptions in the HB, and specifically in the Book of Job and in God's speeches.

Transformation of Conventional Metaphors

The description of the wild animals in Job 38–39 does not include humans. Most interpreters agree that this challenges an anthropocentric worldview.[3] Clines states that this description shows that God, according to the author of the Book of Job, could describe the construction of the universe by omitting humans but not by omitting the wild animals.[4]

Perdue maintains that Job 38–39 deconstructs the metaphor of humanity as the king of the world and that the parts of the world perceived as chaotic from an anthropocentric perspective are, instead, described as being under God's providential care.[5] Kang claims that Job is forced out of his anthropocentric worldview to acknowledge his own limitations to renew his trust in God.[6] Through God's speeches, Job realizes that he is not the center of creation, but that he is cared for, just like the wild animals. God's speeches describe the ambivalence of creation as both ordered and chaotic. According to Kang, God is neither a hunter nor a tamer, but a protector and caretaker in Job 38–39.[7] Clines suggests that Behemoth is a representation of the whole non-human creation, and that Behemoth is created by

---

[3] Perdue 1991, 212–18; Oeming 1996, 159–60; Keel and Schroer 2015, 167–68; Kang 2017, 309–11; Huff 2019, 249–50.
[4] Clines 2013, 3.
[5] Perdue 1991, 212–18.
[6] Kang 2017, 257, 308–11.
[7] Kang 2017, 282–83.

God, just as Job. This would teach Job that he cannot view himself as more important than these animals.[8]

Newsom argues that the wild animals challenge Job's moral imagination. The care of animals that symbolize wickedness and moral disorder, such as the lion, wild asses, and ostriches, challenges traditional values and images. The wild animals do not fit into Job's moral landscape or the social hierarchies in which he sees himself as the center. This forces Job into the liminal spaces of the earth, where he realizes that these areas are not forsaken by God.[9] Doak discusses how God's speeches also depict an existence where God does not need to follow any covenant, moral code, or doctrine of retribution.[10] God is close to creation and reveals to Job a cosmos that is both thrilling and reassuring. Doak claims that God's identity is intertwined with the identity of the animals, suggesting that God, like the animals, is also thrilling and free.[11]

Hawley undertakes an extensive exploration of animal metaphors in the Book of Job (omitting Leviathan and Behemoth). He investigates occurrences of metaphors using predatory and non-predatory animals such as lions, wild asses, and birds as their source domains. He argues that the description of the animals in Job 38:39–39:30 undercuts the animal metaphors used in the dialogue which associate predatory animals with destruction, punishment, and enmity. Instead, God's speeches reveal an order of creation that includes these animals, showing that God cares for them and that they, in turn, care for their young.[12] Huff also discusses how God's speeches transform the perception of these animals. He notes that, in ancient West Asia as well as in the HB, these animals are commonly symbols of persecution and desolation. The birds described in God's speech, for example, are considered unclean in the HB. However, according to Huff, God's speeches offer a different perspective, expressing God's delight in these animals instead.[13]

To summarize: Earlier interpretations have discussed how God's speeches challenge an anthropocentric worldview and deconstruct the metaphor of humanity as the king of the world. Neither Job nor any human is at the center of the description, which concerns only animals, the wilderness, and alien parts of creation. The display of the wild animals teaches Job that he is cared for just as God cares for

---

[8] Clines 2013, 9–10.
[9] Newsom 2003, 234–48.
[10] Doak 2014, 229–32.
[11] Doak 2014, 202–3.
[12] Hawley 2018. For a discussion of how Job 38–39 undercuts conventional metaphors, see especially 185–209.
[13] Huff 2019.

them. It also challenges the conventional metaphors that depict animals as symbols of danger, persecution, and desolation.

Lord of the Animals

The major discussion on wild animals in Job 38:38–39:30 centers on whether it should be interpreted based on the "lord of the animals" motif. Keel presented this interpretation in 1978; although he has since modified his understanding of Job 38–41, his influential 1978 interpretation will be presented first, followed by a discussion of his revised perspective alongside others who have challenged it.

The "lord of the animals" motif pictures a man, woman, god, or goddess in the middle, holding onto an animal in each hand. This motif implies, according to Keel, that God controls the animals. Keel explores how this motif is used on seals and other images in ancient West Asia, from the middle of the second millennium to the Persian era. The animal pairs in these motifs can vary, including lions, onagers, ostriches, birds of prey, or composite beings.[14] Keel presents the "lord of the animals" motif as an expression of the combat motif, where the animals represent the chaotic forces which the lord(ess) in the middle needs to control.[15] He interprets God's speeches as describing God as the lord who controls the wild animals. Keel describes these animals as anarchic, chaotic forces that are "menschenfeindlich" (hostile to humanity). He characterizes Behemoth and Leviathan as evil and as "diabolische Wesen" (diabolical beings).[16] God holds Chaos in a bridle until God will secure a longstanding and steadfast order of creation.[17] Keel claims that God's speech is a promise that the cultivated land of the humans will never become a wilderness, because God has ordered creation, and set the limits to the sea, the wild animals, and to Leviathan. The world contains evil and chaotic forces, but Job, and humans in general, must trust in God's sovereignty.[18] Dick follows Keel's interpretation of God's speeches, but he connects the Job 38–39 motif to the Assyrian royal hunt. The royal lion hunt evolved into a religious ritual, symbolizing control over wild animals, political enemies, and destructive mythological forces.[19]

---

[14] Keel 1978, 86–125; Keel and Schroer 2015, 165–67. The horse is very seldom depicted in the "lord of the animals" motif. Keel displays only two seals that portray a man holding onto horse-like animals (Keel 1978, 108–9).

[15] Keel 1978, 114.

[16] Keel 1978, 85–86, 155.

[17] Keel 1978, 125.

[18] Keel 1978, 61, 155–58.

[19] Dick 2006.

The "lord of the animals" motif has been adopted by many, but it has also been challenged, similarly to how the combat motif in Job 38–41 has been questioned. It has been argued that the "lord of the animal" motif is used in an ironic way, that the motif also implies that the lord cares for and protects the animals, and it has been rejected as an interpretive frame for Job 38–41. Instead, God is said to care for the wild animals as a game keeper or a parent. Fuchs and Oeming argue that the "lord of the animals" motif is behind the description in Job but inverted and used in an ironic way.[20] Fuchs discusses the expressions of the combat motif in the Book of Job and concludes that God's display of the wild animals, Behemoth, and Leviathan is a reinterpretation of the combat myth in which the traditionally chaotic forces are included in God's order of creation. There is no battle between God and the chaotic forces. God is superior and the sea is depicted as an infant, and Leviathan as a pet and someone who God makes a covenant with. According to Fuchs, God's speeches are characterized by God's humor, goodness, and care for the creation.[21] Oeming argues that the description of the wild animals turns the hunting motif or the "lord of the animals" motif upside down, because it is God who hunts on behalf of the lion instead of hunting it down.[22] He states that there are no descriptions of God subduing the animals in Job 38–39; instead, God is depicted as their caretaker. He therefore suggests that Job 39 depicts God as a good father, zookeeper, a game warden, or a wildlife manager.[23] Fuchs and Oeming's critique has been followed by others. Neumann-Gorsolke rejects the idea that Job 38–39 depicts the animals as chaotic or in need of being tamed or hunted. She emphasizes God's role as a creator, and that God has given the wild animals their freedom and space in creation.[24] Kang accentuates that God is a protector and a sustainer and criticizes the interpretation that God should be a tamer or a hunter.[25] Hawley acknowledges similarities between Job 38:39–39:30 and the "lord of the animals" motif. He states that while God dominates the animals, this domination is done with care. God also cares for animals that humans consider dangerous and alien. Hawley suggests that God is depicted as a wildlife manager, though he notes that this is not how ancient people conceptualized God.[26] Keel has modified his interpretation of God's speeches since 1978. He and Schroer now claim that the

---

[20] Fuchs 1993, 25, 220, 262; Oeming 1996, 158.
[21] Fuchs 1993, 22–25, 210–20, 261–64.
[22] Oeming, "צוד," *TDOT* 12:274–75.
[23] Oeming 1996, 158.
[24] Neumann-Gorsolke 2012, 147–49.
[25] Kang 2017, 282–83.
[26] Hawley 2018, 192.

description in Job 38–39 diverges from the common use of the "lord of the animals" motif.[27] God does not control the wild animals by subduing them. God is instead portrayed as the creator and sustainer of the wild, and as the one who defends its existence. However, Keel and Schroer still refer to the combat motif, particularly in their discussion of Leviathan. They argue that God battles chaos, even though chaos retains some "degree of freedom."[28]

The idea that gods have a special relationship with animals is found in many cultures. The god associated with animals is often believed to be the one who created them. Gods are believed to subdue and control the wild animals but also to protect them. This leads to portrayals of gods as hunters, or as mothers or fathers to the animals.[29] Lang discusses the "lord of the animals" motif in the ancient West Asian context and shows how gods interact with animals in ways other than controlling and fighting them. He explores images that picture gods who protect, dance, and play with wild animals.[30] Lang argues that the image of a person holding onto two animals may express that the person plays with them or tries to mediate peace among them.[31] He refers to Sumerian texts that describe the mountain goddess Ninḥursaga as the goddess of the wild. Her name means "Lady of the Foothills" and she was seen as the mother goddess of the wild animals. Later she also was considered a mother of domesticated animals and to humans.[32] She is said to be the spouse of Shulpae, the king of wild beasts in the desert. Lang describes Ninḥursaga thus:

> As the mother of Wildlife, she gives form to the unborn animals, and helps their mothers to give birth. After birth, she continues to love her animal children and laments their loss, whether they are killed by hunters or captured and tamed.[33]

This description is very similar to the description of God in Job 38–39. Lang does not explicitly discuss the similarities between God in Job 38–39 and this image of a mother goddess, but he notes that in Job, God is depicted as the provider of food

---

[27] Keel and Schroer 2015, 159–70.
[28] Keel and Schroer 2015, 170.
[29] Zerries 2005.
[30] Lang refers to three images: one of a goat-man, a figure with horns and a beard, pictured among wild animals, seeming to dance and play with them. Another image depicts a man, presumably a god, embracing an animal as a sign of protection. A third image shows a god playing the flute while animals live in harmony, with a gazelle and a lion appearing to kiss (Lang 2002, 77–81).
[31] Lang 2002, 86.
[32] Ninḥursaga and the mother goddess Nintur seem to been assimilated, see pages 310–11.
[33] Lang 2002, 81.

and overseer of birth. He connects God's first speech with Ps 104, and calls God the divine gamekeeper. Lang points out how God is portrayed as the creator who blesses and protects the wild animals in several texts in the HB.[34] He discusses God's blessing of the wild animals in Gen 1:22 and how the blessing concerns both procreation and protection. God as a creator is proud of the wild animals and expresses that they are good. He refers to Isa 11:6–8 as an example of how God gives the animals peace. His examples of different contents of the "lord of the animals" motif shows how it does not necessarily imply a God who controls the animals. Instead, Lang provides us with a wider understanding of how gods in ancient West Asia relate to the wild animals and how God is depicted in the HB.

To summarize: The "lord of the animals" motif of a person holding an animal in each hand is a widespread motif in images from ancient West Asia. In 1978, Keel suggested that Job 38–41 is best understood as an expression of this motif. The wild animals were understood as chaotic forces which God controlled and subdued. This interpretation has been questioned, and it has been argued that Job 38–41 uses the motif in an ironic way, and it has been reinterpreted to also include care and protection of the animals. God is then instead depicted as a caretaker, wildlife manager, or a parent to the wild animals in Job 39.

Animals and Metaphors

To interpret Job 38:39–39:30, we need to discuss whether the animals are used as metaphors or as a description of nature. I will here give an overview of how animals are used in metaphors in the HB and end by presenting how previous research has reasoned whether the wild animals in Job 38–39 should be viewed as metaphors or not.

Animals are used in the HB to depict human behavior, both unwanted and exemplary; this is seen in Job 3–37. Animals are often used as source domains in descriptions of human behavior which implies the metaphor HUMANS ARE ANIMALS. Animal metaphors are used to describe the wicked (Job 4:10–11; 24:5), and to teach about right behavior (Job 12:7–10). Dell discusses how animals are used in wisdom literature and in the psalms. One thing she points out is that animals are said to behave as expected, in regular ways (Job 6:5; 11:12), but they are also depicted with ways that are unknown and mysterious (Job 38:39–39:30; Prov 30:18–19).[35] She also discusses how the animals' relationship with God can be used as a model for the relationship between God and humans, as in Ps 104, where God's provision

---

[34] Lang 2002, 81–86. In addition to the ones mentioned here, he refers to Pss 23; 50:10–11.
[35] Dell 2000, 284–86.

for the animals is paralleled with God's provision for humans. Animals are also used in images describing suffering and God's punishment or attack on humans (Job 10:16; Ps 22:12–14).[36] Schafer makes an important observation in her investigation of how animals are used metaphorically and non-metaphorically in Isaiah. She describes how domesticated animals are used to depict subjugation and loyalty and are described as dominated by humans. The wild animals, on the other hand, are not subordinate to humans but instead are accountable to God. She describes them as human peers who, in a sense, compete with humans for God's attention and for possession of the land. The wild animals are depicted as praising God and relating to God on their own terms (Isa 43:20).[37]

Hawley discusses whether Job 38:38–39:30 should be viewed as metaphorical according to the metaphor HUMANS ARE ANIMALS. He argues that it should not be viewed as such because the target domain of HUMANS is not mentioned in the text. Instead, the description of the wild animals undercuts other metaphors that depict humans as animals by changing how the animals are conceptualized.[38] Horne notes that even if they are not to be understood as metaphorical, both animals and humans share the basic biological needs such as to give birth, provide food, and raise their young. He discusses the language of anthropomorphism in the description of the animals. The animals are given human traits, such as the raven who cries to God (שׁוע), the young animals who are called children (יְלָדִים), the wild ass, the ostrich and the war horse who laugh (שׂחק), and the horse who even talks, saying "Hurrah" (יֹאמַר הֶאָח).[39] This may imply the metaphor ANIMALS ARE HUMANS which connects animals to humans even when humans are not explicitly mentioned.

Job is often compared to animals, and they are said to teach him about himself and the world. Horne discusses how the use of anthropomorphism encourages the reader to draw parallels between the animals and Job.[40] Clines states that the animals teach Job that he is not more important than they are.[41] Kang argues that the wild animals demonstrate to Job that God cares for him just as God cares for them.[42] Doak claims that the animals are depicted as literal animals, not as metaphors, yet they can teach Job how to be human because they too experience the

---

[36] Dell 2000, 287–90.
[37] Schafer 2016.
[38] Hawley 2018, 204–9.
[39] Horne 2005, 129, 136–39.
[40] Horne 2005, 136–39.
[41] Clines 2013, 8–9.
[42] Kang 2017, 283.

struggles of life and parenthood. Job could learn how to survive the harshness of wilderness and live without any promises of protection or any covenants that regulate his relationship with God.[43]

To summarize: The metaphor HUMANS ARE ANIMALS is used in the HB both to encourage positive conduct and to describe destructive behavior. God's speeches are said to teach Job about God and how to survive in a harsh environment without any protection from God. The animals are not metaphors but serve as examples of how humans can relate to God. They are described in anthropomorphic terms, which may imply that they are Job's equals.

Open Questions from Earlier Interpretation

Earlier interpretations of the description of wild animals in Job 38–39 can be summarized into three main discussions. The first explores how these descriptions transform dominant metaphors, such as humanity being the king of the world. The second examines whether and how Job 38–39 should be interpreted according to the "lord of the animals" motif. The third investigates whether the animals should be understood metaphorically, and if they represent humans.

I agree with the critique of the interpretation which accentuates God's control and subjugation of the wild animals. It is obvious that God's speeches instead express a relationship which is characterized by the freedom of the animals and by God's admiration and care. In my discussion of Job 38 I have shown how the scene of the birth of the sea alludes to the combat motif to oppose and replace it. It is also evident that Job 38:39–41 turns the expected relationship between God and the predators upside down. It is implied that God hunts for the lion or at least provides it with food, which contradicts the view that God should protect humans from lions, real as well as metaphorical. Lang's exploration of how gods relate to animals in ancient West Asia provides a new perspective on how to interpret Job 38–39. The images of the mother goddess as the overseer of birth and as the defender of the wild animals' freedom fit well with the description of the wild animals in Job 38–39. I will explore this further in my investigation.

I also support the conclusion that wild animals are not metaphors describing humans. However, the description shares questions and themes with the rest of the Book of Job. There are parallels, both analogies and disanalogies, between how God treats Job and how God treats these animals, and between how Job views these animals and how they are described in God's sight. This would imply that

---

[43] Doak 2014, 199, 217–18, 229–32.

the description of the animals would bring a new understanding to Job and to humans in general, based on a comparison between him and the animals. Earlier interpretations have recognized how God shares the thrilling and dangerous aspects of the wild animals. What has been overlooked is that the rhetorical questions also imply that God shares characteristics with the wild animal parents. This issue will be explored in depth below. At the end of this chapter, I will discuss how Job relates to the animals and how his disappointment in God's role as a midwife at his birth parallels God's actions as a midwife among the animals.

The background to how Job 38–39 is presented in earlier interpretations is important in the research on the birth metaphors and how God meets the needs of the young animals. The research of birth metaphors and God's relationship with the young animals will also contribute to the overall discussion of how God relates to the creation in Job 38–39.

The Wild Animals in Job 38–39

Before I turn to my metaphor analysis of the birth metaphors, I need to present their context. The immediate context, its description of the 10 animals, its themes, and motifs, influences the constructions of the birth metaphors. An inventory of the domain of WILD ANIMALS will help determine whether Job 39 employs familiar features of the animals or introduces new ones. The speech is designed by rhetorical questions and God's actions is not described explicitly. Therefore, a discussion on the interpretation of these questions must precede the analysis of birth metaphors and how God meets the needs of young animals.

The collection of animals in Job 38–39 contains both predators and peaceful animals. These animals are lion, raven, mountain goat, deer, wild ass, wild ox, ostrich, war horse, hawk, and vulture. One might see them as presented in pairs, which is most obvious in the description of the mountain goats and deer who are presented together.[44] The other pairs are connected by a similar theme but are presented separately. The lion and the raven are linked by the theme of providing food for the young ones. The mountain goats and deer give birth, and their offspring grow and eventually leave their parents. The common theme for the wild ass and

---

[44] Keel structures the animals in five pairs in Keel 1978, 37–38. Newsom follows this structure (Newsom 2003, 244). Van der Lugt argues that that it is ordered by alternating between the care of the young and the freedom of the animals. He misses that the of freedom is already part of the birth description, but I agree with him that there is an alteration between the focus of the young and the older animals (van der Lugt 1995, 385–89).

the wild ox is their freedom from bonds and from human control. The ones who receive the most attention are the ostrich and the wild horse, both of which are portrayed as fearless and laughing. Although the war horse is not typically considered to be a wild animal, in this description it is portrayed as autonomous and unrestrained from human influence. The ostrich is depicted as foolish, and she abandons her eggs and treats her offspring harshly. The panorama of animals ends with descriptions of the hawk and the vulture, highlighting their high-flying nature and the vulture's practice of feeding its young with blood from the slain. The lion and the vulture frame the description of the wild animals, both focusing on how these creatures provide their young with food. Since the animals are discussed as separate species, they do not interact or threaten each other. There are no explicit references to animals killing each other; this is only a subtle undertone, as all readers understand that lions kill their prey and vultures feed on corpses. None of the animals are described as hostile, but as animals which God provides for.

The themes in the description of the wild animals cover procreation, provision of food, and the freedom of the wild animals. The young ones are mentioned in descriptions of six animals, three of which concern procreation and three provision of food. The freedom of the animals is emphasized, explicitly in the descriptions of the young mountain goats and deer, the wild ass, and the wild ox, and implicitly in the actions of the ostrich and the war horse. The description of the wild animals accentuates the contrast between God's wisdom and Job's ignorance. Job cannot know how these animals live, hunt, and certainly not how the shy mountain goats give birth. It is a mystery to him. God on the other hand, knows and oversees the animals.

The Domain of ANIMALS in the Hebrew Bible

There are several texts in the HB that portray God as the creator, provider, and protector of animals, both domesticated and wild. In Gen 1:20–25, God creates animals of all kinds, wild and domesticated, and blesses them. Psalm 36:6 says that God saves both humans and animals. Psalm 50:10–11 states that all animals belong to God, including those in the forest, hills, fields, and skies. Psalm 147:9 declares that God provides food for the animals and responds to the cry of the young ravens. The image of the young ravens who cry to God for food also occurs in Job 39. Psalm 148 commands the whole of creation to praise God, both the wild animals and the cattle.

Many of the animals depicted in Job 38–39 are also mentioned in Ps 104. This is the closest biblical parallel to Job 38–39.[45] These two texts share many motifs, but Ps 104 describes God's role in creation in declarative clauses, while God's involvement in Job 38–39 is mainly implied by rhetorical questions. Psalm 104 is presumably an earlier text which the Book of Job alludes to.[46] The relation between these two texts helps us to understand that God is the actor behind most of the rhetorical questions in Job 38–39. Psalm 104 describes how God provides food for wild animals, cattle, and humans. It refers to birds, land-living animals, and to the creatures in the sea including Leviathan. It is a harmonic description of creation where none of the animals are described as hostile. Job 38–39 describes only wild animals, and many of them are predators who hunt prey and eat dead corpses. Both Ps 104:21 and Job 38:39 refer to lions and their prey with the words כְּפִיר, "young lion," and טֶרֶף, "prey." This implies an image of lions as predators that hunt and kill their prey; however, Ps 104:21 does not explicitly mention the hunt, simply that the lion seeks its prey from God. Both Ps 104 and Job 38:39–39:30 concern how God provides animals with food. A significant difference, however, is that the Book of Job mentions many young animals and depicts their births, whereas the psalm only refers to the young lions.

Rhetorical Questions in God's First Speech

The use of rhetorical questions to describe the creation and God's relationship to it is allusive. There are only a few explicit descriptions of God's acts and knowledge in Job 38–39. God instead inquiries Job: Do you know? Can you do this or that? Have you been there? For example, God asks who delivers precipitation, hunts for the lions, and whether Job can guide the stars. The rhetorical questions have commonly been interpreted as implying that God knows and performs the things being asked.[47] Clines, however, doubts that God actually carries out all the tasks mentioned in the questions.[48] His objection calls for a discussion on what grounds we can assume that God knows and does what these questions convey.

When it comes to the questions of knowledge, it is obvious that God knows the things out of reach of Job. The introduction of God's speech already

---

[45] For parallels to Job 38, see chapter 8, page 236. For an overview of the similarities between Psalm 104 and the book of Job, see Frevel 2013.

[46] Frevel 2013, 159.

[47] That God performs the tasks of questions is presumed, for instance, in Lévêque 1970, 519; Newsom 2003, 245–46; Habel 1985, 529–32.

[48] Clines 2011, 1093, 1118.

establishes that Job lacks the knowledge possessed by God when God asks Job "Who is this that darkens counsel by words without knowledge?" (Job 38:2). Even if God's speeches display creation through rhetorical questions, it is still a description which is expressed by the character God. This implies that God knows the answer to the questions.

However, the fact that God knows all the answers does not imply that God executes all the things God asks whether Job can handle, nor does it mean that God is necessarily the answer to who performs various roles in creation. Clines argues that God is not the one who lets the wild ass free, because it is free from birth, and that God does not hunt for the lions because they hunt by themselves.[49] In my analysis of Job 38, I have shown that God is not the answer to the question of who gives birth to the hoarfrost in Job 38:29, but is the answer to the question of who shuts the doors to the sea in Job 38:8. Job 38 explicitly refers to God as the one who broke the limit and set the bar to the sea in verse 10, and that God stores snow in the storehouses in verse 23. This supports the conclusion that God is the answer to the questions of who stores and releases the precipitation and opening the bonds of the stars in Job 38:22–38. The explicit references to God's actions help us to understand the rhetorical questions. In Job 39, it is explicitly said that God gave the wild ass the wilderness as its home and that God has not given wisdom to the ostrich (Job 39:6, 17). The statement that God has given the wild ass its land continues the questions about who has set the wild ass free, suggesting that God is also responsible for unleashing it (Job 39:5–6). The unleashing of animals is an act of opening bonds, which is coherent with how God is said to open the womb of the sea and the bonds of the stars in Job 38:31. This supports the idea that God is the one who releases the animals in Job 39. The questions about the provision of food for the lion and the raven is best understood from the tradition of God as the provider of prey for the lion and food for the raven, which is also expressed in Pss 104:21 and 147:9. If God then is the one who hunts for the lions, or only provides them with food, cannot be discerned. The allusiveness of the rhetorical questions leads the reader to a sense of uncertainty, which accentuates the fact that God has knowledge that humans can never comprehend.

Birth, Parenthood, and Young Wild Animals

This chapter will examine the birth metaphors, the interactions between adults and young animals, and God's role both at birth and in the care of the young. The

---

[49] Clines 2011, 1122.

analysis consists of three parts. The first concerns the birth metaphors in the description of the mountain goats and deer giving birth in Job 39:1–4. This description uses the metaphor THE UNBORN IS TIED WITH ROPES and describes birth as breaking out of the womb. These metaphors accentuate the freedom of the animals, and depict God as the midwife who oversees their birth. The second part analyzes the depiction of the ostrich in Job 39:13–18, focusing on her neglect of her eggs and offspring. The portrayal of the ostrich does not contain any birth metaphors, but uses the ostrich as an example of bad parenthood. She is a counter-image to how the other wild animals act in Job 38–39 and to parental care in general. The final section investigates the young wild animals and the image of God as their caretaker alongside with their parents. It has been suggested that God's care for the young implies that God is the parent to the animals, but this has not been explored. I will investigate how this image is derived from God's shared characteristics with the animal parents, and how it corresponds to how mother goddesses are described in ancient West Asia and ancient Greece. I will also show how the parent metaphor relates to the metaphor of a midwife, freedom of the animals, and to the references to hunting.

Birth Metaphors in Job 39:1–4

Text and Translation of Job 39:1–4

1	הֲיָדַעְתָּ עֵת לֶדֶת יַעֲלֵי־סָלַע	Do you know the time when mountain goats give birth?
	חֹלֵל אַיָּלוֹת תִּשְׁמֹר	Do you supervise the labor of the deer?
2	תִּסְפֹּר יְרָחִים תְּמַלֶּאנָה	Do you count the months that they fulfill,
	וְיָדַעְתָּ עֵת לִדְתָּנָה	and do you know the time when they give birth,
3	תִּכְרַעְנָה יַלְדֵיהֶן תְּפַלַּחְנָה	when they kneel and make their children break out,
	חֶבְלֵיהֶם תְּשַׁלַּחְנָה	and their cords are unleashed?
4	יַחְלְמוּ בְנֵיהֶם	Their young ones are strong,
	יִרְבּוּ בַבָּר	they grow up in the open
	יָצְאוּ וְלֹא־שָׁבוּ לָמוֹ	they go out, and do not return to them.

Literary Structure and Comments

The deer and mountain goats are the second pair of animals presented. They are preceded by the lions and ravens and followed by the wild ass and wild ox. The mountain goats, deer, wild ass, and wild ox are the wild counterparts to domesticated sheep, goats, horses, and cattle. In Job 38, they are also connected with the motifs of releasing bonds and freedom.

Horned animals are associated with fertility, beauty, vitality, and strength (Prov 5:18–19; Song 3:5; Isa 35:6). Gazelles are also used to describe speed and a rapid flight (2 Sam 2:18). An Akkadian birth incantation refers to a quick and easy birth as a birth of a gazelle, and there are Ugaritic images of nursing scenes of young horned animals fed by a goddess.[50] The associations between horned animals and birth, fertility, and care for the young may explain the choice of using these animals to describe God's involvement in procreation and birth. They were also known to be shy and to give birth in areas inaccessible to humans.[51] This aligns with the aim of the speeches: to illuminate Job's limited knowledge of creation. God is said in 39:1 to supervise the birth of these animals. The verb used is שׁמר, "watch over," "preserve," "take care of." The same verb is used in Job 10:12, where God is said to preserve Job's spirit during his formation. God's speech emphasizes that God's involvement extends beyond the birth of Job or humans to include the birth of wild animals as well.

Verse 3 has been seen as problematic. The verb פלח, "split," "cleave," has not been seen as fitting into a birth scene. It has also been debated whether the expression חֶבְלֵיהֶם refers to the noun חֵבֶל, "labor pains," "fetus" or to חֶבֶל, "cord," "rope." Additionally, the mix of feminine and masculine suffixes in this verse has been considered problematic.[52] Nevertheless, the verb פלח, "split," and the noun חֶבֶל, "cord," "rope," correspond to Akkadian birth metaphors, which will discussed in my investigation below.

Verse 4 contains the expression יִרְבּוּ בַבָּר. The verb רבה probably means "grow" as it does in Ezek 16:7, where a newborn is said to grow like a plant from the field.[53] *HALOT* translates בַּר, "open field," as a fourth root of בַּר.[54] This is the only occurrence of this root in the HB and it is an Aramaism. Hamp questions the interpretation of בַּר as "open land" and instead refers to the root as meaning "be free," which he argues is the meaning of the original root of ברר.[55] I translate the expression יִרְבּוּ בַבָּר, "grow in the open," but the association of being free also fits the context.

---

[50] Veldhuis 1991, 9, 41–42; Day 1992, 187–90.
[51] Habel 1985, 544–45.
[52] Clines 2011, 1070.
[53] *HALOT* s.v. "רבה I."
[54] *HALOT* s.v. "בַּר IV."
[55] Hamp, "בָּרַר," *TDOT* 2:312.

In Job 39:1–4 there are several motifs that occur in birth descriptions in other cultures in ancient West Asia, such as the counting of the months of the pregnancy, the birth position kneeling, babies as breaking themselves out of the womb, and the need for the unborn to be untied from the womb.

Counting the Months of a Pregnancy

The question whether Job knows the time (עֵת) when the animals give birth is repeated twice (vv. 1, 2) and is combined with the question of whether Job supervises (שָׁמֹר) their births or counts the months of their pregnancies. These questions imply that God is the one who supervises the births, knows the time, and counts the months. The knowledge of birth is generally attributed to midwives. The theme of counting the months of a pregnancy is a well-known motif in Akkadian, Ugaritic, and Hittite myths, in which it is the mother goddess (who also are the midwives among the gods) or the god who is the father of the child, who counts the days or the months of the pregnancy.[56] The rhetorical question in Job 39:2 implies that God counts the months and therefore acts as the father or as a mother goddess in the relationship with the wild animals.

Birth Position

The birth description in Job 39:3 refers to the birth position with the verb כרע, "crouch." The same verb is used to describe a woman giving birth in 1 Sam 4:19, and it is also the birth position for the women giving birth to Dusk and Dawn in the Ugaritic myth.[57] It is a natural birth position for a woman but not for bovines, deer, and goats. However, the myths describing the cow of Sîn giving birth describe the cow as kneeling as well as trembling.[58] Job 39:1 uses the verb חיל, "be in labor," which also means "tremble" or "writhe" in pain. This also refers to the experience of a woman in childbirth rather than to animals giving birth.[59]

Breaking Out of the Womb and Untying the Bonds

When the mother goats and deer kneel, their young are born. This is described by the expressions יַלְדֵיהֶן תְּפַלַּחְנָה and חֶבְלֵיהֶם תְּשַׁלַּחְנָה whose meanings have been

---

[56] For an overview of the motif "counting the day of a pregnancy," see Chapter 4, pages 99–100.

[57] "Dawn and Dusk," line 61 (*COS* 1.87:282).

[58] For the Middle Assyrian texts of Cow of Sîn, see Veldhuis 1991, 10–13. For a further discussion of כרע, "crouch," in the HB, see Chapter 3, page 75.

[59] VAT 8869 (Veldhuis 1991, 9). *HALOT* s.v. "חיל I."

discussed. The verb פלח, "split," "pierce," has been seen as problematic. It is elsewhere used to describe how the liver, kidneys, and inner parts of a human are pierced, how the earth breaks, and how wild gourds are cleaved before they are cooked (Job 16:13; Prov 7:23; Ps 141:7; 2 King 4:39). *HALOT* gives three suggestions for how to translate פלח (Piel) in Job 39:3: "split the womb," "give birth," and "drop offspring."[60] Fohrer and Jenni suggest that it is a splitting of the cervix.[61] Clines points out that if פלח is interpreted as "splitting of the womb" then it cannot have יַלְדֵיהֶן, "their young," as its object.[62] Driver suggests that פלח is an Aramaism for פתח, "open (the womb)" and omits the object יַלְדֵיהֶן. He translates verse 3: "they crouch, they open (their wombs), they bring forth their young."[63] A common interpretation is to emend תְּפַלַּחְנָה to תְּפַלֵּטְנָה. The verb פלט (Piel) is used in the context of birth in Job 21:10, meaning calving. The emendation of פלח to פלט has had the most impact on translations of this verse, and leads to translations such as "bring forth," "giving birth," and "deliver."[64] I suggest that the word פלח (Piel) in Job 39:3 should be understood as an act of splitting, and the Piel should here be understood as causative, as the birth mothers make their children break out of the womb. The analyses of the metaphors and the syntax below will explain why this is the most plausible interpretation.

The expression חֶבְלֵיהֶם has been disputed. It is commonly interpreted as referring to חֵבֶל, understood either as "labor pain" or as "fetus" or "offspring," both of which can serve as synonyms for יֶלֶד.[65] These interpretations must consider the fact that the masculine suffix הֶם in חֶבְלֵיהֶם cannot refer to the birth mothers. The masculine suffix might be interpreted as an objective genitive, indicating the labor pains are caused by the children. However, the masculine suffix is problematic if חֵבֶל is interpreted as "fetus." Good suggests a third interpretation and translates it "expel their cords" based on the word חֶבֶל which he interprets as the umbilical cords.[66] I also suggest that חֶבְלֵיהֶם refers to חֶבֶל but not to the umbilical cord. The noun חֶבֶל is a common word for "rope," "cord," used in various contexts, such as snares, ropes on ships, and ropes used to bind someone (Josh 2:15; Isa 33:23; Ps

---

[60] *HALOT* s.v. "פלח."

[61] Fohrer 1963, 493; Jenni 1968, 180.

[62] Clines 2011, 1070.

[63] Driver 1969, 92–93.

[64] Give birth: NRSV; Clines 2011, 1050. Bring forth: KJV; NIV; Gray 2010, 469. Deliver: Habel 1985, 519.

[65] Labor pain: EUE; NIV; Bibel 2000. Fetus/offspring: NRSV; Tur-Sinai 1957, 540; Dhorme 1984, 598; Habel 1985, 519; Gray 2010, 472.

[66] Good 1990, 160–61.

119:61). I suggest that it refers to the image of unborn babies as tied to the womb by ropes, which aligns with the suffix הֶם (indicating "the ropes of the children") and the verb שׁלח (Piel), meaning "set free," or "expel." This will be supported by the analysis below.

The interpretations of the verb פלח as an act of splitting and חֶבְלֵיהֶם as referring to the ropes of the children can be explained by how birth was conceptualized in ancient West Asia, as expressed in Akkadian birth incantations and the HB. The act of breaking is part of birth descriptions in the HB, as in Isa 66:9 and in the birth scene when Perez is born in Gen 38:29. Akkadian birth incantations also describe births as acts of breaking. Additionally, they depict the baby as tied to the womb with cords which need to be untied at the time of birth. The Old Babylonian incantation (YBC 4603) refers to the baby's arms as bound, and the god Asalluḫi is said to have "opened his tight-bound bonds."[67] The compendium from Assur states the necessity of slackening the mooring rope of the boat. The boat depicts the baby, and the baby is said to be "the sealed one." Asalluḫi unties the knots and opens the doors. To open the doors, loosen the bonds, and relax the muscles are parallel expressions in the compendium from Assur.[68] The metaphors of opening the doors of the womb, breaking the womb like a pot, and untying the bonds reflect the need to release the baby and the potential danger if the baby becomes stuck in the womb. The metaphors of doors and ropes go back to two different image schemas of how someone is held back. The first one is CONTAINMENT: the one enclosed cannot leave the container. The other one is ATTACHMENT: the one attached cannot move. The experience of attachment is also described in non-metaphorical descriptions of the muscles and flesh which need to be slackened at birth in this incantation. Figure 9.1 depicts the birth metaphors used in Akkadians incantations, which provides an interpretive frame for how metaphors in Job 39:1–4 are constructed, which will be displayed in Figure 9.2.

---

[67] van Dijk 1973, 503; Stol 2000, 11. See Chapter 4, pages 95–99.
[68] Ebeling 1923; Stol 2000, 65.

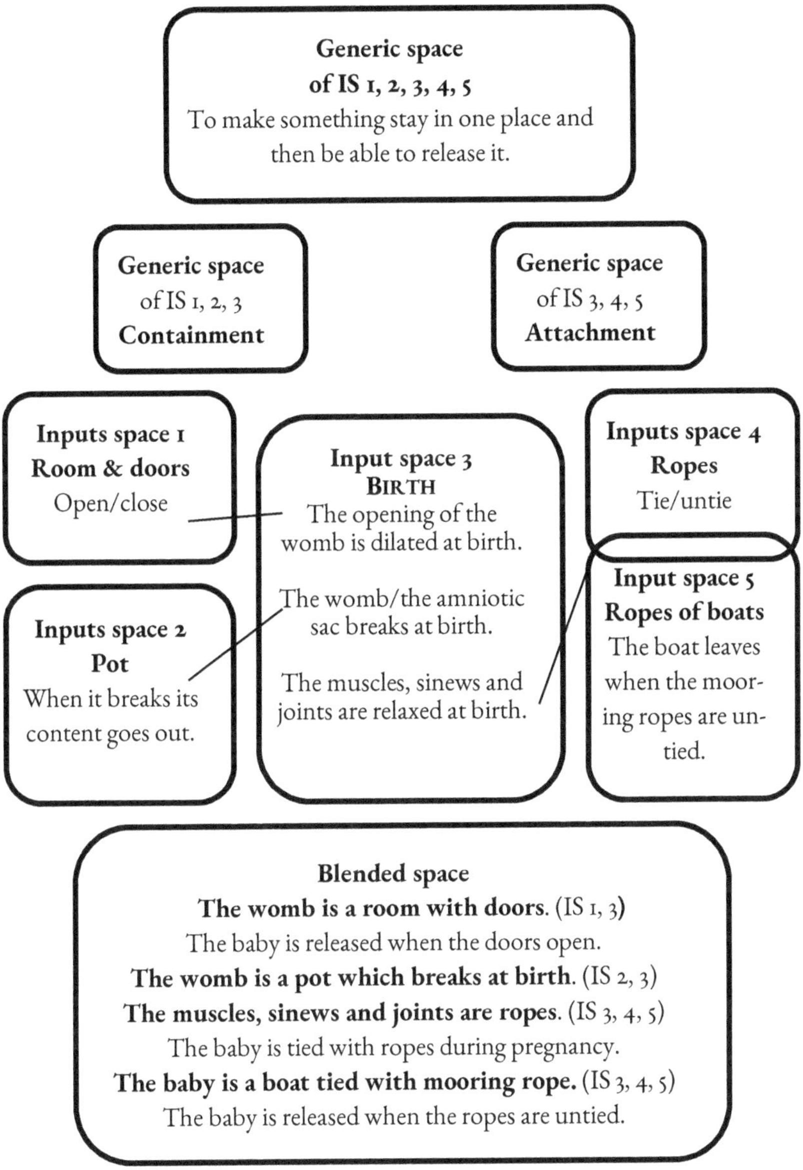

Birth Metaphors in Job 39:1–4

**Generic space
of IS 1, 2, 3, 4, 5**
To make something stay in one place and then be able to release it.

**Generic space
of IS 1, 2, 3
Containment**

**Generic space
of IS 3, 4, 5
Attachment**

**Inputs space 1
Room & doors**
Open/close

**Input space 3
BIRTH**
The opening of the womb is dilated at birth.

The womb/the amniotic sac breaks at birth.

The muscles, sinews and joints are relaxed at birth.

**Inputs space 4
Ropes**
Tie/untie

**Inputs space 2
Pot**
When it breaks its content goes out.

**Input space 5
Ropes of boats**
The boat leaves when the mooring ropes are untied.

Blended space
The womb is a room with doors. (IS 1, 3)
The baby is released when the doors open.
The womb is a pot which breaks at birth. (IS 2, 3)
The muscles, sinews and joints are ropes. (IS 3, 4, 5)
The baby is tied with ropes during pregnancy.
The baby is a boat tied with mooring rope. (IS 3, 4, 5)
The baby is released when the ropes are untied.

Figure 9.1 The Akkadian birth metaphors THE WOMB IS A ROOM WITH DOORS, THE WOMB IS A POT, THE BABY IS A BOAT TIED WITH MOORING ROPE, and THE MUSCLES, SINEWS AND JOINTS ARE ROPES.

This blending schema shows the conceptualization of how a baby can stay in the womb during the pregnancy and then be released at birth. The image schema CONTAINMENT is depicted by the sources ROOM WITH DOORS and POT. The image schema ATTACHMENT is depicted as ROPES. The domain of BOAT is a source of the target BABY, and the image schema ATTACHMENT OF THE BABY is depicted by the input space ROPES and specified as MOORING ROPES. The source input spaces ROOM WITH DOORS and POT are blended with the target WOMB and the source ROPES with the target MUSCLES AND FLESH OF THE WOMAN IN LABOR in the input space BIRTH. One might expect that the umbilical cord is the experience behind the motif of a baby being tied to the womb but in the Akkadian birth incantations there are no such indications. According to the Akkadian descriptions, it is rather the experience of the muscles and limbs relaxing and the womb opening up during birth that leads to the perception of ropes being unleashed.

The Akkadian metaphors explain how to interpret the verb פלח and the expression חֶבְלֵיהֶם in Job 39:3. The verb פלח refers to an act of splitting and חֶבְלֵיהֶם to the noun חֶבֶל, "rope," "cord," which in the context of birth must refer to the cords of the children which tie them to the wombs during pregnancy. This is supported by the syntax of the verse. A closer look at the syntax of verse 3 suggests that יַלְדֵיהֶן תְּפַלַּחְנָה and חֶבְלֵיהֶם תְּשַׁלַּחְנָה are subordinate clauses which both specify the verb, כרע.

C   B   A

Eising points out that כרע usually refers "to an act that goes beyond simple kneeling" and that it is often used in sequences with other verbs which point out what happens when someone kneels.[69] In 1 Sam 4:19, the verb כרע is followed by the verb ילד in the description of the wife of Phinehas giving birth. In Job 39:3, the verb כרע is used with the verbs פלח and שלח to describe what happens when the animals kneel, similar to how the verb ילד describes the purpose of Phinehas' wife kneeling. While 1 Sam 4:19 uses the wayyiqtol form of ילד to point out what happens when she kneels, Job 39:3 instead uses two subordinate clauses.[70] There are no conjunctions in the sentence and both B and C are, accordingly, asyndetic

---

[69] Eising, "כרע," *TDOT* 7:336–37.
[70] For the function of wayyiqtol as a specification of a previous action, see Arnold and Choi 2018, 100.

subordinate clauses to A. The clauses B and C are grammatical parallels, and they both contain a noun with a suffix and a verb in Piel. In addition, the verbs rhyme. Since B and C are subordinate clauses containing verbs that specify כרע, it follows that both describe what occurs when the mothers kneel to give birth.

The act described in clause B is the act when female goats give birth by making their babies break out from the womb.[71] The Piel of פלח must here be understood as causative. This is suggested by *BDB*, which, based on Job 39:3, presents a second meaning of פלח in Piel, as "cause to cleave open."[72] There are five occurrences of פלח in the HB, with only one in the Qal stem, found in Ps 141:7, where its meaning is unclear. The other three examples of פלח in the Piel stem have objects that are assumed to be split or pierced: the liver in Proverbs 7:23 (וַיְפַלַּח חֵץ כְּבֵדוֹ, "an arrow pierced its liver"), the kidneys or inner part of a human in Job 16:13 (יְפַלַּח כִּלְיוֹתַי, "he pierced my kidneys"), and some sort of wild cucumber or gourd in 2 King 4:39 (וַיְפַלַּח אֶל־סִיר, "and cut (the wild gourd) to the pot"). In these examples, the direct objects—kidneys, liver, and gourd—are the things being split. In Job 39:3, however, the direct object is "their children" (יַלְדֵיהֶן), who should not be assumed to be split or cleaved. If Piel of פלח is interpreted as causative, then the children are not pierced but instead pushed to split their ways out of the womb. Their mothers make them break out. Driver and Gray argue that if פלח is correct, it must be understood in a causative sense, where the mothers cause their young to cleave open. However, they dismiss this interpretation due to the lack of other occurrences with a causative meaning, and instead, they suggest emending the text to פלט.[73] Even if this causative interpretation of the Piel stem of פלח can be questioned because of its singularity, it is still the most plausible interpretation.[74] It would not demand an emendation and it is coherent with how births are described as a breaking out of the womb both in the HB (Gen 38:29; Job 38:10; Isa 66:9) and in Mesopotamian birth descriptions.

---

[71] This may be compared with the use of the word מלט, "save," in the context of birth and procreation. In Isa 66:7, it is used in the Hiphil form to mean "giving birth," while in Isa 34:15, it is used in the Piel form to mean "laying eggs."

[72] *BDB*, s.v. "פלח." The Piel stem is commonly referred to as factitive (for intransitive verbs in Qal) or resultative (for transitive verb) but may also have a more causative function like Hiphil. Blau describes the function of the Piel and Hiphil as "blurred" (Blau 2010, 229).

[73] Driver and Gray 1921, 314–15.

[74] I argue that the Piel stem of פלח could also be interpreted as causative in Job 16:13. In this case, the kidneys are said to be made to break out, which actually serves as a closer parallel to its parallel expression יִשְׁפֹּךְ לָאָרֶץ מְרֵרָתִי, "he poured out my gall to the ground," than interpreting the kidneys as being pierced. The metaphor of inner parts of the body being poured out is common in the HB, which closely aligns with the image of inner parts breaking out of the body.

The Piel stem of שלח usually refers to humans or animals who are released and freed, such as the scapegoat in Lev 16:22, the mother bird in Deut 22:7, the people in Egypt in Exod 4:23, and the slaves in Deut 15:12. It is used in this sense later in Job 39:5, when God asks "who let the wild asses free" (מִי־שִׁלַּח פֶּרֶא חָפְשִׁי) which is paralleled with the expression "who opened the bonds of the wild asses?" (וּמֹסְרוֹת עָרוֹד מִי פִתֵּחַ). In Job 30:11, the Piel stem of שלח refers to letting loose or taking off the bridle (רֶסֶן), paralleling the action of loosening the bowstring (יִתְרוֹ פִתַּח). Similarly, Job 39:3 can be understood as the bonds of the children being loosened or untied.

Clines refers to the fact that the suffix in יַלְדֵיהֶן is feminine plural, and the suffix in חֶבְלֵיהֶם is masculine plural, as an oddity.[75] However, this is not strange if we recognize the metaphor of the unborn as tied to the womb with bonds. In clause B, the female goats are the subject and the feminine suffix הֶן refers to them, it is their children. The masculine suffix הֶם in clause C refers instead to the children. It is the cords of the children in the womb that need to be unleashed.

This is the only occurrence in the HB of the metaphor AN UNBORN IS TIED WITH CORDS. The need to untie the unborn is here paralleled with the act of the babies breaking out of the womb, just as in Akkadian birth incantations the metaphor of loosening the band is connected with the act of the baby breaking out. It is not strange that this metaphor appears in the context of depicting animals, in Job 39 which emphasizes the freedom of the wild animals. Job 39:4 continues to describe how the kids grow in the open. As discussed above, the word בַּר, "in the open," has the connotation of someone being free.

Verse 4 ends by stating that the young ones "go out and do not return to them" which can either be a reference to how they go out from the womb at birth or a description of how they leave their parents when they have grown. The verb יצא, "go out," is a general verb which also is used to describe when a baby goes out of the womb (Job 1:21; 10:18; 38:10, 29). Verse 4 might therefore refer to birth and to the fact that when the young are born then they cannot go back to the womb. However, while the preceding reference is to their growth in the open, I believe it is more likely that it refers to how they leave their parents once they have matured. Following the verses about the mountain goats and deer being unleashed, the description shifts to the wild ass, asking who loosens the bonds of the wild ass. This analogy between how animals are freed from bonds and the conceptualization of a baby being untied from the womb explains the choice of the metaphor AN

---

[75] Clines 2011, 1070.

UNBORN IS TIED WITH CORDS in verse 3. In the compendium from Assur the baby is depicted as a boat which is tied with a mooring rope but in Job 39 the ropes of the womb are not specified. In the context of Job 39 it is natural to think of the bonds as bonds which are used to tie animals. Verse 3 contains metaphors which go back to the image schemas ATTACHMENT and CONTAINMENT. They are coherent with the Akkadian metaphors depicted above (Figure 9.1) and are depicted in Figure 9.2.

Figure 9.2 displays a blending schema similar to the one in Figure 9.1. It also refers to the image schemas ATTACHMENT and CONTAINMENT. But it does not refer to the metaphor A WOMB IS A HOUSE WITH DOORS, instead it refers to an unspecified container that breaks at birth. It might allude to the metaphor THE WOMB IS A POT WHICH BREAKS AT BIRTH, but it is not explicitly said. Verse 3 does not specify the ropes of the womb, it does not refer to the target MUSCLES or FLESH, and it does not explicitly refer to the source ROPES OF BONDED ANIMALS. However, the general topic THE BIRTH OF AN ANIMAL and the analogy to verse 5 give us input space 4 which is a specification of input space 3, of what kinds of ropes that are used. Input space 2 and 4 both refer to the more general domain of ANIMALS. The ROPES OF THE BONDED ANIMALS then become the source of the target ATTACHMENT OF THE KIDS IN THE WOMB. The blending schema in Figure 9.2 shows once again how the Book of Job shares metaphors with Akkadian birth texts, and how these metaphors provide essential background for understanding the metaphors and specific linguistic expressions in the Book of Job.

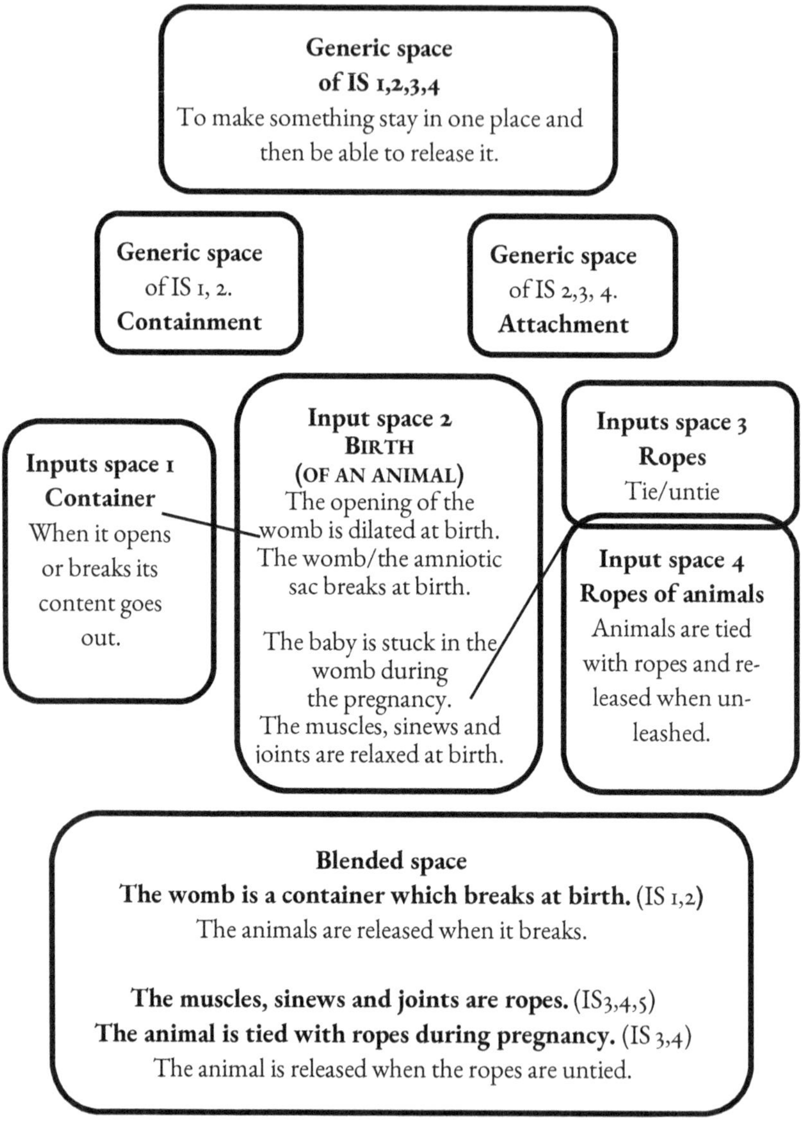

9. Birth Metaphors in Job 39

Generic space of IS 1,2,3,4
To make something stay in one place and then be able to release it.

Generic space of IS 1, 2.
Containment

Generic space of IS 2,3, 4.
Attachment

Inputs space 1
Container
When it opens or breaks its content goes out.

Input space 2
BIRTH (OF AN ANIMAL)
The opening of the womb is dilated at birth. The womb/the amniotic sac breaks at birth.

The baby is stuck in the womb during the pregnancy.
The muscles, sinews and joints are relaxed at birth.

Inputs space 3
Ropes
Tie/untie

Input space 4
Ropes of animals
Animals are tied with ropes and released when unleashed.

Blended space
The womb is a container which breaks at birth. (IS 1,2)
The animals are released when it breaks.

The muscles, sinews and joints are ropes. (IS 3,4,5)
The animal is tied with ropes during pregnancy. (IS 3,4)
The animal is released when the ropes are untied.

Figure 9.2. The metaphors THE WOMB IS A CONTAINER WHICH BREAKS AT BIRTH, THE MUSCLES, SINEWS AND JOINTS ARE ROPES, and THE ANIMAL IS TIED WITH ROPES DURING PREGNANCY.

God and the Birth of the Wild Animals

God's role in Job 39:1–4 is to supervise and care for the pregnant animals and their offspring. The description of God as the one who counts the days shows that God is closely engaged in the pregnancies of the animals. God then acts as a mother goddess, midwife, or as a father. In Job 38:8–11, God is actively breaking limits and shutting the doors, but whether God is also involved in unleashing the bonds and helping the young to break out is unclear. On the one hand, the wild animals usually manage to deliver their offspring without any participation of a midwife. Births of wild animals were seen as easy and quick as in the compendium from Assur, which refers to a safe and quick birth in terms of being born like a gazelle.[76] Thus, wild animals giving birth would not need someone to untie their babies' bonds or open their wombs. On the other hand, the wild animals are described as humans giving birth, they kneel (כרע) and tremble in pain (חיל), in a similar manner as the cow of Sîn who needs divine assistance.[77] The anthropomorphism used in the birth scene accentuates the hardship at birth and is coherent with the need of God's supervision and help at birth. That God assists and unties the ropes for the offspring is also supported by the other references to God as the one who unties bonds in Job 38–39, especially to the reference of the loosing of the bonds of the wild ass (Job 39:5). The description of the opening of the bonds of the unborn can be seen as a literary transition from the birth of the mountain goats to the freedom of the wild ass. The wild ass in verses 6–8 embodies the freedom of the newborn kids in verse 4. Wild animals are only bound when they are in the womb, and they are only dependent on their parents for a short while before they can leave. The freedom of the wild animals is part of their nature.

Summary: Birth Metaphors in Job 39:1–4

Job 39:1–4 depicts births among mountain goats and deer. The verb פלח, "split," and the noun חֶבֶל, "cord" in verse 3 have commonly been seen as unfitting for a birth scene. These elements are explained by the metaphors BIRTH IS AN ACT OF BREAKING and THE UNBORN IS TIED WITH ROPES WHICH MUST BE LOOSENED AT BIRTH. Verse 3 then describes how the female animals make their children break out and how the cords binding the children are unleashed. God's role in this birth scene is to count the months of the pregnancies and oversee the births among the animals. It is also most likely that God is imagined as the one who unleashes the

---

[76] Veldhuis 1991, 9, 41–42.
[77] Veldhuis 1991, 9, 11.

cords to release children from the womb. God's involvement at birth corresponds to how midwives and mother goddesses are traditionally described: knowing the time of birth, counting the months of pregnancy, assisting, and overseeing the birth process. Verse 4 continues to describe the freedom of the animals once they are born. It describes how they grow in the open and that "they go out, and do not return to them." This final line of the birth scene may refer to the irreversible nature of birth—once born, one cannot return to the womb. Alternatively, it can describe how young animals leave their parents when they are old enough. Job 39 then shifts to ask who has unleashed the bonds of the wild ass. Both the description of birth and the portrayal of the wild ass and wild ox emphasize the freedom of wild animals.

The Ostrich in Job 39:13–18

Text and Translation of Job 39:13–18

13	כְּנַף־רְנָנִים נֶעֱלָסָה	The ostrich's wings flap joyfully,
	אִם־אֶבְרָה חֲסִידָה וְנֹצָה	her pinions and plumage are gracious,
14	כִּי־תַעֲזֹב לָאָרֶץ בֵּצֶיהָ	because she leaves her eggs on the ground
	וְעַל־עָפָר תְּחַמֵּם	and lets them be warmed in the dust,
15	וַתִּשְׁכַּח כִּי־רֶגֶל תְּזוּרֶהָ	She forgets that a foot may crush them,
	וְחַיַּת הַשָּׂדֶה תְּדוּשֶׁהָ	and that a wild animal may trample them.
16	הִקְשִׁיחַ בָּנֶיהָ	She deals harshly with her young,
	לְלֹא־לָהּ	as if they were not her own.
	לְרִיק יְגִיעָהּ בְּלִי־פָחַד	She does not fear that her labor is in vain,
17	כִּי־הִשָּׁהּ אֱלוֹהַּ חָכְמָה	because God made her to forget wisdom,
	וְלֹא־חָלַק לָהּ בַּבִּינָה׃	and gave her no share in understanding.
18	כָּעֵת בַּמָּרוֹם תַּמְרִיא	When she rouses her plumes,
	תִּשְׂחַק לַסּוּס וּלְרֹכְבוֹ׃	she laughs at the horse and its rider.

Literary Structure and Comments

The ostrich is paired with the wild horse. These two animals receive the most attention among the animals. They are both said to have received their specific characteristics from God (vv. 17, 19). The ostrich is happy, foolish, fearless, and careless. The horse is fearless, strong, and seeks battle. Their fearlessness, along with the ostrich's foolishness, grants them the freedom to act without considering the consequences of their actions. The ostrich is commonly an animal of desolation and grief in the HB (Lam 4:3; Mic 1:8). Job identifies himself with the ostrich in Job

30:29, in a context that describes his grief and how he has become an outcast. In contrast, God's speech portrays the ostrich as a happy animal. The ostrich's reputation as a poor parent is also mentioned in Lam 4:3, where it is described as cruel, in contrast to the jackal, which is depicted as a good parent that provides for its young. The verses about the ostrich, Job 39:13–18, are missing in the LXX, and there is a shift in both content and rhetoric in this passage. Unlike the surrounding passages, this section lacks rhetorical questions, refers to God in the third person, and does not depict the ostrich as a good parent. The strange behavior of the ostrich fits with the break in the rhetorical pattern. Although there are no rhetorical questions in this passage, it implies that Job lacks understanding of the life of the ostrich.

The common word for ostrich is בַּת הַיַּעֲנָה or simply יַעֲנָה, but in verse 13a it is called רְנָנִים which is a *hapax legomenon*, from the root רנן, "cry," "rejoice." I interpret עלס as the ostrich flapping joyfully, which aligns with calling her רְנָנִים.[78] There have been various suggestions on how to interpret verse 13b. The word חֲסִידָה means "stork," but it may also be read as the adjective חָסִיד, "kind," "gracious."[79] It has been emended and interpreted to mean that the pinions lack feathers (from חָסֵר).[80] My translation above follows Tur-Sinai, Dhorme, and Habel, who interpret חֲסִידָה as an adjective.[81] Furthermore, the conjunction אִם in verse 13 is problematic. It may indicate a question, but verse 14 starts with another conjunction, כִּי, which indicates that verse 13 is a statement describing how the ostrich flaps joyfully. Verse 14 provides an explanation of why she behaves joyfully. It is because she does not care about her eggs. Similarly, verse 17 starts with כִּי and gives the reason why the ostrich treats her offspring harshly. It is because God has made her foolish. Verses 13 and 18 frame the description by describing how the ostrich is spreading its plumes and acting joyfully.

God and the Negligent Parent

The ostrich is described as an anomaly in creation. It flaps its wings but does not fly, it does not fear the hunter, it neglects its offspring, and is stupid. Its stupidity is described as a gift from God, resulting in the ostrich being unafraid and

---

[78] *BDB*, s.v. "עָלַס."

[79] Dhorme and Habel translate חֲסִידָה "gracious" and Tur-Sinai "beautiful" (Tur-Sinai 1957, 544–45; Dhorme 1984, 603; Habel 1985, 519).

[80] Pope 1973, 304. He translates v. 13b "though her pinions lack feathers." Clines translates v. 13 "The wings of the ostrich are beautiful, but are they the pinions of stork or falcon?" (Clines 2011, 1051).

[81] Tur-Sinai 1957, 544–45; Dhorme 1984, 603; Habel 1985, 519.

negligent. Dell argues that animals are used in psalms and wisdom literature either to embody expected behavior or to embody the unanticipated and the mystery in creation.[82] The description of the ostrich is clearly used to describe unexpected behavior. The ostrich is here characterized by traits that oppose human values such as wisdom and fear. However, the emphasis is on how it is not described as a good parent. Human and animal parents do not treat their offspring as if they were not their own (v. 16). Parents should care for their offspring and not abandon them until they have matured, as described in verse 4 concerning the young mountain goats and deer. The ostrich is also a contrast to the lioness, raven, and the vulture who provide food for their young and are concerned with keeping them alive. That the ostrich neglects its offspring is also noted in Lam 4:3, which might have been a common image of the ostrich in ancient West Asia. The description of the ostrich being a bad parent may be grounded in the fact that ostriches lay their eggs in communal nests. The male ostrich mates with all the hens of his flock who then lay their eggs in the same nest. Only the dominant female ostrich stays and incubates the eggs, together with the male ostrich. The other must leave the nest which may be understood as if they do not care for their eggs and chickens.

The ostrich is described as happy, a happiness which is caused by the fact that she does not need to worry about her young. An animal with young ones usually becomes more cautious and defensive. The caring parents are not as free and joyous as the stupid careless ostrich.

God's role with respect to the offspring of the ostrich is not clear. The description deals with the characteristics and the actions of the adult ostrich rather than with the young. Greenstein argues that God is responsible for the negligence of the parents and therefore is the one who deliberately put the young ostriches at risk.[83] Stump, on the other hand, argues that God steps in as the caretaker for the offspring of the ostrich, and remembers them when the ostrich neglects them.[84] It is a possible interpretation which coheres with God's care for the other young animals. The young ravens cry to God and the young ostriches may do the same. Stump argues that they will not survive unless God intervenes to protect them.[85] However, the text does not state that God will step in. The absence of any questions about who takes care of the young ostriches suggests that this role is not attributed to God.

---

[82] Dell 2000, 284–85.
[83] Greenstein 2009, 355.
[84] Stump 2010, 189.
[85] Stump 2010, 189.

The ostrich serves as a counter-image to the parental care displayed by the other animals in Job 38–39, and also as a contrast to God. Job has accused God of being a creator who does not care for the ones God has created. The ostrich acts as a negligent parent because of its foolishness, but God, in contrast, is all-knowing and wise. Unlike the ostrich, God would not neglect Job as the ostrich does with its offspring.

To summarize: Job 39:13–18 describes the foolish happy ostrich as a bad parent. This description does not contain any birth metaphors, but rather references to her eggs and offspring. The ostrich stands as an example of the unexpected and the alien parts of creation. She is an anomaly, opposing important values such as wisdom and being a caring parent. God is the one who has made the ostrich foolish, but there are no explanations of why God created her this way, nor any indication that God watches over her eggs and offspring.

The Young Wild Animals in Job 38–39

There are references to the young animals in six out of ten animal descriptions in 38–39. Besides the images of the births of the mountain goats and the deer, and the ostrich's treatment of its offspring discussed above, there are references to the provision of food for the young lions, ravens, and vultures.

Text and Translation of Job 38:39–41 and 39:27–30

Lions and ravens

38:39	הֲתָצוּד לְלָבִיא טָרֶף		Do you hunt prey for the lioness,
	וְחַיַּת כְּפִירִים תְּמַלֵּא		and satisfy the appetite of the young lions?
38:40	כִּי־יָשֹׁחוּ בַמְּעוֹנוֹת		When they crouch in their lair,
	יֵשְׁבוּ בַסֻּכָּה לְמוֹ־אָרֶב		lie in ambush in the thicket?
38:41	מִי יָכִין לָעֹרֵב צֵידוֹ		Who provides for the raven its food
	כִּי־יְלָדָו [יְלָדָיו] אֶל־אֵל יְשַׁוֵּעוּ		when his children cry to God,
	יִתְעוּ לִבְלִי־אֹכֶל		and stagger from lack of food?

The vulture[86]

39:27	אִם־עַל־פִּיךָ יַגְבִּיהַּ נָשֶׁר		Is it by your word the vulture mounts up,
	וְכִי יָרִים קִנּוֹ		and makes its nest high up?

---

[86] The noun נֶשֶׁר could refer to either an eagle or a vulture, as both birds fly high, have impressive wings, and possess keen eyesight. Additionally, they can nest in both trees and rocks. However, the description of the birds on the battlefield in verse 30 makes it more likely that the reference is to a vulture (Kronholm, "נֶשֶׁר," *TDOT*, 10:78–79).

39:28	סֶלַע יִשְׁכֹּן	It lives on the rock,
	וְיִתְלֹנָן עַל־שֶׁן־סֶלַע וּמְצוּדָה	and stays at the sharp rock, its stronghold.
39:29	מִשָּׁם חָפַר־אֹכֶל	From there he searches for food
	לְמֵרָחוֹק עֵינָיו יַבִּיטוּ	from far away his eyes see.
39:30	וְאֶפְרֹחָיו יְעַלְעוּ־דָם	His chicks lick up the blood,
	וּבַאֲשֶׁר חֲלָלִים שָׁם הוּא	and where the slain are, there he is.

Literary Structure and Comments

The depictions of the first two animals, the lion and the raven, and the last, the vulture, concern the provision of food for their young. These descriptions frame the portrayal of the wild animals. It is striking that it is the feeding of the predators and scavengers that is depicted, with the lion first. This underscores the theme of God's care for even the most dangerous animals, right from the beginning. The young animals are always referred to in the plural, while the adult and parents are mentioned in the singular, except for the mountain goats and deer. The parents include both males, such as the raven and vulture, and females, such as the mountain goats, deer, ostrich, and presumably the lion as well.

The young animals in Job 38–39 are depicted at various stages of development. The young mountain goats and deer are described at birth and then at the time when they leave their parents. The young lions are shown at a transitional stage, learning to hunt and fend for themselves, while the birds are portrayed as dependent on their parents or on God for food. The offspring of the mountain goats and deer are referred to as בֵּן, "son," and יֶלֶד, "child." The noun יֶלֶד is also used for the offspring of the raven, and בֵּן is applied to the young ostrich. The offspring of the vulture is referred to as אֶפְרֹחַ, "chick."[87] The use of יֶלֶד as a reference to young animals is rare. It only occurs here and in Isa 11:7. A more common word for the young goats is גְּדִי, "kid" (Gen 27:9; Deut 14:21; Isa 11:6).[88] To refer to young animals with the word בֵּן is, on the other hand, common (Deut 22:6–7; Pss 114:4; 147:9).

The lions are referred to as כְּפִיר, "young lion," in 38:39 and not as גּוּר, "cub." Hawley and Clines suggest that כְּפִיר in Job 38:39 refers to cubs waiting in the thicket for their parent to bring home food.[89] However, it is more likely that they

---

[87] *HALOT*, s.v. "אֶפְרֹחַ."
[88] Botterweck, "גְּדִי," *TDOT* 2:386.
[89] Clines 2011, 1119; Clines 2013, 6; Hawley 2018, 188.

are young lions waiting to attack the prey that God provides for them.⁹⁰ The young lion, כְּפִיר, is mentioned several times in the HB, often in contexts that emphasize their danger and desire to hunt (Job 4:10; Pss 17:12; 58:7; Isa 5:29). Nahum 2:12–13 refer to the cubs, the baby lions who are provided with food by their parents, with the word גּוּר, "cub."⁹¹ In Ezek 19:3 it is said that a גּוּר grows into כְּפִיר. In Job 4:10–11, Eliphaz describes the young lion together with the fierce adult lions, and not among the cubs of the lioness (בְּנֵי לָבִיא). The young lions (כְּפִיר) mentioned in Job 38:39 are thus the young lions who are trained to hunt rather than small cubs who are provided with food by their parents. They are at a transitory age when they start to become independent of their parents. Job 38:39 first asks, "do you hunt prey for the lion(ess) (לָבִיא)?" and then whether Job satisfies the appetite of the young lions. The word לָבִיא refers to a grown-up lion, presumably a lioness, but it may also refer to a male lion.⁹² It is likely that the לָבִיא (lioness) in verse 39 hunts for her cubs, but the text does not mention any cubs or specify whether she is the mother of the young lions lying in ambush. In the following questions about the raven, it is explicitly asked who provides food for the raven when his children cry to the Lord. The young ravens turn directly to God to express their need and hunger. The word used for the food given to the raven is צַיִד, which has connotations of hunting. Another root of צַיִד means "game" and the noun צַיָּד means hunter.⁹³ Ravens are omnivorous; they eat berries, eggs, small mammals, and also carrion. The ravens and vultures are both seen as scavengers (Prov 30:17).

Earlier Interpretation of the Young Animals

The fact that Job 38:39–39:30 largely refers to young animals has been overlooked by previous interpretations. Although often mentioned, it has not been discussed in detail, with the focus instead being on the adult animals.⁹⁴ Van der Lugt argues

---

⁹⁰ The suggestion that כְּפִיר refers to young lions who search for prey on their own is also supported by Botterweck, "אֲרִי," *TDOT* 1:376.

⁹¹ *HALOT* s.v. "גּוּר I."

⁹² It is common to translate לָבִיא as lioness, but it has also been suggested that לָבִיא refers to the Asiatic lion (Botterweck, "אֲרִי," *TDOT* 1:377). Clines seems to be hesitant to translate לָבִיא as lioness. He states that there are feminine form such as לְבִיָּא and לְבָאָה which would more clearly indicate a female lion (Clines 2013, 6).

⁹³ *HALOT* s.v. "צַיִד I, II," "צַיָּד."

⁹⁴ For example, Hawley points out that the focus is on the young animals and their need to be provided for in the description of the lion and raven. However, this observation does not influence his discussion of whether the depiction of wild animals coheres with their references in the dialogue. He does not explore how the birth of the mountain goats and deer, along with the

that the speech about wild animals alternates between the themes of care for the young and the animals' freedom, but he does not elaborate further on the care of the young.[95] Clines discusses the motherhood of the animals and argues that the ibex, ostrich, and the lioness are depicted in traditional roles for women, giving birth and providing food.[96] Horne points out that most of the questions asked about the animals concern the young. He concludes that their descriptions accentuate the risks to life and the exposure to death that all creatures share. He notes that humans and animals share basic needs and discusses how the use of anthropomorphism encourages the reader to draw parallels between the animals and Job.[97] Doak refers to the parenthood of the animals as a characteristic they share with Job.[98] Neither Doak nor Horne discuss whether parenthood is also a feature present in the relationship between the wild animals and God. I will explore how the young animals contribute to God's speeches and whether they imply anything about God's relationship with the animals, humans, and Job.

The Domain of YOUNG ANIMALS in the Hebrew Bible

The young animals are mainly used in the HB to intensify the sense of safety and harmony, and in images of God's care. They were imagined to be vulnerable and in need of protection. A safe place is described as a place where the animals can bring their young and where predators and prey can be close to each other. Isaiah 11:6–8 refers to three kinds of young animals: lamb, kid, and young bull, and also to a human infant. They interact safely with predators without being harmed. Ezekiel 31:6 depicts the harmony under the tree in Lebanon by describing how all kinds of animals make their nests and give birth in its shade. When the HB refers to young birds it is often in descriptions of care and provision. The young ravens cry for food and God provides for them (Ps 147:9). The swallow makes a nest for her young ones at the altars of God (Ps 84:4). God's protection of the people is described in the image of an eagle or a vulture who hovers over its young (Deut 32:11). The young lion and the young raven are the only animals that are said to cry out to God (Pss 104:21; 147:9).

---

description of their young, contributes to the metaphors of the wild animals. Instead, he emphasizes their shyness and habitat in inaccessible areas, presenting them as a counter-image to the domesticated animals in Job 1 (Hawley 2018, 187–92, 203–9).

[95] van der Lugt 1995, 385–89.
[96] Clines 2013, 6–7.
[97] Horne 2005, 136–39.
[98] Doak 2014, 2, 204, 217–18.

The animal parents are depicted as caring for their young, even the jackal in Lam 4:3. A mother's instinct to protect her children can make her extremely dangerous when she is threatened (Hos 13:8). There are prohibitions against killing the animal parent together with its young in Lev 22:28 and Deut 22:6–7. Breier claims that these texts are derived from sympathy and respect for the relationship between parents and their offspring.[99] Sherman concludes from Breier's reasoning that the parent-progeny relation is a transspecies experience.[100]

Young Wild Animals and Their Deities

The description in Job 38–39 of how God relates to several young animals and their needs does not have any counterpart elsewhere in the HB. Descriptions of how gods relate to young animals in other cultures in ancient West Asia and in ancient Greece may give us clues as to how the needs of young animals were conceptualized and how gods were said to respond to these needs. These myths may not have influenced the Book of Job directly, but provide us with general patterns, on a phenomenological level, of how young animals and their gods were characterized in ancient West Asia. It must be assumed that such general conceptualizations also influenced Job 38–39, both where the text coheres and clashes with them.

The deities who relate to wild animals in Mesopotamian, Ugaritic, and Greek myths are mainly goddesses. The care of young wild animals is primarily the concern of the mother goddess. The goddesses of hunting have a general responsibility for wild animals which may include care for the young. The male gods such as the Mesopotamian Dumuzi and the Greek Pan are mainly seen as gods of domesticated animals.

Lang refers to the Sumerian mother goddess in his exploration of the "lord of the animals" motif.[101] The mother goddess has a special responsibility for young animals. Lang summarizes her function as the one who gives form to the unborn, helps at birth, and cares for young animals. The Sumerian mother goddess has many names, and Jacobsen discusses how two of them, Nintur and Ninḫursaga, express that she is the goddess of both wild and domesticated animals.[102] The name Nintur means "Lady of the birth hut," which refers to the birth hut in a cow pen

---

[99] Breier 2018, 174–77.
[100] Sherman 2020, 41.
[101] Lang 2002, 80–81.
[102] In his article "Notes on Nintur," he argues that Nintur and Ninḫursaga refer to two different mother goddesses, but later in his book he claims that these two names refer to the same deity (Jacobsen 1973, 285; Jacobsen 1976, 104–10).

where domesticated animals were brought when they were sick or in labor. The Sumerian sign "tur" is also used to refer to "give birth," "being ill," "the kid of a goat," and metaphorically also to depict a womb.[103] The name Ninḫursaga is more connected with the wild and wild animals, and means "Lady of the foothills" or "Lady of the stony ground."[104] Jacobsen refers to texts that portray her searching for her child, a young wild ass. As a mother to wild animals, she mourns when she loses them, whether they are tamed or killed. The mother goddess Nintur is depicted as the midwife of the gods and the one who forms the unborn in the womb.[105]

The mother goddess was one of the high gods of the Sumerian pantheon in the third millennium BCE.[106] She was later replaced by other gods who took over her traits and functions, especially Enki, and she became a helper to him.[107] As demonstrated in my overview of Akkadian birth metaphors, she shared her role as a midwife with Asalluḫi/Marduk.[108] The goddess Inanna/Ishtar became more prominent as the significance of the mother goddess diminished. Ambiguous in nature, she embodies both fertility and war, bringing life while also causing death. She is associated with lions, symbols of her strength and ferocity. As a goddess of love and sexuality, she grants fertility among humans and animals, yet she is not depicted as involved with births, young animals, or children. Her role does not extend to being a mother, midwife, or birth goddess.[109] Even though the mother goddess lost her status, the concept of a goddess overseeing birth and the fertility of both animals and humans did not disappear. She remained a part of the tradition, mentioned in texts and depicted in art from the seventh and sixth centuries BCE.[110]

---

[103] Jacobsen 1973, 279.

[104] Jacobsen 1976, 104.

[105] Jacobsen 1976, 104–10.

[106] Jacobsen 1976, 95–116; Rodin 2014, 34–40. Both Rodin and Jacobsen refer to An, Enki, Enlil, and Ninḫursaga as the highest deities.

[107] For an analysis of the decline of the status of the goddesses, see Frymer-Kensky 1992, 70–80; Rodin 2014, 34–40, 299–300. They suggest that the decline of the mother goddess figures was linked to the broader patriarchal and political transformations in Mesopotamian society such as the centralization of power from local urban leaders to kings.

[108] See chapter 4, 95–102.

[109] Abusch 1999.

[110] One of the curses in the Vassal Treaties of Esarhaddon includes a curse that Belit-ili, the mother goddess, should put an end to childbirth in the land. Additionally, the mother goddess is a key figure in the Atraḫasis epic, which continued to be copied and influential even as late as the fifth century BCE (Frymer-Kensky 1992, 75–76). Amulets featuring the symbol of the mother

The goddess Anat plays a prominent role in Ugaritic texts. She is the sister of Baal and the goddess of war, hunting, and revenge. Descriptions of her usually accentuate her violent personality. Traditionally she is viewed as a fertility goddess and as the consort of Baal, but this has been disputed.[111] She is referred to as a *btlt*, "virgin," a young woman who has not given birth. Day describes Anat "as the mistress of the wild" and that she has both "a predatory and protective aspect."[112] In her role as a huntress, she primarily fulfills the predatory aspect, but Day also claims that Baal gives Anat a herd. The herd comes from a cow who Baal has impregnated, and Anat is present at its birth and rejoices over it.[113] Day argues that Anat has a special responsibility for the young animals, especially the firstlings. She refers to *KTU* 1.13 in which Anat may be the one who pronounces a blessing of the newborn.[114] The tablets containing the text that may describe Anat in this role are badly damaged, and while Day's interpretation is plausible, it should be noted that Anat's role as a violent hunter is more prominent. Even if she oversees the birth of her herd and cares for its firstlings, this only suggests that she tends the domesticated animals, with no mention of her concern for wild ones. In the Canaanite pantheon, there is a group of birth goddesses called Kotharat. They oversee conceptions and births and are also goddesses of weddings and marriages, but they are not said to have a special responsibility for young animals.[115]

Ugaritic iconography contains images of a goddess who feeds animals, especially goats, rams, and cows. These pictures show that the "mistress of the animals" motif was present also in Canaan.[116] Other images depict mother cows feeding their sucklings. Day identifies the goddess who feeds the animals with Anat and

---

goddess, characterized by an omega-shaped symbol, have been found in Judean graves dating from Iron Age IIC (ca. 700–586 BCE) (Keel and Uehlinger 1998, 26).This demonstrates the enduring importance of the mother goddess in Mesopotamian mythology and religious practices.

[111] Day 1999, 36–37. For a critique of viewing Anat as goddess of love and fertility, see Day 1992, 182–86; Walls 1992, 154–59. They for example, oppose the idea that Anat and Baal are sexual partners and reject the notion that the texts equate the cow Baal impregnates with Anat.

[112] Day 1992, 181.

[113] *KTU* 1.10; 1.11. Day says that tablet 1:10 is badly damaged. These tablets have by others been interpreted as describing Anat as the cow, a translation both Day and Walls reject (Day 1992, 185; Walls 1992, 154–59).

[114] Day 1992, 185–86.

[115] *KTU* 1.11; 1.24 (Watson and Wyatt 1999, 201, 248, 558).

[116] Day 1992, 187–90.

Keel suggests that the cow feeding her young represents Anat.[117] These two kinds of images illustrate, at least, that rams and goats are associated with fertility and nursing, and the care of a goddess who feeds them.

The Greek mother goddess Cybele originates from the Phrygian mother goddess.[118] The Phrygian mother goddess was both a huntress and the Matar Kubileya, "the mother of the mountains." The myth of Cybele and Attis originates from Anatolia, but is only preserved in Greek and Latin texts. Cybele is said to be born in the wild and fed by wild animals. She is known for her care of young animals and children. This has given her the epithet mother even if she is not a birth goddess.[119]

In Greek mythology, the goddess Artemis is called the "queen of the wild beast." Homer uses this title for Artemis in the Iliad.[120] She is at home in wild places such as the mountains, uncultivated fields, and at the edge of the sea.[121] She is a huntress and, just as Anat, she is a virgin, and she is not depicted as a mother, but she has a special responsibility for the young animals. Aeschylus describes her relationship to wild animals: "So very kindly disposed is the Fair. One to the unfledged seed of fiery lions, and so delightsome to the suckling whelps of all beasts that roam the wild."[122] She is called Kourotrophos, "nurse of the young" which applies both to animals and humans. She guides the young children into adulthood. She oversees the initiation of young girls and is also described as the goddess of birth. She is the one who women in labor ask for help and is called Locheia "she of the childbed."[123]

Male gods could also have a responsibility for young animals, but it is less frequent. Dumuzi is depicted as a shepherd; his name means "producer of healthy young ones," and he is depicted as the god of domesticated animals, and cares especially for the lambs.[124] The Greek half god Pan is the deity of shepherds and goat

---

[117] Day 1992, 187–90; Keel 1980, 136–37. Keel suggests that the mother cow may be seen as a representation of Anat, referring to KTU 1.6 ii 6–9, where Anat's love for Baal is compared to a cow's love for its calf and an ewe's love for its lamb.
[118] Roller 1999, 39, 48, 69.
[119] Roller 1999, 6, 239.
[120] Homer, *Il.* 21.470 (trans. Murray and Wyatt 1999, 438–39).
[121] Vernant 1993, 420.
[122] Aeschylus, *Ag.* 140–143 (trans. Sommerstein 2008, 18–19).
[123] Vernant 1993, 420–21; Hard 2004, 187.
[124] Jacobsen 1993, 513.

herds. He was less important than Artemis but is also associated with the wilderness and the high hills. He feeds his herds and oversees their birth.[125]

To summarize: In different myths from ancient west Asia and Greece the responsibility for young wild animals is mainly attributed to mother goddesses. The exception is Artemis, who is a young woman, and her youth makes her suitable to care for the young. She is also the goddess of hunting. This is also a characteristic attributed to the mother goddess Cybele. The goddesses meet the needs of the young by helping at birth, providing food, and protecting their freedom. The male gods are typically associated with domesticated animals.

General Patterns in the Care for Young Wild Animals

The roles of being a mother, huntress, and being a young adult entail different associations, which explain why they are used in relation to the care of young animals. They relate to different domains, which overlap when it comes to the care of young wild animals. The characteristics of a mother that are used in these descriptions are fertility, giving birth, assisting other women in childbirth, and care for the children. She becomes the mother of the wild animals, who either gives birth to them or assists at their births. She cares for and provides food for them. The huntress brings other characteristics to the description, which explain why they are associated with wild animals. She is at home in the wild and knows how animals behave in nature. She shares characteristics with the predatory animals and is strong, furious, and knows how to kill. Artemis also shows how she, as a young woman, is close to young animals and children and helps them in their transition to adulthood.

The roles and characteristics of the one who cares for the young ones are mainly derived from the domain of NEEDS OF THE CHILDREN. The young need someone who helps them at birth, protects them, provides for them, and helps them into adulthood. Different goddesses in the descriptions above fulfill different needs. When the youth of the animals is accentuated, it is natural that it is paired with someone who takes care of them. That motherhood is a dominant characteristic among the goddesses who care for young animals reflects a culture where the mother is the primary caretaker. More surprising than connecting young animals to the mother goddess is the fact that the care of the young is combined with the feature of hunting, as in the Greek myths of Cybele and of Artemis. This is explained by the fact that a huntress knows the wild and how the animals behave,

---

[125] Hard 2004, 214–18.

shares characteristics with the wild animals, and also needs to oversee the animals to ensure there are enough to hunt. These shared characteristics do not respond to a need among the young animals but are derived from the identification between the gods and the wild animals. Artemis also responds to the need for help at the transition between childhood and adulthood.

God and the Young Wild Animals in Job 38–39

The depiction of how God relates to several young animals stands out from the rest of the HB. Only Isa 11:6–8 also refers to several young animals. It depicts a harmonic state between the animals, and how young animals lay close to predators without being harmed. The young animals are not used in Job 38–39 to depict peace between the animals. The animals are not interacting with each other. Instead, the different species are depicted separately. There are references to hunting and war, but it is not explicitly stated which animals are eaten by the predators, except for the vultures who eat the blood of the killed, presumably from those who have fallen on the battlefield of the horse. The depiction of the young animals emphasizes their needs, and the care provided by their parents and God. It mentions several birds, notable as birds are associated with God's providential care in the HB. The numerous references to young animals in Job 38–39 indicate a focus on the care for the animals.

I have shown how different cultures, close to ancient Israel, associate the care of the young wild animals with goddesses. The characteristics of a goddess taking care of young wild animals respond to common needs among children and refer to the domains of BIRTH, TRANSITION FROM CHILDHOOD TO ADULTHOOD, KNOWLEDGE OF THE WILD, PROVIDING THE YOUNG WITH FOOD, and HUNTING. I will below discuss how these domains also are part of the description of how God meets the needs of the young wild animals in Job 38–39. I argue that God's role can be understood in terms of parenthood, where God can be seen as a parent god, a parent to the wild animals, and a co-parent with the animal parents. I have already shown that God acts as a mother goddess at birth by counting the months, knowing the time of birth, and helping the unborn to be released from the womb.

God is not directly called a parent to the wild animals, but the rhetorical questions imply that God is a provider of food for the young just as their parents. The raven and the lion are associated with God's provision in Pss 104:21 and 147:9, and that the ravens cry directly to God in Job 38:41 underscores that God is seen as their provider. At the same time, the parents themselves are the ones who hunt for and feed their young. This dual understanding makes the reader merge the image of God with that of the animal parents. The animal parents are not metaphors for God in this description; they are depicted simply as the animals they are. However, God's involvement in providing food for the young creates a blend between God and the animal parents, resulting in the metaphor GOD IS A PARENT, depicted in Figure 9.3.

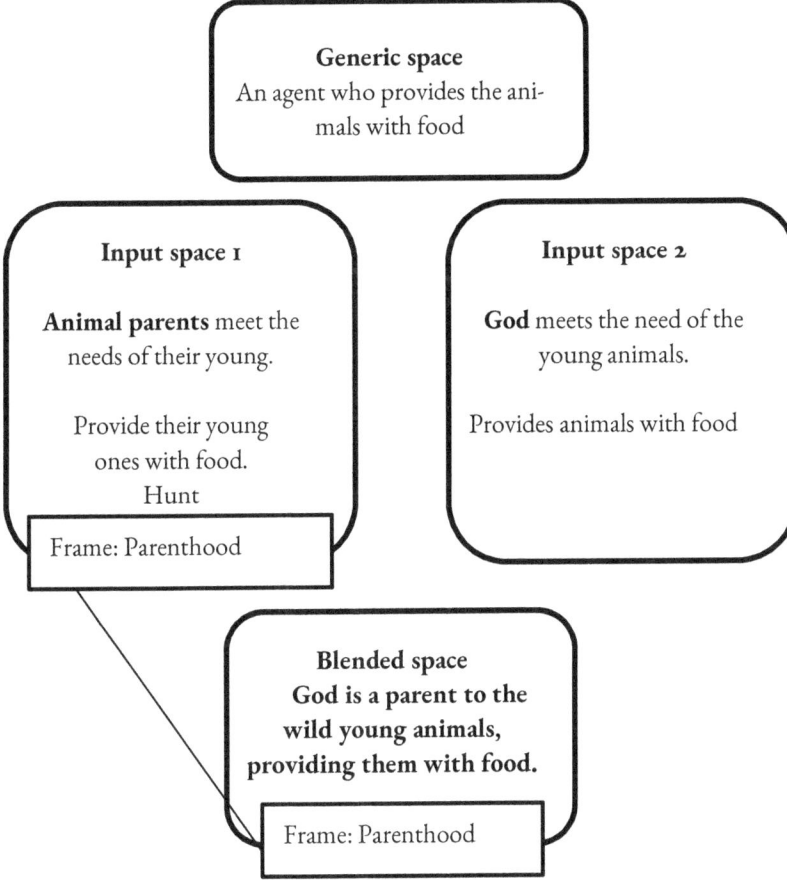

Figure 9.3. The blend of the domains of ANIMAL PARENTS and GOD, and the metaphor GOD IS A PARENT TO THE WILD YOUNG ANIMALS.

The questions of who hunts for the animals or provides the animals with prey have two answers: it is both God and the animal parents. They become the input spaces in the network of the metaphor and blend into the metaphor GOD IS A PARENT.

The metaphor is structured by the organizing frame PARENTHOOD. God is depicted in the characteristics of parenthood, as one who provides food for the young. God helps the animal parents by acting as a parent.

God's provision for the young is evident in Job 38:39–41, and the theme of providing food for the young also concludes the portrayal of wild animals in Job 39:29–30. The questions asked then are whether it is on Job's command the vulture mounts high and makes its nest high up on the rock. This is followed by a description of how the vulture feeds its young with the blood of the slain. In this context, God is the one who guides the parents to build safe nests and to feed their young, rather than directly providing the food. Nonetheless, the focus remains on the needs of the young animals, with God assisting the parents in meeting those needs. Furthermore, the description of the wild ass depicts how she finds grass to eat in the wilderness, in the territory God has given her (Job 39:6–8). This implies that God also provides for the adult animals, just as God cares for the young.

God supports the mothers and the fathers among the wild animals. God becomes an extra or a co-parent with the wild animals, a role which is similar to how mother goddesses generally were conceptualized. God is associated with the animal parents, both the fathers and the mothers. The parents' responsibility for their young is part of the descriptions of the ravens, mountain goats, deer, and the vultures, and possibly also in the description of the lioness. Clines points out that the ibexes and the ostrich are clearly female. He also refers to the lion as female and argues that the rest of the animals are seen as male because of the masculine forms of the nouns, verbs, and prefixes.[126] He claims that the female animals are depicted in a stereotypical way as good and bad mothers. He overlooks the fact that the raven and the vulture, which he points out as male, are also providers for the young. The vulture and the raven are more clearly depicted as providers for the young than the lioness. It is not explicitly stated that the lioness provides her cubs with food, nor that she is the mother of the young lions. The raven, on the other hand, feeds its young, and the vulture is said to satisfy its young ones with blood from the battlefield. The role of caring for the young animals is not a specific role of the mother in Job 38–39, which portrays God as helper of both fathers and mothers and as a parent god rather than a mother goddess.

The roles of caring for the young, providing them with food, and being involved in their births are characteristics which are used in metaphors of God's parenthood in the HB. The description of God in Hos 11:1–4 describes how God

---

[126] Clines 2013, 6. Clines seems to be hesitant to translate לָבִיא as lioness, see page 309.

cared for the young Israel, called נַעַר, "young boy" and בֵּן, "son," and how God taught them to walk, carried them, and provided them with food. In Num 11:12–14 Moses implies that God has given birth to the people and therefore also must carry them and provide food for them. Deuteronomy 32:1–19 refers to God as the father and creator, and Israel as God's בֵּן, "son." God is said to be the rock that gave birth to the Israelites. It describes how God had protected them and provided food for them. However, there is one significant feature in the description of God's relationship with the young wild animals in Job which deviates from the common pattern of depicting God as a parent in the HB: the freedom granted to the animals.

The freedom of the animals in Job 38–39 is described both in terms of young animals leaving their parents and in the freedom given to the adult animals. The mountain goats are released from the womb and when they are old enough, they leave their parents for good. God is implied to be the one who has loosened the bonds of the wild ass. The young lions are trained to hunt to be able to provide for themselves. Parenthood includes being able to set the children free and help them to establish a new life or a family of their own. This is a universal experience of parenthood, even if the forms of when and how the grown-up child leaves are culture specific.

Freedom is not a common trait among descriptions of parenthood in the HB. The father and child relationship usually emphasizes obedience and the hierarchy between the superior father and his children. In Job 38–39, the conventional parent metaphor is extended and uses an unused part of the domain of PARENTHOOD by including the domain of FREEDOM into the description of the young animals leaving their parents. The extension of freedom is inspired and a projection from the domain of WILD ANIMALS. The wild animals are free. It is an essential feature of the definition of all wild animals. When they are bonded or tamed, they turn into domesticated animals. Therefore, any form of parenthood for these animals must allow them to be free. This is seen in the myths of Ninḫursaga who cherishes freedom of the wild animals and mourns when they are tamed. The freedom among the animals is highlighted in Job 38–39. It is a crucial element in the description of adult wild animals without children. The wild animals have been released by God, just as all children need to learn to be self-dependent. This image accentuates the wild animals' autonomy from both their parents and God.

Job 38–39 depicts God as primarily responding to the needs of the young animals, while also caring for the adult animals, with several characteristics of parenthood. God is the caretaker, the provider of food, overseer at birth, and the one who helps the young to leave the home. This forms the image of God as the parent to the wild animals as it is depicted in Figure 9.4. It is a more extensive blending schema than Figure 9.3 and includes birth, freedom, and hunting as characteristics of God's parenthood. It also extends the metaphor by including adult animals as recipients of God's care, providing for them, and granting them freedom. God's care for the adult animals can be seen either as God assisting the animal parents as a co-parent or as God acting as a parent to the adult wild animals as well. The blending schema in Figure 9.4 shows which characteristics of parenthood are highlighted in the description of God and the wild animals. God is the creator of both predators and prey, which leads to the image of God as the parent to both predators and the prey. God oversees the birth, provides them with food, and gives them freedom. The characteristic of freedom in the blend is induced by the domain of WILD ANIMALS, where it is an essential feature. It also belongs to the domain of PARENTHOOD, even if it is not a common feature in depictions of parenthood in the HB. The hunting to provide for the young is also induced from the domain of WILD ANIMALS. Even though humans also hunt for food, hunting is more prominent among animals as a way to provide for themselves and their young. The hunting activities depicted in Job 38–39 do not concern the rivalry between animals fighting for the same territory, nor killing for self-protection. Therefore, the motif of hunting is subordinate to the parent metaphor.

The domain of PARENTHOOD dominates the blend and highlights God's care, and structures the blend with its organizing frame. It can therefore be argued that it is a single-scope blend where the frame PARENTHOOD alone structures the blend. If so, then the frame PARENTHOOD includes the elements of freedom of the children and the hunting for food, but their projection to the blend is induced because freedom and hunting are essential traits of wild animals. However, it can also be seen as a double-scope blend where the organizing frame of the blend is a mix of the organizing frame THE WILD ANIMALS and PARENTHOOD. If so, then the frame PARENTHOOD is the dominant organizing frame of the blend, but the elements of freedom and hunting from the frame THE WILD ANIMALS are also included in the frame of the blend.

The Young Wild Animals in Job 38–39 321

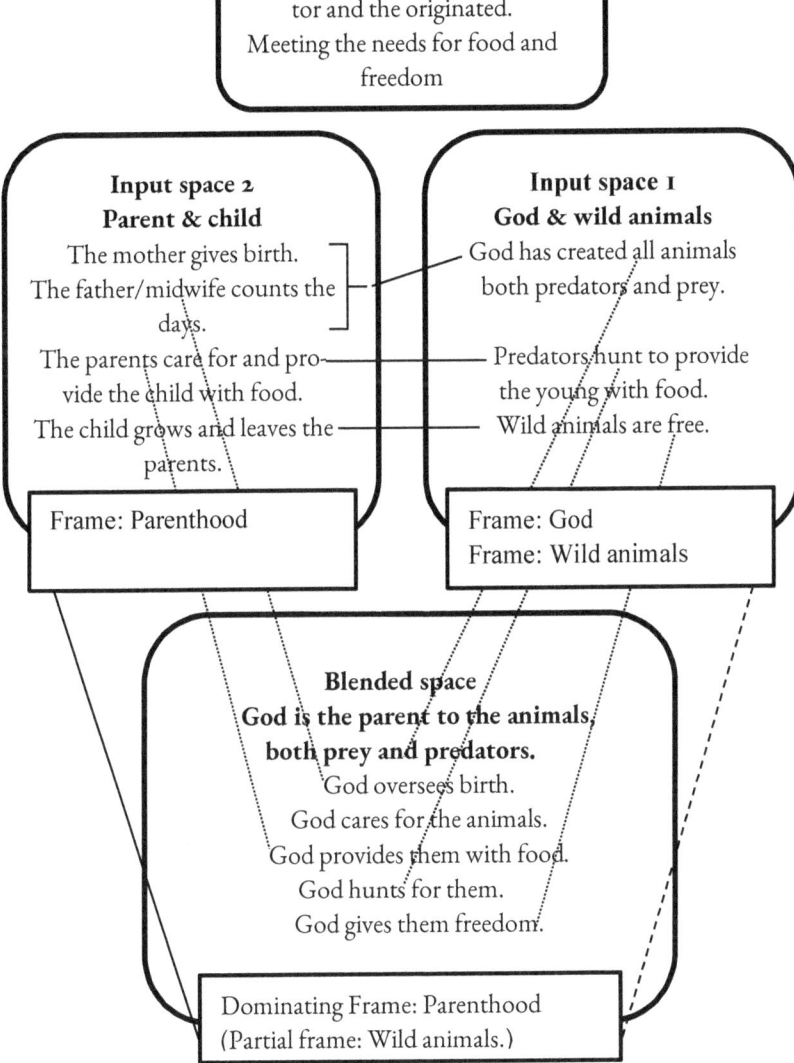

Figure 9.4 *The metaphor* GOD IS THE PARENT TO THE WILD ANIMALS. *An extensive blend of God's parenthood including* BIRTH, HUNTING, *and* FREEDOM.

The description of the wild animals includes the predatory aspect of them and of God. The provision of prey to the predator's young implies that other animals are killed. References to animals who eat their prey create tension between the predators and the non-predators in the text, even if they are described separately. The mountain goats, deer, wild asses, and wild oxen may be the prey of the lions, and the ravens may eat the leftovers after the lions have eaten.[127] The vulture gives his children food to eat from slain humans.[128] The war horse participating in a battle also refers to the predatory aspects of creation. Its description is the most extensive among the animals at seven verses, and it is described as mighty, terrifying, joyous, and unfearful. God seems to admire these terrifying animals, and the war horse is described in theophanic language.[129] This image implies that God is associated with the wild forces and identifies with the wild parts of creation. Job 38–39 then both portrays God as a parent god in relationship with the animals, but also as a god of the wilderness who shares characteristics with the wild animals, predators, and mythical beasts. This mix, caring for the young and being a God of war and hunt, is seen in other myths as well. This responds to the reality of the living conditions in the wilderness.

God is seen as the creator of the animals and responsible for their living conditions and characteristics (39:6, 17). As a parent, God needs to provide the wild animals with food. This implies a hunt sanctioned by God, and that animals are killed. The parenthood of all animals makes God unable to protect all of them. This is a deviation from the traditional parent metaphor in which protection is an essential feature. God is a parent to all wild animals and cares for them all, even if God cannot protect them. Kang argues that God is described as a protector of the wild animals, but this is only partially true.[130] Providing animals with food protects them from starvation, and assisting at birth safeguards the mothers and their young, but there are no descriptions of God protecting the animals from each other or from other dangers.

---

[127] Miller 1991.

[128] The word for slain, חָלָל, refers only to human corpses, not to animal corpses, according to Clines 2013, 1133.

[129] The horse is described with theophanic characteristics such as "strength" (גְּבוּרָה), "majestic" (הוֹד), "power" (כֹּחַ), and "earthquakes" (רַעַשׁ). These same words are also used to depict God. For example, "strength" (גְּבוּרָה) is used in Ps 65:7, "majestic" (הוֹד) and "strength" (גְּבוּרָה) in 1 Chr 29:11, "power" (כֹּחַ) in Exod 15:6, and "earthquakes" (רַעַשׁ) refers to the earth quaking when God is angry in Ps 18:8.

[130] Kang 2017, 282–83.

The wild animals are not metaphors depicting God, but God shares characteristics with the animals. God becomes a parent and a co-parent and is portrayed as the master of freedom who gives freedom to the animals. The adult animals are free and rejoice in their freedom. The ass and ostrich laugh at the animals who have a driver, and the war horse is depicted without a rider. Here is a possible connection to the prologue. The Accuser's question of whether Job serves God freely is here matched with an answer that at least the wild animals act freely in relationship with God. The freedom of the animals may also imply that God acts freely and is not bound by commitments.[131] God is free and acts freely towards humans and animals.

God's speeches present the wilderness and the wild animals with a tone of admiration. God is proud of what God has created, and cherishes the various characteristics of the wild animals. God's admiration of the wild is congruent with the image of God as a parent. If the admiration is interpreted as a feature of parenthood, then God would be a proud parent who cherishes the resilience of the wild ass, the thunderous glory of the war horse, how the goats give birth, and even the foolishness of the ostrich.[132]

To summarize: The description in Job 38–39 depicts God as responding to the needs of the young animals and their parents. The images of the animal parents and God are merged into the metaphor GOD IS A PARENT. The overview of how goddesses meet the needs of wild young animals shows how they relate to the domains of BIRTH, PROVIDING THE YOUNG WITH FOOD, HUNTING, and TRANSITION FROM CHILDHOOD TO ADULTHOOD. These are also part of the description in Job 38–39. God shares characteristics with mother goddesses, and acts as a coparent to the adult animals. God is the caretaker, provider of food, overseer at birth, and the one who helps the young to leave the womb and their parents. The references to hunting in Job 38–39 are also part of the description of parenthood. The purpose of hunting is to provide the wild animals with food, not to dominate them. The freedom of the wild animal is highlighted through the description. It diverges from traditional metaphors of God as a parent in the HB, but can be seen as an overlap between the domains of PARENTHOOD and WILD ANIMALS. God is the parent to the wild animals who cares for them but cannot protect them all from dangers.

---

[131] Horne argues that the freedom of the animals corresponds to the question of whether Job serves God freely (Horne 2005, 139–40). Doak argues that the relationship between the wild animals and God is characterized by their reciprocal freedom (Doak 2014, 229–32).

[132] Brown suggests that God admires the wild animals as a proud mother in Brown 2010, 129.

Birth in Job 39 and Job's Speeches

The birth metaphors in God's first speech are responding to Job's speeches and complaints. The themes of birth and creation are important in Job 3 and 9–10. In these chapters Job describes how he was brought to life by God only to experience misery and God's attacks on him. Job argues that God who has formed him is obliged to continue to provide him with life and loyalty (Job 10:8–12). Job 38:39–39:30 describes a god who oversees births of animals and continues to care for the animals when they are born. The theme of birth and God's care or absence of care unites Job's speeches with God's first speech. Even if the animal parents and their young are not metaphorical descriptions of God and Job, they do portray God's relationship with those God has created and brought out of the wombs. The references to the young wild animals as children (יְלָדִים) in the references to the young mountain goats, ravens, and the ostrich are unusual and make them more human-like. The birth position is also an anthropomorphism. Job's complaint of being born to misery and oppression is contrasted with the image of the young wild animals being released from the womb and the wild ass who enjoys freedom in the harsh environment of the wilderness. The images of birth, divine care, and the use of anthropomorphic language for the wild animals invite the reader to reflect on the relationship between God and Job in light of God's relationship with the animals.

Job complains that God is a neglectful creator. The role of being a neglectful parent is assigned to the happy ostrich, who lays eggs but does not care about them. The ostrich is a negligent parent, but it is because God has made it foolish. God, on the other hand, is wise and not like the ostrich. God is a parent who cares for the children; however, even then, they are not protected from death and destruction. Job has accused God of being a sadist who takes pleasure in oppressing Job and crushing him without reason.

Job's answer to the suffering is a wish that he had stayed in the womb, disconnected from life and the world. God's perspective is different. God instead cherishes the unleashing of the bonds and the freedom in creation. The wild ass enjoys the freedom which Job only thinks is possible if he had died in the womb. The wild ass scorns the noise of the city and does not hear the shouts of the oppressor (נֹגֵשׂ, as in Job 3:18). God is the parent who lets creation free and does not control it as a dominant ruler. The description of the freedom assigned to the wild animals destabilizes the hierarchical thinking which depicts God as the one who controls the creation, or as a parent who controls their children. Freedom is necessary if

God is a parent to all animals. The lion, the raven, the hawk, and the vulture need prey to eat, and, as their god, God needs to let them free and let them hunt.

The emphasis on the freedom of the animals is at the cost of their protection. This is a contrast to how God is said to have put up fences around Job to protect him in the prologue. The aspect of freedom and promises of protection are hard to combine. However, Job 38–39 shows how the parents care for their children and how God cares for the free and wild animals even if they are not protected. This might also be true of Job in his relationship with God. God is a caring God even if Job is unprotected.

Summary and Conclusions

This chapter has discussed the birth metaphors used in the birth scenes of the mountain goats and the deer, the ostrich as a counter-image of parental care, and how God relates to the young animals in Job 38–39. It has shown how God's acts as a midwife relate to the image of God acting as a parent to the young animals. The two birth scenes in Job 38 are followed by one birth scene in Job 39. God is seen as a midwife also in Job 39, but this image is complemented with depictions of God's care for the young wild animals. The metaphor GOD IS A MIDWIFE is not an isolated metaphor but belongs to the metaphors GOD IS A CO-PARENT and GOD IS A PARENT TO THE WILD ANIMALS.

Job 39:3 has been considered in need of emendations to be interpretable. The understanding of how birth was conceptualized in ancient West Asia helps explain how to interpret this verse. It employs standard metaphors that describe births in terms of unleashing of bonds and as a breaking out of the womb. Verse 3 entails the metaphors THE WOMB IS A CONTAINER WHICH BREAKS AT BIRTH, and THE UNBORN IS TIED WITH ROPES DURING PREGNANCY. The verses referring to the mountain goats and deer describe God as the overseer at birth, and as the one who unleashes the bonds that ties the unborn kids to the womb. This entails the metaphor GOD IS A MIDWIFE. The argument that God is a midwife who loosens the ropes at birth is strengthened by the questions about the wild ass, which imply that God also releases the wild ass from its bonds. God is the one who counts the months of the pregnancy, similar to how mother goddesses or the father of the unborn are portrayed in ancient West Asian myths.

The long description of the ostrich highlights different aspects of parenthood. She is depicted as a bad parent who leaves her eggs unattended and is cruel to her offspring. The contrast between the ostrich and the other animal parents makes them appear even better.

This chapter has paid special attention to the young animals. Besides the description of the mountain goats and deer, there are three references to how the young are provided with food. Young animals and especially young birds are used in the HB to highlight God's acts of care and provision, as is the case here. The description of the wild animals and God in Job 38–39 shares features with descriptions of how goddesses care for the young wild animals in myths in ancient West Asia and ancient Greece. The main characteristic of the goddesses who care for the young animals is motherhood. Sometimes the reference to motherhood also includes being able to assist at birth. Hunting goddesses relate to wild animals in general, with some also having a special responsibility for the young and assisting them in the transition to adulthood. Job 38–39 also relates to the domains of BIRTH, TRANSITION FROM CHILDHOOD TO ADULTHOOD, PROVIDING THE YOUNG WITH FOOD, and HUNTING. In Job 38–39, God fulfills the same role as the mother goddess Ninḫursaga, acting as a parent associated with birth and care for the young, while also protecting the freedom of the animals. Freedom is not a common attribute in the metaphors of parenthood in the HB and the parenthood metaphor is extended here to include how the children eventually leave their parents. A feature which instead is commonly used in descriptions of parenthood is protection. It is absent in the description of the young animals. The animals are neither described as threatened nor as protected. The act of protection and freedom are two features that are hard to combine.

I have accentuated the identification between God and the animal parents. God as well as the parents meets the needs of the young animals. This makes God a co-parent in the description of the wild young animals. The description in Job includes male animals as the caretakers of the young. Therefore, I prefer to refer to the metaphor GOD IS A PARENT and a parent god, rather than as God the mother or a mother goddess, even though midwifery traditionally refers to the domain of WOMEN. Horne and Doak refer to the parenthood of the animals as a characteristic that they share with Job.[133] The metaphor GOD IS THE PARENT TO THE WILD ANIMALS instead makes Job to identify himself with the young animals. God would then act as a parent who cares for Job as God cares for the free and young animals.

The interpretation that the birth metaphors and God's relations to the animals are characterized by parenthood and freedom shares arguments with the interpretation which describes the beauty and tragic sublime in the speeches. First, they share the criticism of the image of God as dominating creation and combating the

---

[133] Horne 2005, 137; Doak 2014, 217–19.

destructive forces and instead propose a God who cherishes the freedom of the wild parts of creation. Second, they share the insight that the animals are described independently from each other. This has been interpreted as a description of a polycentric world. Third, destructive forces are part of creation. The focus in the discussion of the sublime is how to cope with the destructive parts of creation and that God seems to admire these parts of creation. It refers to how Job is transformed by exposure to the danger and beauty in creation. The discussion in this chapter shifts the focus from the destruction and danger in creation to a perspective that views the world through the eyes of the animal parents and God as a parent. As a parent, God cares but cannot protect the animals; God does not control the animals but lets them free and admires the mountain goats who give birth, the resilient wild ass, foolish ostrich, as well as the dangerous war horse. Even if the world in Job 38–39 portrays the powerful sea and predators it does not portray the conflict between them and other inhabitants of the world. The enemy is not even depicted in the scene with the warhorse. The emphasis is on their care for their young and their freedom. God is accordingly portrayed as a caring parent to all animals and as a master of freedom.

10. Summary and Conclusions

This concluding chapter will summarize the findings of the study and link the different chapters more closely together. It will begin with a discussion on how blending theory has been applied throughout the study, and how background information on birth has been gathered from descriptions and metaphors in the HB and other ancient texts, as well as from shared embodied experiences of birth. Next, it will provide an overview of how this detailed investigation of birth metaphors offers new perspectives on Job's speeches in Job 1, 3, and 10, and on God's first speech in Job 38–39. The chapter will also address the interaction between the birth metaphors and other metaphors, and will conclude with remarks on how the insights gained from this study can inform future biblical research.

The Application of Blending Theory

This study has analyzed metaphors using blending theory. This theory, along with conceptual metaphor theory, explores metaphors at the conceptual level. Therefore, general patterns of how birth has been conceptualized have been investigated, rather than focusing on textual interdependence with other texts. Background information has been sought from sources as close to the time and culture of the Book of Job as possible. Akkadian birth incantations have been the most valuable source outside of the HB. These texts have been complemented with other texts from ancient West Asia, and on two occasions, I also refer to general experiences of midwifery and childbirth.

Blending theory offers a closer look at the construction of metaphors than conceptual metaphor theory, particularly evident in discussions of metaphorical creativity. The Book of Job shares many birth metaphors with Akkadian texts, but also employs them in new and creative ways. Lakoff and Turner's concept of "extension" has been valuable in discussions of how a new metaphor is created from other parts of the domains than the original metaphor. However, when a metaphor is extended, it is important to use a blending schema to clarify what other associations of the input spaces that are now projected contribute to the blend, the new metaphor. Displaying these relationships in a blending schema becomes even more important when discussing reversed metaphors. When a metaphor switches the target and source domains, it prompts a revaluation of the elements projected into the blend and how the metaphor should be interpreted. For example, when the sea rushes out of the womb as amniotic fluid or as a baby, the danger of the sea is downplayed. Conversely, when the amniotic fluid is said to be a sea, the danger is highlighted.

This study displays metaphorical constructions that are not acknowledged by traditional conceptual metaphor theory, but which work well within blending theory. For instance, the metaphor SOLIDIFICATION OF WATER INTO ICE IS FORMATION OF A FETUS demonstrates that a source domain can be more abstract than its target. The most significant insight from blending theory is that a metaphor is not about experiencing one thing through another thing, but is a new image created from a blend of both. This holds true even in single-scope blends, where only the organizing frame of the source structures the blend. Both the source and the target play active roles in the metaphorical network. This is evident in the metaphor GOD IS THE PARENT TO THE WILD ANIMALS, which can be presented as a single-scope blend where the element of freedom is part of the organizing frame of PARENTHOOD, yet it is inspired by the inherent freedom of wild animals in the domain of WILD ANIMALS. Most of the blends in this study are presented as single-scope blends. This is not surprising, given that several metaphors portray God or death. Metaphors with abstract targets, such as God, are formed from the need to project structure and characteristics from the source to the target, because the organizing frames of their targets are weak. The classification of metaphors as single or double-scope networks has been done pragmatically. Blending schemas of integration networks should reveal the decisive pattern of the metaphor. When the frame of a metaphor can be explained solely by the source frame, it is depicted as a single-scope metaphor. A metaphor is presented as double-scope blend when both the target and the source clearly project different parts to the image—as in the metaphor of God dressing Job in skin and flesh—or when the emergent structure and the content of the metaphor cannot be explained without the organizing frames of the target, as in the metaphor THE WOMB IS A GRAVE. This metaphor has the dominant frame GRAVE but also uses parts from the frame of the target WOMB. It uses the collision between the frames GRAVE and WOMB to highlight an important feature in Job's argumentation. The womb is expected to be life-giving and is an antonym of the grave, and this collision creates an emergent structure that emphasizes Job's despair and his resentment toward life. The collision between Job's wish that God had closed the doors and the common prayer for a safe birth is another example of how Job's speeches use conflicting frames to question both Job's life and God's treatment of him. The comical and provocative effect of the metaphor THE SEA IS A BABY is explained by its emergent structure, formed from the collision between the sea, described as a dreaded enemy, and the image of the sea as an infant. Collisions between a conventional frame, depicting the expected belief or scenarios, and the frame of the source domain of a new metaphor, are used to question conventional metaphors, such as the combat motif.

An advantage of blending theory is that the understanding of metaphors is not seen as a separate process of thought but as integrated into how we think in general. This helps us acknowledge other cognitive processes that are integral to the construction of metaphors. The exploration of metaphors depicting death as a negation of life and birth demonstrates how we can form metaphors based on counterfactual blends. I also depict the blending schemas of the mental process of integrating God's dual roles as both a watcher and a midwife.

BIRTH in Ancient Texts

Understanding how birth was conceptualized in the cultural context of the Book of Job is essential for analyzing the birth metaphors within it. The chapters on birth metaphors in the HB and other texts from ancient West Asia explore various descriptions of birth and illuminate the metaphors used in these descriptions. The exploration of metaphors in the HB demonstrates how the domain of BIRTH is used in relation to the domains of GOD, CREATION, PLANTS, DEATH, WAR, and EXILE. One conclusion drawn from the discussion of birth metaphors in the HB is that descriptions of birth are often abbreviated. Metaphorical descriptions that use BIRTH as their source domain provide deeper insights into how birth was experienced and conceptualized, a tendency also evident in the Book of Job. The birth metaphors related to creation are notably richer than those referencing Job's own birth.

The examples of birth metaphors in the HB have shown that the metaphors of God as a midwife and birth as an act of breaking were familiar images. This supports the interpretation of Job 38:8–11, where God is portrayed as a midwife breaking the limit to the sea. The exploration of the domain of BIRTH and its metaphors in the HB also uncovers assumptions about birth metaphors that are not valid, such as the concept of Mother Earth as an entrenched metaphor in the HB or the belief that the womb is always associated with fertility and life. Instead, this study demonstrates that birth and the womb are used in depictions of both death and life, drawing on associations with both stillbirth and healthy birth, in both Job and the HB as a whole.

Knowledge of how birth was depicted in Akkadian birth incantations provides valuable insights into the birth metaphors in the Book of Job. In particular, Job 38–39 shares several metaphors with Akkadian birth incantations. The analyses of the metaphors in Job 38–39 explore how these shared metaphors are used creatively, mainly by extending and reversing them. Birth incantations refer to how women in labor are aided by their gods. Several metaphors describe the birth experiences of women in labor and their wishes for a safe birth. The target domain of BIRTH and the more specific targets such as WOMB, AMNIOTIC FLUID, and BABY'S MOVEMENTS, are described using different metaphors, such as THE WOMB IS A ROOM WITH DOORS, MIDWIVES OPEN THE DOORS AND UNTIE BONDS AT BIRTH, GODS ARE MIDWIVES, THE AMNIOTIC FLUID IS A SEA, THE BABY WHO COMES FORTH FROM THE WOMB IS A RUSHING RAINFALL, and THE FORMATION OF THE FETUS IS COAGULATION OF FLUID. In the Book of Job, some of these metaphors are reversed, such as using the domain of BIRTH as a source domain for describing the creation of the sea and the solidification of water into ice.

Embodied Experiences of Birth

This study uses cross-cultural documented experiences of birth and midwifery to complement the birth metaphors found in ancient texts. Some of the birth metaphors in the Book of Job can be explained by universal experiences of childbirth that are also attested to in texts from ancient West Asia. Metaphors depicting a baby breaking itself out or complications of a baby being stuck in the womb are derived from the physical experience of childbirth and are also used in Akkadian birth incantations. The depiction of God as a midwife who both holds the baby back and opens the womb at birth is unique and not found in other ancient West Asian texts. I interpret the shutting of doors in Job 38:8–11 as analogous to the practice of a midwife pressing her hand on the perineum during delivery, even though this is first attested to in a midwife instruction from 200 CE. This suggestion is based on the fact that this practice is used among midwives in different cultures. The experience of a newborn covered with a layer of vernix may provide a background for metaphors of the birth of hoarfrost or the fetus being imagined as cheese. These are more speculative associations and are less significant for interpreting the text in Job than the dual act of the midwife.

New Perspectives on Job's Speeches

This study provides new insights into how the domain of BIRTH interacts with the domains of DEATH, CREATION, and FORMATION OF A FETUS in Job 1, 3 and 10. The use of counterfactual blends to analyze Job 1:21 and the womb-grave metaphor in Job 3 reveal how death is conceptualized as the reversal of the features of birth and life. A careful analysis of Job's wish to destroy his day of birth in Job 3 shows that Job is not attempting to invert all of creation. Furthermore, examining the metaphors related to the formation of the fetus shows how these metaphors highlight God's role as a creator while also complementing each other by referring to different qualities of the human body. The birth metaphors in Job's speeches are used to underscore God's actions as absurd and unjust, and Job's anguish and resentment of life.

BIRTH and DEATH

In Job 1 and 3, death is described in negated terms of birth or life. In Job 1:21, Job first refers to his birth, saying, "Naked, I came from my mother's womb," and then to his death with, "and naked I will return there." This reflects a mental process known as a counterfactual blend, a common process we tend to do unconsciously. Although Job 1:21 has been called enigmatic, it is actually straightforward: if birth is going out from the womb, then "returning there" refers to the opposite state—death. It is not necessary or accurate to interpret Job 1:21 as a blend of SHEOL and WOMB or as a reference to Mother Earth. The text contains no depictions of the existence in the womb or the land of the dead. The womb is not described at all and cannot be said to be either devouring or protective.

The term "naked" is highlighted in Job 1:21. That Job is said to be naked at both birth and death suggests a reversal of dressing, with someone dressing the newborn and undressing the dead. The nakedness at death symbolizes exposure and vulnerability rather than literal nakedness, as the dead were not buried unclothed. Here, "nakedness" refers to Job's loss of wealth and children, which leaves him vulnerable to death. Unlike in Ps 49:18, where death deprives a person of their possessions, Job's loss occurs at the height of his life. His loss brings him closer to death. Job 1:21 does not express a longing for death but rather Job's exposure to it.

In Job 3, Job wishes he had died in the womb, making it his grave. This wish does not express a longing to return to the protective womb, as previous research suggested. Instead, Job wishes he had died before his life began. The womb is blended with the grave into the metaphor THE WOMB IS A GRAVE. This blend is built on shared associations between the domains of WOMB and GRAVE as enclosed, dark spaces containing bodies. However, the organizing frame of the grave, with its associations of death, structures the blend. The collision of the frames of grave and womb highlights the absurdity of wishing that the womb, the origin of life, would become the place of death. The grave is not depicted in terms of the womb, and no positive associations of the womb are projected onto the grave. Instead, the existence of the dead is described as the opposite of Job's miserable life, with no confinement, sighs, turmoil, or unrest, leading to a positive description of death as freedom, joy, and rest. In contrast, Job 10 presents another view of death as a place of no order and darkness. The state in the womb and the existence in the land of the dead are not described in the same terms, nor are they blended in Job 10. Job describes his formation in the womb as a time when God treated him with loyalty and gave him life. He neither longs to return to the womb nor wishes for death itself; he laments being born and wishes he had never lived, thereby escaping God, his watcher. Job wonders why God brought him out of the womb and why he did not die before any eyes saw him. He wishes that he had been carried from the womb directly to the grave. The womb and the grave were imagined as two separate places, and Job wishes to minimize the life in between.

The analysis of how the domains of BIRTH and DEATH relate to each other in the Book of Job shows that this is not done in only one conventional way. The domains do not project the same content or associations to the blends in these different metaphors. In Job 1:21, death is a reversal of birth. In Job 3, the womb is seen as a grave, a chamber of death, with death depicted positively as the negation of Job's miserable life. In Job 10, death is described negatively, yet Job wishes he had died at birth so that God never would have seen him. These varied depictions demonstrate that metaphors must be interpreted in context and that birth and womb metaphors do not necessarily bring associations of life and protection. On the contrary, when womb and death are blended, the womb is perceived as a grave.

BIRTH and CREATION

Both the language of creation and the language of birth share associations of life and of an originator, and they use metaphors of darkness and light. This makes them suitable to blend in various metaphors. Previous interpretations claim that Job's wish to destroy his day of birth and night of conception implies that he wants to destroy all of creation. Job 3 has been seen as a reversal of Gen 1–2:4a. This idea stems from interpreting the expression "let it be darkness" in Job 3:4 as a reversal of God's creative words "let there be light" in Gen 1:3. However, Job is not discussing the entirety of creation; instead, he uses the language of creation to imagine the destruction of his day of birth. The metaphorical analysis of Job 3 clarifies which input space serves as the source and which as the target. The target of a metaphorical blend must be consistent with the context. The focus of Job 3:4, as well as the entire chapter, is Job's day of birth. The creation of the world is not mentioned in Job 3. Therefore, JOB'S DAY OF BIRTH must be the target and CREATION the source domain. However, I have also presented how the expression "let it be darkness" can be interpreted from the background that God calls all days into existence with light or as an expression of the metaphor DESTRUCTION IS DARKNESS.

The Formation of the Fetus Job

There is a clear difference in how the formation in the womb is presented in Job 3 and Job 10. Job 3 expresses Job's despair over his conception and birth, while Job 10 conveys his anguish over God's actions after he was born. In Job 3, the womb is depicted as a place of death, whereas Job 10 describes the formation of Job in the womb in positive terms. Job 3 does not describe how Job was formed, while Job 10 contains the most detailed account of fetal formation in the entire HB.

In Job 3, descriptions of the womb do not reference the formation or growth of the embryo during pregnancy. Job's only concern is how the womb brings death to one who is stuck in it. Job expresses a wish to destroy the night of his conception, the night when it was said, "a man is conceived." The choice of the word גֶּבֶר meaning "(adult) man," instead of a word for son or boy, indicates that Job identifies himself as an adult with the embryo. The embryo's identity is blended with that of the suffering adult Job, leading him to believe it would have been better if the fetus had never existed. Job does not wish to return to the womb or to the time of his conception; he only wishes that his conception and birth had never occurred.

In contrast, Job 10 describes his formation in the womb in positive terms, as a counter-image to the misery Job experiences later in life. His suffering begins only after he leaves the womb. The womb was associated with life and loyalty (חֶסֶד). Several metaphors are used to describe the target domain of FORMATION OF A FETUS (JOB). God's role as a creator is accentuated by describing God as a handcrafter who shapes Job out of clay, forms him like cheese, and intertwines his bones and sinews into a woven fabric, rope, or booth. It is also said that God clothes Job with skin and flesh. The clay and cheese metaphors refer to the idea that the formation of a fetus is a process of solidification. While the cheese metaphor is unique in the HB, it appears in other cultures as a metaphor for the formation of a fetus from the fluids of the man and woman. God is not depicted as the begetter but as the handcrafter, consistent with the surrounding metaphors. This study demonstrates how the cheese metaphor is particularly suitable in Job 10:8–12 because it simultaneously depicts God as a handcrafter and the process of fetal formation in terms of coagulation. The intertwining metaphor can be understood in different ways. Traditionally, it is seen as weaving, with God as the weaver, but it could also refer to rope plaiting or booth building. All three metaphors are grounded in how the word סכך is used non-metaphorically in later Jewish Aramaic and Hebrew texts. Regardless, all three metaphors suggest inner stability and how bones and sinews are connected. The booth metaphor also implies the construction of a protective covering. The dressing metaphor complements the intertwining metaphor, highlighting the body's outer protection. Together, these metaphors portray Job as a distinct, well-formed object with protective boundaries and inner strength. The clay and booth metaphors also convey the transience of human life.

The metaphors of handcrafting emphasize the absurdity of destroying something one has carefully created. Job's formation is used as an appeal for God to vindicate him and cease his suffering. Handcrafters do not destroy their creations unless they are flawed, yet God destroys Job even though he is innocent and merely mortal.

Conceptualizations of Birth and the Womb

Job's words in Job 1, 3, and 10 do not provide extensive information on how the womb was conceptualized, but it is still possible to derive some insights on this topic. Greenstein and Langton have shown that Job 3 depicts the womb as a room with doors, similar to imagery found in Akkadian birth incantations. Although Job 3 does not explicitly state that the womb is dark, this is implied by the contrast with the description of light outside the womb and the parallel between the closed womb in 3:10 and the never-ending night in 3:9. Job 1 does not describe the characteristics of the womb; Job 3 portrays it as a place where Job could have died; and Job 10 portrays it as the site of Job's formation, where God cared for him.

In Job 3, Job expresses a desire to destroy the day of his birth and the night of his conception, reflecting his strong aversion towards them. The wordplay in Job 3:8, where the usual word pair "the sea and Leviathan" is replaced with "the day and Leviathan," illustrates how Job associates his birth with the destruction and danger typically associated with the sea. In Job 3:10, Job questions why God did not shut the doors of the womb when he was born, and in Job 10:18, he asks why God brought him out of the womb. These verses imply that God is viewed as a midwife. A midwife is expected to care for the newborn, and in other biblical texts, such as Psalms and Isaiah, God as a midwife shows mercy to those God delivers. However, in Job 3 and 10, the metaphor of the midwife is used to highlight that God is not fulfilling these expectations. This is consistent with how Job 10:8–12, where God is depicted as a creator and handcrafter who, instead of caring for Job, destroys him.

New Perspectives on God's First Speech

Metaphors which refer to BIRTH are prominent in God's first speech. The two birth scenes in Job 38 use the domain of BIRTH as the source domain in the images of the emergence of the sea into the world and the formation of ice. The scene of the birthing mountain goats and deer in Job 39 contains metaphors describing the birth process in which BIRTH is the target domain, but it also depicts God in the image of the midwife or mother goddess who oversees the birth. The theme of birth and its metaphors unite Job 38 and 39, connecting the three areas of creation presented in these chapters: creation in primeval times, the maintenance of precipitation, and the lives of wild animals. This study's investigation of birth metaphors offers new insights into interpreting the Masoretic text of two of the birth scenes. It shows how the combat motif is replaced by birth metaphors and illustrates how the image of God as a midwife is integrated into the role of God as a co-parent or parent to the wild animals.

New Understanding of Job 38:10 and 39:3

Job 38:10 is previously interpreted as God setting limits and doors to the sea. The verb וָאֶשְׁבֹּר, meaning "I broke," has been emended, commonly to words meaning "I set." However, if we recognize that וָאֶשְׁבֹּר refers to the birth of the sea, the word can be understood as God breaking the limit to the sea. The concept of birth as an act of breaking is attested in both the HB and Akkadian birth incantations. God also shuts and sets the doors to the sea in verse 8, but not so tightly as to prevent it from rushing out. These actions are analogous to those of a midwife, who both holds back the baby and opens the way for it. Therefore, there is no need to change the word וָאֶשְׁבֹּר, "I broke."

The metaphor of a baby breaking out of the womb and the Akkadian metaphor of bonds tying the unborn to the womb explain Job 39:3. It depicts how the mountain goats kneel to help their young break out and how the cords of the young are unleashed at birth. Without these metaphors, it has been difficult to explain how the words פלח (Piel), "split," and חֶבֶל, "rope," fit the context of birth.

Birth Replaces the Combat Motif

Earlier research has often suggested that the underlying theme in Job 38–39 is the order in creation and that God controls destructive forces such as the sea and the wild animals. The combat motif has shaped interpretations of God's actions against the sea, emphasizing how God restricts the dangerous and chaotic sea, even when portrayed as a midwife. Similarly, wild animals are seen as being controlled, with God viewed as "the lord of the animals." However, both the combat motif and the "lord of the animals" motif have been criticized. New interpretations highlight themes such as the beauty and danger of creation and God's care for wild animals. Job 38 is usually interpreted as describing the fundamental order of creation, while Job 39 presents the dangerous and destabilizing forces allowed to run wild within this order.

This study emphasizes the freedom of wild animals in creation while also noting that God released the sea and caused it to gush out when the world was created. I argue that Job 38:8–11 is best understood as a birth scene rather than through the lens of the combat motif. This perspective provides a different image of God's relationship with the sea and creation. The sea is not depicted as a chaotic enemy but as a child whom God cares for and swaddles in divine garments. The danger of the sea is downplayed, and to God, it is as harmless as an infant to its midwife or caretaker. The metaphors of the sea as amniotic fluid and an infant, with God as the one delivering the sea, is both comical and provocative. They belittle the sea and its ability to harm and instill fear. On the other hand, they also depict how God assists the wild sea in its out bursting, which must have been terrifying for ancient readers.

The metaphor of God as a midwife explains God's actions in Job 38:8–11, where God closes the doors and lets the sea gush out, both breaking and barricading the doors, and instructing the sea when to move forward and when to stop. The combat motif can only account for why God shuts the doors, not why God allows the sea to rush out by breaking its limits. The act of shutting the doors aligns with the combat motif, but within the context of BIRTH, it is better understood as a midwife's action to slow down the birth to prevent harm when the baby emerges from the womb. The midwife metaphor incorporates both breaking the limit and shutting the doors of the womb, the acts of both protecting creation and causing the powerful sea to gush out. There are allusions to the combat motif that surprise the reader with expressions challenging expectations, such as God breaking the limit and swaddling the sea. While there is a sense of restriction in God delivering the sea, control is neither the purpose nor the goal of a midwife's actions. The purpose is a safe birth for both mother and child. The goal of God's actions in Job 38:8–11 is to allow the sea to stream out of the womb, for the sea to fulfill its purpose in creation and to exist as a sea in its own right The collision with the conventional combat motif emphasizes the shift from a God who dominates creation to a God who embraces the wild parts of creation and rejoices in their birth and existence. It highlights God's care for the wild parts of creation and the freedom God grants them. The speech continues by describing God as a midwife and co-parent among the wild animals, who are also said to be released from their bonds.

The Cry of the Young Wild Animals

The motif of God as a midwife who assists at birth and cares for the young continues in Job 39. Here, the focus is on the birth of shy mountain goats and deer, not the destructive forces. This description highlights the role of a midwife or mother goddess by implying that God counts the months of their pregnancies and releases their offspring from the cords of the womb at birth. God's role as the midwife and caretaker of the newborn sea provides an interpretive framework for the understanding the birth of the mountain goats and deer and the care of other young wild animals. God is depicted as a caretaker who supports the parents and relates to the animals with the characteristics of a parent.

This study offers new perspectives on God's first speech by exploring the young wild animals and what it means that God responds to their needs and supports their parents. The questions about who provides food for the young can be answered by referring to both the parents and God, thereby blending the image of God with that of the parents into the metaphor GOD IS A PARENT. The overview of deities responsible for young wild animals in ancient West Asian and Greek myths shows that these roles were primarily associated with female deities who combined motherhood, birth assistance, and in some cases hunting. Given that mothers were the primary caretakers of children in these cultures, it is not surprising that motherhood is a key characteristic of a goddess who cares for the young. However, motherhood has not commonly been used to interpret how God relates to wild animals in Job 38–39. In the description of the wild animals, God fulfills similar roles as the mother goddess Ninḥursaga, meeting the needs of the young animals by assisting at birth, caring for them, and protecting their freedom. God also helps the young in their transition to adulthood, a characteristic also found in descriptions of the hunting goddess Artemis. Even if these goddesses are from different time periods and may not have been known to the author of the Book of Job, they demonstrate a general pattern that characterizes a god who meets the needs of young wild animals. The depiction of God in this role suggests an image of God with characteristics of motherhood or, more accurately, parenthood. I use the gender-neutral term "parenthood" because the description of wild animals includes both mothers and fathers caring for the young, identifying God with both parents. God is not labeled a mother goddess in this study because it is unclear whether Job 38–39 is modeled after a belief in a mother goddess. However, it can be said that God shares traits with her, as both respond to the cries of young wild animals.

The domain of HUNTING is also part of God's parenthood of the wild animals. It is a way for the parents to provide food for their children, not to control or dominate the animals. It is subordinate to the metaphor of parenthood in Job 38–39. The overview of the goddesses shows that the responsibility for wild animals may be combined with being a huntress. The huntress is familiar with the wild and shares a predatory side with the wild animals. In Job 38–39, God is also associated with hunting and the wild animals, sharing characteristics with them, especially with the wild horse, who is described using theophanic language.

Freedom is an essential characteristic of wild animals and must be included in God's relationship with them. Job 39 contains three major images of how the animals are released: at birth as they are released from the bonds of the womb, when they leave their parents, and, finally, the release of the wild ass. Freedom among the animals is also part of the descriptions of the wild ox, the ostrich, and the war horse. The domain of FREEDOM is part of the descriptions of birth, transition into parenthood, and wild animals in general.

The replacement of the combat motif with the birth scene, followed by images of God as a midwife and caring parent, demonstrates a conscious shift from the image of a dominant God to one of birth, care, and freedom. Job 38–39 does not dismiss the dangers of the world. The image of God as a parent to all animals and one who grants them freedom shows that God cares, even if God is not able to protect the children from hurting or killing each other.

The Mysteries of Creation

Birth metaphors illustrate the mysteries and wisdom beyond Job's understanding. Rhetorical questions about creation emphasize the gap between Job's knowledge and God's wisdom. The mystery of how water turns to ice and dew becomes hoarfrost is depicted through the metaphor of formation in the womb. The womb serves as a fitting metaphor for a container of precipitation, as it is both a space for containment and transformation. The abstract source domain accentuates the mystery of the origin of ice; just as no one fully comprehends how a fetus forms within the hidden womb, Job cannot explain how water turns into ice.

God's questions about the pregnancies and births of mountain goats and deer also highlight the inaccessible parts of creation. These shy animals presumably retreat to a safe, hidden space to give birth, away from human observation. While humans do not witness these births, God is present, knowing the timing of their pregnancies and aiding in the delivery of their young. The midwife's wisdom was respected, and in Akkadian, as in many other cultures, she was called wise, possessing knowledge of the inside of the body and the womb. The portrayal of God as a wise midwife resonates with the underlying theme of divine wisdom that runs throughout God's speeches.

Conceptualizations of Birth and the Womb

The descriptions of creation using BIRTH as a source domain, along with the imagery of births among mountain goats and deer, offer profound insights into how birth was conceptualized. These descriptions include various metaphors illustrating different aspects of the domain of BIRTH such as the WOMB IS A ROOM WITH DOORS, THE UNBORN IS TIED WITH BONDS TO THE WOMB, THE MIDWIFE OR A GOD OPENS AND CLOSES THE DOORS OF THE WOMB; THE MIDWIFE OR A GOD UNTIES THE ROPES OF THE WOMB AT BIRTH, and FORMATION OF A FETUS IS SOLIDIFICATION OF FLUIDS.[1] It is also described how the midwife counts the months in pregnancies and regulates births by both holding back the baby and opening the way for it. Behind the imagery of the sea rushing out from the womb is presumably the experience of the breaking of water. In the descriptions of Job's birth, we find some of these metaphors, such as THE WOMB IS A DARK ROOM WITH DOORS and FORMATION OF FETUS IS SOLIDIFICATION, but the most detailed information in Job about how birth was conceptualized is found in God's first speech.

Interaction between Metaphors

Metaphors in a text can trigger, allude to, or complement other metaphors in its literary context. They may refer to the same target domain, source domain, or image schema, or they may collectively contribute to the flow and plot of the text. One metaphor might specify another, more general metaphor. The interaction among metaphors contributes to the understanding of specific metaphors.

---

[1] FORMATION OF A FETUS IS SOLIDIFICATION OF FLUIDS is only implied by its reversed counterpart SOLIDIFICATION OF WATER INTO ICE IS FORMATION OF A FETUS.

Job 3 uses the domains of DARKNESS and LIGHT in a chain of metaphors. Darkness is associated with destruction and death, while light represents life and creation. Job wants to destroy his day of birth and night of conception by invoking darkness as a destructive force. He wishes that God had never sought the day or allowed light to shine upon it. This suggests a metaphor of God commanding days into existence by giving them light. The idea of God summoning the days leads to images of the night as not being summoned or counted among the months and days, effectively erasing it from the calendar. Job's longing for an unending night, or a morning that never begins, transforms into a wish that he had remained in the dark womb. While the womb is not explicitly described as dark, there are descriptions of the light outside the womb that Job wished he never had seen. The wish of not seeing light at birth is repeated in more general terms later in Job 3, when Job questions why light is given to those in misery.

The interplay between birth metaphors and precipitation metaphors in Job 38 is crucial for understanding God's role as a midwife. Precipitation, like snow, hail, and rain, is described as stored in pots, heaven, or storehouses, with God as the keeper who opens and closes these containers, just as God opens and closes the wombs of the sea, ice, and hoarfrost. The description of birthing mountain goats and deer in Job 39:3 includes the metaphor THE UNBORN IS TIED WITH BONDS TO THE WOMB. The conclusion that God is the one who unleashes them is reinforced by questions about who opens and loosens the bonds of the stars (38:31) and who releases the bonds of the wild ass (39:5).

Birth metaphors also interact with expressions of God's protective acts of shutting in Job. The verbs for shutting in (שׂוך, סגר, סכך) describe God's actions of fencing in, either for protection or attack, as well as in references to birth and the closing of the doors of the womb. The verb סכך also conveys the idea of intertwining used when Job's formation is described as an intertwining of bones and sinews.

The birth metaphors in Job explain each other. A prime example is how the birth metaphor of forming ice in the womb and the cheese metaphor illuminate one another. Similarly, the image of God delivering the sea supports the interpretation of God as a midwife, also evident in Job 39:2–3. The birth metaphors link Job's initial speeches with God's first speech. Job accuses God of opening the womb and bringing him into misery, whereas the birth metaphors in Job 38–39 portray God as one who frees the sea and the wild animals from the womb. Job claims that God is a negligent creator who carefully formed him and brought him out of the womb, only to expose him to suffering. Job therefore wishes he had remained in the womb, disconnected from life and the world. God, instead, cherishes the unleashing of bonds and the freedom in creation. The wild ass enjoys a freedom that Job believes would have been possible only if he had died in the womb. God's first speech demonstrates that God is not a negligent creator but one deeply involved in creation, caring for those God has formed and delivered, even after birth.

Further Discussions

This study emphasizes the importance of accurately interpreting metaphors through methods grounded in metaphor research. It is crucial to examine the context in which metaphors were likely conceptualized in ancient times, as well as their literary context. Metaphors cannot be studied intuitively or in isolation; doing so leads to misinterpretations. Although this is not a new insight, previous research discussed in this study demonstrates how easily metaphors are misunderstood when not contextualized. Blending theory, theories of metaphorical creativity, and the understanding that new metaphors can convey novel ideas that challenge conventional beliefs are essential tools in the study of metaphors.

This study reveals how the HB employs images drawn from women's experiences. Birth, midwifery, and motherhood are universal experiences, and it is not surprising that they are used in myths and biblical texts. There is still a need to detect them and recognize how they may alter the overall interpretation of a text. Metaphors depicting God as a midwife and caretaker have been questioned due to their associations with womanhood and procreation.

The exploration of metaphors in this book demonstrates the importance of taking new metaphors that contradict conventional ones seriously. New metaphors arise from the need to express new ideas. While birth metaphors have been previously acknowledged in research on the Book of Job, they are often interpreted as subordinate to the conventional metaphors of how God limits and controls the wild parts of creation. Although the comical portrayal of the sea as an infant and God as a midwife has been noted, the challenge to traditional metaphors has been downplayed. Viewing God as a midwife and caretaker of young wild animals provides new perspectives on the perception of God.

The purpose of this study has been to examine the birth metaphors. I have discussed their relation to other metaphors, primarily within the same chapter and between the birth metaphors in Job's speeches and God's first speech. The next step is to explore more extensively how these metaphors relate to other prominent metaphors in the Book of Job. For instance, the birth metaphors in God's first speech can be compared to the prominent metaphors in God's second speech. The descriptions of Behemoth and Leviathan do not include any references to birth or parenthood. Instead, there are many references to their strength, weapons used to control Leviathan, and the danger of Leviathan. To achieve a more comprehensive interpretation of the diverse images of God and the wild in God's speeches, the study of birth metaphors in Job 38–39 need to be complemented by a closer examination of the metaphors describing Behemoth and Leviathan.

The Book of Job is a rich text, with poetry dense in metaphors. This study has demonstrated the importance of thoroughly examining birth metaphors to understand Job's speeches in Job 1, 3, and 10, as well as God's first speech in Job 38–39. Blending theory is a pragmatic tool for exegesis that needs to be used and developed in the future.

Appendix A: Sources for Ancient Texts

Below is a list of selected ancient texts discussed in this book, along with a selected bibliography for them.

Sumerian and Akkadian Texts

Alphabetical List	Selected Bibliography
Against Lamashtu YOS 11, 19 (YBC 4601), Atraḫasis	Foster 2005, 174; Dijk, et al. 1985. Lambert, et al. 1999; Foster 2005, 227–80; *COS* 1.130 (trans. Foster)
BAM 240	Scurlock, 1991.
Babylonian Theodicy	Oshima 2014, 115–154. *COS* 1.154 (trans. Foster).
CBS 1509, 10489, 10756	Finkel 1980.
Cow of the Sîn It is included in: UM 29-15-367 Neo-Assyrian compendium for a woman in Childbirth from Assur/ Nineveh) Ligabue Tablets KUB IV. 13	Veldhuis 1991; Lambert 1969; Stol 2000, 60–70; Foster 2005, 1007–8.
Creation of Pickax	Simkins 2014
Descent of Ishtar	*COS* 1.108 (trans. Dalley).
Enki and Ninḫursaga	Kramer and Albright 1945; Rodin 2014, 329–37.
Enki and Ninmaḫ	*COS* 1.159 (trans. Klein).
Enki and the World Order	Dickson 2007: *COS-Sup* 4:91 (trans. Averbeck); Stol 2000, 110–12.
Enuma Elish (Epic of Creation)	*COS* 1.111 (trans. Foster) Lambert 2013; *ANET*.
Hymn to Nungal	Sjöberg 1973; Couto-Ferreira 2018, 49–50.

K 5208 (Mother mourning her son Tammuz)	Jacobsen and Nielsen 1992, 188–189.
KUB IV. 13	Veldhuis 1991.
Lamentation over the Destruction of Ur	Jacobsen and Nielsen 1992, 189–191.
Ludlul-Bel-Nemeqi (Let Me Praise the Lord of Wisdom, The poem of the righteous Sufferer) The second tablet is often called the Babylonian Job.	Oshima 2014, 1–114. *COS* 1.153 (trans. Foster).
Ligabue Library tablets	Lambert 1969; Veldhuis 1991; Foster 2005, 1006 .
Neo Assyrian Compendium for a Women in Childbirth Compendium from Assur (VAT 8869, see below) Compendium from Nineveh (K 2413)	Veldhuis 1989; Veldhuis 1991; Stol 2000, 66–72.
SpbTU I no. 44:67	Hunger 1976; Stol 2000, 29.
UM 29-15-367	van Dijk 1975; Stol 2000, 60–61; Cunningham 1997.
VAT 8381 (VS 17, 33)	van Dijk 1975; Stol 2000, 60–61.
VAT 8869 (*BAM* 248) (Compendium from Assur)	Ebeling 1923; Stol 2000, 64–66; Veldhuis 1991; Foster 2005, 1007–9.
VAS 10 189	Finkel 1980; Johandi 2019, 94.
YBC 4603 (YOS 11, 86)	van Dijk 1973; Stol 2000, 11.
YBC 5636	Finkel 1980.

Hittite Texts

Alphabetical list	Selected Bibliography
Appu and His Two Sons	*COS*, 1.58 (trans. Hoffner).
Songs of Kumarbi–Song of Emergence	*COS-Sup* 4.6A (trans. Hoffner).
Sun God and the Cow	Stol 2000, 68.

Ugaritic Texts

Order in KTU(CAT)	Selected Bibliography
1.1–1.6—Baal cycle	*KTU*; *COS* 1.86 (trans. Pardee); Moor 1987; Smith 1994; Smith and Pitard 2009.
1.10—Baal Fathers a Bull	Parker 1997, 181–86.

Appendix A: Sources for Ancient Texts 347

1.11—A Birth	Parker 1997, 186–87.
1.13—A Hymn to Anat	Wyatt 2002, 169–173.
1.17–19— Aqhatu legend	*COS* 1.103 (trans. Pardee); Parker 1997, 49–80.
1.23—Dawn and Dusk	*COS* 1.87 (trans. Pardee)
1.101—Baal enthroned on his mountain Sapan	Smith and Pitard 2009, 65.

Greek Texts

Alphabetical List	Author	Translations
Agamemnon (*Ag.*)	Aeschylus	Sommerstein 2008
Generation of Animals (*Gen. An.*)	Aristotle	Peck 2014.
Homeric Hymns	unknown	Hine 2005.
Iliad (*Il.*)	Homer	Murray and Wyatt 1999.
Libation-bearers (*Cho.*)	Aeschylus	Sommerstein 2008.
Nature of the Child (*Nat. Puer.*)	Hippocrates	Potter 2012.
Theogony (*Theog.*)	Hesiod	Most 2018.
Works and days (*Op.*)	Hesiod	Most 2018; Hine 2005.

Scripture

Hebrew Bible	Hebrew text: HBS. LXX: Rahlfs and Hanhart 2006. Translations: German: EUE (Einheitsübersetzung) English: KJV; NIV; NRSV Swedish: Bibel 2000
Sirach	Hebrew texts: BENSIRA-C; https://www.bensira.org/ Greek texts: LXX (See above)

Bibliography

Dictionaries, Lexica, and Selected Text Collections

ANET: Pritchard, James B. 1969. *Ancient Near Eastern Texts: Relating to the Old Testament*. 3rd ed. with supplement. Princeton: Princeton University Press.

BDB: Brown, Francis, Charles A. Briggs, and Samuel Rolles Driver. 1979 [1952]. *A Hebrew and English Lexicon of the Old Testament: With an Appendix Containing the Biblical Aramaic*. Oxford: Clarendon.

BENSIRA-C: BenSira C (Bensira-c, Bensira-m, Bensira-e and Sirapesh). Hebrew text of Sirach (Ecclesiasticus) in canonical order transcribed from original MSS. Grammatical tagging by Dr. Martin Abegg and Casey Toews. Accordance.

BHS: Elliger, Karl, and Wilhelm Rudolph, eds. 1983. *Biblia Hebraica Stuttgartensia*. Stuttgart: Deutsche Bibelgesellschaft.

CDA: Black, Jeremy, Andrew George, and Nicholas Postgate. 2000. *A Concise Dictionary of Akkadian*. 2nd corrected ed. Wiesbaden: Harrassowitz.

CDCH: Clines, David J. A., ed. 2009. *The Concise Dictionary of Classical Hebrew*. Sheffield: Sheffield Pheonix.

COS 1: Hallo, William W., and K. Lawson Younger, eds. 1997. *Canonical Compositions from the Biblical World*. Vol. I of *The Context of Scripture*. Leiden: Brill.

COS-Sup: Younger, K. Lawson, ed. 2016. *Supplements*. Vol. 4 of *The Context of Scripture*. Leiden: Brill.

HALOT: Koehler, Ludwig, Walter Baumgartner, and Johann J. Stamm. 1994–1999. *The Hebrew and Aramaic Lexicon of the Old Testament*. Translated and edited under the supervision of Mervyn E. J. Richardson. 4 vols. Leiden: Brill.

Jastrow Dictionary: Jastrow, Marcus. 1903. *A Dictionary of the Targumim, the Talmud Babli and Yerushalmi and the Midrashic Literature*. London: Luzac & Co.

KTU: Dietrich, Manfried, Oswald Loretz, and Joaquín Sanmartín, eds. 2013. *Die keilalphabetischen Texte aus Ugarit, Ras Ibn Hani und anderen Orten* [*The Cuneiform Alphabetic Texts from Ugarit, Ras Ibn Hani and Other Places*]. Third, enlarged edition. Alter Orient und Altes Testament 360/1. Münster: Ugarit-Verlag.

LSJ: Liddell, Henry George, and Robert Scott. 1996. *A Greek-English Lexicon: with a Revised Supplement*. 9th ed. Oxford: Clarendon.

SpbTU I: Hunger, Hermann, ed. 1976. *Spätbabylonische Texte aus Uruk T.1*. Vol. 9 of *Ausgrabungen der deutschen Forschungsgemeinschaft in Uruk-Warka*. Berlin: Gebr. Mann.

TDOT: Botterweck, G. Johannes, and Helmer Ringgren, eds. 1974–2006. *Theological Dictionary of the Old Testament*. Translated by John T. Willis et al. 8 vols. Grand Rapids: Eerdmans.

TUAT II/2: Kaiser, Otto, Rykle Borger, and Walter Farber, eds. 1987. *Texte aus der Umwelt des Alten Testaments* Bd 2: *Religiöse Texte*. Lief. 2: *Rituale und Beschwörungen, I*. Vol. 2. Gütersloh: Mohn.

Literature

Abusch, Tzvi W. 1999. "Ishtar." Pages 452–56 in *Dictionary of Deities and Demons in the Bible*. Edited by K. van der Toorn, Bob Becking, and Pieter Willem van der Horst. 2nd and revised ed. Leiden: Brill; Grand Rapids: Eerdmanns.

Alter, Robert. 2011. *The Art of Biblical Poetry*. Rev. ed. New York: Basic Books.

Andersen, Francis I. 1976. *Job: An Introduction and Commentary*. Tyndale Old Testament Commentaries. London: Inter-Varsity.

Andrews, William A. 2014. "'Don't Think of a Voice!' Divine Silence, Metaphor, and Mental Spaces in Selected Psalms of Lament." Pages 47–72 in *Cognitive Linguistic Explorations in Biblical Studies*. Edited by Bonnie Howe and Joel B. Green. Berlin: de Gruyter.

Arnold, Bill T., and John H. Choi. 2018. *A Guide to Biblical Hebrew Syntax*. 2nd ed. Cambridge: Cambridge University Press.

Balentine, Samuel. 2006. *Job*. Edited by Mark K. Gammons and Keith Mc Elroy. Smyth & Helwys Bible Commentary. Macon, GA: Smyth & Helwys.

—. 2013. "Job and the Priests." Pages 42–53 in *Reading Job Intertextually*. Edited by Katherine Dell and Will Kynes. LHBOTS 574. New York: T&T Clark.

Barkay, Gabriel. 1988. "Burial Headrests as a Return to the Womb—A Reevaluation." *BAR* 14.2: 48–50.

Basson, Alec. 2006a. *Divine Metaphors in Selected Hebrew Psalms of Lamentation*. FAT II: 15. Tübingen: Mohr Siebeck.

—. 2006b. "'People Are Plants': A Conceptual Metaphor in the Hebrew Bible." *OTE* 19: 573–83.

—. 2009. "A Few Metaphorical Source Domains for Emotions in the Old Testament." *Scriptura* 100: 121–28.

Bergmann, Claudia D. 2007. "We Have Seen the Enemy, and He Is Only a 'She': The Portrayal of Warriors as Women." *CBQ* 69: 651–72.

—. 2008. *Childbirth as a Metaphor for Crisis: Evidence from the Ancient Near East, the Hebrew Bible, and IQH XI, 1–18*. BZAW 382. Berlin: de Gruyter.

—. 2010. "'Like a Warrior' and 'Like a Woman Giving Birth': Expressing Divine Immanence and Transcendence in Isaiah 42:10–17." Pages 38–56 in *Bodies, Embodiment, and Theology of the Hebrew Bible*. Edited by S. Tamar Kamionkowski and Wonil Kim. LHBOTS 465. New York: T&T Clark.

Blau, Joshua. 2010. *Phonology and Morphology of Biblical Hebrew: An Introduction*. LSAWS 2. Winona Lake, IN: Eisenbraun.

Boddy, Janice. 1982. "Womb as Oasis: The Symbolic Context of Pharaonic Circumcision in Rural Northern Sudan." *American Ethnologist* 9: 682–98.

Boris, Lazzaro. 2020. "If the Blind Walk: The Cognitive Metaphor 'Knowing is Seeing' and Its Elaboration in Isa 42,16." Pages 61–77 in *Networks of Metaphors in the Hebrew Bible*. Edited by Danilo Verde and Antje Labahn. LHBOTS 309. Leuven: Peeters.

Boss, Jeffrey. 1961. "The Antiquity of Caesarean Section with Maternal Survival: The Jewish Tradition." *Medical History* 5: 117–31.

Bowdle, Brian, and Dedre Gentner. 2005. "The Career of Metaphor." *Psychological Review* 112: 193–216.

Breier, Idan. 2018. "Animals in Biblical and Ancient Near Eastern Law: Tort and Ethical Laws." *Journal of Animal Ethics* 8: 166–81.

Breitkopf, Alexander W. 2020. *Job: From Lament to Penitence*. Sheffield: Sheffield Phoenix.
Brenner, Athalya. 1981. "God's Answer To Job." *VT* 31: 129–37.
Brettler, Marc Zvi. 2009. *God Is King Understanding an Israelite Metaphor*. JSOTSup 76. Sheffield: Sheffield Academic.
Brown, William P. 2000. "Creatio Corporis and the Rhetoric of Defense in Job 10 and Psalm 139." Pages 107–24 in *God Who Creates: Essays in Honor of W. Sibley Towner*. Edited by William P. Brown and S. Dean McBride. Grand Rapids: Eerdmans.
—. 2010. *The Seven Pillars of Creation: The Bible, Science, and the Ecology of Wonder*. New York: Oxford University Press.
Burnight, John. 2013. "The 'Reversal' of Heilsgeschichte in Job 3." Pages 30–41 in *Reading Job Intertextually*. Edited by Katherine Dell and Will Kynes. LHBOTS 574. London: T&T Clark.
Burns, John Barclay. 1993. "Cursing the Day of Birth." *Proceedings, Eastern Great Lakes and Midwest Biblical Societies* 13: 11–22.
Butz, Kilian. 1982. "Altbabylonische Beschwörungen, um den Blasensprung bei Graviden herbeizuführen." *OrAnt* 21: 221–26.
Caballero, Rosario. 2017. "Genre and Metaphor: Use and Variation Across Usage Events." Pages 193–205 in *The Routledge Handbook of Metaphor and Language*. Edited by Elena Semino and Zsófia Demjén. London: Routledge.
Caird, George Bradford. 1980. *The Language and Imagery of the Bible*. London: Duckworth.
Campbell, John, and Albert Katz. 2006. "On Reversing the Topics and Vehicles of Metaphor." *Metaphor and Symbol* 21: 1–22.
Chilton, Paul, and George Lakoff. 1995. "Foreign Policy by Metaphor." Pages 37–59 in *Language and Peace*. Edited by Christina Schäffner and Anita Wenden. Aldershot: Dartmouth.
Cho, Paul K. K. 2019. *Myth, History, and Metaphor in the Hebrew Bible*. Cambridge: Cambridge University Press.
Claassens, L. Juliana M. 2012. *Mourner, Mother, Midwife: Reimagining God's Delivering Presence in the Old Testament*. Louisville: Westminster John Knox.
—. 2014. "The Rhetorical Function of the Woman in Labor Metaphor in Jeremiah 30–31: Trauma, Gender and Postcolonial Perspectives." *JTSA* 150: 67–84.
Clines, David J. A. 1989. *Job 1–20*. Word Biblical Commentary 17. Dallas: Word.
—. 2006. *Job 21–37*. World Bible Commentary 18A. Nashville: Nelson.
—. 2011. *Job 38–42*. Word Biblical Commentary 18B. Nashville: Nelson.
—. 2013. "The Worth of Animals in the Divine Speeches of the Book of Job." https://www.academia.edu/2437878/The_Worth_of_Animals_in_the_Divine_Speeches_of_t he_Book_of_Job.
—. 2021. "Alleged Female Language about the Deity in the Hebrew Bible." *JBL* 140: 229–49.
Cooper, Alan. 1997. "The Sense of the Book of Job." *Prooftexts* 17: 227–44.
Couto-Ferreira, Erica M. 2014. "She Will Give Birth Easily: Therapeutic Approaches to Childbirth in 1st Millennium BCE Cuneiform Sources." *Dynamis* 34: 289–315.
—. 2018. "Uterine Architectures: Womb and Space in Sumero-Akkadian Sources." Pages 35–55 in *Cultural Constructions of the Uterus in Pre-Modern Societies, Past and Present*. Edited by M. Erica Couto-Ferreira and Lorenzo Verderame. Newcastle upon Tyne: Cambridge Scholars.
Croft, William, and D. Alan Cruse. 2004. *Cognitive Linguistics*. Cambridge Textbooks in Linguistics. Cambridge: Cambridge University Press.

Cunningham, Graham. 1997. *Deliver Me from Evil: Mesopotamian Incantations, 2500–1500 BC.* Studia Pohl Series 17. Rome: Pontificio Istituto Biblico.
Curtis, Robert I. 2001. *Ancient Food Technology.* Leiden: Brill.
Dahlen, Hannah, Caroline Homer, Nicky Leap, and Sally Tracy. 2010. "From Social to Surgical: Historical Perspectives on Perineal Care during Labour and Birth." *Women and Birth: Journal of the Australian College of Midwives* 24: 105–11.
Dahood, Mitchell. 1974. "Northwest Semitic Texts and Textual Criticism of the Hebrew Bible." Pages 11–37 in *Questions disputées d'Ancien Testament. Méthode et théologie.* Edited by Chris Brekelmans. BETL 33. Leuven: Leuven University Press.
Dancygier, Barbara, and Eve Sweetser. 2014. *Figurative Language.* Cambridge Textbooks in Linguistics. New York: Cambridge University Press.
Day, John. 1985. *God's Conflict with the Dragon and the Sea: Echoes of a Canaanite Myth in the Old Testament.* UCOP 35. Cambridge: Cambridge University Press.
Day, Peggy L. 1992. "Anat: Ugarit's 'Mistress of Animals'." *JNES* 51: 181–90.
—. 1999. "Anat." Pages 36–43 in *Dictionary of Deities and Demons in the Bible.* Edited by K. van der Toorn, Bob Becking, and Pieter Willem van der Horst. 2nd and revised ed. Leiden: Brill; Grand Rapids: Eerdmanns.
Dell, Katharine J. 2000. "The Use of Animal Imagery in the Psalms and Wisdom Literature of Ancient Israel." *SJT* 53: 275–91.
DesCamp, Mary Therese. 2007. *Metaphor and Ideology: Liber Antiquitatum Biblicarum and Literary Methods through a Cognitive Lens.* Edited by R. Alan Culpepper and Ellen van Wolde. BibInt 87. Leiden: Brill.
DesCamp, Mary Therese, and Eve E. Sweetser. 2005. "Metaphors for God: Why and How Do Our Choices Matter for Humans? The Application of Contemporary Cognitive Linguistics Research to the Debate on God and Metaphor." *Pastoral Psychology* 53: 207–38.
Dhorme, Edouard. 1984. *A Commentary on the Book of Job.* Nashville: Nelson.
Dick, Michael Brennan. 2006. "The Neo-Assyrian Royal Lion Hunt and Yahweh's Answer to Job." *JBL* 125: 243–70.
Dickson, Keith. 2007. "Enki and Ninhursag: The Trickster in Paradise." *JNES* 66: 1–32.
DiFransico, Lesley R. 2016. *Washing Away Sin: An Analysis of the Metaphor in the Hebrew Bible and Its Influence.* BTS 23. Leuven: Peeters.
Dijk, J.J.A. van. 1972. "Une variante du thème de 'l'Esclave de la Lune.'" *Or NS* 41: 339–48.
—. 1973. "Une incantation accompagnant la naissance de l'homme." *Or NS* 42: 502–7.
—. 1975. "Incantations accompagnant la naissance de l'homme." *Or Ns* 44: 52–79.
Dijk, J.J.A. van, Albrecht Goetze, and Mary Inda Hussey, eds. 1985. *Early Mesopotamian Incantations and Rituals.* Yale Oriental Series: Babylonian Texts 11. New Haven: Yale University Press.
Dille, Sarah. 2004. *Mixing Metaphors: God as Mother and Father in Deutero-Isaiah.* Edited by David J. A. Clines, Philip R. Davies, and David M Gunn. Gender, Culture, Theory 13. London: T&T Clark.
—. 2010. "The Rock that Gave You Birth." *Classical Bulletin* 86: 37–65.
Doak, Brian R. 2014. *Consider Leviathan: Narratives of Nature and the Self in Job.* Minneapolis: Fortress.

Driver, G. R. 1969. "Problems in the Hebrew Text of Job." Pages 72–93 in *Wisdom in Israel and in the Ancient Near East: Presented to Harold Henry Rowley by the Society for Old Testament Study in Association with the Editorial Board of Vetus Testamentum in Celebration of His 65th Birthday 24 March 1955*. Edited by Martin Noth and David Winton Thomas. Leiden: Brill.

Driver, Samuel Rolles, and George Buchanan Gray. 1921. *A Critical and Exegetical Commentary on the Book of Job*. Vol. 2. International Critical Commentary Series. Edinburgh: T&T Clark.

Dunn, Jonathan. 2015. "Modeling Abstractness and Metaphoricity." *Metaphor and Symbol* 30: 259–89.

Ebeling, Erich. 1923. "Keilschrifttexte medizinischen Inhalts. IV." *Archiv für Geschichte der Medizin* 14.3/4: 65–78.

Eckstein, Juliane Maria. 2019. "'Why Did Knees Meet Me?' Giving Birth on One's Knees in Job 3:12." *CBQ* 81: 381–404.

Eidevall, Göran. 1996. *Grapes in the Desert: Metaphors, Models, and Themes in Hosea 4–14*. Stockholm: Almqvist & Wiksell.

—. 2019. "Trees and Trauma: On the use of Phytomorphic Metaphors in Prophetic Descriptions of Deportation and Exile." Pages 217–31 in *Images of Exile in the Prophetic Literature*. Edited by Jesper Høgenhaven, Frederik Poulsen, and Cian Power. FAT II 103. Tübingen: Mohr Siebeck.

Erickson, Amy. 2013. "'Without My Flesh I Will See God': Job's Rhetoric of the Body." *JBL* 132: 295–313.

Evans, Vyvyan. 2019. *Cognitive Linguistics: A Complete Guide*. Edinburgh: Edinburgh University Press.

Fauconnier, Gilles, and George Lakoff. 2009. "On Metaphor and Blending." *Cognitive Semiotics* 5: 393–99.

Fauconnier, Gilles, and Mark Turner. 1996. "Blending as a Central Process of Grammar: Expanded Version." Pages 113–30 in *Conceptual Structure, Discourse, and Language*. Edited by Adele Goldberg. Stanford, CA: CLSI.

—. 1998. "Conceptual Integration Networks." *Cognitive Science* 22.2: 133–87.

—. 2002. *The Way We Think: Conceptual Blending and the Mind's Hidden Complexities*. New York: Basic Books.

Finkel, Irving L. 1980. "The Crescent Fertile." *AfO* 27: 37–52.

Fisch, Harold. 1988. *Poetry with a Purpose: Biblical Poetics and Interpretation*. Bloomington: Indiana University Press.

Fishbane, Michael. 1971. "Jeremiah IV 23–26 and Job III 3–13: A Recovered Use of the Creation Pattern." *VT* 21: 151–67.

Flynn, Shawn W. 2018. *Children in Ancient Israel: The Hebrew Bible and Mesopotamia in Comparative Perspective*. Oxford: Oxford University Press.

Fohrer, Georg. 1963. *Das Buch Hiob*. Kommentar zum Alten Testament 16. Gütersloh: Mohn.

Foster, Benjamin R., ed. 2005. *Before the Muses: An Anthology of Akkadian Literature*. 3rd ed. Bethesda: CDL.

Fox, Michael V. 2013. "Gods Answer and Job's Response." *Biblica* 94:1–23.

Franke, Chris. 2009. "'Like a Mother I have Comforted You': The Function of Figurative Language in Isaiah 1:7–26 and 66:7–14." Pages 35–55 in *The Desert Will Bloom: Poetic Visions in Isaiah*. Atlanta: Society of Biblical Literature.

Frevel, Christian. 2013. "Telling the Secrets of Wisdom: The Use of Psalm 104 in the Book of Job." Pages 157–68 in *Reading Job Intertextually*. Edited by Katharine Dell and Will Kynes. LHBOTS 574. New York: T&T Clark.

—. 2016. *Gottesbilder und Menschenbilder: Studien zur Anthropologie und Theologie im Alten Testament*. Neukirchen-Vluyn: Neukirchener Verlag.

Frymer-Kensky, Tikva Simone. 1987. "The Planting of Man: A Study in Biblical Imagery." Pages 129–36 in *Love and Death in the Ancient Near East: Essays in Honor of Marvin H Pope*. Edited by John H. Marks and Robert M. Good. Guilford, CT: Four Quarters.

—. 1992. *In the Wake of the Goddesses: Women, Culture, and the Biblical Transformation of Pagan Myth*. New York: Free Press.

Fuchs, Gisela. 1993. *Mythos und Hiobdichtung: Aufnahme und Umdeutung altorientalischer Vorstellungen*. Stuttgart: Kohlhammer.

Garroway, Kristine Henriksen. 2014. *Children in the Ancient Near Eastern Household*. EANEC. Winona Lake, IN: Eisenbrauns.

Gault, Brian P. 2019. *Body as Landscape, Love as Intoxication: Conceptual Metaphors in the Song of Songs*. AIL 36. Atlanta: Society of Biblical Literature.

George, A. R., ed. 2016. *Mesopotamian Incantations and Related Texts in the Schøyen Collection*. CUSAS 32. Bethesda, MD: CDL.

Gibbs, Raymond W., ed. 2016. *Mixing Metaphor*. Metaphor in Language, Cognition, and Communication 6. Amsterdam: Benjamins.

—. 2017. *Metaphor Wars: Conceptual Metaphors in Human Life*. Cambridge: Cambridge University Press.

Gibson, John C. L. 1985. *Job*. The Daily Study Bible Old Testament. Edinburgh: Saint Andrew Press.

—. 1988. "On Evil in the Book of Job." Pages 399–419 in *Ascribe to the Lord: Biblical and Other Studies in Memory of Peter C Craigie*. Sheffield: Sheffield Academic.

Glucksberg, Sam, and Boaz Keysar. 1990. "Understanding Metaphorical Comparisons: Beyond Similarity." *Psychological Review* 97:3–18.

Goering, Greg Schmidt. 2014. "Sapiential Synesthesia: The Conceptual Blending of Light and Word in Ben Sira's Wisdom Instruction." Pages 121–43 in *Cognitive Linguistic Explorations in Biblical Studies*. Edited by Bonnie Howe and Joel B. Green. Berlin: De Gruyter.

Gomola, Aleksander. 2018. *Conceptual Blending in Early Christian Discourse: A Cognitive Linguistic Analysis of Pastoral Metaphors in Patristic Literature*. Germany: De Gruyter.

Good, Edwin M. 1990. *In Turns of Tempest: A Reading of Job, with a Translation*. Stanford: Stanford University Press.

Goossens, Louis. 2002. "Metaphtonymy: the Interaction of Metaphor and Metonymy in Expressions for Linguistic Action." Pages 349–77 in *Metaphor and Metonymy in Comparison and Contrast*. Edited by René Dirven and Ralf Pörings. Cognitive Linguistics Research 20. New York: De Gruyter.

Gordis, Robert. 1969. "The Temptation of Job: Tradition Versus Experience in Religion." Pages 74–92 in *The Dimensions of Job: A Study and Selected Readings*. Edited by Nahum N. Glatzer. New York: Schoken Books.

—. 1978. *The Book of Job: Commentary, New Translation and Special Studies*. New York: Jewish Theological Seminary of America.

Gordon, Cyrus H. 1966. "Leviathan: Symbol of Evil." Pages 1–10 in *Biblical Motifs: Origins and Transformations*. Edited by Alexander Altmann. Cambridge, MA: Harvard University Press.
Grady, Joseph E., 1997a. *"Foundations of Meaning: Primary Metaphors and Primary Scenes."* PhD diss. ,University of California, Berkeley.
—. 1997b. "Theories are Buildings Revisited." *Cognitive Linguistics* 8: 267–90.
Grady, Joseph E., Todd Oakley, and Seana Coulson. 1999. "Blending and Metaphor." Pages 101–24 in *Metaphor in Cognitive Linguistics: Selected Papers from the Fifth International Cognitive Linguistics Conference, Amsterdam, July 1997*. Edited by Raymond W. Gibbs and Gerard Steen. Amsterdam: John Benjamins.
Grant, Jamie A. 2019. "Complaint and Transformation: Decreation at the Outset of Job." *Southeastern Theological Review* 10.2: 59–76.
Gray, John. 2010. *The Book of Job*. Edited by David J. A. Clines. Sheffield: Sheffield Phoenix.
Green, Alberto R. W. 2003. *The Storm-God in the Ancient Near East*. BJSUCSD 8. Winona Lake, IN: Eisenbrauns.
Green, Barbara. 2012. "Cognitive Linguistics and the 'Idolatry-Is-Adultery' Metaphor of Jeremiah 2–3." Pages 11–38 in *Daughter Zion: Her Portrait, Her Response*. Edited by Mark J. Boda, Carol J. Dempsey, and LeAnn Snow Flesher. AIL 13. Atlanta: Society of Biblical Literature.
Green, Stefan. 2019. "Zion as a Mother in the Restored Relationship between God and God's People: A Study of Isaiah 66:7–14a." Pages 266–97 in *God and Humans in the Hebrew Bible and Beyond: A Festschrift for Lennart Boström on his 67th Birthday*. Edited by David Willgren. Sheffield: Sheffield Phoenix.
Greenstein, Edward L. 2003. "The Language of Job and Its Poetic Function." *JBL* 122: 651–66.
—. 2004. "Jeremiah as an Inpiration to the Poet of Job." Pages 98–110 in *Inspired Speech: Prophecy in the Ancient Near East: Essays in Honor of Herbert B. Huffmon*. Edited by John Kaltner and Louis Stulman. LHBOTS 378. London: T&T Clark.
—. 2009. "The Problem of Evil in the Book of Job." Pages 333–62 in *Mishneh Todah: Studies in Deuteronomy and Its Cultural Environment in Honor of Jeffrey H. Tigay*. Edited by Nili Sacher Fox, David A. Glatt-Gilad, and Michael J. Williams. Winona Lake, IN: Eisenbrauns.
—. 2017. "The Book of Job and Mesopotamian Literature: How Many Degrees of Separation?" Pages 143–58 in *Subtle Citation, Allusion, and Translation in the Hebrew Bible*. Edited by Ziony Zevit. Sheffield: Equinox.
Grogan, Geoffrey. 2008. *Psalms*. The Two Horizons Old Testament Commentary. Grand Rapids: Eerdmans.
Grohmann, Marianne. 2007. *Fruchtbarkeit und Geburt in den Psalmen*. FAT 53. Tübingen: Mohr Siebeck.
—. 2010. "Metaphors of God, Nature and Birth in Psalm 90,2 and Psalm 110,3." Pages 23–33 in *Metaphors in the Psalms*. Edited by Pierre Van Hecke and Antje Labahn. BETL 231. Leuven: Peeters.
—. 2019. "Metaphors of Miscarriage in the Psalms." *VT* 69: 219–31.
Gunkel, Hermann and Heinrich Zimmern. 2006. *Creation and Chaos in the Primeval Era and the Eschaton: A Religio-Historical Study of Genesis 1 and Revelation 12*. Translated by K. William Whitney. The Biblical Resource Series. Grand Rapids: Eerdmans.
Habel, Norman C. 1985. *The Book of Job*. The Old Testament Library. Philadelphia: Westminster.

Halvorson-Taylor, Martien A. 2010. *Enduring Exile: The Metaphorization of Exile in the Hebrew Bible*. VTSup 141. Leiden: Brill.
Ham, T. C. 2013. "The Gentle Voice of God in Job 38." *JBL* 132: 527–41.
Hankins, Davis. 2015. *The Book of Job and the Immanent Genesis of Transcendence*. Diaeresis. Evanston, IL: Northwestern University Press.
Hard, Robin. 2004. *The Routledge Handbook of Greek Mythology: Based on H.J. Rose's Handbook of Greek Mythology*. London: Routledge.
Hartley, John E. 1988. *The Book of Job*. The New international Commentary on the Old Testament. Grand Rapids: Eerdmans.
—. 2013. "Yahweh Instructs Job on the Character of the Creation (Job 38:1–39:30)." *Biblica et Patristica Thoruniensia* 6: 37–49.
Hawley, Lance R. 2018. *Metaphor Competition in the Book of Job*. JAJpSup 26. Göttingen: Vandenhoeck & Ruprecht.
Hays, Christopher B. 2012. "'My Beloved Son, Come and Rest in Me': Job's Return to His Mother's Womb (Job 1:21a) in Light of Egyptian Mythology." *VT* 62: 607–21.
Hine, Daryl, ed. and trans. 2005. *Works of Hesiod and the Homeric Hymns*. Chicago: University of Chicago Press.
Horne, Milton. 2005. "From Ethics to Aesthetics: the Animals in Job 38:39–39:30." *Review and Expositor* 102: 127–42.
Horst, Friedrich. 1968. *Hiob 1–19*. Biblischer Kommentar: Altes Testament 16. Vol 1. Neukirchen-Vluyn: Neukirchener Verlag.
Hossfeld, Frank-Lothar, Erich Zenger, and Klaus Baltzer. 2011. *Psalms 3: A Commentary on Psalms 101–150*. Hermeneia. Minneapolis: Fortress.
Howe, Bonnie, and Joel B. Green, eds. 2014. *Cognitive Linguistic Explorations in Biblical Studies*. Berlin: De Gruyter.
Huff, Barry R. 2019. "From Societal Scorn to Divine Delight: Job's Transformative Portrayal of Wild Animals." *Int* 73: 248–58.
Hulster, Izaak J. de, and Brent A. Strawn. 2015. "Figuring YHWH in Unusual Ways: Deuteronomy 32 and other Mixed Metaphors for God in the Old Testament." Pages 117–33 in *Iconographic Exegesis of the Hebrew Bible/Old Testament: An Introduction to Its Method and Practice*. Edited by Izaak J. de Hulster, Brent A. Strawn, and Ryan P. Bonfiglio. Göttingen: Vandenhoeck & Ruprecht.
Häner, Tobias. 2020. "Job's Dark View of Creation: On the Ironic Allusions to Genesis 1:1–2:4a in Job 3 and Their Echo in Job 38–39." *OTE* 33: 266–84.
Jacobsen, Thorkild. 1973. "Notes on Nintur." *Or NS* 42: 274–98.
—. 1976. *Treasures of Darkness*. New Haven: Yale University Press.
—. 1993. *Dumuzi*. Pages 512–13 in vol. 4 of *The Encyclopedia of Religion*. Edited by Mircea Eliade and Charles J. Adams. 16 vols. Complete and unabridged ed. New York: Macmillan Reference USA.
Jacobsen, Thorkild, and Kirsten Nielsen. 1992. "Cursing the day." *SJOT* 6: 187–204.
Jäkel, Olof. 2002. "Hypotheses Revisited: The Cognitive Theory of Metaphor Applied to Religious Texts." *Metaphorik.de* 2: 20–42.
Janowski, Bernd. 2010. "Das Licht des Lebens: Zur Lichtmetaphorik in den Psalmen." Pages 87–113 in *Metaphors in the Psalms*. Edited by Pierre Van Hecke and Antje Labahn. BETL 231. Leuven: Peeters.

Jenni, Ernst. 1968. *Das hebräische Pi'el: syntaktisch-semasiologische Untersuchung einer Verbalform im Alten Testament*. Zürich: EVZ-Verlag.
Jindo, Job Y. 2010. *Biblical Metaphor Reconsidered: A Cognitive Approach to Poetic Prophecy in Jeremiah 1-24*. HSM 64. Winona Lake, IN: Eisenbrauns.
Johandi, Andreas. 2019. *The God Asar-Asalluḫi in the Early Mesopotamian Pantheon*. School of Theology and Religious Studies. Tartu: University of Tartu Press.
Johnson, Mark. 1987. *The Body in the Mind: The Bodily Basis of Meaning, Imagination, and Reason*. Chicago: University of Chicago Press.
Jones, Peter Murray, and Lea T. Olsan. 2015. "Performative Rituals for Conception and Childbirth in England, 900–1500." *Bulletin of the History of Medicine* 89: 406–33.
Joode, Johan de. 2018. *Metaphorical Landscapes and the Theology of the Book of Job: An Analysis of Job's Spatial Metaphors*. VTSup 179. Leiden: Brill.
Kang, Chol-Gu. 2017. *Behemot und Leviathan: Studien zur Komposition und Theologie von Hiob 38,1-42,6*. WMANT 149. Göttingen: Vandenhoeck & Ruprecht.
Katz, Dina. 2003. *The Image of the Netherworld in the Sumerian Sources*. Bethesda, MD: CDL.
Kazen, Thomas. 2014. "The Role of Disgust in Priestly Purity Law: Insights from Conceptual Metaphor and Blending Theories." *Journal of Law, Religion and State* 3: 62–92.
—. 2023. "Malachi's Metaphorical Divorce: Reading Marital Faithlessness as Cult Criticism with a Little Help from Blending Theory." Pages 116–37 in *Metaphors in the Prophetic Literature of the Hebrew Bible and Beyond*. Edited by David Davage, Mikael Larsson, and Lena-Sofia Tiemeyer. JAJSup 36. Paderborn, Germany: Brill Schöningh.
Keel, Othmar. 1978. *Jahwes Entgegnung an Ijob: eine Deutung von Ijob 38-41 vor dem Hintergrund der zeitgenössischen Bildkunst*. FRLANT. Göttingen: Vandenhoeck & Ruprecht.
—. 1980. *Das Böcklein in der Milch seiner Mutter und Verwandtes: im Lichte eines altorientalischen Bildmotivs*. OBO 33. Freiburg Göttingen: Vandenhoeck & Ruprecht Universitätsverlag.
—. 1987. "The Peculiar Headrests for the Dead in First Temple Times." *BAR* 13.4: 50–53.
Keel, Othmar, and Silvia Schroer. 2015. *Creation: Biblical Theologies in the Context of the Ancient Near East*. Translated by Peter T. Daniels. Winona Lake, IN: Eisenbrauns.
Keel, Othmar, and Christoph Uehlinger. 1998. *Gods, Goddesses, and Images of God in Ancient Israel*. Minneapolis: Fortress.
Keller, Catherine. 2002. *The Face of the Deep: A Theology of Becoming*. London: Routledge.
Kim, Brittany. 2018. *'Lengthen Your Tent-Cords': The Metaphorical World of Israel's Household in in the Book of Isaiah*. Siphrut 23. University Park, PA: Eisenbrauns.
Kimmel, Michael. 2010. "Why We Mix Metaphors (and Mix Them Well): Discourse Coherence, Conceptual Metaphor, and Beyond." *Journal of Pragmatics* 42: 97–115.
Kindstedt, Paul S. 2017. "The History of Cheese." Pages 3–19 in *Global Cheesemaking Technology: Cheese Quality and Characteristics*. Edited by Photis Papademas and Thomas Bintsis. Hoboken, NJ: John Wiley & Sons.
King, Philip J., and Lawrence E. Stager. 2001. *Life in Biblical Israel*. LAI. Louisville: Westminster John Knox.
Kitz, Anne Marie. 2014. *Cursed Are You! The Phenomenology of Cursing in Cuneiform and Hebrew Texts*. Wionna Lake, IN: Eisenbrauns.
Kotzé, Zacharias. 2009. "A Cognitive Linguistic Approach to the Emotion of Anger in the Old Testament." *HTS* 60.3: 21.

Kövecses, Zoltán. 2005. *Metaphor in Culture: Universality and Variation*. Cambridge: Cambridge University Press.
—. 2010. *Metaphor: A Practical Introduction*. 2nd ed. Oxford: Oxford University Press.
—. 2013. "The Metaphor-Metonymy Relationship: Correlation Metaphors are Based on Metonymy." *Metaphor and Symbol* 28: 75–88.
—. 2015. *Where Metaphors Come from: Reconsidering Context in Metaphor*. Oxford: Oxford University Press.
—. 2020. *Extended Conceptual Metaphor Theory*. Cambridge: Cambridge University Press.
Krainer, Antonia. 2020. "Gottesbilder in Psalm 102: Netzwerke von Metaphern, Metaphors for God in Ps 102 as Networks." *PzB* 29: 1–25.
Kramer, Samuel N., and W. F. Albright. 1945. *Enki and Ninḫursag: A Sumerian 'Paradise' Myth*. BASORSup 1. New Haven: American Schools of Oriental Research.
Krebernik, Manfred. 1993. "Muttergöttin." Pages 502–16 in *Reallexikon der Assyriologie und vorderasiatischen Archäologie*. Edited by D. O. Edzard. Berlin: De Gruyter.
Krolokke, Charlotte H. 2010. "On a Trip to the Womb: Biotourist Metaphors in Fetal Ultrasound Imaging." *Women's Studies in Communication* 33: 138–53.
Kruger, Paul A. 2015. "Emotions in the Hebrew Bible: A Few Observations on Prospects and Challenges." *OTE* 28: 395–420.
Kubina, Veronika. 1979. *Die Gottesreden im Buche Hiob: ein Beitrag zur Diskussion um die Einheit von Hiob 38,1–42,6*. Freiburger theologische Studien 115. Freiburg im Breisgau: Herder.
Kynes, Will. 2012. *My Psalm Has Turned into Weeping: Job's Dialogue with the Psalms*. Berlin: de Gruyter.
Lakoff, George. 1987. *Women, Fire, and Dangerous Things: What Categories Reveal About the Mind*. Chicago: University of Chicago Press.
—. 1993. "The Contemporary Theory of Metaphor." Pages 202–51 in *Metaphor and Thought*. Edited by Andrew Ortony. Cambridge: Cambridge University Press.
—. 2008. "The Neural Theory of Metaphor." Pages 17–38 in *The Cambridge Handbook of Metaphor and Thought*. Edited by Raymond W. Gibbs. Cambridge: Cambridge University Press.
Lakoff, George and Mark Johnson. 2003. *Metaphors We Live by*. Rev. ed. Chicago: University of Chicago Press.
Lakoff, George and Mark Turner. 1989. *More than Cool Reason: A Field Guide to Poetic Metaphor*. Chicago: University of Chicago Press.
Lakoff, Gerorge, Jane Espenson, and Alan Schwartz. 1991. "Second Draft Copy of Master Metaphor List." Edited by Cognitive Linguistics Group: University of California at Berkeley.
Lam, Joseph. 2016. *Patterns of Sin in the Hebrew Bible: Metaphor, Culture, and the Making of a Religious Concept*. New York: Oxford University Press.
Lambert, David A. 2015. *How Repentance Became Biblical: Judaism, Christianity, and the Interpretation of Scripture*. New York: Oxford University Press.
Lambert, Wilfred G, Alan R Millard, and Miguel Civil, eds. 1999. *Atra-ḫasīs: the Babylonian Story of the Flood*. Winona Lake, IN: Eisenbrauns.
Lambert, Wilfred G. 1969. "A Middle Assyrian Medical Text." *Iraq* 31: 28–39.
— ed. 2013. *Babylonian Creation Myths*. Winona Lake, IN: Eisenbrauns.
Lamprecht, At. 2021. "Unipolar Conceptual Metaphors in Biblical Hebrew." *JSem* 30.2: 1–20.

Lancaster, Mason D. 2021. "Metaphor Research and the Hebrew Bible." *CurBR* 19: 235–85.
Lang, Bernhard. 2002. *The Hebrew God: Portrait of an Ancient Deity*. New Haven: Yale University Press.
Langacker, Ronald W. 2008. *Cognitive Grammar: A Basic Introduction*. Oxford: Oxford University Press.
Langton, Karen. 2012. "Job's Attempt to Regain Control: Traces of a Babylonian Birth Incantation in Job 3." *JSOT* 36.4: 459–69.
Leonard, Jeffery M. 2019. "Let the Day Perish: The Nexus of Personification and Mythology in Job 3." *JSOT* 43.2: 247–69.
Lev-Tov, Justin. 2022. "Animal Husbandry: Meat, Milk, and More." Pages 77–98 in *T&T Clark Handbook of Food in The Hebrew Bible and Ancient Israel*. Edited by Jangling Fu, Cynthia Shafer-Elliott, and Carol Meyers. London: T&T Clark.
Levenson, Jon D. 1988. *Creation and the Persistence of Evil: the Jewish Drama of Divine Omnipotence*. Princeton: Princeton University Press.
Lévêque, Jean. 1970. *Job et son dieu: essai d'exégèse et de théologie biblique*. Etudes Bibliques. Paris: Gabalda.
Linafelt, Tod. 2006. "The Wizard of Uz: Job, Dorothy, and the Limits of the Sublime." *BibInt* 14: 94–109.
Lindström, Fredrik. 1983. *God and the Origin of Evil: A Contextual Analysis of Alleged Monistic Evidence in the Old Testament*. Lund: Gleerup.
Longrigg, James. 1985. "A Seminal 'Debate' in the Fifth Century B.C.?" Pages 277–87 in *Aristotle on Nature and Living Things: Philosophical and Historical Studies: Presented to David M. Balme on His Seventieth Birthday*. Edited by Allan Gotthelf. Pittsburgh: Mathesis Publications; Bristol: Bristol Classic.
Loon, Hanneke van. 2018. *Metaphors in the Discussion on Suffering in Job 3–31: Visions of Hope and Consolation*. BibInt 165. Boston: Brill.
Lugt, Pieter van der. 1995. *Rhetorical Criticism and the Poetry of the Book of Job*. Old Testament Studies 32. Leiden: Brill.
Lundhaug, Hugo. 2010. *Images of Rebirth: Cognitive Poetics and Transformational Soteriology in the Gospel of Philip and the Exegesis on the Soul*. Nag Hammadi and Manichaean Studies 73. Leiden: Brill.
—. 2014. "The Fruit of the Tree of Life: Ritual Interpretation of the Crucifixion in the Gospel of Philip." Pages 73–97 in *Cognitive Linguistic Explorations in Biblical Studies*. Edited by Bonnie Howe and Joel B. Green. Berlin: De Gruyter.
Macky, Peter W. 1990. *The Centrality of Metaphors to Biblical Thought: A Method for Interpreting the Bible*. Lewiston, NY: Mellen.
Maier, Christl M. 2012. "Zion's Body as a Site of God's Motherhood in Isaiah 66:7–14." Pages 225–42 in *Daughter Zion: Her Portrait, Her Response*. Edited by Mark J. Boda, Carol J. Dempsey, and LeAnn Snow Flesher. AIL 13. Atlanta: Society of Biblical Literature.
Malul, Meir. 1990. "Adoption of Foundlings in the Bible and Mesopotamian Documents: A Study of Some Legal Metaphors in Ezekiel 16:1–7." *JSOT* 15.46: 97–126.
Mathewson, Dan. 2006. *Death and Survival in the Book of Job: Desymbolization and Traumatic Experience*. LHBOTS 450. New York: T&T Clark.
McFague, Sallie. 1987. *Models of God: Theology for an Ecological, Nuclear Age*. Philadelphia: Fortress.

McKane, William. 2014. *Jeremiah 1–25*. International Critical Commentary. London: T&T Clark.
Mettinger, Tryggve N. D. 1976. *King and Messiah: The Civil and Sacral Legitimation of the Israelite Kings*. Lund: Gleerup.
—. 1987. *Namnet och Närvaron: Gudsnamn och Gudsbild i Böckernas Bok*. Örebro, Sweden: Libris.
—. 1988. *In Search of God: The Meaning and Message of the Everlasting Names*. Philadelphia: Fortress.
—. 1992. "The God of Job: Avenger, Tyrant, or Victor?" Pages 39–49 in *The Voice from the Whirlwind: Interpreting the Book of Job*. Edited by Leo G. Perdue and W. Clark Gilpin. Nashville: Abingdon.
Meyer, Nicholas A. 2021. "Born of Woman, Fashioned from Clay: Tracking the Homology of Earth and Womb from the Hebrew Bible to the Psalms of Thanksgiving." *DSD* 28: 135–178.
Mies, Francoise. 2022. *Job ou sortir de la cendre: Etude exégétique, littéraire, anthropologique et théologique de la mort dans le livre de Job*. BETL 324. Leuven: Peeters.
Miller, James E. 1991. "Structure and Meaning of the Animal Discourse in the Theophany of Job (38,39–39,30)." *ZAW* 103: 418–21.
Moor, Johannes Cornelis de, ed. 1987. *An Anthology of Religious Texts from Ugarit*. Leiden: Brill.
Most, Glenn W., trans. 2018. *Theogony; Works and Days; Testimonia*. Loeb Classical Library 57. Cambridge, MA: Harvard University Press.
Moughtin-Mumby, Sharon. 2008. *Sexual and Marital Metaphors in Hosea, Jeremiah, Isaiah, and Ezekiel*. Oxford: Oxford University Press.
Murray, A. T., and William F. Wyatt, trans. 1999. *Iliad: Volume II: Books 13–24*. Loeb Classical Library 171. Cambridge, MA: Harvard University Press.
Neumann-Gorsolke, Ute. 2012. *Wer ist der "Herr der Tiere"? Eine hermeneutische Problemanzeige*. Biblisch-Theologische Studien 85. Göttingen: Vandenhoeck & Ruprecht.
Newsom, Carol A. 1996. "The Book of Job: Introduction, Commentary and Reflections." Pages 318–637 in *The New Interpreter's Bible*, V 4: 1 and 2 *Macabees, Introduction to Hebrew Poetry, Job, Psalms*. Nashville: Abingdon.
—. 2003. *The Book of Job: A Contest of Moral Imaginations*. Oxford: Oxford University Press.
Nõmmik, Urmas. 2014. "Thinking of Water in the Book of Job: A Fluvial Introduction to the Job Literature." Pages 279–98 in *Thinking of Water in the Early Second Temple Period*. BZAW 461. Germany: De Gruyter.
O'Connor, Kathleen M. 2003. "Wild, Raging Creativity: The Scene in the Whirlwind (Job 38–39)." Pages 171–79 in *A God So Near: Essays on Old Testament Theology in Honor of Patrick D. Miller*. Edited by Brent A. Strawn and Nancy R. Bowen. Winona Lake, IN: Eisenbrauns.
Oeming, Manfred. 1996. "'Kannst du der Löwin ihren Raub zu jagen geben?' (Hi 38,39): Das Motiv des 'Herrn der Tiere' und seine Bedeutung für die Theologie der Gottesreden Hi 38–42." Pages 146–63 in *"Dort ziehen Schiffe dahin ...": Collected Communications to the XIVth Congress of the International Organization for the Study of the Old Testament, Paris 1992*. Frankfurt am Main: Lang.
Oorschot, Jürgen van. 2019. "Nudity and Clothing in the Hebrew Bible: The Ecological and Anthropological Aspects." Pages 237–49 in *Clothing and Nudity in the Hebrew Bible: A Handbook*. Edited by Christoph Berner. London: T&T Clark.
Osborne, William R. 2018. *Trees and Kings: A Comparative Analysis of Tree Imagery in Israels Prophet*. BBRSup 18. Winona Lake, IN: Eisenbrauns.

Oshima, Takayoshi. 2014. *Babylonian Poems of Pious Sufferers: Ludlul Bel Nemeqi and the Babylonian Theodicy.* ORA 14. Tübingen: Mohr Siebeck.

Pantoja, Jennifer Metten. 2017. *The Metaphor of the Divine as Planter of the People: Stinking Grapes or Pleasant Planting?* BibInt 155. Leiden: Brill.

Parker, Simon B., ed. 1997. *Ugaritic Narrative Poetry.* WAW 9. Atlanta: Scholars.

Patton, Corrine. 2001. "The Beauty of the Beast: Leviathan and Behemoth in Light of Catholic Theology." Pages 142–67 in *The Whirlwind: Essays on Job, Hermeneutics and Theology in Memory of Jane Morse.* Edited by Stephen L. Cook, Corrine L. Carvalho, James W. Watts, and Jane Morse. JSOTSup. London: Sheffield Academic.

Paul, Shalom. 2013. "Two Notes on Biblical and Mesopotamian Imagery." Pages 171–77 in *Built by Wisdom, Established by Understanding: Essays on Biblical and Near Eastern Literature in Honor of Adele Berlin.* Edited by Adele Berlin and Maxine L. Grossman. Bethesda, MD: University Press of Maryland.

Pease, Anna S., Peter J. Fleming, Fern R. Hauck, Rachel Y. Moon, Rosemary S. C. Horne, Monique P. L'Hoir, Anne-Louise Ponsonby, and Peter S. Blair. 2016. "Swaddling and the Risk of Sudden Infant Death Syndrome: A Meta-Analysis." *Pediatrics* 137.6: 1–9.

Peck, A. L., trans. 2014. *Generation of Animals.* Loeb Classical Library 366. Cambridge, MA: Harvard University Press.

Pelham, Abigail. 2012. *Contested Creations in the Book of Job: The-World-as-It-Ought-and-Ought-Not-to-Be.* BibInt 113. Leiden: Brill.

Perdue, Leo G. 1986. "Job's Assault on Creation." *HAR* 10: 295–15.

———. 1991. *Wisdom in Revolt: Metaphorical Theology in the Book of Job.* BLS 29. Sheffield: JSOT.

Pettys, Valerie Forstman. 2002. "Let There Be Darkness: Continuity and Discontinuity in the 'Curse' of Job 3." *JSOT* 26.4: 89–104.

Philip, Gill. 2016. "Conventional and Novel Metaphors in Language." Pages 219–232 in *The Routledge Handbook of Metaphor and Language.* Edited by Elena Semino and Zsófia Demjén. London: Routledge.

Pinker, Aron. 2020. "An Examination of a Breaking (אשבר) in Job 38:10." *RB* 127: 196–214.

Plantin, Lisa. Forthcoming-a. "God Breaks the Water: The Creative Use of Akkadian Birth Metaphors in Job 38." In *Biblical Job in the Literary Network of the Ancient Near East.* Edited by Andreas Johandi and Urmas Nõmmik. Kasion. Münster: Zaphon.

———. Forthcoming-b. "God Hears the Cry of the Young Wild Animals: An Analysis of the Young Animals in Job 38–39 and God's Relationship to Them." In *Job Unveiled and Reimagined: Current Issues, New Paradigms, and Future Horizons.* Edited by James Kwon JiSeong and Tobias Häner. FAT II. Tübingen: Mohr Siebeck.

Pope, Marvin H. 1973. *Job: Introduction, Translation and Notes.* The Anchor Bible. Garden City, NY: Doubleday.

Potter, Paul, trans. 2012. *Generation. Nature of the Child. Diseases 4. Nature of Women and Barrenness.* Loeb Classical Library 520. Cambridge, MA: Harvard University Press.

Pyeon, Yohan. 2003. *You Have Not Spoken What Is Right About Me: Intertextuality and the Book of Job.* StBibLit 45. New York: Lang.

Pyrhönen, Heta. 2005. "Thematic Approaches to Narrative." Pages 597–98 in *Routledge Encyclopedia of Narrative Theory.* Edited by David Herman, Manfred Jahn, and Marie-Laure Ryan. London: Routledge.

Quick, Laura. 2022. "'Like a Garment Eaten by Moths' (Job 13:28): Clothing, Nudity and Illness in the Book of Job." *BibInt* 30: 46–65.

Rahlfs, Alfred and Robert Hanhart. 2006. *Septuaginta: id est Vetus Testamentum graece iuxta LXX interpretes, Editio altera.* Stuttgart: Deutsche Bibelgesellschaft.

Rancour-Laferriere, Daniel. 2021. "Death Imagined: From Mother Earth to Dust and Ashes in the Mind of Job." *American Imago* 78: 1–53.

Reece, William David. 1989. "The Concept of Light in the Old Testament: A Semantic Analysis." PhD diss., University of California.

Regt, Lénart J. de. 1996. "Discourse Implications of Rhetorical Questions in Job, Deuteronomy and the Minor Prophets." Pages 51–78 in *Literary Structure and Rhetorical Strategies in the Hebrew Bible.* Edited by Lénart J. de Regt, J. de Waard, and J. P. Fokkelman. Winona Lake, IN: Eisenbrauns.

Ricoeur, Paul. 1975. "Biblical Hermeneutics." *Semeia* 4:29–148.

Robinette, S. J. 2014. "Looking beyond the Tree in Jeremiah 17:5–8." Pages 25–46 in *Cognitive Linguistic Explorations in Biblical Studies.* Edited by Bonnie Howe and Joel B. Green. Berlin: De Gruyter.

Rodin, Therese. 2014. *The World of the Sumerian Mother Goddess: An Interpretation of Her Myths.* Uppsala: Acta Universitatis Upsaliensis.

Roller, Lynn E. 1999. *In Search of God the Mother: The Cult of Anatolian Cybele.* Berkeley: University of California Press.

Ross, William A. 2019. "David's Spiritual Walls and Conceptual Blending in Psalm 51." *JSOT* 43.4: 607–26.

Rowley, Harold Henry. 1981. *The Book of Job.* New Century Bible Commentary. Grand Rapids: Eerdmans.

Sasson, Vanessa R., and Jane Marie Law. 2008. "A Womb With a View: The Buddha's Final Fetal Experience." Pages 55–72 in *Imagining the Fetus: The Unborn in Myth, Religion, and Culture.* New York: Oxford University Press.

Schafer, Rahel A. 2016. "Co-Creaturely Associates or Peers? The Nature of Animals as Portrayed in Isaiah." Pages 64–101 in *Meeting with God on the Mountains: Essays in Honor of Richard M. Davidson.* Edited by Jiří Moskala. Berrien Springs, MI: Old Testament Department, Seventh-day Adventist Theological Seminary, Andrews University.

Schifferdecker, Kathryn. 2008. *Out of the Whirlwind: Creation Theology in the Book of Job.* HTS 61. Cambridge, MA: Harvard University Press.

Schlimm, Matthew R. 2011. *From Fratricide to Forgiveness: The Language and Ethics of Anger in Genesis.* Siphrut 7. Winona Lake, IN: Eisenbrauns.

Schmid, Konrad. 2007. "Innerbiblische Schriftdiskussion im Hiobbuch."*https://www.academia.edu/1541276/Innerbiblische_Schriftdiskussion_im_Hiobbuch.*

Schmidt, N. F. and P. J. Nel. 2016. "Divine Darkness in the Human Discourses of Job." *AcT* 36: 125–47.

Scholnick, Sylvia Huberman. 1976. "Lawsuit Drama in the Book of Job." PhD diss., Brandeis University.

—. 1992. "The Meaning of *Mišpāṭ (Justice)* in the Book of Job." Pages 349–58 in *Sitting with Job: Selected Studies on the Book of Job.* Edited by Roy B. Zuck. Grand Rapids: Baker.

Schultz, Richard L. 2013. "Job and Ecclesiastes." Pages 190–203 in *Reading Job Intertextually.* Edited by Katharine Dell and Will Kynes. LHBOTS 574. New York: T&T Clark.

Scurlock, JoAnn. 1991. "Baby Snatching Demons, Restless Souls and the Dangers of Childbirth: Magico-Medical Means of Dealing with Some of the Perils of Motherhood in Ancient Mesopotamia." *Incognita* 2: 137–85.

— ed. 2014. *Sourcebook for Ancient Mesopotamian Medicine.* WAW 36. Atlanta: Society of Biblical Literature.

Semino, Elena, and Gerard Steen. 2008. "Metaphor in Literature." Pages 232–46 in *The Cambridge Handbook of Metaphor and Thought.* Edited by Jr Raymond W. Gibbs. Cambridge: Cambridge University Press.

Seow, Choon-Long. 2013. *Job 1–21: Interpretation and Commentary.* Illuminations. Grand Rapids: Eerdmans.

Shead, Stephen L. 2011. *Radical Frame Semantics and Biblical Hebrew: Exploring Lexical Semantics.* BibInt 108. Leiden: Brill.

Sherman, Phillip. 2020. "The Hebrew Bible and the 'Animal Turn.'" *CurBR* 19.1: 36–63.

Simkins, Ronald A. 2014. "The Embodied World: Creation Metaphors in the Ancient Near East." *BTB* 44: 40–53.

Sjöberg, Åke W. 1973. "Nungal in the Ekur." *AfO* 24: 19–46.

Smith, Mark S. 1994. *The Ugaritic Baal Cycle: Introduction with Text, Translation and Commentary of KTU 1.1–1.2.* Vol. I. VTSup 55. Leiden: Brill.

Smith, Mark S. and Wayne Thomas Pitard. 2009. *The Ugaritic Baal Cycle: Introduction with Text, Translation and Commentary of KTU/CAT 1.3–1.4.* Vol. II. VTSup 114. Leiden: Brill.

Sommerfeld, W. 1928. "Marduk: A. Philologisch. I. In Mesopotamien." Pages 360–70 in *Reallexikon der Assyriologie und vorderasiatischen Archäologie.* Edited by Erich Ebeling, Bruno Meissner, Ernst F. Weidner, Wolfram von Soden, and Dietz Otto Edzard. Berlin: De Gruyter.

Sommerstein, Alan H., trans. 2008. *The Oresteia: Agamemnon, Libation-Bearers, Eumenides.* Loeb Classical Library 146. Cambridge, MA: Harvard University Press.

Soskice, Janet Martin. 1985. *Metaphor and Religious Language.* Oxford: Clarendon.

Spieser, Cathie. 2018. "Aspects of the Womb and Embracing the Dead in Ancient Egypt." Pages 87–99 in *Cultural Constructions of the Uterus in Pre-modern Societies, Past and Present.* Edited by Erica M. Couto-Ferreira and Lorenzo Verderame. Newcastle upon Tyne: Cambridge Scholars.

Steen, Gerard. 2017. "Deliberate Metaphor Theory: Basic Assumptions, Main Tenets, Urgent Issues." *Intercultural Pragmatics* 14: 1–24.

Stol, Marten. 1993. "Milk, Butter, and Cheese." *Bulletin on Sumerian Agriculture* 7: 99–113.

—. 2000. *Birth in Babylonia and the Bible: Its Mediterranean Setting.* Groningen: Styx.

Stordalen, Terje. 2010. "Mother Earth in Biblical Hebrew Literature: Ancient and Contemporary Imagination." Pages 113–29 in *The Centre and the Periphery: A European Tribute to Walter Brueggemann.* Edited by Jill Middlemas, David J. A. Clines, and Else Kragelund Holt. Sheffield: Sheffield Phoenix.

Stump, Eleonore. 2010. *Wandering in Darkness: Narrative and the Problem of Suffering.* Oxford: Oxford University Press.

Sweetser, Eve, and Mary Therese DesCamp. 2014. "Motivating Biblical Metaphors for God: Refining the Cognitive Model." Pages 7–23 in *Cognitive Linguistic Explorations in Biblical Studies.* Edited by Bonnie Howe and Joel B. Green. Berlin: De Gruyter.

Tilford, Nicole L. 2017. *Sensing World, Sensing Wisdom: The Cognitive Foundation of Biblical Metaphors.* AIL 31. Atlanta: Society of Biblical Literature.

Trible, Phyllis. 1978. *God and the Rhetoric of Sexuality.* Overtures to Biblical Theology. Philadelphia: Fortress.

Tönsing, Detlev. 1996. "The Use of Creation Language in Job 3, 9 and 38 and the Meaning of Suffering." *Scriptura* 59: 435-49.
Tromp, Nicholas J. 1969. *Primitive Conceptions of Death and the Nether World in the Old Testament*. Biblica et Orientala 21. Rome: Pontifical Biblical Institute.
Tsevat, Matitiahu. 1966. "The Meaning of the Book of Job." *HUCA* 37:73-106.
Tur-Sinai, Naphtali H. 1957. *Book of Job: A New Commentary*. Jerusalem: Kiryath Sepher.
Turner, Mark. 2008. "Frame Blending." Pages 13-32 in *Frames, Corpora, and Knowledge Representation*. Edited by Rema Rossini Favretti. Bologna: Bononia University Press.
Vall, Gregory. 1993. *From Womb to Tomb: Poetic Imagery and the Book of Job*. Department of Semitic and Egyptian Languages and Literatures. Washington DC: Catholic University of America.
—. 1995a. "The Enigma of Job 1,21a." *Bib* 76: 325-42.
—. 1995b. "'From Whose Womb Did the Ice Come Forth?' Procreation Images in Job 38:28-29." *CBQ* 57: 504-13.
Van Hecke, Pierre. 2005a. "Conceptual Blending: A Recent Approach to Metaphor." Pages 215-31 in *Metaphor in the Hebrew Bible*. Edited by Pierre Van Hecke. BETL 187. Leuven: Leuven University Press; Peeters.
—. 2010. "'Is My Flesh Bronze?' (Job 6:12): Metaphors of Fluidity and Solidity in the Description of the Body in the Book of Job." *The Classical Bulletin* 86: 101-15.
—. 2011. "'I Melt Away and Will No Longer Live': The Use of Metaphor in Job's Self-Descriptions." *ET Studies* 2: 91-107.
Van Hecke, Pierre and Antje Labahn, eds. 2010. *Metaphors in the Psalms*. BETL 231. Leuven: Peeters.
Veldhuis, Niek. 1989. "The New Assyrian Compendium for a Woman in Childbirth." *ASJ* 11: 239-60.
—. 1991. *A Cow of Sîn*. Library of Oriental Texts. Groningen: Styx.
Verde, Danilo and Antje Labahn, eds. 2020. *Networks of Metaphors in the Hebrew Bible*. BELT 309. Leuven: Leuven University Press; Peeters.
Vernant, Jean-Pierre. 1993. "Artemis." Pages 420-21 in vol. 1 of *The Encyclopedia of Religion*. Edited by Mircea Eliade and Charles J. Adams. 16 vols. Complete and unabridged ed. New York: Macmillan Reference USA.
Viberg, Åke. 1992. *Symbols of Law: A Contextual Analysis of Legal Symbolic Acts in the Old Testament*. Stockholm: Almqvist & Wiksell.
—. 2021. "Metaphors of Evil: An Application of Cognitive Metaphor Theory on Imagery of Evil in the Book of Psalms." Pages 241-57 in *Sin, Suffering, and the Problem of Evil*. Edited by David Willgren and Blaženka Scheuer. FAT II. Tübingen: Mohr Siebeck.
Vogels, Walter. 1994. "Job's Empty Pious Slogans (Job 1.20-22, 2, 8-10)." Pages 369-76 in *The Book of Job*. Edited by Wim Beuken. BETL 114. Leuven: Peeters.
Wälchli, Stefan. 2013. "Job 3: Metaphors Turned Into Their Contrary." Pages 63-67 in *Conceptual Metaphors in Poetic Texts: Proceedings of the Metaphor Research Group of the European Association of Biblical Studies in Lincoln 2009*. Edited by Antje Labahn. PHSC 18. Piscataway, NJ: Gorgias.
Walls, Niel. 1992. *The Goddess Anat in Ugaritic Myth*. Dissertation Series. Atlanta: Scholars.
Watson, Rebecca Sally. 2005. *Chaos Uncreated: A Reassessment of the 'Theme of Chaos' in the Hebrew Bible*. BZAW 341. Berlin: de Gruyter.
Watson, Wilfred and Nicolas Wyatt eds. 1999. *Handbook of Ugaritic Studies*. Leiden: Brill.

Weiss, Andrea L. 2006. *Figurative Language in Biblical Prose Narrative: Metaphor in the Book of Samuel.* VTSup 107. Leiden: Brill.
Weiss, Meir. 1984. *The Bible from Within: The Method of Total Interpretation.* Jerusalem: Magnes Press, Hebrew University.
WHO. 2018. *WHO Recommendations: On Intrapartum Care for a Positive Childbirth Experience.* Geneva: World Health Organization.
Wikander, Ola. 2010. "Job 3,8 – Cosmological Snake-Charming and Leviathanic Panic in an Ancient Near Eastern Setting." *ZAW* 122: 265–71.
Wilson, Gerald Henry. 2007. *Job.* Understanding the Bible Commentary Series. Grand Rapids: Baker Books.
Wilson, Lindsay. 2015. *Job.* Two Horizons Old Testament Commentary. Grand Rapids: Eerdmans.
Wolde, E. J. van. 2006. "Towards an 'Integrated Approach' in Biblical Studies, Illustrated with a Dialogue between Job 28 and Job 38." Pages 355–80 in *Congress Volume Leiden 2004.* Edited by A. Lemaire. VTSup 109. Leiden: Brill.
Würzbach, Natascha. 2005. "Motif." Pages 322–23 in *Routledge Encyclopedia of Narrative Theory.* Edited by David Herman, Manfred Jahn, and Marie-Laure Ryan. London: Routledge.
Wyatt, Nicolas. 2002. *Religious Texts from Ugarit.* 2nd ed., BibSem 53. London: Sheffield Academic.
Zerries, Otto. 2005. "Lord of the Animals." Pages 5512–16 in vol. 8 of *Encyclopedia of Religion.* Edited by Lindsay Jones. 15 vols. 2nd ed. Detroit: Macmillan Reference USA.
Zwan, Pieter van der. 2017. "Some Psychoanalytical Meanings of the Skin in the Book of Job." *Verbum et Ecclesia* 38.1:1–8.
—. 2019a. "Job's Emotional Struggle with the Womb: Some Psychoanalytic Interpretations." *JSem* 28.2:1–21.
—. 2019b. "Scanning the Body Image of Job Psychoanalytically." *HTS* 75.3: 1–8.

Index of Ancient Literature

Hebrew Bible
Genesis

1	229, 235
1–2:4a	138–141, 147, 150–51, 175, 334
1:3	139, 152–55, 334
1:7	139
1:11	*84*
1:12	*84*
1:14	139
1:20	75
1:20–25	289
1:21	139, *236*
1:22	285
1:26	139
1:28	*84*
2:2	139
2:6–7	185
2:7	123, 185
2:9	165
2:22	214, 216
3:16	*84*
3:19	108, 111–12, 116, 122–24, 185
3:21	201
4:25–26	75
7:4	235
7:11	*260*
8:2	*260*
8:7	108
9	229
9:13–16	*239*
13:16	185
15:15	*149*
16:2	76, 215
18:8	194, 267
20:18	76
21:24	194
25:6	*82*
26:5	240
27:9	308
27:28	235
29:31	76
29:6	194
30:2	76, *84*
30:3	215
30:22	76,
30:22–23	*161*
35:16–18	74
38:9	76, *84*
38:27–30	74, 250
38:29	82, 296, 299
49:25	118,
49:25–26	*84*,
50:23	164

Exodus

1:14	185
1:15	73
1.16	73
2:1	214
2:12	162
3:8	194
4:22	*79*
4:23	300
9:25	235
15:1–18	236
15:6	*322*
15:8	192

16:14	235, 272	28:3–6	84
16:31	*84*	28:4	76
21:22	75	28:24	185
23:26	75	32	29, 80
24:15–16	239	32:1–19	319
25:20	206	32:5	*79–80*
26:236	208	32:6	*79*, 80
28:41	201	32:10	*79*
32:13	183	32:11	310
38:23	208	32:13–14	*79–80*
40:13	201	32:18	*69, 69, 78, 80, 82*
40:34	239		

Leviticus

		Judges	
12:2	*76*	3:22	77
15:16	*76, 84*	4:19	194
16:22	300	13:15	*85*
20:24	194	16:13–14	208
22:28	311		
23:43	215	Joshua	
26:4	*84*	2:15	295
		7:21	162

Numbers

		Ruth	
5:28	76	4:16	164
11:12	*79*		
11:12–14	*79*, 319	First Samuel	
11:13	*79*	1:5	77
12:10–12	271	1:5–6	*161*
12:12	77	1:20	75
16:30	186	4:19	294, 298
20:26	201	4:19–22	74–75
20:26–28	126	4:22	*79*
		17:18	194

Deuteronomy

		Second Samuel	
4:11	239	2:18	293
5:22	239	7:11	214
6:3	194		
8:5	*80*	First Kings	
8:6	*80*	11:27	77
11:14	235	12:26	214
11:17	235	20:12	214
14:21	308		
15:12	300	Second Kings	
22:6–7	308, 311	2:14	201
22:7	300	2:21	75
25:9	214–15		

4:39	295, 299	3:5–9	151–52
13:7	185	3:6	139, 145, 154
		3:6–7	136
First Chronicles		3:6–9	148
7:23	75	3:7	160
29:11	322	3:8	139, 151, 155–58, 176, 336
Job		3:8–9	136
1	21–22, *236*, 329, 333, 34	3:9	145, 148, 153–54, 166, 336
1:2–5	129	3:10	32, 94, 136, 140, 146, 151, 163–64, 166–67, 169, 173, 220, 241, 336
1:2–3	129		
1:7–8	*222*		
1:10	127, 217, 239	3:10–11	86, 94, 144, 152
1:10–19	127	3:10–12	166–67, 169, 173
1:20	108	3:10b–12	166
1:21	32, 32–33, *84*, 107–131, 133, 144, 204, 218, 220, 300, 333–34	3:10–15	172, 177
		3:10–19	161, 169, 171, 173
		3:10–23	166
1:21a	108, 110–111, 114–15, 119–20, 122	3:10–26	228
		3:11	143–44, 146, 161–64, 169, 220
1:21aa	107–8, 110, 112		
1:21ab	107, 109, 110, 124, 130	3:11a	*162*
1:21b	111, 122, 125, 131	3:11–12	151
1:21ba	107–8, 120	3:11–19	135–37, 147
1:21bb	107–8	3:11–26	137
2:3	186	3:12	144, 154, 163–65, 176
2:4–5	201, 204	3:12–25	141
2:9	129	3:13	139, 143, 149, 171–173, 177
3	21–22, 32, 34, 114, 131, 133–77, 179, 219, 223–24, 230–31, 274, 329, 333–37, 342, 344	3:13–15	32, 136, 161, 167, 169, 173, 175
		3:13–19	223
3–37	285	3:14–15	171, 172
3:1	158	3:16	77, 86, 137, 146, 148–49, 151–52, 163–64, 166–67, 169, 173, 177, 220, 223
3:1–9	150–61		
3:1–10	150		
3:3	136, 151, 159–60		
3:3–9	158, 161, 169	3:16–19	172, 177
3:3–10	135–37, 142, 147, 155, 159	3:17	111, 158, 169, 173
		3:17–18	136
3:3–11	140	3:17–19	149, 161, 167, 172–73, 175, 177
3:3–13	138		
3:4	139, 145–46, 148, 150–55, 175, 334	3:18	173, 324
		3:19	111, 172–73
3:4–5	136		

3:20	137, 163, 167, 173, 220, 223	10:8–11	182
		10:8–12	179, 181–219, 221, 223, 225, 324, 336–37
3:20–26	135, 141, 147, 161, 169		
3:21	162, 167, 173	10:8–17	228
3:21–22	223	10:9	75, 108, 123, 182, 184, 188, 190
3:22	169, 173		
3:21–23	137	10:9–10	204, 207
3:23	137, 159, 173	10:9–11	179, 182–83, 197, 201, 218
3:24	173		
3:25	173	10:9–12	182
3:24–26	137, 159, 173	10:10	76, 179, 186, 191–200, 267–68, 272
3:26	158, 173		
4:10	309	10:11	75, 180, 204–5, 207, 210, 217, 239, 248
4:10–11	285, 309,		
4:14	205	10:11a	200, *200*, 207, 210
4:19	185, 215	10:11b	200, 207–8, *200*, 215
5:6–7	*22*	10:12	180, 182, 219, 222, 293
5:9–10	266	10:13–17	182, 219
6:5	285	10:14	219, 224
6:12	207	10:14–19	222
6–7	20	10:16	219, 286
7:3	163	10:18	90, 108, 143, 166, 219, 223, 300, 336
7:5	201–2, 204		
7:6	208, 216	10:18–19	86, 179–181, 184, 219–25
7:7	183		
7:12	253	10:19	168, 219, 223–24
7:17–21	219	10:20	184
8:22	201	11:12	285
9–10	182, 220	12:7–10	285
9:2–3	188	12:14–15	253
9:4–12	228	12:17–21	126
9:12	188	14:1	*22*
9:20–23	190	14:3	219
9:24	224	14:13	87, 169
9:25–26	184	15:7	*22*
10	21–22, 76, 179–226, 274, 329, 333–37, 344	15:14	*22*
		15:35	*22*
10–12	182	16:8	201–2, 204
10:2–7	190	16:13	295, 299, *299*
10:3	182	17:15	224
10:3–8	184	17:16	123
10:4–5	183	18:10	162
10:5	184	19:9	126
10:7	182	19:13–19	202
10:8	182, 186, 203	19:20	205
10:8–9	186	19:20–26	201

20:11	*119*, 204–5	38:6b	238
20:17	267	38:8	78, *81*, 108, 140, 220, 241, 243–44, 250, 258, 336–37
21:10	*22*, 295,		
21:23–24	205		
21:24	195–96, *196*	38:8–9	240–42
21:26	123	38:8–10	32, 166, 220
22:21	201	38:8–11	166, 227, 229, 237–59, 265, 274–76, 303, 331–32, 338–39
24:5	285		
24:5–12	126		
24:20	*22*, 143	38:9	239–42, 248, 258, 336
25:4	*22*	38:9–11	241
26:8	*239*, 248	38:10	240–41, 249–50, 299–300, 336–37
26:10	240		
26:10–12	253	38:10a	248–49
26:10–13	235	38:10–11	240–42, 248–50, 258
26:12	158	38:12	145, 154, 262
26:12–13	236	38:16	253, 262
27:16	185	38:17	262
29–31	127	38:22	262
29:14	201	38:22–23	266
30:11	300	38:22–30	253
30:17	205	38:22–38	*235*, 238, 291
30:30	201, 205	38:22–23	259
31:13–15	172	38:23	233, 235, 272
31:15	*22*	38:25	263
33:6	185	38:25–26	259
34:15	123	38:25–27	260, 272
34:22	111	38:28	261, 266
36:29	266	38:28a	261, 264–65
36:27–37:22	234	38:28b	261
37:10	267, 273	38:28b–29	265
37:11	*260*	38:28–29	32, 166, 183, 192, 195–96, *199*, 227, 230, 233, 259–77,
38	21–22, 32, 71, 227–77, 329, 337		
38–39	227, 279–327, 332, 337–42	38:29	108, 220, 261, 291, 300
38–41	228, 283, 285, 344	38:29a	261,
38:2	291	38:29b	261,
38:2–3	237	38:30	267–68, 272
38:2–39:20	237	38:31	291, 342
38:4–7	238	38:34	260
38:4–11	*235*, 238	38:36	263
38:4–21	237	38:37	260, 263
38:5	263	38:39	290, 308, 309
38:5–6	238	38:39–41	*279*, 287, 307, 318
38:6	263	38:39–39:30	*235*, 238, 279–327

39	21–22, 79, 228, 276, 279–327, 329, 337–41	22:10	*81*, 81–82, *239*
		22:10–11	220, 226
39:1	293–94	22:10–12	183
39:1–3	273	22:12–14	286
39:1–4	279, 292–304	22:14	*219*
39:2	294	23	199, *285*
39:2–3	342	25:6	183
39:3	293–95, 298–300, 325, 337, 342	27:5	214
		27:10	*79*, 79
39:4	108, 293, 300	28:5	214
39:5	303, 342	34:21	204
39:5–6	291	35:17	*219*
39:6	254, 291, 322	36:6	289
39:6–8	303, 318	45:15	208
39:13	305	46:4	236
39:13a	305	48:7	80, *89*
39:13b	305	49:18	129, 333
39:13–18	292, 304–7	50:10–11	*285*, 289
39:14	305	51	29
39:16	306	52:7	215
39:17	291, 304–5, 322	57:5	*219*
39:18	305	58:7	309
39:19	304	58:9	75, 77, 162
39:27–30	307–8	65:7	*322*
40:17	204, 210, 216	65:8	236
40:18	205, 207	65:10	235
40:22	206	68:6	*79*
40:23	239	69:16	186
40:26	236	71	31, *81*
40–41	228, 276	71:2–6	183
41:9	267	71:6	*81*, 81–82, 220, *239*
		74:12–14	235–36
Psalms		77:15–21	236
2:6	206, 239	78:48	235
2:6–7	*206*	84:4	310
2:7	31, 78, *79*, 83	87:4	236
2:9	185	88	*119*
7:3	*219*	88:6	*119*
9:12	183	88:7	*119*
9:18	111	88:15	*119*
10:9	*219*	89:10–11	235–36
13:4	*119*	89:27	*79*
17:12	*219*, 309	89:48	183
18:8	*322*	90:2	31, 78, 82–83
18:10–12	239	90:3	123
22	31, *81*	90:3–6	185

91:4	206, 214	148	289
93	236	148:6	240
93:1–4	236		
95:5	183	Proverbs	
96	236	1:12	86
97:2	239	3:22	*79*
98	236	5:18–19	293
102	29	7:23	295, 299
102:27	126	8:23	206–7, 239
103:13	*79*	8:23–24	82, *206*
103:14–15	185	8:27–29	235
104	*235*, 236, 285, 290	22:2	172
104:2–9	*235*	27:20	86
104:6–9	236	30:4	248
104:9	240	30:15–16	86, *119*
104:10–13	*235*	30:17	309
104:11–30	*235*	30:18–19	285
104:21	290–91, 310, 316	30:33	194
104:26	236, *236*	31:19	208
104:29	123, 185		
105:32–33	235	Ecclesiastes	
106:7–12	236	3:30	123–24
109:29	201	5:13	129
110	83	5:14	108–9, 116, 118, 125,
110:3	31, 78, 82–83, *83*, 235,		129,
	264, 270	6:3	75, 77, 162, 168
114:4	308	11:5	205
114:3–8	236	12:7	123
119:61	295		
132:9	201	Song of Songs	
132:18	201	4:11	195
135:7	*260*	3:5	293
139	76, 180, 218, 222	5:1	195
139:13	*76*, 76, 179, 183, *200*,		
	205–8, 239	Isaiah	26, 31
139:13–15	84, 112–13, 116, 118,	1:2	*79–80*
	172, 199, 216	1:4	*80*
139:13–16	268	5:14	86
139:15	76, 85, 118, 130, 204,	5:29	309
	208, 216	10:6	185
141:7	295, 299	11:6	308
146:4	111, 123, 185	11:6–8	285, 310, 316
147:9	289, 291, 308, 310, 316	11:7	308
147:16	271	13:8	80, *89*
147:16–17	235	13:18	76
147:16–18	267	20:3–4	126

21:3	*89*	51:15	158
24:18	260	55:9	90
25:12	185	55:10	84, *84*, 235
26:5	185	55:11	108
26:16–19	*149*	58:11	204
26:17	*89*	61:10	201
26:17–18	87	63:8	79
26:17–19	118	63:16	79
26:17–20	86–87	64:7	79, 80, 185, 190
26:18	*162*	64:7–8	183
26:19	85, 87, 123	66:7–14	88
26:20	87	66:7	*299*
27:1	236	66:8	*82*
28:26	*80*	66:9	78, *81*, 81–82, 88, 90, 106, 220, 241, 249, 296, 299
29:16	185		
30:1	*79–80*		
30:9	*79–80*	66:9–10	226
30:14	186	66:9–13	89
32:12	*84*	66:13	79
33:23	295		
34:15	*299*	Jeremiah	26
35:6	293	3:4	79
38:1	204	3:19	79
38:9	239	4:31	*89*
38:12	208, 215–16	5:22	235, 240
41	26	6:24	*89*
41:25	185	10:13	260
42:13–14	81	10:20	215
42:14	80, 89	12	26
43	26	13:21	*89*
43:20	286	16:3	*81*
44:22	*239*	17:5–8	29
45:10	79	18:1–11	186
45:9–10	78, 80, 183–84, 188, 199	18:4	185
		18:6	185
45:9–11	185	20:14–18	86, 146, 159
45:11	79	20:15	73, 159, *159*
48:4	204	20:17	86, 162–63
48:7	80	22:28	185
49:13–15	*89*	23:9	204
49:15	79	30:6	80, *89*
49:20–21	88	31:9	79
50:9	126	31:15–16	*149*
51:2	82	31:20	79
51:9	236	35:2	214
51:14	*149*	42:10	214

48:41	*89*	Joel	
49:24	*89*	2:2	239
50:43	*89*		
51:34–37	236	Amos	
		5:8	*260*
Lamentations			
3:6	*119*	Jonah	
3:42	206	2:3	87
3:44	*239*	4:5	214
4:3	304–6, 311		
		Micah	26
Ezekiel		1:8	304
13:11	235	4:9–10	*89*
16	75	4:10	*81*, 239
16:4	126, 239	6	26
16:4–5	75		
16:7	293	Nahum	
16:10	201, 248	3:13	185
16:37–39	126		
19:3	309	Habakkuk	
23:29	126	3:16	204
26:16	208		
28:18	185	Zephaniah	
32:2	239	1:15	239
32:22–30	111		
34:12	239	Zechariah	
36:27	240	14:6	192
37:6–9	205		
38:9	*239*	Malachi	30
38:16	*239*	1:6	*79*
41:26	240	2:10	*79*

Hosea	
2:1	*79*
2:5	109, 126
4:16	28
5:14	*219*
6:4	*239*
11:1	*79*
11:1–4	318–19
11:3	*79*
13:7	*219*
13:8	311
13:13–14	86–87, *149*
14:6–8	83

Apocrypha

Wisdom of Solomon	
7:1–2	192
9:15	215
Sirach	
40:1	87–88, 112, 116–17
43:19–20	267, *267*
43:20	102

Sumerian and Akkadian Texts

Atraḫasis	84, 100–101, 104, 145, 184, 191, 273, *312*
I 202–214	*184, 191*
I 277–89	101
I iv 46–49	104
III iii 32–37	145
III iii 33	*273*
Enuma Elish	157, 191, 228, 235, 236
IV 101	236
IV 36–38	*236*
IV 95	*236*
IV 137–139	241
VI 5–6	*191*

Babylonian Theodicy
26

BAM 240 250

CBS
1509   *250*
10489   *250*
10756   *250*

Creation of Pickax
104

Descent of Ishtar 126

Enki and Ninḫursaga
100

Enki and Ninmaḫ *191*

Enki and the World Order
103–4

Hymn to Nungal 104

KUB IV. 13   *99*

Ligabue Tablets   *99*, 101, 255

Lamentation over the Destruction of Ur
145

Ludlul-Bel-Nemeqi
26, *26*

SpbTU I no. 44:67
165

UM 29-15-367   97–98, *97–99*, 191, *191*, *242–43, 260*

VAS 10 189   *250*

VAT
8381   *97, 191, 242–43*
8869 (BAM248)   94, *94*, 96–100, *100*, *242–43*, 243, *270, 294*, 296, 301, 303

YBC
4603   95, *95*, 242, 296
5636   *250*

YOS 11, 19   103

Hittite Texts

Appu and His Two Sons
100

Songs of Kumarbi 100

Sun God and the Cow
99

Ugaritic Texts (*KTU*)

1.1–1.6	*99*, 228, 235–36, *239*, 263, 266
1.3	
i 22–27	263
ii 40–41	260
iii 38–42	236
iv 43–44	260
1.4	
iv.54–57	263
vii 17–19	260
vii 25–28	260
vii 59–60	260
1.5	
i 1–8	236
v 2–6	239
v 17–25	99
v 23–26	239
1.6	
ii 6–9	*314*
1.10	*313*
1.11	*313*
1.13	313
1.17–19	100
1.23	100, *294*
1.101	
3–4	*260*

Rabbinic Literature

Mishnah
m. Shabb. 7:2	207
m. Sukkah 1:4	207

Palestinian Talmud
y. Shabb. 7:2, 10c	207

Babylonian Talmud
b. Ber. 62b	207
b. Menah. 97a	207

Leviticus Rabbah 193

Greek Literature

Aeschylus
Cho. 127–29	116–17
Ag. 140–143	*314*

Aristotle
Gen. An.
II, 4 739B	192
II, 4 737A	*192*
II, 4.735 A–B	*193*

Homer
Il.
	314
21.470	*314*

Homeric Hymns *87*

Hesiod
Theog.	116, 164
126–45	*116*
Op.	*87*
609–614	260

Hippocrates
Nat. Puer.
VII 486	*192*

Index of Modern Authors

Abusch, Tzvi W 312
Alter, Robert 22, 32, 142, 147–48, 230, 233, 262–63
Andersen, Francis I. 110, 264
Andrews, William A. 29
Arnold, Bill T. 205, 238, 298

Balentine, Samuel 110, 115, 139, 180, 198, 241–42
Barkay, Gabriel 113–14
Basson, Alec 27
Bergmann, Claudia D. 28, 31, 74–75, 81, 89, 94, 100, 255
Beyse, K.-M 204
Blau, Joshua 299
Boddy, Janice 105
Boris, Lazzaro 27
Boss, Jeffery 74
Botterweck, Johannes G 308–9
Bowdle, Brian 40
Breier, Idan 311
Breitkopf, Alexander W. 137, 139
Brenner, Athalya 229
Brettler, Marc Zvi 27
Brown, William P. 180, 183, 225–26, 228, 232, 323
Burnight, John 141, 150
Burns, John Barclay 146
Butz, Kilian 250

Caballero, Rosario 62
Caird, George Badford 27
Campbell, John 66
Caquot, A. 194
Chilton, Paul 214

Cho, Paul K. K. 236, 247, 254
Choi 205, 238, 298
Claassens, L. Juliana M. 31, 81, 89
Clines, David J. A. 25, 78, 109–13, 115, 129, 140, 142, 149–50, 156, 158–60, 163, 182, 196, 198, 205, 230, 241, 262–63, 267, 280–81, 286, 290–91, 293, 295, 300, 305, 308–10, 318, 322
Cooper, Alan 262
Couto-Ferreira, Erica M. 94, 104–5
Croft, William 44
Cruse, Alan 44
Cunningham, Graham 191
Curtis, Robert I. 193–94

Dahlen, Hannah 251
Dahood, Mitchell 156
Dancygier, Barbara 47, 68
Day, John 229
Day, Peggy L. 293, 313–14
Dell, Katharine J. 285–86, 306
Descamp, Mary Therese 28–30, 47, 60, 69
Dhorme, Edouard 109, 112, 115, 156, 159, 163, 182, 198, 200, 264, 267, 295, 305
Dick, Michael Brennan 282
Dickson, Keith 104
DiFransico, Lesley R. 28
Dijk, J.J.A. van 93–97, 99, 103, 191, 242–43, 260, 296
Dille, Sarah 27–28, 31, 69, 79, 85, 185
Doak, Brian R. 242, 281, 286–87, 310, 323, 326
Driver, G. R. 295
Driver, Samuel Rolles 110, 299

Dunn, Jonathan 66

Ebeling, Erich 94, 97, 242–43, 270, 296
Eckstein. Juliane Maria n 32, 144, 162–65
Eidevall, Göran 27
Eising, Herman 298
Erickson, Amy 201
Evans, Vyvyan 36, 40–42, 47, 55, 57

Fauconnier, Gilles 43–48, 52, 54–57, 59, 64, 69, 119, 124, 160
Finkel, Irving L. 250–51
Fisch, Harold 198
Fishbane, Michael 138–40, 150–51, 155–56, 158, 176
Flynn, Shawn W. 168
Fohrer, Benjamin R. 110, 156, 163, 295
Foster, Sahwn W. 98, 100, 103–4, 191, 250, 255
Fox, Michael V. 262
Franke, Chris 81, 88
Freedman, David N. 91
Frevel, Christian 180, 193, 195, 272, 290
Frymer-Kensky, Tikva Simone 84, 312
Fuchs, Gisela 283

Garroway, Kristine Henriksen 168
Gault, Brian P. 27
Gentner, Dedre 40
George, A. R. 96
Gibbs, Raymond W. 41, 61, 68
Gibson, John C. L. 229, 263–64
Glucksberg, Sam 40
Goering, Greg Schmidt 47
Gomola, Aleksander 30, 47, 69
Good, Eswin M. 295
Goossens Louis 42
Gordis, Robert 110, 156, 179–80, 198, 205, 231
Gordon, Cyrus H 229
Grady, Joseph E. 40, 43, 50, 59, 218
Grant, Jamie A. 139
Gray, George Buchanan 110, 299
Gray, John 200, 264, 295
Green, Alberto R. W. 266

Green, Barbara 27
Green, Joel B. 29
Green, Stefan 81, 88
Greenstein, Edward L. 32, 94–95, 146, 156, 159, 166, 241, 306, 336
Grogan, Geoffery 200
Grohmann, Marianne 29, 31, 78, 81–83
Gunkel, Hermann 156

Habel, Norman C. 25, 110, 112, 139, 156, 158–59, 163, 180, 182, 198, 205, 210, 222, 229–30, 241–42, 247, 264, 266–67, 290, 293, 295, 305
Halvorson-Taylor, Martien A. 28, 88, 149
Ham, T. C. 263
Hamp, Vinzen 293
Häner, Tobias 140–42, 150
Hankins, Davis 232–33
Hard, Robin 314–15
Hartley, John E. 110, 115, 163, 180, 198, 240–41, 262
Hawley, John E. 28, 69, 281, 283, 286, 308–10
Hays, Christopher B. 104, 114
Hine, Daryl 87
Horne, Milton 286, 310, 323, 326
Horst, Friedrich 109, 156, 163
Hossfeld, Frank-Lothar 83, 200
Howe, Bonnie 29
Huff, Barry R. 280–81
Hulster, Izaak J. de 29, 69

Jacobsen, Thorild 102, 144–45, 311–12, 314
Jäkel, Olof 28
Janowski, Bernd 28
Jenni, Ernst 295
Jindo, Job Y. 27–28
Johandi, Andreas 250
Johnson, Mark 28, 35–42, 61, 68
Jones, Peter Murray 105
Joode, Johan de 27

Index of Modern Authors

Kang, Chol-Gu 22, 280, 283, 286, 322
Katz, Dina 66, 117
Kazen, Thomas 29–30
Keel Othmar 22, 32, 85, 87, 110, 113–14, 229, 280, 282–85, 288, 313–14
Keller, Catherine 241–42
Kellerman, Diether 240
Keysar, Boaz 40
Kim, Brittany 28
Kimmel, Michael 68–69
Kindstedt, Paul S. 193–94
King, Philip J. 184
Kitz, Anne Marie 145
Kotzé, Zacharias 27
Kövecses Zoltán 35–39, 41–42, 44, 47, 51, 59–66
Krainer, Antonia 23, 29
Kramer, Samuel N. 100
Krebernik, Manfred 117
Krolokke, Charlotte H. 105
Kronholm, Tryggve 91, 307
Kruger, Paul A. 27
Kubina, Veronika 155, 229
Kynes, Will 180, 183, 225–26

Labahn, Antje 27–28
Lakoff, Gerorge 28, 35–42, 61, 64–66, 68, 70, 84, 149, 214, 329
Lam, Joseph 28
Lambert, David A. 108
Lambert, Wilfred G. 98–101, 145, 184, 191, 241, 255, 273
Lamprecht, At 27
Lancaster, Mason D. 27–28
Lang, Bernhard 284–85, 287, 311
Langacker, Ronald W. 36
Langton, Karen 32, 94–95, 142–43, 147, 152, 165–67, 169, 336
Law, Jane Marie 105
Leonard, Jeffery M. 139, 159
Levenson, Jon D. 229
Lévêque, Jean 85, 110, 113, 264, 290
Lev-Tov, Justin 193
Linafelt, Tod 232

Lindström, Fredrik 229
Longrigg, James 192
Loon, Hannecke van 141
Lugt, Pieter van der 288, 309–10
Lundhaug, Hugo 30, 47, 69
Lundholm, J. R. 91

Macky, Peter W. 27
Maier, Cristl M. 88
Malul, Meir 75
Mathewson, Dan 115, 224
McFague, Sallie 27
McKane, William 146
Mettinger, Tryggve N. D. 229, 241, 247, 263–64
Meyer, Nicholas 32, 198
Mies, Francoise 115
Miller, James E. 322
Moor, Johannes Cornelius de 239, 260
Most Glenn W. 116, 260
Moughtin-Mumby, Cornelius 27
Murray, A. T. 314

Nel. P. J. 28, 156
Neumann-Gorsolke, Ute 283
Newsom, Carol A. 33, 85, 110, 112, 114, 156, 158, 200, 228–29, 231–32, 241–42, 254, 264, 266, 281, 288, 290
Nielsen, Kirsten 144–45
Nier, H. 126
Nõmmik, Urmas 234

O'Connor, Katheen M. 231
Oeming, Manfred 280, 283
Oorschot, Jürgen 125–26
Osborne, William R. 27
Oshima, Takayoshi 26
Ottoson, Magnus 90
Otzen, B. 164

Pantoja, Jennifer Metten 27
Patton, Corrine 231
Paul, Shalom 4–5, 95
Pease, Anna S. 248

Peck, A. L. 192–93
Pelham, Abigal 140, 158, 181
Perdue, Leo G. 110, 139–41, 155, 158, 240, 263–64, 280
Pettys, Valarie Forstman 139, 142
Pinker, Aron 249
Plantin, Lisa 3, 6, 8, 227, 279
Pope, Marvin H. 109, 111, 115, 156, 163, 198, 241, 264, 267, 305
Potter, Paul 192
Preuss, Horst-Dietrich, 90
Pyeon, Yohan 139
Pyrhönen, Heta 22

Quick, Laura 126

Rancour-Laferriere, Daniel 114, 129, 198
Reece, William David 148–49
Regt, Lénart de 264–65
Ricoeur, Paul 67
Ringren, Helmer 185
Robinette, S. J. 29, 47
Rodin, Therese 100, 117, 312
Roller, Lynn E 314
Ross, William A. 29
Rowley, Harold Henry 110, 264

Sasson, Vanessa R 105
Schafer, Rahel A. 286
Schifferdecker, Kathryn 32–33, 114, 230, 241–42
Schlimm, Matthew R. 27
Schmid, Konrad 140, 158
Schmidt, N. F. 28, 156
Scholnick, Sylvia Huberman 228
Schreiner, J. 90, 261
Schroer, Silvia 32, 85, 87, 110, 113, 280, 282–84
Schultz, Richard L. 109
Scurlock, JoAnn 74, 93, 102–3, 250–51
Semino, Elena 63–64
Seow, 110, 112, 139–40, 142, 156, 159, 163, 194, 198, 200
Shead, Stephen L. 23, 27

Sherman, Philip 311
Simkins, Ronald A. 104, 151
Sjöberg, Åke W. 104
Sommerfeld, W. 101
Sommerstein, Alan H. 117, 314
Soskice, Jamet Martin 27
Spieser, Cathie 104
Steen, Gerard 40, 63–64
Stol, Marten 73–75, 93–95, 97–103, 165, 168, 191–94, 198, 242–43, 251, 270, 273, 296
Stordalen, Terje 32, 85, 110, 116, 118
Strawn, Brent A 29, 69
Stump, Eleonore 306
Sweetser, Eve 28–29, 47, 60, 68

Tilford, Nocole L. 27
Tönsing, Detlev 139
Trible, Phyllis 263
Tromp, Nicholas J. 57, 88, 109, 149, 175
Tsevat, Matitiahu 262–63
Turner, Mark 43–48, 52, 54–57, 64–66, 69–70, 84, 119, 124, 149, 160, 329
Tur-Sinai 110–11, 159, 241, 249, 264, 295, 305

Uehlinger, Christoph 113, 313

Vall, Gregory 32, 84–85, 109–16, 118, 144, 180–81, 187–88, 195–96, 224, 262–63, 265
Van Hecke, Pierre 27–28, 69, 148, 180, 188, 198, 207, 212
Veldhuis, Nick 93–94, 97–100, 102–3, 293–94, 303
Verde, Danilo 27–28
Vernant, Jean-Pierre 314
Viberg, Åke 8, 29, 163
Vogels, Walter 108

Wagner, Siegfried 215
Wälchli, Stefan 141, 148
Walls, Niel 313
Watson, Wilfred 313
Watson, Rebecca Sally 236

Weiss, Andrea L. 23
Weiss, Meir 84
Wikander, Ola 156–57
Willoughby, B. E. 239
Wilson, Gerard Henry 263
Wilson, Lindsay 264
Wolde, E. J. Wolde 262

Würzbach, Natascha 22
Wyatt, William F. 313–14

Zenger, Erich 83
Zerries, Otto 284
Zwan, Piter van der 32, 85, 114, 143–44, 147, 169, 181, 201, 204, 224

Index of Subjects

accusation (accuse) 21, 24, 136, 156, 179–82, 219–20, 222, 224–26, 228–29, 274, 342
afterbirth 90, 102–3
Akkadian birth incantations 23, 25, 32, 93–99, 102, 105, 142–43, 166–67, 227, 234, 241, 249–50, 258, 270, 279, 293, 296, 298, 300, 329, 332, 336–37
Akkadian birth metaphors 105–6, 167, 258, 293, 297, 312, 361
amniotic sac 102, 104, 195, 249
amniotic fluid 23, 95–97, 99, 143, 195, 234, 242–59, 270, 275, 277, 330, 332, 338
Anat 313–14
animals
 – domesticated 284, 286, 293, 310–15, 319
 – wild 21, 33, 227–29, 232–38, 253–54, 265, 273–27, 330, 337–43
anthropomorphism 63, 286–87, 303, 310, 324
Asalluḫi 5–97, 100–101, 250, 296, 312

Baal 236, 239, 263–66, 313–14
barren 76, 85–88, 92, 118–19, 134–36, 160–61, 272
begetter 23, 78–80, 91, 183–84, 198–200, 217, 233, 261, 266, 271–72, 335
Behemoth 204, 210, 228–29, 231, 253–54, 276, 280–83, 344
birth
 – and combat 255–58
 – and creation 82, 138, 150–52, 324, 334
 – and death 85–88, 112–125, 131, 140–41, 333, 334
 – and exile 81, 88
 – and precipitation 230, 261
 – as rainfall 96–99, 105–6, 234, 243–44, 259, 270, 275, 332
 – as breaking 23, 26, 74, 77, 81–82, 91, 94, 97, 102, 104, 106, 186, 234, 237, 245–59, 275, 279, 292–303, 325, 331–32, 337–38, 341
 – as untying ropes 96–97, 99, 296–303, 332, 341
 – complications 71, 74, 88, 98–99, 106, 162, 167, 252
 – goddess 101, 117, 312–14
 – incantations (see Akkadian birth incantations)
 – stones (birth stool) 73, 75–76, 91, 93, 102
 – of the sea 21, 227, 228, 233, 237–259, 266, 268, 270, 274, 276, 287, 337
 – of wild animals 273, 276, 293, 303
birthing custard (see vernix)
blended space 44–50, 53–55, 58, 67, 69, 121, 128, 153, 157, 170, 174, 187, 189, 197, 203, 209, 211, 213, 221–22, 243–44, 246, 252, 256–57, 269, 297, 302, 317, 321
blending schema 24, 45–70, 128, 154, 171, 177, 198, 221–22, 244–45, 247, 251, 255, 298, 301, 320, 329–31
blending theory 21–30, 33, 35, 39–41, 43–72, 107, 147, 175, 329–31, 343–44
blood 75, 89, 92, 98, 106, 184, 191–92, 250, 255–56, 270, 277, 289, 308, 316, 318
body fluids 192, 199, 218, 268–273
body parts 37, 63, 96, 180, 188, 196, 200–217

bonds 95–99, 254, 260, 279, 288, 291–96, 300–304, 319, 324–25, 332, 337, 339–43
bone (bones) 76, 95–97, 181, 191, 200–218, 225, 335–36, 342
booth 206–7, 212–18, 225, 335–36
breastfeeding 163–65, 176, 192, 196
build 32, 37, 42, 91, 207, 212–18, 225, 235, 336

caretaker 21, 120, 176, 247, 280, 283, 285, 292, 306, 315, 320, 323, 326, 338–39, 343
ceramic 123, 185–90, 198, 218, 225
chaos 133, 138–40, 151, 155–56, 158, 176, 228, 230–31, 233, 280, 282, 284
cheese 179–81, 183, 188, 191–200, 202, 204, 207, 209, 212, 214, 217–18, 225, 268, 271–72, 332, 335–36, 342
cheesemaker 179–82, 191–200, 202, 209, 214, 216–17
clay 76, 80, 93, 123, 145, 179, 181, 183–91, 196, 198, 200, 202–4, 207, 209, 212, 214, 216–18, 225–26, 335–36
clothe (clothes) (see dress) 48, 52, 108, 120–31, 181, 201–4, 208, 210, 212, 216–17, 225, 238–39, 248, 274–75, 335
cloud 67, 133, 230, 237, 239, 248, 259, 266, 275
coagulate (coagulation) 183, 191–200, 209, 212, 215, 217–18, 225, 234, 267–69, 271–74, 332, 336
combat motif 22, 24, 227–29, 233, 237, 240, 246–55, 258–59, 274–76, 282–84, 287, 331, 337–40
combat myth 235–36, 254, 283
compendium for a woman in childbirth 94, 99–101, 345–46
conceive 73, 79, 90–91, 133–36, 150, 158–61, 169, 176, 179, 335
conception 21, 76–78, 83, 90, 93, 106, 133–37, 143, 146, 148, 150–51, 154–55, 158–61, 165–66, 175, 192, 199, 313, 334–36, 342
correlation metaphors 37–40, 42–43, 59, 61, 64, 69, 84

counterfactual blends 29, 57–58, 71, 119–22, 124, 130, 173–75, 177, 331, 333
creator 80, 82, 91, 139, 172, 182–85, 188, 198, 204, 216, 219–26, 283–85, 289, 307, 319–20, 322, 324, 333, 335, 337, 342–43
cross-cultural metaphors (see universal metaphors) 83, 105, 131, 184
curdle 188, 191–92, 194, 197, 271
curse 107–8, 129, 131, 133–77, 312

darkness 28, 32, 37, 43, 88, 94–95, 99, 119, 133–55, 160–61, 165–67, 170, 175–76, 223–24, 226, 230, 237, 239, 248, 259, 275, 334–35, 342
day of birth 135–36, 138, 140, 142, 144–46, 150–58, 165, 175–76, 333–35, 342,
day of creation 17, 133, 151–55, 176
death
 – as return 112, 122–24, 130
 – as negation of birth 121–22, 125, 130, 175, 331, 333–5
 – as negation of life 57, 119, 173– 177, 331
 – as sleeping 49, 54, 65, 119, 148–49, 171–72, 177
deer 21, 279, 288–89, 292–304, 306–9, 318, 322, 325, 337, 339, 341–42
dew 82–83, 86, 91, 234, 235, 260–73, 340
deliver (delivery) 21, 23, 33, 73–74, 81–82, 86–87, 89, 97, 103, 106, 162, 164, 182, 219–22, 227, 229, 237, 242–53, 258, 265, 269, 271–75, 290, 295, 303, 332, 337–38, 341–42
double-scope blend 47–69, 171–72, 177, 202, 208, 320, 330
dress 120, 126, 179–80, 182, 200–205, 207, 210, 214–18, 225, 239, 248, 274, 330, 333, 336
dresser 203, 216, 225
dusk 100, 294
dust 85–86, 97–98, 102, 107–13, 122–24, 130, 149, 181, 184–86, 234, 267, 272, 304

eagle 80, 307, 310

elaboration 39–40, 55–56, 60, 62, 64–67, 70, 172, 177, 234, 245
emergent structure 45–51, 55–58, 170–71, 177, 221–22, 246–47, 252, 330–31
entailment 28, 38–39, 59, 68, 71, 200, 218, 270
extension 30, 54, 65, 67, 199, 215, 248, 250, 258–59, 271, 274–75, 319–20, 326, 329

fertility 31, 76, 84–85, 92, 117–18, 130, 141, 161, 266, 293, 312–15, 331
firstborn 74, 77, 79
formation of a fetus/Job 21, 23, 31, 76–77, 82, 84–85, 113, 118, 160, 171, 179–226, 234, 239, 248, 260, 266–71, 273–74, 276, 293, 330, 332–37, 340–42
freedom 24, 76, 150, 230, 276, 279, 283–84, 287–89, 292–93, 300, 303–4, 310, 315, 319–21, 323–27, 330, 334, 338–40, 343
frost (see frozen precipitation) 192, 264–65, 267, 272
frozen precipitation 18, 234, 260, 266, 269–70, 272

generic space 44–70, 121, 128, 153, 157, 170, 174, 187, 189, 197, 203, 209, 211, 213, 221–22, 243–44, 246, 252, 256–57, 269, 297, 302, 317, 321
gestation 76–77, 91, 93, 180–81, 191, 193–96, 198–200, 217–18
God
– as begetter 79–80, 91, 183, 198–200, 217, 272, 335
– as booth builder 207, 213–218
– as caretaker 320, 323
– as cheesemaker 191, 196–200, 217–18
– as co-parent 316, 318, 323, 325–26, 337–39
– as dresser 200, 203, 216, 225
– as handcrafter 76, 183, 196, 199, 200, 207, 210, 212, 225, 335, 336
– as midwife 31, 33, 34, 81–82, 88, 92, 220–26, 237, 239–53, 258, 259, 273–77, 325, 331, 337–43

– as parent 27–29, 64, 68, 79–81, 89, 199, 262, 263, 292, 317–27, 330, 339–40
– as potter 76, 80, 123, 183–90, 199, 202, 216
– as rope plaiter 210–14, 216, 225
– as watcher 219, 221, 223–26, 274, 331, 334
– as weaver 76, 200, 208–10, 212, 215, 225
– opens and shuts wombs 77, 245–54, 265, 341, 342
Grim Reaper 52–54, 65, 67

hail (see frozen precipitation) 97, 102, 234–35, 259, 265–66, 272, 276, 342
handcrafter (crafter) 76, 183, 196, 215–16, 225, 335–37
hardship 77–78, 85–88, 96, 148–50, 173–77, 223, 303
hawk 288–89, 324
hoarfrost (see frozen precipitation) 21, 192, 195, 227, 230, 233–35, 260–61, 266, 268–73, 276–77, 291, 332, 340, 342
humans are plants 54, 76, 85, 92, 118, 123, 185
Hunt (hunting, hunter, huntress) 219, 236, 279–92, 305, 307–9, 311, 313–17, 319–24, 326, 339–40

ibex (see deer, mountain goats) 310, 318
ice (see frozen precipitation) 21, 78, 184, 191–99, 227, 230, 233–35, 260–62, 264, 266–77, 330, 332, 337, 340–42
image schemas 41, 60, 260, 301
incantations (see Akkadian birth incantations)
infertility (see barren) 23, 88, 161
innocence (innocent) 26, 179–81, 183–84, 189–90, 216, 218–19, 225–26, 336
input space 30, 43–70, 73, 78, 121, 128, 153, 156–57, 160, 169–71, 174, 187, 189, 197, 199, 202–3, 209, 211, 213, 221–22, 243–44, 246, 252, 256–57, 268–69, 297–98, 301–2, 317, 321, 329, 335

Index of Subjects

integration network 29, 45–60, 68, 70, 330, 353
intertwine 23, 76, 179–83, 199–201, 204–7, 210–15, 217–18, 225, 281, 335–36, 342
inversion
– of Akkadian birth incantations 32, 143, 167
– of creation 32, 34, 138–41, 147, 150, 333
– of conventional metaphors 141, 147–48, 150
irony 141, 144, 219, 241, 255, 263, 283, 285
kneeling 73, 75, 91, 93, 164, 292, 294, 298–99, 303, 337

labor pain 23, 26, 71, 82, 293, 295
Lamaštu 99, 103, 250
Lament (lamentation) 21–22, 26, 34, 86, 117, 129, 131, 133, 137, 142, 145–48, 162, 177, 180, 201, 204, 225, 274, 284, 334
Leviathan 134–35, 139–40, 151, 155–58, 176, 228–36, 240, 247, 253–54, 276, 281–84, 290, 336, 344
lion 219, 223, 226, 276, 281–84, 287–92, 307–10, 312, 314, 316, 318–19, 322, 324
– young 290, 308–10
loosen bonds 96–97, 279, 300, 303, 319, 325, 342
lord of the animals 22, 279–80, 282–85, 287, 311, 338

Marduk 26, 98, 101, 157, 191–92, 235–36, 241, 248, 312
mental space 43–45, 54, 56, 58–60, 69–70
metonymy 40–43, 52, 69, 77, 115
midwife (midwifery) 21, 23, 31, 33–34, 73–82, 88, 90–106, 117, 145, 163, 167, 219–26, 234, 237, 239, 242–304, 312, 321, 325–26, 329, 331–43
Mother Earth 32, 34, 85, 87, 107, 109–19, 124, 130, 331, 333
mother goddess 96, 100–104, 113–18, 145, 184, 266, 279, 284, 287, 292–94, 303–4, 311–18, 323, 325–26, 337, 339–40,

mountain goats 21, 279, 288–89, 292–304, 306–9, 318–19, 322, 324–25, 327, 337, 339, 341–42

naked (nakedness) 107–9, 114, 119–20, 122, 125–31, 204, 333
night of conception 135–36, 146, 150, 154, 160, 165, 175, 334, 342
Ninḫursaga 96, 100–101, 113, 117, 284, 311–12, 319, 326, 339
Nintur 113, 284, 311–12

organizing frame 43–69, 160, 171, 187–88, 192, 197, 200, 202, 209, 242, 251, 256, 268, 318, 320, 330, 334
ostrich 279, 286, 288–89, 291–92, 304–8, 310, 318, 323–27, 340

perineum (perinial tears) 74, 77, 102, 250–51, 332
personification (personify) 52, 54, 67, 116, 159, 161, 233, 243, 258
plaiter 207–18, 225, 336
plants 53–54, 73, 76–78, 83–85, 90–92, 104, 116, 118, 123, 185, 206–7, 212–17, 331
plants are humans 84–85
plea (petition) 82, 137, 158, 180, 183
postpartum care 101, 103–6
potter 76, 80, 123, 179, 183–90, 192, 198–99, 202, 214, 216, 225
pottery 179, 182, 184–90, 197, 199, 209
precipitation 77, 227, 234–35, 238, 253, 259–77, 290–91, 337, 340, 342
predators (predatory) 29, 148, 281, 287–88, 290, 308, 310, 313, 315–16, 320–22, 327, 340
pregnancy 83, 86, 93, 100, 102, 146, 159–60, 168, 171, 195, 242–43, 245, 251, 294, 297–98, 302, 304, 325, 335
pregnant 90, 96, 98, 103, 303
prey 282, 289–91, 307, 309–10, 317, 320–22, 324

primary metaphor 40, 218

Index of Subjects

procreation 32–34, 77–78, 84, 93, 116, 152, 184, 218, 263, 265–66, 280, 285, 289, 293, 299, 343

rain 67, 84, 90, 145, 212, 227, 230, 234–35, 243–44, 259–66, 268, 270–73, 342
raven 286, 288–89, 291–92, 306–10, 316, 318, 322, 324
rennet 192–94, 196
resemblance metaphors 37–39, 59, 69
return to dust 110, 112, 122–24
reversed metaphors 58, 65–66, 70, 92, 138, 243, 245, 255, 270, 330

sea 21, 33, 34, 78, 87, 95, 96, 99, 139, 140, 143, 156–58, 167, 176, 220, 227–77, 282, 283, 287, 290, 291, 314, 327, 330–32, 336–43
seed 76, 84, 92, 191–92, 314
semen (sperm) 76, 84, 90, 92, 104, 180, 183, 191–200, 218, 269–71
sinews 76, 96, 181, 200–202, 204–18, 225, 297, 302, 335–36, 342
single-scope blend 47–69, 320, 330
skin 77, 127, 181, 200–218, 241, 248, 271, 274, 277, 330, 335
snow (see frozen precipitation) 195, 227, 233–35, 259, 265–67, 271–72, 276, 291, 342
solidification 180, 182, 184, 188, 191–200, 207, 210, 212, 214, 217, 260–62, 266–71, 273, 277, 330, 332, 335, 341
source domain 23, 29, 36–69, 77, 91, 104, 150, 152, 186, 193, 199–200, 202, 208, 217, 227, 249, 254, 259–60, 270, 273, 276, 330–32, 335, 337, 340–41
spell 103, 156–57
stillbirth 75, 86, 118, 133, 162–72, 223, 271, 332
storehouses (storerooms) 67, 234, 259–60, 265–66, 291, 342
sublime 228, 231–32, 276, 326–27
suffering 86–87, 108, 133, 137, 141, 156–60, 163, 167, 169, 176, 179, 183–84, 190, 201, 218, 220, 226, 231–32, 285, 324, 335–36, 342
swaddling 75, 229–30, 237, 239, 241–43, 248–49, 252, 254, 258–59, 270, 274–75, 338

target domain 22–23, 27, 29, 36–69, 76–77, 88, 91, 96, 175, 193, 199–200, 208, 217, 259, 270, 273, 276, 286, 332, 335, 337, 341
Tiamat 157, 235, 241, 248

undressing (unclothe) 120–22, 126, 128, 131, 333
universal metaphors (see cross-cultural metaphors) 40–41, 149, 166, 203, 214–15

vernix (birthing custard) 195, 269–73, 277, 332
vital relations 54–56, 160
vulture 80, 276, 288–89, 306–10, 316, 318, 322, 324
vulva 97, 102, 104–5, 162, 251

weave (weaving) 30, 76, 179–80, 200, 205–16, 218, 336
weaver 76, 200, 208–9, 214, 216, 225, 336
wild ass 281, 286, 288–89, 291–92, 300–304, 312, 318–19, 322–25, 327, 340–43
wilderness 214, 228, 231, 260, 266, 272, 276, 281–86, 291, 315, 318, 322–24
wild horse 289, 304, 340
wildlife manager 24, 283, 285
wild ox 288–89, 292, 304, 322, 340
womb
– and the grave/Sheol 86, 88, 92, 105, 116, 118, 142, 144, 167–82, 223–24, 226, 234, 330, 333–34
– and earth 85, 104, 115, 118, 130
– as pot 67, 98–99, 260, 297, 301
as room 32–33, 77, 94–96, 99, 105, 165–66, 241, 248–49, 258, 260, 275, 297, 301, 332, 336, 341
young wild animals 80, 279, 286, 288, 290–92, 304–26, 339–40, 343

Dissertationes Theologicae Holmienses

1. Eurell, John-Christian. *Peter's Legacy in Early Christianity: The Appropriation and Use of Peter's Authority in the First Three Centuries.* DTH 1. Stockholm: Enskilda Högskolan Stockholm, 2021.
2. Mannerfelt, Frida. *Co-preaching: The Practice of Preaching in Digital Culture and Spaces.* DTH 2. Stockholm: Enskilda Högskolan Stockholm, 2023.
3. Appelfeldt, Joel. *Dopet som hantverk: Gudstjänstkreativitet och liturgisk taktik i Svenska kyrkan och Equmeniakyrkan.* DTH 3. Skellefteå: Artos Academic, 2023.
4. Gobena, Abate. *Sanctity and Environment in Ethiopian Hagiography: The Case of Gedle Gebre Menfes Qiddus.* DTH 4. Stockholm: Enskilda Högskolan Stockholm, 2023.
5. Lockneus, Elin. *Kyrkbänksteologi.* DTH 5. Skellefteå: Artos Academic, 2023.
6. Asserhed, Björn. *Gardens in the Wasteland: Christian Formation in Three Swedish Church Plants.* DTH 6. Stockholm: Enskilda Högskolan Stockholm, 2024.
7. Hallonsten, Simon. *Online Small Groups as Sites of Teaching: An Action Research Dissertation into Christian Religious Education in the Church of Sweden.* DTH 7. Stockholm: Enskilda Högskolan Stockholm, 2024.
8. Plantin, Lisa. *Birth Metaphors in the Book of Job: A Blending Theory Analysis.* DTH 8. Stockholm: Enskilda Högskolan Stockholm, 2024.

www.ingramcontent.com/pod-product-compliance
Lightning Source LLC
Chambersburg PA
CBHW071438300426
44114CB00013B/1488